THE

ECONOM...

BY

W. W. ROSTOW

SECOND EDITION

The Norton Library

W · W · NORTON & COMPANY · INC ·

NEW YORK

Books That Live
The Norton imprint on a book means that in the publisher's
estimation it is a book not for a single season but for the years.
W. W. Norton & Company, Inc.

SBN 393–00176–8

Printed in the United States of America

4 5 6 7 8 9 0

PREFACE

IT IS gratifying to see this book made available to a wider audience more than a decade after the first edition was put to bed. For the author it represented a first and basic effort to break into the problem of economic growth in ways that would force a systematic confrontation of the economic and non-economic factors whose interaction determines the path of growth.

This was, evidently, an area of thought about which there was much more to learn in 1951; and the Second Edition (1959) reflected further development, including the concept of definable stages of growth. The author was by no means alone in his concern with this problem during the 1950's. That decade saw a remarkable surge in the field of economic growth as well as new efforts to analyze the political and social evolution of non-western societies as they move towards modernization. And a few scholars have begun systematically to relate the empirical data relating the economic and non-economic dimensions of the modernization process.

In the vocabulary of this book the forces determining "the propensities" as well as "the yields" are being studied and related.

Meanwhile, governments in the West have deepened their commitment to assist the developing areas and are now increasingly involved in the process of modernization in both its economic and non-economic aspects. It is operationally as well as intellectually clear that economic growth is not an antiseptic economic process — that the most apparently technical of acts (tax reform, for example) is inextricably linked to the social and political life of societies.

Out of the counterpoint between intellectual life and the working experience of governments we can hope to develop in the 1960's a much firmer grasp on the total process of development and modernization than we now command. I would hope that the present book would remain at least suggestive, as this effort unfolds.

W. W. Rostow

Washington, D. C.
June, 1962

PREFACE TO SECOND EDITION

THIS edition is designed to serve two purposes: to make available a text now out of print; and to bring within covers certain further developments of the lines of thought which the first edition contained. Chapters XI–XIV are based on essays written between 1953 and 1959, here substantially reprinted by the kind permission, respectively, of the International Economic Association and the editors of the *Economic Journal*, the *Economic History Review*, and the *Journal of Economic History*.

The two basic derivations from the original analysis are the concept of leading growth sectors, expounded in Chapter XI, and the concept of definable and general stages of growth presented in Chapters XII and XIII. The reader will find that both flow directly from the effort to render the classical theory of production more dynamic and flexible, via sectoral analysis, in Chapter IV. In addition, the stages of growth bring the concept of the propensities (Chapters II and III) to bear, in an organized way, around the non-economic aspects of the transition of a traditional to a growing society.

The stages of growth sequence is both an effort to fill the gap in contemporary thought noted at the end of the introduction to the first edition—that is, an alternative to Marxism —and a way of giving tolerable order to the Marshallian long period.

Since there has been a basic continuity in the development of my ideas, the other chapters stand in their original form. The argument in Chapter X, concerning policy towards the underdeveloped areas, has, however, been much further elaborated in *A Proposal: Key to an Effective Foreign Policy* (Harpers, New York, 1957), written with Max F. Millikan. And the concept of the stages of growth, summarized in Chapter XIII, is developed and applied at length in *The Stages of Economic Growth* (Cambridge University Press, 1960).

The interval between the two editions of this book has seen a most remarkable surge of thought centred on the process of economic growth. Although it would be inappropriate here to review that literature it may be useful to exploit the perspective afforded by these years to underline certain characteristics of this particular approach to the analysis of economic growth.

First, sectoral analysis. The central theoretical effort here is to provide a systematic way of breaking through the aggregates, which we have inherited from Keynesian income analysis, in order to grip dynamic forces at work in the particular sectors on which growth depends. The judgement is that consumption and saving, consumer goods and capital goods, are insufficient categories for the analysis of growth, cycles, or trends; and that the static cast of traditional production theory must be broken. The treatment of the terms of trade, in Chapters VIII and IX, is to be viewed as an extension of this basis perspective to price analysis. Income analysis and all its refined tools are not rejected in this way of looking at things. On the contrary. But the intellectual problem of making a theoretical framework for growth analysis is taken to be the problem of orderly disaggregation, within a dynamic model which links the broad income aggregates to the concept of sectoral equilibrium.[1]

Second, the propensities. The propensities are merely a way of rendering realistic and flexible the arbitrary or evasive assumptions with which the theory of capital formation is usually hedged about. In growth analysis it is useless to assume that all available, relevant, and profitable technology is being regularly brought within the capital stock by the existing corps of entrepreneurs; for it is the failure to exploit these technological possibilities which substantially explains why certain economies fail to grow or grow at lesser rates than they might. Therefore the concept of the propensity to accept innovations was introduced to reflect degrees of variation in a society's effective exploitation of the technological and resource possibilities available to it. Similarly, it is necessary, in a closed system, to account for the generation

---

[1] This theme is developed in 'Some General Reflections on Capital Formation and Economic, Growth', a chapter in *Capital Formation and Economic Growth, A Conference National Bureau of Economic Research, Princeton, N.J., 1955.*

of both basic science and the inventions on which the innovation process ultimately depends. Therefore the propensities to develop fundamental science and to apply science to practical ends are introduced.

On the supply side of the capital market it was thought necessary to modify the conventional profit-maximization assumption and to allow for variations in the willingness of lenders to take risk. Thus the propensity to seek material advance, reflecting the calculus between security and more risky, higher yields.

Finally, it was judged necessary to introduce an independent variable, which would reflect differences in attitude towards family size, since similar objective economic circumstances have been marked by a variety of birth-rates; thus the propensity to have children.

The propensities do not represent, then, some kind of discovery, which can be assessed one way or another. The proposition here is that no statement about the course of population or about the level of productivity or about the scale and composition of capital formation can be made, in a world of changing production functions, unless it contains implicit or explicit assumptions about the strength and the position of the propensities. The purpose of the propensities is to make those assumptions explicit and render it possible for them to be realistic; for in a world of change the state of the arts is not fixed, and profit maximization in no way covers what is involved in borrowers' or lenders' risk. Capital formation is not merely a matter of profit maximization: it is a matter of a society's effective attitude towards and response to basic science, applied science, and the risk-taking of innovation and innovational lending. The reader interested in the relation between the propensities and Keynesian income analysis may wish to note, particularly, pp. 66–69.

The third special feature of this approach is its substitution of the goal of process for that of conventional theory, a theme elaborated at some length in Chapter XIV. I would hold that, given the minimum inescapable number of variables directly relevant to growth, and given the fact that the human decisions which determine growth are not maximization decisions (but, rather, decisions of balance), the goal of a theory of growth is likely to be unattainable or attainable only at the cost of abstractions so high and assumptions so restrictive as to render the theory one of extremely limited usefulness, at least for the historian or for the contemporary planner of economic development. The objective here is to provide a framework of theoretical concepts within which the variety of growth experiences can be systematically arrayed, similarities and differences systematically isolated. The goal is, in short, a kind of biological theory, of process and pattern, rather than a rigid Newtonian derivation from a few axiomatic assumptions.

W. W. R.

Marshall Library,
Cambridge, England

March 1959

PREFACE TO FIRST EDITION

THIS book has arisen directly from the give and take of my graduate seminar in economic history at M.I.T., and its first acknowledgement should be to the students of that seminar in 1950–1. One of them, Mr. H. A. J. Green, served as my assistant in preparing the text, and, notably, in preparing the materials for the discussion of growth patterns in Chapter IV and Appendix I.

I have profited greatly from the comments of economists and historians whose work and thought have led them to consider, from one perspective or another, the issues with which this book is concerned. In particular, I should like to acknowledge valuable exchanges with D. S. Ballantine, R. M. Goodwin, J. R. Hicks, Albert Kervyn, C. P. Kindleberger, S. S. Kuznets, D. H. Robertson, Joan Robinson, E. V. Rostow, P. A. Samuelson, and J. E. Sawyer, as well as a working party in Cambridge, England, assembled *ad hoc* by R. F. Kahn. I have also had the benefit of observations from A. H. Cole, K. W. Deutsch, A. D. Gayer, H. Heaton, R. K. Lamb, E. S. Mason, J. B. Rae, and A. M. Schlesinger, Jr.

A special acknowledgement is required for Chapter VII. Its substance was presented by the author as the last of a series of lectures organized by W. K. Hancock at Oxford, in 1947, on the theme: War and Economic Change. The pre-1815 era was covered by F. W. D. Deakin, K. B. Macfarlane, J. O. Prestwich, H. G. A. V. Schenk, L. Stone, and Miss L. S. Sutherland. Professor Hancock introduced the series. Whatever virtues the analysis may contain are largely theirs, although they bear no responsibility for the manner in which their scholarship and ideas have been exploited.

The substance of Chapters VIII and IX has appeared in the *Economic History Review*, whose editors have kindly permitted republication. The author is similarly indebted to the editors of the *American Economic Review*, the *Economic Journal*, and the *Journal of Economic History* for permission to reprint portions of articles here contained, in modified form, within Chapters V and X.

The contribution of my wife, Elspeth Davies Rostow, has been of major importance to this book. As an historian she has used her influence to develop such concreteness as the abstract argument of Part I attains; as the reader's friend she has patiently sought to increase the clarity of the text.

W. W. R.

Cambridge, Massachusetts
October 1951

CONTENTS

APPENDIXES

INTRODUCTION

THIS is an historian's book about economic theory. Its connexion with history is both direct and oblique.

The argument set forth in Part I arose directly from the requirements of the author's graduate seminar in economic history at M.I.T. That seminar is addressed to the pattern of evolution of the world economy since the mid-eighteenth century. Modern economic theory offers its students no agreed framework for disciplining such a story of growth and fluctuation. The concepts abstractly presented in Part I have been used in the past two years to bring order to a wide range of questions. For example, they have been applied, in a general way, to the classic story of the British Industrial Revolution; to the reasons for the differential rates of growth of Britain, the United States, Germany, and France in the first half of the nineteenth century; to the process whereby Latin America, Australasia, China, and Japan were drawn into the world economy; to the complex of forces that detonated the United States into rapid industrialization after the mid-century; to the world-wide network of trends from 1873 to the mid-nineties, and their reversal down to 1914; to the pathological but historically recognizable patterns of events during the inter-war and post-war periods.

The origin of this theoretical apparatus in the study and teaching of history in no way can justify such inadequacies as it may contain as a logical structure; and its believed usefulness to one teacher of economic history by no means guarantees general persuasiveness or applicability. Nevertheless, it is a theoretical analysis generated at no great distance from bodies of agreed fact; and its purpose is to assist in framing further empirical investigation.

The analysis also has a more remote connexion with history. The historian shares one central problem with the maker of public policy. He must take as unique events, in their full complexity, the situations he confronts. Like the policy-maker, the historian brings, certainly, to those events implicit or explicit suppositions which determine his view of what the facts are, what relative importance they may have, and what underlying forces may link them causally. Nevertheless, the historian, by the nature of his profession, must use theoretical models in a special way. He may find them invaluable guides to the organization of his materials and immensely helpful in sorting out strands of connected events. He must deal, like the theorist, with the philosophic problem of theory's relation to fact; and, perhaps, the historian should be more aware of that inescapable problem. The empirical aura of modern historiography induces a dangerous evasiveness concerning the theoretical presuppositions which are at work in the conventions of history. Nevertheless, on balance, the historian's loyalty must remain to his perception of the facts.

This bias—at once the historian's glory and his limitation as a scientist—has a special meaning for economic analyses conducted in the present day. The most vital and fully articulated bodies of modern economic thought have been developed within Marshallian short-period assumptions; that is, the social and political framework of the economy, the state of the arts, and the levels of fixed capacity are assumed to be given and, usually, fixed. Except for an extremely limited range of problems, these are intolerable assumptions for the historian. The economic historians, from their formal nineteenth-century beginnings, have in fact mainly devoted themselves to telling the story of how the social and political framework of the economy, the state of the arts, and the levels of fixed capacity have changed in various regions of the world. It is this fundamental divergence of interest and outlook as between economists and economic historians which accounts, principally, for the limited nature of their useful professional exchanges in recent decades.[1]

Even when the historian turns to problems which might appear more susceptible of treatment with short-period tools

---

[1] It will be recalled that J. H. Clapham's famous attack on economic theory ('On Empty Boxes', *Economic Journal*, 1922) centred on the failure of the Marshallian concepts to grip the essential facts and the dynamic processes summarized under the cases of increasing and decreasing returns in particular industries. Clapham's challenge, which played a part in generating the theory of imperfect competition, remains still to be met.

(for example, the narrative of business cycles), he finds that the long-period factors are much with him, however short the historical time period he may choose to consider.[1]

When one poses the question, How has the world economy of the past two centuries evolved, and what forces have mainly determined its changing shape? then it is obviously necessary to deal somehow with long-period factors and the social and political framework of the economy. So far as theory is concerned, this book is an effort to explore how such factors may be linked systematically with the received bodies of short-period analysis without doing undue violence to the latter.

The author's inclination to pursue this theme has been strengthened from what he has been able to learn of the problems of policy that confront the post-war world, in the Department of State, in the United Nations Economic Commission for Europe in Geneva, and as an American teacher at Oxford and Cambridge, for various periods over the past five years. It is the author's conviction that an appropriate scientific framework for the making of public policy, at present and over the foreseeable future, requires the development of improved tools for the handling of long-period factors and for relating social and political forces to the body of economics. This judgement is elaborated and briefly illustrated in Chapter X.

In such an effort a writer at the present time is by no means alone. There is a ferment in the world of economics which appears to centre on these issues. From different initial interests, academic theorists in many parts of the world are beginning to pose a new set of questions addressed, roughly, to the process of economic growth, and the character of its relation to short-period income analysis. Then there is an accumulating body of empirical data; for example, the papers delivered at the Social Science Research Council meeting on the Quantitative Description of Technological Change (May 1951), and the growing collection of historical analyses of

---

[1] See, for example, the author's essays on *The British Economy of the Nineteenth Century*, Oxford, 1948, especially pp. 52–53, and 145–60 (subsequently referred to as *B.E.N.C.*).

entrepreneurship. There are the publications of the United Nations economists in Geneva, Santiago, Bangkok, and New York, directed toward the issues of economic growth by the pressure of current events and the expressed will of governments. Similarly, there are the government economists, throughout the non-Communist world, wrestling to create formulations appropriate to problems of future raw materials supply, the development of under-developed countries, and so on. This book is to be regarded, then, as an effort to contribute, from an historian's perspective, to a widespread effort.

In entering this complex terrain, where variables long firmly nailed down are set in motion, economists may take a certain comfort. These new interests constitute a return to some of the oldest issues in formal economic thought. Looked at from the present day, *The Wealth of Nations*, in one of its aspects, is a dynamic analysis and programme of policy for an under-developed country. Adam Smith was concerned to see created a social and political framework appropriate to a policy of sustained economic growth in Britain and the world. He used history not simply to illustrate static relationships but to illuminate the processes whereby the wealth of nations may increase or decrease. He was much concerned, as were most of the early modern economists, with the probable long-period course of the yield from new investment. He focused on 'the accumulation of stock', on the 'natural progress of opulence', and he discussed at length the appropriate distribution of investment among the sectors of the economy. He was concerned not only with the relation of public policy to the rate of economic development, but also with what we would call social policy and social attitudes. His attack on the system of education in eighteenth-century England was not only a reprisal for a Scotsman's dissatisfactions with his days at Oxford; it incorporated, also, the notion that education, for good or ill, is one of the determinants of the efficiency of the working force and, thus, the rate of growth of an economy. It is not a distortion of *The Wealth of Nations* to regard it as a dynamic analysis of the forces determining change in long-period factors, placed in a setting of the social and political forces relevant to economic development.

Strong elements of this approach to economic analysis remained within the tradition down to John Stuart Mill. Although the formal structure of economic thought had been crystallized and much advanced since the days of Adam Smith, Mill not only considered the forces determining the long-period course of wages and of interest from capital; but he considered at some length the social and political setting of the economy. With free trade freshly triumphant, however, he was less concerned with the old inhibitions on the freedom of enterprise than he was with the 'future of the labouring class' (Book IV, Chap. V) and with public finance (Book V). As pointed out later, in another context,[1] Mill considered in Book I, Chapter X, the relation between what he called the 'effective desire of accumulation' and the rate of growth of capital. He was aware that societies existed where potentially productive forms of investment were not exploited for lack of will or for lack of an appropriate institutional environment. Believing, as well he might, that this was not a major problem for the England of his day, he quickly set aside these issues of social and political analysis; and he turned to clarifying, from Ricardo's formulations, the laws governing a society where the assumption of profit maximization was, roughly, realistic, and to the problem of mitigating the worst consequences of such a society for the working classes.

Although the passages are often ignored in the teaching of Marshall, his *Principles* contains an extended discussion of long-period factors and of the role of social forces in determining the level of and changes in the productivity of the labour supply and of capital investment. Book IV constitutes perhaps the most extensive and rigorous statement of the factors governing changes in the rate of growth and productivity of the factors of production that exists in the literature of economics.

Marshall's influence in these matters, however, has been much affected by his inability to deal formally and graphi-

---

[1] See below, pp. 248–50.

cally with the long period. Appendix H in *The Principles*, and Appendix J, paragraphs 8 and 10, in *Money, Credit, and Commerce* bring to sharp focus his frustration in this regard.[1] The latter appendixes are entitled, significantly: 'Hindrances to the isolation for separate study of tendencies to Increasing Return to capital and labour in the production of a country's exports' and 'Diagrams representing the case of Exceptional Supply, in which the exports of a country show strong general tendencies to Increasing Return, are deprived of practical interest by the inapplicability of the Statical Method to such tendencies'. Marshall was impressed by the wide range of forces that might affect the long-period course of output and price. In both Appendix H and his treatment of the case of Exceptional Supply, he referred to the impact on demand of habits built up over time by the nature and cheapness of supplies available. He noted, for example, the price inelasticity of British demand for cotton during the American Civil War, which in part could be attributed to the previous decline in price and growth in the habit of cotton using it induced. More generally, long-period analysis troubled him because historical developments were not fully reversible. Equilibrium could not be exhibited, as he noted, in terms of a static analysis.

Marshall's awareness of the difficulties of dealing with long-period phenomena by means of the techniques that could be neatly applied in short-period analyses has no doubt contributed to the tradition among economists of dealing with long-period forces on an *ad hoc* and descriptive basis; or, in certain formal structures, of treating them as exogenous to their systems. The present analysis would by no means pretend to have solved fully the issues of multiple dynamic causation which a formalization of long-period analysis demands. The approach to long-period analysis developed in this study, however, and notably the analysis of equilibrium in sectors of the economy presented in Chapter

[1] The author is indebted to Professor D. H. Robertson for drawing his attention to the significance of Appendix J in Marshall. He is also indebted to Professor Robertson for warnings of the pitfalls inherent in a systematic approach to the long period, warnings which, if not wholly heeded, contributed to an awareness of the extreme complexity of the problem.

IV, may permit certain of the issues of long-period analysis to be brought within the scope of systematic treatment.

In a larger sense, the whole of Part I of this book is an effort to explore a method for permitting the introduction of long-period factors into economic analysis, including within them the changing social and political framework of the economy. Part II of the book consists of a few exploratory and illustrative exercises in this approach. They are designed, like the illustrative material in Part I, to give some concreteness to the abstract notions developed in the course of this study. A more appropriate body of illustration would consist in a general historical analysis of the evolution of the world economy in modern times. This is a task to which the author hopes to address himself in the future. The occasional pieces included in Part II may, nevertheless, assist the reader in judging the usefulness of the apparatus erected in Part I.

As Marshall was aware, and as every historian must know, the introduction of long-period factors into economic analysis multiplies vastly the number of variables and reduces the possibilities for strict theoretical statement. The multiplicity of factors which might determine the long-period course of an economic system is such that a modest, descriptive approach, centred on limited problems and time periods, would appear to be most sensible and useful. And, in any case, a theoretical formulation of this character can pretend to no more than the posing of a set of related questions whose answers might permit a more coherent and unified treatment of particular situations and problems. The author, as noted earlier, has been driven to attempt the formulation of this extensive structure from the necessities of teaching history and from a reading of certain issues of public policy in our time. In the end, the usefulness of this argument must be measured in terms of such insights as it may afford into historical and contemporary situations.

The achievement of a workable analytic structure has demanded one device which deserves explicit comment. A range of what are here called 'propensities' is introduced into the analysis. The propensities summarize the effective response of the society in six directions to the economic possibilities open to it. Included among them is the familiar Keynesian propensity to consume. Behind the propensities, and mainly unanalysed here, lies the whole living process whereby men and societies balance material objectives against other objectives. These propensities, defined from the perspective of economic analysis, are meant to do no more than pose certain issues for analysis by the sociologist, the historian, and others concerned with the non-economic aspects of society. It may properly be objected that the propensities themselves tell us nothing about the social and political workings of a society. Whether the other purposes they serve are worth their introduction is, of course, for the reader to decide. The author's reason for introducing these arbitrary variables should, however, be understood. They stem from a belief that, in the present state of knowledge, co-operation among different disciplines within the social sciences is likely to be achieved not by the making of a single universal hypothesis, into which the facts may be fitted, but rather by forcing the application of the best techniques of analysis available around a given problem. Here the problem is economic growth. The technical issue that must be faced is how to bring to bear on this problem the accumulated knowledge and methods of the non-economic social scientists. If the problem is approached, as it were, all at once, the number of variables that would have to be treated would be immense. It has been judged wiser to proceed by leaving within economic analysis a set of variables whose strength and course of change cannot be deduced from the formal assumptions of economics alone. They are designed to constitute a link among those working, with different disciplines, on the problem of economic growth.

There are a variety of grounds on which the adequacy of the propensities as a tool of analysis might be criticized. The author would only suggest that if some such device of linkage is not adopted the analysis of growth faces the danger of a multiplicity of variables too great for useful analysis; the adoption of some crude, generalized schema which has marked so much Teutonic thought in the social sciences; or a continuance of present specialized procedures, which fail to yield an adequately full view of the process of economic growth.

It may, finally, be proper in this introduction to call attention to an issue which arose in the context of this analysis and which historians and social scientists must face if they are to make progress in many important directions, including the analysis of economic growth; namely, the inadequacies of the Marxist analysis of the relations among the sectors of society and the need for an alternative general view. It is the author's judgement that Marx's framework for relating economic, social, and political factors has found its way much more deeply into Western academic thought than most practitioners are aware. Its harshness and oversimplicity is, of course, often softened by *ad hoc* references to moral, idealistic, and individualistic 'factors' that operate in history or in particular situations. Nevertheless, if political analysis, social analysis, and economic analysis are to be made to converge on a given problem, the issue of dynamic causation in society cannot be thus evaded. It has arisen here in attempting to discuss the forces which might cause changes in the propensities: and, more generally, in a brief consideration of the range of forces, other than changes in the yield from natural resources, that might determine acceleration or deceleration in economic growth. The author has by no means solved the problem of formulating an alternative to the Marxist system; but he would argue that the focusing of attention on this problem of formulating an alternative to the Marxist system;[1] Further, its solution appears essential both for a full understanding of the process of economic growth in the past and for the formulation of adequate public policy designed to sustain or accelerate economic growth in the many portions of the world where this is the majority will of peoples and the enunciated aim of their governments.

[1] Between the publication of the first and second editions of this book the author came to feel he had solved, at least *ad interim*, the problem of an alternative to Marxism, the result being summarized in Chapter XIII.

PART I

AN ANALYSIS OF ECONOMIC GROWTH

I

A SUMMARY OF THE ARGUMENT

THE analysis elaborated in Part I of this book (Chaps. I–VI) is designed to state the determinants of economic growth; to formulate the dynamic process of growth; and to isolate those factors which have determined two characteristics of the process of growth in the Western world over, roughly, the past century and a half—namely, the regular recurrence of business cycles and the alternating sequence of secular trends.

The argument hinges on one version of a simple, classical relationship. Output is taken as determined by the scale and productivity of the working force and of capital. Included within capital, for purposes of this analysis, is land and other natural resources, as well as scientific, technical, and organizational knowledge. The rate of growth of an economy is thus viewed as a function of changes in two enormously complex variables. Chapters II and III analyse the forces which appear to determine the level of these variables and changes in them. Chapter IV considers the nature of the conditions required for a steady rate of growth in an economy where the decisions to invest and to consume are taken discretely by individuals and private institutions, as well as the character of forces likely to cause acceleration and deceleration in the over-all rate of growth. Chapter V seeks to state, against the background of the process of growth, the conditions which have caused the regular appearance of business cycles; while Chapter VI considers the nature of the trend periods which characterize modern economic history. Without pretence to an exhaustion of the literature, the text refers at each stage to other views on these matters; and an effort is made to relate the present argument to certain alternative formulations.

It is central to the perspective of this book that the economic decisions which determine the rate of growth and productivity of the working force and of capital should not be regarded as governed by the strictly economic motives of human beings. Economic action is judged the outcome of a complex process of balancing material advance against other human objectives. Further, both history and contemporary events indicate that actions which result in economic advance need not be motivated by economic goals. Excepting certain tentative observations in Chapters II and III, however, this book does not consider systematically the human determinants of economic action. The present purpose, in this region of general social analysis, is extremely limited. It may be defined as an effort to introduce into formal economic analysis variables which incorporate the human response to the challenges and material opportunities offered by the economic environment. These variables are designed to constitute a link between the domain of the conventional economist on the one hand, and the sociologist, anthropologist, psychologist, and historian on the other. They aim to force the economist to ask and answer (or have others answer) certain essential questions, before proceeding with the analysis of economic problems of the real world, whether historical or contemporary. They also aim to provide a focus for the efforts of non-economic analysts interested in economic phenomena, which would permit them to bring their data and techniques to bear in such a manner that their conclusions might be absorbed directly into a general analysis of the growth and fluctuations of economies.

The device chosen for this linkage consists in six propensities:

The propensity to develop fundamental science (physical and social).

The propensity to apply science to economic ends.

The propensity to accept innovations.

The propensity to seek material advance.

The propensity to consume.

The propensity to have children.

The propensities summarize the effective response of a

society to its environment, at any period of time, acting through its existing institutions and leading social groups; and they reflect the underlying value system effective within that society. But the propensities imply nothing whatsoever about the motives of a society or the individuals who constitute it. It is left for the non-economic social scientists to disentangle the motives and societal processes which might determine the effective strength and course of change of these variables under various circumstances. These are an economist's terms, not those of a sociologist or political scientist: they are designed to pose questions, not to answer them.

The use of quasi-sociological terminology in the foundations of this argument does not imply that the political process is judged to be unimportant in the evolution of the economic system, or that politics is a simple, automatic reflex of the social structure and social attitudes. It is, simply, more convenient in the exposition of the stylized argument of Part I to assume that the political process and political institutions are one of the possible means by which the propensities effective in a society have their consequences for the economy. The tax structure and fiscal policy of a country may often, for example, be decisive to the course of its economic development and in any full analysis require detailed, separate consideration. Nevertheless, it is not unrealistic in a formal analysis to regard these factors as reflecting, in one of their aspects, the effective propensities of a society. Politics is, on this view, simply one arena within which men seek to make felt their scales of values. Since the general view taken here is that societies are thoroughly interacting in their operation, no priority in time or in causation attaches to economic over social forces, or to social over political forces. Chapter X, in Part II, seeks explicitly to bring this view to bear on certain current issues of public policy.

The consideration of the propensities (Chap. II) is confined, in the first instance, to their definition. In particular, an effort is made to clarify their separability from the economic decisions to which they relate and which they help to determine. Their quantitative character and the probable extent of their measurability is then examined. And, finally, the nature of their determinants, in the context of a moving society, is tentatively considered, including the extent of their predictability in the present state of knowledge. Since the propensities reflect the value system of a society, as effectively operative through its social and political institutions, the analysis of changes in the propensities requires, strictly speaking, a general dynamic theory of societal change. Chapters II and III contain limited observations on this vast issue. Accepting the scientific criteria of measurability and of predictability, it is concluded that the present state of knowledge probably permits of significant quantitative statement of change, if not full measurability; and of a limited but perhaps useful degree of predictability.

Chapter III, which relates the propensities to the decisions on which growth depends, also indicates the basis for their choice. They are judged the minimum groupings of social and political behaviour necessary to analyse the rate of change in the size and productivity of the working force and of the capital stock. The essential economic subvariables are taken to be the following:

Related to Current Changes in the Size and Productivity of the Working Force

1. The (prior) birth-rate.
2. The (prior and current) death-rate.
3. The role of women and children in the working force.
4. The skill of the working force.
5. The degree of effort put forward by the working force.

Related to Current Changes in the Size and Productivity of the Capital Stock

1. The yield from additions to the capital stock (including natural resources, fundamental and applied science, organizational techniques, &c.).
2. The (prior) volume of resources devoted to the pursuit of fundamental science.
3. The (prior) volume of resources devoted to the pursuit of applied science.

4. The proportion of the flow (and pool) of potential innovations accepted.

5. The volume of resources allocated to current investment.

6. The appropriateness of the desired level of consumption in relation to 5 above.

The long-run yield from additions to the capital stock differs from the other variables in its determination. Despite some brief consideration of the question of diminishing and increasing returns in various segments of the capital stock, the trend in long-run marginal yields is left exogenous to the system, in the sense that this argument does not accept a generalization to all forms of capital of classic long-run diminishing returns to land. All the other variables are judged to be the outcome of the interplay of various economic yields or incentives and one or another of the propensities (or sectoral aspects of them). Short-run fluctuations in yield are regarded as dependent on deviations of actual capacity in sectors of the economy from that capacity appropriate to the rate of growth of the economy, tastes, and the potentialities for innovations, with the strength of the propensities given.

The decisions to allocate resources to fundamental and to applied science, and to accept innovations, can be viewed, at this stage, as sectoral aspects of the whole investment process. The structure is thus capable of a generalization which would absorb the first, second, and third propensities as sectoral aspects of the fourth. Similarly, the yields to be derived from fundamental and applied science and from the acceptance of innovations can be regarded as sectoral aspects of the yield from new investment in general. The isolation of these elements for separate analysis is judged necessary in the first instance, however, because it is believed that they relate to economic decisions (concerning the resources allocated to fundamental and applied science and the proportion of innovations accepted) which help determine, with a time lag, the productivity of investment possibilities currently offered.

For any period of time, the level of investment is judged to be determined by the interplay in the capital markets between a profitability curve (or curves) exhibiting the rate of return over cost for those investment projects actually brought forward, given the propensity to accept innovations, and a finance supply curve (or curves) exhibiting the disposition of those resources not consumed, as among objectives to which attach differing degrees of profit and risk. This manner of presenting the short-run determinants of the level of investment is designed to bring to the centre of economic analysis a factor often left implicit among the formal assumptions—namely, the quality of enterprise. In particular, it is designed to dramatize the fact that societies, presented by the environment around them with similar investment possibilities, involving ranges of risks and degrees of change in existing productive methods, will exploit those possibilities in differing degree. The analysis also envisages the possibility of comparing the response to profit possibilities, not only as among different societies but as among sectors of the same economy at the same period of time, and the response within a sector of a given economy at different periods of time. It is believed that the Keynesian mode of exhibiting the level of investment as determined by the intersection of a marginal efficiency of capital curve and the rate of interest may be modified to take account of these factors (*a*) by introducing an optimum curve which would show the demand for investment resources if all possibilities for innovation were effectively offered in the markets; and (*b*) by deductions from the marginal efficiency of capital curve appropriate to the (lenders') risk premium attached by the economy to different acts of investment, including the influence of public authorities on these deductions.

The argument of Chapters II and III can be summarized in the form of the following six propositions:

1. The level of the output of an economy, at any period of time, is a function of the size of its working force and of its stock of capital (including its stock of applied knowledge). Embraced within these stocks, conceptually quantitative, are the productivity factors attaching to them.

2. The rate of growth of an economy is a function of the rate of change in these stocks.

3. These rates of change, in turn, may be regarded as

resulting from the interplay of certain yields and the effective strength of the following propensities, as they operate
through the existing economic, social, and political institutions in the society: the propensity to develop fundamental
science; the propensity to apply science to economic ends;
the propensity to accept innovations; the propensity to seek
material advance; the propensity to consume; the propensity
to have children. The first three propensities may in a
generalized manner be regarded as sectoral aspects of the
propensity to seek material advance. Further, the interplay
of the propensity to seek material advance and the propensity
to consume determine the extent to which material resources
are fully or steadily employed, whether inflation occurs, and
in what proportion the propensity to seek material advance
is, in fact, effective in causing real investment to take place.

4. The effective strengths of the propensities, in turn, are,
at any moment of time, or for any limited period, a function
of the prior operation of economic, social, and political forces,
which determine the current social fabric, institutions, and
effective political policy of the society.

5. For a given complex of institutions controlling them, the
propensities, in the course of their own long-period life, may
have a built-in tendency to follow an approximation of a
curve of growth, stagnation, and decline. Whatever their
course, it is essential to this argument that the propensities,
which enter directly and technically into economic decisions,
are not to be investigated or analysed in terms of wholly
economic variables or motives.

6. Quite apart from the possibility of built-in deceleration
within the propensities, in a given society, diminishing
returns may, in the long run, operate on the size and quality
of the working force, on the extractive industries, and possibly but not surely on agricultural and industrial investment
as a whole.

Against this analysis of the determinants of the rate of
growth, Chapter IV considers the formal conditions under
which a steady rate of growth would obtain, and the relation
between sectoral rates of growth and the over-all rate of
growth. Further, this chapter considers the nature of the

forces which might cause acceleration or deceleration in the over-all rate of growth.

The concept of sectoral levels of capacity appropriate to a given rate of growth is elaborated. This requires the taking into account of demands for particular goods and services which depend upon population growth and over-all changes in real income (and tastes), as well as the potentialities offered in the form of innovations. This conception of appropriate capacity levels in sectors of the economy requires, however, that the process of innovation be viewed as an internal response of the system rather than as an exogenous factor. In these terms, two 'optimum' patterns of growth are considered: one under the assumption of steady full employment; the other under the realistic assumption that the system moves forward with cyclical fluctuations in employment—that is, with a margin of resources unemployed, on average.

This view is compared with several recent formulations of the process of growth, notably that of Harrod. The demonstration, in these analyses, of the unlikelihood of steady rates of growth, with uninterrupted full employment, is accepted. An effort is made here, however, to treat changes in the rate of growth as determined by the workings of the fundamental variables in the system, rather than as the consequence of exogenous forces. The chapter concludes by examining briefly the nature of the take-off of an economic system into industrialization, and the question of secular stagnation.[1] The forces which might operate to produce such changes in the over-all rate of growth are grouped under the general headings of changes in yields and changes in the propensities, the latter being given somewhat greater weight than is conventional in economic analyses.

Chapter V constitutes an analysis of the relation between business cycles and the process of growth, as developed in the previous chapters. The cyclical character which growth has assumed historically in societies where the decisions to consume and to invest were discretely taken by private

---

[1] The term 'take-off' is here used to describe the transition of a society from a preponderantly agricultural to an industrialized basis, or, more generally, a sustained rate of increase in output *per capita*. See Chapter XII.

individuals and institutions is traced to (*a*) certain lags within the economic process; and (*b*) certain psychological and sociological aspects of the behaviour of individuals and institutions in the private investment markets. The lag believed most relevant is that between the commitment to undertake an act of investment and its completion. The characteristics of the investment markets believed most relevant are its tendency to take long-run decisions on the basis of current indications of profitability and its follow-the-leader tendency in selecting the main avenues for current investment. In combination these factors contribute elements of irrationality to the pattern of investment outlays when rationality is defined in terms of an optimum long-run sectoral pattern of growth.

The historical succession of business cycles is seen as the recurrent, disproportionate exploitation by investors of gaps between actual capacity and capacity required (and made profitable) by the process of growth and the potentialities of innovations. These gaps reflect themselves in profit possibilities offered to investors. The lags and the institutional process of investment result in an overshooting of the realistic optimum levels required by the process of growth and its technical possibilities, given the strength of the propensities. The upward turning-point is judged to occur as a result of a falling off of profitability in the lines of investment dominating the boom, caused either by a rise in costs or an appreciation by the investment market that capacity has overshot or is likely to overshoot the sectoral optima in certain directions where the investment markets are heavily committed.

Although linked to a somewhat different exposition of the process of growth than is conventional, the explanation of business cycles is similar to that which is now widely accepted. The present analysis raises, however, the following possibility: that the instability of the boom does not result, in the first instance, from a total level of investment which is too high to be sustained, given the underlying trend of growth; but rather that investment concentrates in certain key sectors disproportionately, in the course of a boom, and that the upper turning-point results primarily from a realization among investors that certain key areas of investment have been carried too far. In both the upswing and the downswing the entrance of investors into these main lines of investment and their withdrawal from them would, of course, have important and familiar secondary repercussions on the total level of investment, income, and employment. This hypothesis, centring on the inappropriate character of investment, is believed relevant to the formulation of a proper counter-cyclical policy, if, in fact, it is sustained by the evidence.

Chapter VI treats the problem of long-period trends in the course of economic growth in the Western world since the end of the eighteenth century. These trends are defined as trends in general and relative prices, relative income distribution, and the direction and average yield from new investment. They are believed to have a common basis in distortions of a peculiarly powerful kind in sectors of the economy, as between actual and realistic optimum capacity. These distortions, in turn, are believed to have come about because of wars and because of certain forms of investment with abnormally long periods of gestation and subject to execution only in very large units; notably, the opening up of areas for the exploitation of agricultural land and raw materials.

Against this background the historical evidence for trends is very briefly surveyed; and exceptions to a systematic trend pattern (such as a fifty-year cycle) are noted. The impact of the trend pattern of growth on international trade is considered; notably, its relation to the trend course of the terms of trade as between industrial and agricultural sectors of the world economy. The relation between this view of trend phenomena and those of Kondratieff and Schumpeter are noted. The approach to trends developed here is, finally, shown to be a generalization, in terms of the world economy, of the trend analysis used by the author in a previous consideration of the British economy of the nineteenth century.

THE PROPENSITIES AND THEIR DETERMINANTS

I

Two relationships are widely accepted by social scientists and historians, although rarely employed with rigour or related to each other. One would regard the social structure of a society, and its politics, as partially determined by its economic life; the other would regard the operation of the economy as partially determined by its social and political framework.

It is widely agreed, for example, that the social structure, political outlook, and culture of the American South, which evolved in the first half of the nineteenth century—the attitudes of its men, the value system of its most powerful groups, the character of its institutions—were, in some meaningful sense, partially caused by the large-scale development of cotton growing, on a plantation basis, after the invention of the cotton gin.[1] It would be similarly agreed that much of social and political life in mid-Victorian England can be traced back causally to the rapid rise of the cotton textile and iron industries, starting in the late eighteenth century.

It would also be widely acknowledged, however, that the character, scale, and capacity for growth of an economy are closely related to the whole society of which it is a part. It is now an accepted convention, for example, to regard the social, scientific, and cultural attitudes of the British commercial middle class in the eighteenth century as among the 'causes' of the Industrial Revolution; the rise of a new national spirit is similarly associated with the German and Japanese industrial revolutions of the nineteenth century; the attitudes of post-Revolutionary peasant and *petite bourgeoisie* in France are accepted among the 'causes' of the sluggish character of modern French economic development.

[1] Even before the coming of the cotton gin, however, plantation life had already developed roots in certain tobacco-growing areas in colonial America.

This chapter seeks to probe further into these two kinds of interacting relationships, at once familiar and largely unexplored, as they relate to economic growth. The exploration of these relationships, as they affect economic growth, is here conducted in separate stages. The initial stage of the argument would seek to establish the manner in which the social frame of a society, taken as given, can be formally introduced into an analysis of the economic decisions of a society, which determine the level of output and the rate of growth. The latter stage considers tentatively the process whereby the wider non-economic variables relevant to economic growth are determined.

The analytic instrument chosen for the first stage of the exposition consists in six propensities, which reflect the behaviour of a given society in certain particular directions: the propensity to develop fundamental science; to apply science to economic ends; to accept the possibilities of innovation; to seek material advance; to consume; and to have children.[1] These propensities have been selected on economic grounds and given economic labels; that is, their justification lies in the belief that they represent aspects of total social behaviour which determine (with given resources and the marginal yields to be derived from increments to them) the level and rate of growth of output. If correctly chosen, they pose the minimum essential questions that the economist must ask and answer (or have answered) of a society's behaviour, in order to proceed with an analysis of its economic output and capacity for growth in the short period. The case for their selection is examined in Chapter III, where the relation of the various propensities to the size and character of the working force and the scale and character of capital resources in an economy is considered. The aim of the present chapter is to

[1] The first three propensities can well be viewed as sectoral aspects of the fourth. The allocation of resources to fundamental and to applied science and the acceptance of innovations are aspects of the investment process. They are here arbitrarily separated in order to explore the manner in which the productivity of current investment is determined, to the extent that it does not depend on the current yield from natural resources. At a higher level of generality, however, the basic propensities are: to seek material advance; to consume; and to have children.

make clear the nature of these propensities and to consider tentatively, in generalized terms, the forces which appear to determine their effective strength at a given period of time and their course of change. It cannot be too strongly emphasized that the argument of this chapter is not designed to answer fully the questions posed. The long and complex task of establishing the facts concerning the social determinants of economic growth, at different times and places, and of ordering them, still lies, largely, before us. The present limited concern is to explore one possible method for introducing social and political forces into the analysis of economic growth.

The introduction of new concepts carries with it special responsibilities and should be greeted, *prima facie*, with scepticism. In the social sciences, notably, the development of systematic thought has often been hampered by eccentricities of vocabulary, which consisted merely in substituting your own pet phrases for those commonly used by others, or in elevating observed phenomena to a specious analytic generality. The verbal landscape of modern economics is already sufficiently cluttered. The suggested role of the propensities in economic analysis must be set out, therefore, with some care.

II

For any given period of time it is possible to say of a society that it devotes a certain proportion of its current resources to the development of fundamental science; that it devotes a certain proportion of its current resources to developing from science applications useful in its economy; that, of the flow (and pool) of potential innovations coming forward (or available) it accepts for application a certain proportion, within the total volume of its current investment; that it devotes certain proportions of its current resources to investment and to consumption; and that it exhibits a certain birth-rate in relation to its total population. Although difficulties of definition may attach to certain of these conceptions, and practical difficulties in measurement would exist for certain of them, these are reasonably unequivocal and conceptually measurable aspects of a society's behaviour for any given period of time.

Fundamental science, in this context, is taken broadly as the pool and flow of knowledge from which applications for the economy might be drawn. It would include the pursuit of knowledge in the physical and social sciences not directed toward specific, practically applicable results. In reality of course, fundamental science might well shade off into, and be difficult to disentangle from, efforts to derive practical results for the economy. The lines between the physical sciences and engineering, psychology and industrial relations, economics and political economy are not easy to draw. Nevertheless, it appears useful (not least in America of the twentieth century) to distinguish the two types of effort and to emphasize the economic significance of fundamental science. The fact that the conclusions of fundamental science are, relatively, a free good in the world economy for any particular consumer—country, region, industry, or individual—does not diminish the economic importance for everyone of allocations of resources to its pursuit, in certain regions. If one were to set up a theoretical model for the growth of a closed economy, such allocations would certainly have a central place.

Further, it is not difficult to conceive of societies where the proportion of resources devoted to fundamental science is relatively high while the proportion of resources (including, of course, first-rate human talent) devoted to the development of practical applications is relatively low; and vice versa. Britain and the United States in modern times might well prove, on examination, to differ relatively in some such manner. Although it would be difficult to measure the proportions of total resources going to fundamental and applied science in any exact way, it should not be difficult to derive indexes showing changes in such proportions, which would be comparable as between different societies.[1] With respect

[1] See, for example, S. C. Gilfillan's analysis of the scale and financial sources of organized research in the United States and United Kingdom, 'The Lag Between Invention and Application', an unpublished paper delivered before the Conference on Quantitative Description of Technological Change (Social Science Research Council), Apr. 1951.

to sectors of a given economy, measurement of the resources devoted to applied science should prove easier.[1]

The conception of a total pool or flow of potential innovations, of which a certain proportion are selected for application, is even more difficult to visualize as measurable for a society as a whole. Nevertheless, indexes reflecting changes in the flow of potential innovations (e.g. patents) might prove of use; and more precise comparisons of potential innovations with current practice might be possible within sectors of the economy, where a realistic maximum technical performance, in the light of existing possibilities, might be defined.[2]

The notion of proportions of current income devoted to investment and consumption are adequately familiar, as is the birth-rate.

If the propensities are to be regarded as valid working tools they must be distinguished firmly from the decisions of a society which they help determine at any moment in time. For example, the propensity to apply resources to fundamental science is something different from the proportion of resources actually applied at a given time; just as the most familiar of the propensities, the propensity to consume (or consumption function) differs from the proportion of income consumed in any given economy for any given time period. In the short period the propensity to consume would reflect the changing allocation of current resources to consumption in relation to alterations in income, with income distribution, tastes, &c., fixed. The shape of such a short-period curve showing the propensity to consume reflects and summarizes

[1] See for example, Jacob Schmookler, 'Technical Change and Patent Statistics', unpublished paper delivered before the Conference on Quantitative Description of Technological Change (Social Science Research Council), Apr. 1951; also E. Graue, 'Inventions and Production', *Review of Economic Statistics*, 1943, pp. 221–6, and the extremely interesting long-run analysis of invention in sectors of the economy by R. K. Merton, 'Fluctuations in the Rate of Industrial Invention', *Quarterly Journal of Economics*, 1934–5, pp. 455–74.

[2] See, for example, A. P. Grosse, 'Innovation and Diffusion', and Y. Brozen, 'Invention, Innovation, and Diffusion', unpublished papers delivered before the Conference on Quantitative Description of Technological Change (Social Science Research Council), Apr. 1951. See also Brozen's 'Research, Technology, and Productivity', a chapter in the forthcoming volume *Productivity*, to be published by the Industrial Relations Research Association.

from one perspective the outlook, value judgements, and institutions of a given society. The attention of economists has lately been turned to the manner in which the curve of the propensity to consume might shift its position over a period of time, in response to income changes. Duesenberry has formulated the consumption function in secular terms showing how it might shift upwards with the long-period rise of the level of income, maintaining (in the United States over the period 1869–1929) a relatively constant proportion of income consumed.[1]

There is no reason to believe, however, that a unique relation exists for all societies between the level of income and the level of consumption. Despite the lack of empirical studies, there is ample *prima facie* evidence to justify our regarding the propensity to consume as determined by a much wider range of forces than the level of income alone. The propensities, in general, reflect the actual performance of societies rather than merely the psychic inclinations in individuals or in the social group regarded as an aggregate.[2] The propensities imply nothing and tell us nothing about the motivations of individuals or of groups. It is only the effective performance of a society, operating through existing institutions and its system of political power, that concerns us here. Thus, in a

[1] J. S. Duesenberry, *Income, Saving, and the Theory of Consumer Behavior* (Cambridge, Mass., 1949). See also A. H. Hansen's discussion of the social and institutional forces which might affect the consumption function over long periods, in *Business Cycles and National Income* (New York, 1951), chap. 10, especially pp. 167–70; and G. L. S. Shackle's review of Duesenberry, *Economic Journal* (Mar. 1951). On the obverse of the consumption function see R. F. Harrod's discussion of the motives for saving, *Towards A Dynamic Economics* (London, 1948), pp. 35 ff.

[2] A conception of social and political equilibrium would presumably involve an equating of the actual response of societies and the underlying inclinations of individuals. For examples of implied disequilibrium see p. 44. To be useful, however, in the present context this conception of equilibrium must be dynamically formulated. The discovery of new rich natural resources in a hitherto stagnant and complacent community may, given time, alter its whole value system and political and social aspirations. Even without such a material change in the physical environment and its material potentialities the introduction of new ideas may alter value systems and political and social aspirations. In short, a general system for society must involve a conception of the determinants over time of 'the underlying inclinations of individuals'. For an interesting effort to invoke the concept of political equilibrium in an economic analysis, see C. P. Kindleberger, *The Dollar Shortage* (New York, 1950), Appendix, pp. 255–71.

Communist state, devoting its resources heavily to capital development and armaments, the propensity to consume is a function of the full range and effectiveness of the control apparatus rather than the aggregate response of atomistic individuals. If the psychological bases of the propensity to consume or the fundamental value judgements incorporated in it are allocated to any individuals, they must in this case be allocated to those making the central plan and administering it—although the effectiveness of the administrative machinery for achieving the distribution of resources laid down by the plan, as between consumption and investment, would also be relevant. Similarly, in a relatively backward society, characterized by extremes of wealth and poverty, the propensity to consume would reflect the actual distribution of resources and the tastes and value judgements of those actually disposing of current income, rather than the behaviour which might be observed with a different distribution of income and if the will of the majority were effectively consulted in tax policy and in other fundamental institutional arrangements. In short, although the level of income may be an important and perhaps the chief independent variable which in the short run determines, together with the propensities, the allocation of resources, it does not follow that the allocations themselves are uniquely associated with the level of income. The Duesenberry analysis of secular changes in the consumption function incorporates assumptions about the social framework of the American economy, which are not to be taken as universal in time or with respect to different societies.[1]

It is possible to view the other propensities on analogy with the consumption function; that is, in relation to changes in

[1] Duesenberry's analysis is distinguished by the clarity and explicitness with which its underlying psychological and sociological assumptions are introduced. See especially *Income, Saving, and the Theory of Consumer Behavior*, pp. 23–30, and 112–13. These include behaviour which, while not necessarily unique to the United States, is not universal to all societies at all times. For example, the attainment or maintenance of a higher social status is an important driving force in American society; income is a principal criterion of status; there is a high degree of social mobility; contact with members of status groups other than one's own is sufficiently great for their consumption patterns to affect one's own; and so on.

the level of real income, both short-run and long-run. It is evident, for example, that a curve showing the proportion of total resources allocated to the pursuit of science in different societies at similar *per capita* levels of income might vary widely. The powerful influence of the seventeenth and eighteenth centuries on British and French education and culture might produce a different allocation than in the United States, with its strong empirical bent. An under-developed country, seeking to move ahead as rapidly as possible, might well show a relatively low allocation of resources for fundamental science, as might the Soviet Union, with its special history and peculiar philosophical bias against the notion of pure science. An explanation of the proportion of income devoted to fundamental science in a particular society would thus involve a broad analysis which focused aspects of its economic, social, political, and cultural heritage on a particular facet of its behaviour.

Similarly, a curve showing either the short-period or the long-period allocations of resources to the practical applications of science, in relation to income, could be explained only in terms of a general analysis that embraced factors wider than the level of income. Further, within a given economy one might find striking divergences in the propensity to apply innovations as between different industries. The range of factors that might be relevant in explaining such differences would be very broad indeed: the age of the industry and its rate of growth; the sort of management it possesses; the degree and character of the monopolistic elements in the organization; its outlook on its future prospects; and so forth.[1] A special kind of mixed economic, social, political, and perhaps even biographical analysis would be required to explain the response in a particular industry to the potentialities presented by the flow (and pool) of possible innovations.

The proportion of real income invested might also be

[1] For a partial but illuminating discussion of this problem, see E. Domar, 'Investment, Losses, and Monopoly', in *Income, Employment, and Public Policy, Essays in Honor of Alvin H. Hansen* (New York, 1948), chap. 2; also, B. S. Keirstead, *The Theory of Economic Change* (Toronto, 1948), chap. xi.

exhibited in its relation to short- and long-run changes in the level of real income for different economies; and, again, one would have to invoke the widest form of general analysis to explain the contours of the curves which might thus be derived. In this case, however, we strike an area of economic analysis, familiar in quite other terms. For certain purposes, it is true, the long-run proportion of real income invested has been statistically examined, and this relationship has contributed to various forms of analysis;[1] although the determinants of the long-run proportion of income invested in different economies have not yet been systematically explored. The short-run determination of the level of investment is, however, a highly developed segment of economic thought, central to virtually all theories of economic fluctuation. Short-run changes in the level of investment (with income given) are regarded as the consequence of the interplay between a demand curve for investment, incorporating the (expected) yields to be derived from additional increments of investment, and some form of supply curve (or market interest rate, in the Keynesian case), exhibiting the supply of funds or of real resources made available for investment. As indicated below, analogy with this form of demand-supply analysis is likely to provide a more fruitful approach to the propensities than analogy with the conventional presentation of the consumption function.

It is customary to regard the birth-rate, the last of the fundamental variables, as exhibiting significant short-period fluctuations in relation to current and expected (*per capita* or per family) income. The propensity to have children, however, is an independent parameter subject, in different societies, to a much wider range of causal forces than mere income fluctuations. Not only are there rural-urban differences (which may be partially economic in character as well as social), but also differences depending upon religious outlook, social status, and so on. The long-period course of the birth-rate cannot be taken as uniquely determined by the

[1] See, for example, W. Fellner, 'The Capital-Output Ration in Dynamic Economics', *Money, Trade and Economic Growth, Essays in Honor of John Henry Williams* (New York, 1951).

level of real income any more than can the long-period course of the proportion of income consumed.

This form of presenting the propensities in relation to changes in the level of income is not wholly satisfactory, for it somewhat obscures the character of their short-run relation to the economic decisions which they help to determine. The propensities constitute a formalization of a society's response to certain kinds of economic incentive, given the structure of its value system, as effectively operative through its existing economic, social, and political institutions. Changes in the level of income may, indeed, affect the strength of the economic incentive to invest, in general, or to invest in these particular directions isolated at this stage of the analysis for special treatment; namely, in fundamental or applied science. Changes in income may affect the incentive to accept innovations, the economic attractiveness of consumption versus saving, or the economic attractiveness of having children. And the relation between income changes and the yields to be derived from the allocation of resources in different directions is an important area for analysis. But we come closer, conceptually, to the central process if we regard the basic decisions examined here as resulting from the interplay between a range of possible economic yields (in the form, perhaps, of a conventional demand curve), and a supply curve, reflecting the response of the society to those yields, with income given.

The meaning of this way of looking at the propensities is best seen with respect to the determination of the level of investment. The propensity to seek material advance, as it relates to the volume of current investment, would indicate, at any period of time, with a given level of income, what volume of resources an economy would allocate to investment at alternative levels of expected profits. The alternatives actually open would depend on the combination of yields from natural resources available and the willingness of entrepreneurs to accept innovations. With the effective demand curve (or curves) for the economy thus given one can conceive of the level of investment and the complex of rates of interest as determined by the supply curve (or curves) of finance, showing, with income given, the funds which a society would be prepared to make available at different levels of expected profit and risk.[1] Here again it would be important, in any realistic analysis, to distinguish the response to profit and innovation possibilities in different sectors of the economy which, in the present analysis, would affect the position and shape of supply and demand curves, respectively. To explain the difference in response to similar combinations of profit and risk, as between different sectors of the same economy, or as between different economies, one would have to probe into the whole outlook of those responsible for risk taking and the degree of innovation.

The conventional assumption in economic theory that entrepreneurs will seek to maximize profit does not adequately take into account the possibility that the responsible lenders and entrepreneurial groups may well differ in the premium attached to profit as against risk, as against the disruption to existing routines, as against the sheer effort and energy required to take the required innovational steps, as against the damage innovation in one firm might do to other firms in the industry, and so forth. If one were to explore, for example, differences between the entrepreneurial response of leaders in the American and British coal industries between the wars or between American and French entrepreneurs in the steel industries at the present time or between British and French entrepreneurs as a whole in the first half of the nineteenth century, one would have to take into account an exceedingly broad range of forces which lie outside the field of economics as it is now usually conceived.[2]

It will be recalled that, in one of its aspects, the propensity to seek material advance is taken as a determinant of the

[1] For a more detailed discussion of the determination of the level of investment in this scheme, see pp. 66-69.

[2] An interesting comparative analysis of this character is that of A. W. Menzies-Kitchin, *Labor Use in Agriculture*, University of Cambridge, Dept. of Agriculture, Farm Economics, Branch Report, No. 36 (July 1951). The author concluded that differences in productivity stem not only from certain strictly economic and technical differences between the two countries but also from the differences in social attitudes toward farm labour and from the fact that 'Women on the farms in America provide a spur to additional effort by demanding a higher standard of amenities'.

effective strength of the working force, with the size and technical skill of the working force given. Conventional economic analysis has long allowed for a variable of this kind. In the short period, changes in the effort put forward by a working force in relation to the real return offered have been considered, including the case of a negative response to wage increases: the backward-sloping supply curve of elementary economics courses. And the notion that the response of labour in terms of effort to varying real wage rates may differ as between societies or sectors of an economy is not unfamiliar, although the factors which might determine such differences have by no means been systematically examined.

The other propensities might also be related not to changes in the level of income but to a particular profit curve, indicating the yield to be derived from the allocation of additional units of resources to fundamental science, applied science, &c., with the short-period level of income fixed.[1] Thus, with a given level of income, the volume of resources devoted to fundamental science would be determined by the intersection of two curves: a downward-sloping curve, reflecting, let us say, diminishing yield from additional increments of investment in pure science, and an upward-sloping curve, exhibiting allocation of resources to science with a rise in expected yields. It might be the case that the scale on which fundamental science was pursued was determined wholly by tradition, love of truth, &c.; and that the supply curve of resources for this purpose was inelastic with respect to the economic yield believed to attach to this form of activity. A similar pair of curves might exhibit, with income given, the productivity of application of resources to applied science and the response of the society to such possible yields. The propensity to apply innovations might, again, be shown as an upward-sloping curve, exhibiting the number of innovations applied at different levels of yield and with a given income level; while the possibilities offered might be exhibited by a downward-sloping curve, which arrayed such

[1] In short-period income analysis the expected yield would be the relevant variable. See Chap. V.

possibilities according to yield. The birth-rate, with a given income level, might be shown by the intersection of the economic rate of return over cost for children, including negative positions, and the propensity to have children, as determined by other factors.

It is, thus, not difficult in these partial-equilibrium terms, to formulate the role of the propensities, in relation to the aspects of the investment process here selected as decisive, as the supply response of a society to the yields offered by the operation of the economic system and the productivity of various stocks. The position and slope of the supply curves would summarize within them the complex calculus of human beings weighing the profit possibilities before them against all other forms of activity (or inactivity), economic or otherwise. Profit might not only be weighed against costs, in terms of alternative uses of resources, or the disruption of existing methods; it might be, as it were, reinforced by non-economic satisfactions to be derived from the allocation of resources in certain directions, as, for example, in the pursuit of fundamental science or the having of children.

But can we deal with the consumption function in such terms? The yield to be derived from additional units of consumption is a concept which would plunge us into the old, unsolved problems of the measurement of utility. Abstracting, however, from the question of risk and enterprise, we may take the rate of interest on safe securities as representing the cost of additional units of consumption; and we may then exhibit the propensity to consume as a curve rising inversely with the rate of interest, and, with income fixed, exhibiting the volume of consumption at different (secure) rates of interest.[1] Although this is an awkward means of

---

[1] In her essay, 'The Generalisation of *The General Theory*' (*The Rate of Interest and Other Essays*, London, 1951), Mrs. Joan Robinson exhibits Keynesian equilibrium as determined by a relation between the rate of interest and the marginal efficiency of capital which would hold investment and consumption in an appropriate relationship, and then considers the inadequacy of the interest rate, in fact, as such an equilibrating mechanism. In part this inadequacy stems from the motives for saving. In the present formulation, for example, the propensity to consume would undoubtedly show slight short-run elasticity with respect to the reciprocal of the secure interest rate; and some might judge that the enticements of high interest rates to saving might be fully cancelled out,

approach, the analysis of the consumption behaviour of different societies and different groups with similar income positions in relation to different (safe) interest rates would correctly pose the fundamental issues raised by the conception of the propensity to consume, and permit its formulation in terms symmetrical with the other propensities.

There are, then, two ways of distinguishing the propensities from the economic decisions to which they relate and of indicating the sense in which they may be regarded themselves as conceptually quantitative. We can examine, by one method, the relation between changes in income and the allocation of resources in various directions in different societies (or sectors) both in the short run and in the long run. In the short period, regarded as the response of a society to changes in the level of income, the propensities would define a relation between the level of real income and allocation of resources to fundamental science, applied science, and consumption. The propensity to apply potential innovations would show the quantitative relation between the level of income and the proportion of potential innovations accepted. With a given population, the propensity to have children would define the relation between changes in income and the number of births. The propensity to seek material advance would define, in one of its aspects, the relation between the level of income and the volume of resources devoted to investment; in another aspect, it would exhibit, with a working force of given size, the effective effort associated, in any short period, with alternative levels of real income. In the long period the propensities would indicate the successive positions of the short-period curves or, alternatively, the path of various short-period situations at, say, successive full-employment positions. Concretely, one might exhibit the amount of total resources allocated to fundamental science, applied science, and consumption associated over considerable time periods, within a given society, at full employment with different levels of total real income. Similarly the birth-

and more, by the possibility offered by high interest rates of achieving the security objectives of saving with a diminished outlay of resources drawn from current income.

rate might be charted against the long-period course of real income per family, or *per capita*, as might the proportion of income invested. Finally, one might exhibit the proportions of potential innovations accepted, in relation to the long-period course of real income.

By an alternative method, which is conceptually more precise but less susceptible of statistical investigation, one might regard the propensities as reflecting, for any short period of time, the response of a society to changes in the yields believed to be associated with the allocation of the resources in various directions. This approach involves certain difficulties. There are ambiguities with respect to the yield to be derived from fundamental science; the yield from the having of children is, in most societies, almost certainly negative; and one must regard the yield from additional increments of consumption as related inversely to the interest rate, rather than directly to some utility index for increments of consumption. Nevertheless, in conception, this mode of presenting the propensities appears a possible way of indicating their nature and of isolating them from the fundamental economic decisions which they help to determine.

It is evident that a distinction exists between establishing the quantitative nature of a concept and effectively measuring it. As noted on pp. 22–23, grave difficulties of measurement would exist in certain cases, and in practice even the exact limits of certain of the concepts would have to be decided in a rough and ready way. Nevertheless, the propensities can be quantitatively defined, in the sense, for example, that they may exhibit differing quantitative responses to similar, objective economic possibilities. And since, for practical purposes, it may suffice to consider their increase or decrease, rather than their absolute position, indexes reflecting their movement might serve. It is not the statistical measurement of demand curves which has made them a useful tool but their conceptually quantitative nature, which has permitted meaningful statements concerning their movement and their elasticity. The usefulness of the propensities as working tools of analysis is unlikely to be decided wholly on grounds of difficulty or ease of precise measurement.

The propensities emerge, then, as the summation of the complex response of a society in certain directions to changes in income and/or in (known or believed) profit possibilities; but they are themselves determined by a much wider range of forces in which the long-run course of income is one among numerous possible variables.

III

The use of the propensities in the present analysis involves a frank abandonment of the effort to make economic behaviour solely a function of what are conventionally regarded as economic motives. The propensities exhibit the extent to which the actual economic decisions of a society deviate from those which would obtain if 'economic' motives alone were operative. If such an approach is not to result in chaos, some provision must be made for formal treatment of the wider determinants of the propensities; that is, the character of the interrelated economic, social, and political process which would yield for a given society, at a given period of time, propensities of a particular strength and character.

We are confronted here by the lack of any coherent and agreed theory of societies as a whole. By invoking certain powerful simplifying assumptions concerning the human character (profit maximization and diminishing relative marginal utility) and concerning natural resources (diminishing returns), economists have been able to build, over the past two centuries, a remarkable body of scientific thought. No very useful cause is served by simply repeating the old rallying cry against economic theory, i.e. economics ignores certain basic 'human factors'. Those who would seek to broaden the basis of fundamental assumptions about human behaviour within economic analysis face the heavy responsibility of doing so without violating the accumulated achievement of the most advanced of the social sciences.

The author cannot pretend to knowledge of the precise assumptions about human behaviour which, if formally elaborated, would yield a theory of society within which economics would be one portion. He would, however, define the ultimate theoretical goal of the social sciences in some such terms, while admitting scepticism concerning the likelihood of its early achievement.[1] Progress towards that goal is likely to take shape when the fundamental human motives are clarified and generalized by the maturing, in combination, of psychiatry, social psychology, and sociology. From such a base, a method might be developed for dealing with human and social behaviour, in various circumstances, as a balancing among alternative human objectives when confronted with the challenges and possibilities of different environments. In this balancing process we might find, in the end, that some extended version of the economist's diminishing relative marginal utility plays a part.

Within the present analysis, the need for considering the broad determinants of the propensities has a special importance. An essential part of the structure elaborated here consists in the notion that the propensities are determined by a complex of forces largely independent of the level of income in a given period for a particular society, and largely independent of short-period changes in income. The propensities are regarded as a function of the value system (or groups of value systems) of a society; and thus they are fundamentally connected with the social structure and institutions of a society and the manner in which production has been organized. Only in this roundabout, long-run manner are the propensities linked to the level of income. When sudden changes occur in the propensities, they are believed to be connected with violent and usually revolutionary changes in the effective balance of power among the classes in a society, and often with a shift in the balance of political power.

It will be recalled that the choice of the propensities set forth here has been determined in the light of certain economic variables, and that the case for their choice awaits the exposition of Chapter III. Looking at society from an historian's point of view, or from the perspective of the sociologist,

For observations on this conception of the goal of the social sciences, see K. Boulding, 'A Conceptual Framework for Social Science', delivered Mar. 1951 before the Michigan Academy of Arts and Sciences, to be published in a forthcoming issue of its proceedings; also J. S. Duesenberry, 'Some Aspects of the Theory of Economic Development', *Explorations in Entrepreneurial History*, vol. iii, No. 2, 15 Dec. 1950, pp. 68–74.

for example, the propensities are introduced from an alien system of thought. The economist, in a sense, is simply asking the general analyst of society certain particular questions concerning social behaviour, suggested by the economist's particular interests.

It is possible, therefore, that on investigation the forces determining the strength and position of one propensity might also be directly relevant to the strength and position of other propensities, since their separability stems from economic rather than social analysis. It is quite likely, in a given society, that the general analyst would find the social forces making for increased allocations of resources to fundamental science the same or closely related to those making for increased allocations to applied science; and the same set of forces also operating to increase the propor-tion of innovations accepted, to shift outward the supply curve of finance, and to reduce the death-rate. In a rough way these phenomena are all often associated with the complex of underlying forces which have caused industrial revolutions in Western societies.[1]

The possibility of changes in the strength of the propensi-ties, stemming from common causes, does not, in itself, limit their usefulness or validity. It is essential, however, that the propensities be distinguishable, one from another; that changes in each be capable of separate analysis; and above all, that they be aspects of social and political outlook and behaviour correctly chosen in relation to economic analysis.

The earlier discussion of the propensities within this chap-ter should indicate that the propensities are essentially separ-able, and related to discrete quantitative aspects of a society's performance. Further, reflection on the history of various societies and their contemporary position should indicate the possibility that the propensities might vary in their relative strength within societies of broadly similar structure; and that they might vary as among regions, sectors, and social groups within a given society. In short, regarded as social phenomena relating to a particular society, the propensities

[1] See, for example, T. S. Ashton, *The Industrial Revolution* (London, 1948), especially chap. i.

are not a single package. In talking of the propensities we are not using different names to describe the same variable. They need not all move in a consistent relationship to one another in conformity to some other single variable, for example, the level of real income or the relative size of the middle classes, somehow defined. On the other hand, they are economists' concepts, not those of the sociologist. This means that the sociologist, in dealing with the questions they raise, will undoubtedly desire to relate them to his own concepts and vocabulary; and from his point of view the propensities may represent simply aspects of other phenomena, judged more basic by the sociologist, or complex manifestations not related simply and directly to any one concept or variable in his domain.

The formal position which emerges from the analysis might now be stated in the following terms: The propensities summarize those aspects of social and political behaviour believed to be directly relevant to the level of output and the rate of economic growth; the strength of the propensities and the course of their change are not simple functions of the level of real income or its change; the strength of the propensities and their course of change are determined by a complex inter-relationship among the economic, social, and political forces of a society, long-run and slow-moving in character.

In another place the author has attempted to suggest a rough framework which would indicate the character of the inter-relationships among economic, social, and political factors.[1] The view developed there may be briefly summarized as follows. Economic factors are distinguished with respect to the time period over which they operate on the economy and within this infinite possible array four types of economic forces are arbitrarily distinguished: very long-run economic factors, including geography, climate, natural resources; long-run factors, relating to the methods of production and distribution of the working force; medium-run forces associated with trends longer than, say, a decade; short-run forces,

---

[1] *B.E.N.C.*, pp. 126–44. In the present context the term 'social' embraces the world of ideas, religion, and what is often called the culture of a society, as well as its social structure in a stricter sense.

associated with business cycles, harvest fluctuations, &c. Movements within the economic system—very long-run and long-run in character, the latter related to the composition of the working force and the techniques of production—set the framework within which social life and its concepts evolve, pursuing on the whole a sluggish life of their own. The long-run impulses have their main impact on politics, having worked through the social structure, where they have been generalized, built into institutions, associated with non-economic aspirations, and crystallized into ideas and particular, often structural, political objectives, often of a fundamental, constitutional character. These long-run economic influences, through the workings of the social system, also play back on the economy, either reinforcing or retarding the trend of its development. Similarly, the medium-run or trend impulses imparted from the economic system become associated with wider concepts and objectives before they make their full appearance in politics, often in the form of particular non-structural acts of legislation designed to operate within the existing structural framework of politics. The short-run economic forces tend to strengthen or weaken the relative forces making for or resisting political change; and they thus affect the timing and character of political events. The political level of society receives from the other levels this complex of impulses, and by rules and conventions and ideas which are themselves partially the product of long-run economic and social influences, sorts them out, and seeks to resolve conflicts among them in a manner such as to avoid resort to settlement by trial of brute strength.[1] In performing these functions the political level of society sets the legal terms for both social and economic relationships within it; and, in receiving and disbursing income, it actively engages in current activity of economic and social significance.

[1] While totalitarian states obviously take a different view of individual and group aspirations and wishes than democratic societies, and a different view of the proper scope and techniques of the police power of the state, it can probably be said that practitioners of dictatorship regard the goal of politics as the achievement of their ends by the use of forces other than brute strength (e.g. propaganda), however ready they may be to compromise with methods short of that goal.

This thoroughly interacting structure leaves, at every level, a substantial role for the individual and for adventitious circumstances; and it can thus be regarded as determinist only *ex post*. Although the analysis gives, formally, a special initial position to economic forces, this is an arbitrary aspect of its exposition rather than a matter of causal priority. The analysis would assert that social and political consequences flow from sustained economic changes; but, since the system is interacting, it leaves open the possibility that economic changes themselves are the product of political or social forces. And further, the system gives no special priority to economic motives over the other motives which move men to act.

The propensities belong, in these terms, with the social level of society; and they are designed to help analyse the play-back on the economy of the social structure, at a particular period of time. They reflect the scheme of ideas and values relevant to economic action with which a community equips the individual and which are incorporated in the community's institutions. While these ideas may be modified, rejected, or supplanted by an individual in the course of his life and experience, for profound reasons, which any theory of society must ultimately take into account, these fundamental conceptions and evaluations are altered only slowly.[1]

Since the normally slow-moving character of the propensities, in relation to the potentially more irregular (short-run) movement of economic yields and incentives, is central to this structure, and to such scientific content as it may contain, it is important to array the forces which might account for the slow-moving character of value systems, the institutions which incorporate them, and the propensities which are a manifestation of them.

There are, perhaps, three reasons for the sluggishness of fundamental ideas. First, they appear to be acquired relatively early in life and change relatively slowly thereafter. Keynes's observation about ideas in economics and political philosophy has a wider application: '. . . there are not many who are influenced by new theories after they are twenty-five

[1] *B.E.N.C.*, pp. 126–44, especially pp. 134–7.

or thirty years of age. . . .'[1] Second, but related to this phenomenon, is the role of such ideas in relation to the individual. They serve to bring order to a fundamentally unstable and treacherous world. They are the means by which an individual interprets what he sees around him; and they afford a degree of security and stability in confronting complex and otherwise chaotic circumstances. No general theory of society could be constructed without leaving a place for the security requirement of individuals for stability in fundamental values and for their consequent resistance to their change.[2] As Dr. William C. Menninger has recently said:[3]

When any of us is confronted by an unknown, by a new situation with its new demands for which we have no immediate answer, we become insecure in varying degrees. When there are many rapid and major changes demanded of us—and our scientific progress has done this to all of us—we therefore become more insecure and uncertain. Our individual beliefs and attitudes, and way of life are not something that we easily cast off. They are our personal means of solving our problems, serving an important function in our psychological lives. Whether they are our amulets or prejudices, political leanings or religious faith, they are all important to us and we resist their change—i.e., their loss. It matters not if they are right or wrong, healthy or unhealthy, backward or progressive. The human personality resists change. When it is forced upon us it gives rise to insecurity. Insecurity is increased when the result of change is unknown or, if known, is undesired.

Nevertheless, values do change. And, over time, they appear to change in such a way as to cope with the phenomena that men confront daily in their lives. There appear to be substantial reasons why the ideas men apply to their environment should lag behind actual changes within it;

[1] J. M. Keynes, *General Theory* (New York, 1936), pp. 383-4.
[2] At least one recent analyst takes the view that modern American society is characterized by a failure to implant in its children a set of fundamental values, leaving the individual abnormally subject, as compared with earlier times, to accommodation to the views and behaviour of others. D. Riesman, *The Lonely Crowd* (New Haven, 1950).
[3] 'Social Change and Scientific Progress', Arthur Dehon Little Memorial Lecture, M.I.T. (Cambridge, Mass., 1951), pp. 29-30. See also the illustrations cited by Menninger and relevant to economic growth, pp. 30-32.

nevertheless, there is a hard, long test of empiricism that societies appear to apply to the large ideas they accept.[1]

Accepting the notion that ideas are adjusted to the physical environment by a complex, lagged process, there is, however, a third reason for the slow change of ideas, which can be made apparent under certain simplifying assumptions. Let us assume that all ideas are related to a social system which arises from the nature and composition of output in an economy, i.e. the Marxist half- or quarter-truth. Let us ignore the influence of time lags and of very long-run environmental factors, not necessarily related to the manner of organization of the economy. Then, ideas in the wide sense, or the value system of the society, would be adjusted without friction to the social structure emerging from the current techniques of production and the current balance in the distribution of the working force, taken by broad classes. But techniques of production and the proportionate distribution of a working force themselves alter relatively slowly. This relative sluggishness, in turn, results from the fact that such alterations in the structure of a society stem from the scale and character of current investment. Even economies where the proportion of current income invested is high, and where the composition of current investment differs radically from the over-all (current) composition of capital, exhibit relatively slow changes in the distribution of the working force. Thus, if we choose grossly to simplify the model of a society in such a manner that its fundamental values are made, without friction or time lag, a simple function of the method of output and the distribution of the working force, the propensities would even then emerge as slow-changing phenomena.

The Marxist hypothesis is faulty in two respects at least:[2]

---

[1] For further discussion see the author's *B.E.N.C.*, pp. 135-7.

[2] It may be argued, from certain passages in Marx and Engels, that the Marxist hypothesis allowed for an interacting process in society; and that the independent power of religion, nationalism, and other very long-run cultural forces were given due weight. It is certainly the case that Marx and Engels had some second thoughts about economic determinism, in its simple form (see, for example, Barrington Moore, Jr., *Soviet Politics—The Dilemma of Power* [Cambridge, Mass., 1950], pp. 6-8). It is also the case, however, that from the

it omits, or makes arbitrarily dependent, the role of very long-run forces (which have manifestations, for example, in religion and the consciousness of nationality); and it gives an undemonstrated priority and fundamental causal position to economic motivations and economic processes in social and political life.

History affords cases where the balance of ideas and values effectively operative in a society appear to change rapidly: e.g. in the decade of the 1860's in the United States; in France as a result of the revolution; in Japan as a result of its opening to the Western world and its internal revolution of the late 1860's; in Russia, as a result of the revolution; and in modern Turkey, Israel, Pakistan, &c. The possibility of such relatively rapid changes does not alter the validity of the analysis; for it was only by an alteration in the effective balance of power and the relative influence among social groups that such changes came about; and it is the association of the propensities with specific social groups and their relative balance which gives them their normally slow-changing character. In turn, the possibility of rapid changes in the effective balance of forces in a society usually stems from a prior actual change in the balance, frustrated by the rigidity of the social and political system, and given effective expression by revolutionary changes.

For any period of time, then, an analysis of the propensities must proceed in terms of the forces which determine the relative strength of certain fundamental values and attitudes in a given society and their effective strength. In turn this requires a consideration of the prior long-period inter-rela-

Communist Manifesto forward the practitioners of Marxism have written as if societies were determined by their economic techniques and the composition of output; and that it is via economic changes that changes elsewhere in societies are brought about. Both in the Soviet Union and elsewhere Marxists in responsibility have found this a thoroughly inadequate basis for the exercise of the pursuit of power and have employed heterodox devices without, however, wholly abandoning their dogma. If, in fact, present Soviet practice were to be given a full theoretical foundation, freed of the necessity of maintaining a strand of continuity with Marx, such a theory of society would approximate a conception of political (rather than economic) determinism. In effect, Lenin and Stalin have reversed Marx's effort and set Hegel right side up again. An Hegelian doctrine of societal change is, however, subject to strictures at least as severe as those applicable to a doctrine of economic determinism.

tions among economic, social, and political factors in that society; in short, a consideration of its history.

If the determinants of the propensities are taken to be given by an *ex post* consideration of certain broad forces operating in a society over long periods, to what scientific status can they pretend? In particular, to what extent is the course of their change predictable, from an analysis of their current position and strength?

It is at this stage that we confront the lack of a general theory of society; that is, we do not know enough about the complex inter-relations within a society to predict with any exactness what its attitudes toward fundamental science, applied science, &c., would be, from a knowledge of its other attributes. To put it another way, we must examine as nearly as we can the behaviour of a society at a particular period of time, with respect to allocations of resources to fundamental science, applied science, &c., before we can measure the propensities related to those allocations. The presentation of this structure cannot shirk an underlining of this fundamental, formal weakness.

While a formal prediction of the propensities from other variables is outside our grasp in the present state of knowledge, an explanation of the propensities in terms of the evolution of a given society is possible and, in effect, is usefully conducted in many forms of historical and contemporary analysis. The complex of factors determining attitudes toward the having of children, for example, or toward material advance, or toward science can be reasonably well sorted out in any given case. Moreover, the bases for these attitudes can be traced back into the groups which are attached to them, and to the economic, social, and political process by which they came to hold their relative strength within those groups and, on balance, within the society as a whole. It is often possible, viewing a certain society, to associate certain attitudes and value systems with different classes or groups and, on the basis of the path of economic and social development that society is pursuing, to associate changes in the balance of attitudes in the society with the changing balance of the economic and social system. This sort of connexion is a familiar aspect of analyses which trace the shift of a society from a rural to an urban majority. It figures, for example, in conventional analyses of the background to the American Civil War[1] or the Reform Bill of 1832 in Britain.[2] In short, *ex post*, the propensities can be 'explained' in terms of a decently comprehensive and analytic historical understanding of a society; and, given their roots in certain slow-changing economic and social structural features of a society, the propensities are subject to some degree of prediction.

The historical method is often adequate for fruitful independent analysis of the process whereby the propensities change.[3] For example, it is possible to observe the rise in number and influence of the British industrial middle class during the period of the French wars early in the nineteenth century. We can observe not only its successful struggle for political power but the spread through the country of what might be called its value system: the premium it placed on natural science, on material progress, on education, on the relative independence of the individual as against the State, and so on. *Pari passu* we can observe the relative decline in the value system associated with important segments of the landowning gentry who had, on balance, played so important a part in the previous century.[4] Connected with this shift in

[1] See, for example, S. E. Morison and H. S. Commager, *The Growth of the American Republic* (New York, ed. 1940), vol. i, chaps. xxviii and xxix.

[2] See, for example, D. Thomson, *England in the Nineteenth Century* (London, 1950), pp. 73–76.

[3] If one accepts the notion that the power ideas and values exercise over a society is in some manner positively correlated with the time period over which they have been accepted and applied as a guide to human action, historical analysis would have a special technical importance in determining the character and strength of a society's response to particular situations, at any period of time. Some of the greatest errors in judgement in modern times (e.g. Hitler's misjudgement of the response of Britain to defeat on the Continent in 1940) can be traced back to a failure to give certain attitudes a weight appropriate to the length of time period over which they have operated. In the case of Britain in 1940 Hitler much overrated the weaknesses and schisms revealed during the inter-war years as against a nationalism generated by some nine hundred years of successful and unviolated island life.

[4] In Britain, of course, many landowning gentry of the seventeenth and eighteenth centuries were among the principal contributors to the ideas and even techniques which formed the foundations of the Industrial Revolution.

the balance of social and political forces and with fundamental values, we can observe, and to some extent we might even measure, shifts in the effective strength of the propensities. One of the dynamic determinants of the propensities, over time, was certainly the rise in national income itself, and the importance within total income of its industrial component. The self-reinforcing process envisaged here is analogous to that described and used by Gunnar Myrdal, in another context.[1]

The nature of the forces determining these propensities might decree not only a self-reinforcing rise, as in early nineteenth-century Britain, but a self-reinforcing decline, as in Spain after 1600. The inverse relation between income and family size in certain phases of the history of a number of societies, as well as between urban life and family size, is perhaps the best known of these built-in decelerators affecting the level of the real national income through the propensities. Recent movement of the birth-rate and the propensity

---

[1] *An American Dilemma* (New York, 1944), Appendix 3, pp. 1065–70. In the course of this study of the Negro problem in America Myrdal evolved a dynamic social model, on analogy with the economic model developed in his *Monetary Equilibrium* (London, 1939). He took as his focus, in this social model, the gap between the conception of equality incorporated in the American creed and the actual performance of American society in its treatment of the Negro. The gap, in turn, he found to be determined by some of the *de facto* differences between Negroes and whites; e.g. with respect to education, dress, manner, &c., as well as colour. This array of factors he took to be mutually inter-related. Under these circumstances any force which affected one of these *de facto* differences might have a cumulative effect on the others, and on the gap itself. This social model might, then, spiral in either direction. A boom or a slump affecting the relative economic and social position of the Negro might set it in motion; legislation affecting the educational opportunities of the Negro; war-time arrangements which broke down barriers between Negro and white; and so on. The present exploration of the determinants of the propensities would thus share with Myrdal's analysis its dynamic character; its eclecticism with respect to the forces and motivations which might set in motion a cumulative social (and economic) process; its acceptance of the interacting nature of the relations between the sectors of society. It may be noted that Myrdal defined as the fundamental dynamic force, in altering the character of the Negro problem in America, the American creed: that is, a set of persistent social and political ideals. This selection of a key parameter is not unlike Duesenberry's focusing on a belief in the ability to transform the environment as central to economic growth (see pp. 77–79). Both analyses would leave open, in a sense, the process which determined the emergence and the power of such central dominating conceptions.

to have children, however, suggest, even here, the importance of caution in associating the propensities in any oversystematic way with the level of income alone. Although an analogy of this sort is dangerous, something like the observable waning of the impulse to expand material wealth to be noted in successive generations within families may apply to important segments of society or even to whole societies, affecting particularly the propensity to accept innovations and the propensity to seek material advance.[1] In the balancing which men and societies perform among material advance, security, leisure, &c., a form of diminishing returns to any one objective in relation to the others may operate over time. For example, it is, perhaps, not a too grave distortion of history to regard the post-1945 acceptance in Britain

[1] See, for example, the recent observations on the quality of industrial management in New England by the Committee on the New England Economy (*The New England Economy, a Report to the President*, Washington, 1951, chap. vii), which include the following (pp. 81–82): 'New England needs more enterprising management. The Committee has been told time and again that some firms, especially in the older, declining industries, have often missed the opportunity to extend or even maintain their market positions because of a failure to follow realistic policies in the scrapping and replacing of their obsolete plant and equipment. We have likewise been told that even in the expanding industries some firms have been unwilling to modernize and expand their plant and equipment to take advantage of the opportunities presented.

'Both labor and management have commented on the imperviousness to new ideas of many New England executives. Management responsibility in the hands of third and fourth generations, who often do not show the ability of the original owners, partially explains management deficiencies. In some cases, absentee ownership also contributes to management weakness because of an unawareness of technical problems and plant requirements. On the other hand, in some cases outside management has been the source of renewed vigor and improved management techniques.

'Management weakness in some communities also depends on the lack of opportunity for individuals from all groups in the community to rise to supervisory positions. In the past, but fortunately not to the same extent currently, those with control in the textile and shoe industries did not provide opportunities for individuals irrespective of social groupings to attain management positions. This reflected in part the general social and economic stratification of our textile and shoe communities. We have also been told that New England textile firms have not and are not recruiting their reasonable share of able graduates from our leading textile schools. In fact it has been widely questioned whether New England firms generally are as enterprising as they should be in picking up potential executive and supervisory talent from the local universities. Furthermore, there are frequent complaints that executives are not allowed to participate in the ownership and share in profits.'

of enlarged government responsibility for stimulus to the development and application of innovations, as the society's response to its view of the inter-war situation. It is widely believed in Britain that during the inter-war years, important segments of the economy, notably the older industries, lacked private vigour in the functions of innovation, risk-taking, and investment. It would, indeed, be of interest to examine the sociology of the leadership in various sectors of the British economy during the inter-war years, seeking to segregate the extent to which the difficulties imposed by the world environment of particular industries were responsible for their performance as opposed to the priority placed by their leaders on values other than material efficiency and material advance. In terms of the present vocabulary the issue is the extent to which the difficulties, for example, in the British coal industry between the wars is to be allocated to the state of yields as opposed to the position of the propensities.

Whether or not particular social groups are subject systematically to some 'shirtsleeves to shirtsleeves in three generations' cycle or to a sequence of economic rise and fall like Thomas Mann's Buddenbrooks, the familiar pattern itself illustrates the possibility of changes in the propensities related not to change nor even long-term fluctuations in income alone but to the more complex process whereby individuals, groups, or societies form and balance their schemes of values, in which income changes are not a unique, independent variable.[1]

---

[1] It seems possible that some of the essential analytic issues raised in the empirical study of entrepreneurship might be better gripped by an imaginative consideration of the character and motivations of key industrial and financial leaders than by a detailed and conventional consideration of the strictly economic operations of the firms which they controlled. Marshall's consideration of the 'Agents of Production' (Book IV, *Principles of Economics*) includes a length analysis of the qualitative factors attaching to land, labour, and capital, including entrepreneurship. As Mrs. Robinson points out in her 'Generalisation of *The General Theory*', Marshall was prepared to regard the deterioration in entrepreneurial ability, from one generation to the next, as a factor limiting the growth of firms, a process in which the inadequacies of domestic servants and the self-indulgent habits induced by living in very rich houses play a part (p. 207 n.). In Marshall's formal analysis of the long period, however, these social forces would enter into the rise and fall of trees in the forest; he did not consider systematically the manner in which they might relate to the evolution

IV

This structure of analysis is based on a particular conception of the manner in which the various social sciences might best work together. The author would hold that what is most required at the present exploratory stage of thought are working links which would permit the partial techniques developed out of an era of intellectual specialization in the social sciences to be brought to bear on problems of common interest and concern. A part of the working method for this form of inter-relation of the social sciences consists in the formulation by those concerned with one discipline of questions to be answered by those working in other disciplines, and in the incorporation of the answers into the machinery of the questioning discipline. As suggested earlier, the propensities are meant to represent the questions which an economist concerned with the problem of growth would address to the sociologist and historian.

Social analysis has, however, its own wide and changing interests. Whereas the economist's apparatus is devoted to measuring and explaining the course of the national income, clearly if arbitrarily defined, the social analyst may be examining the relative 'cohesion' of a society, the power and content of its integrating concepts, or some other central variable. A virtue which the propensities formulated here may possess is that they might permit the general analyst of societies to bring his methods to bear more effectively on the determinants of economic growth. Since Max Weber wrote and Tawney complained that 'economic interests are still popularly treated as though they formed a kingdom over which the *Zeitgeist* bears no sway',[1] it has been commonplace to discuss, in one compartment of our knowledge, the wide social framework of economic development. The challenge

of the forest itself, despite the fact that many of his *obiter dicta* in Book IV (especially chaps. vi, vii, xi, and xii) imply the existence of over-all differences in social outlook, educational systems, willingness to accept innovations, &c., which would affect the relative rates of growth of different economies or sectors of economies.

[1] R. H. Tawney, *Religion and the Rise of Capitalism* (London, ed. 1936), p. 277.

now confronted in the social sciences is technical rather than philosophical or even conceptual; namely, how to harness disparate perspectives and techniques so that they contribute effectively to a unified analysis of a given problem.

Contemporary sociologists and social historians have given some attention in their own terms to the issues posed by the propensities.[1] Sawyer's essay on modern France, for example, demonstrates clearly how the current analytic categories of sociology, whatever their inadequacies, can serve as a useful frame for the treatment of economic institutions and attitudes. In the terms developed here Sawyer may be said to analyse the relative weakness in modern France of the propensities to apply science to the economy, to accept innovations, and to seek material advance. He finds French behaviour rooted, in these respects, in certain economic, social, and political patterns and scales of value, carried over from pre-Industrial Revolution times.[2] Sawyer's analysis, although related to a particular country, is broad with respect to time and not developed in detail. Parson's essay on motivation is designed to be even more abstract and exploratory. Would not a more precise and detailed account be possible of (say) the interaction of the French social system and its economy, if the changing course of the propensities were traced? Could we not better account for the impact of the Napoleonic Wars on the French economy; the sluggish years from 1815 to 1848; the relative vigour of the French expansion in the third

---

[1] See, for example, R. K. Merton, *Social Theory and Social Structure*, especially Part IV, 'Studies in the Sociology of Science' (Glencoe, Ill., 1949); T. Parsons, *Essays in Sociological Theory Pure and Applied*, especially chap. ix, 'The Motivation of Economic Activities' (Glencoe, Ill., 1949); J. E. Sawyer, 'Strains in the Social Structure of Modern France', chap. 17 of *Modern France*, edited by E. M. Earle (Princeton, 1951). To the author, a thoroughly non-professional reader of modern sociology, it would appear that, at its present state, progress in that field is mainly confined to the development of descriptive categories or to the development of certain causal relations within the social level of society. No clear or agreed system of thought appears to exist which would formulate the determinants of social phenomena or the mechanics of their inter-relations with the economic and political levels of society or with the individual himself. For a somewhat crude effort to relate social behaviour to the economy, via stages in population growth, see D. Riesman, *The Lonely Crowd* (New Haven, 1950), especially chap. i.

[2] Op. cit., especially p. 303.

quarter of the century? It is for the social and economic historian himself to decide. It is the author's belief, however, that the propensities summarize reasonably precise aspects of social behaviour, quantitative in conception. They may, therefore, be capable of being traced over time, and their use might help sharpen the perspective of social analysis in its relation to the economy and permit the economist to use more effectively the fruits of historical and social analysis. Such an effort might also accelerate the progress of sociologists in making their systems more dynamic and in clarifying the processes by which social phenomena may change.

The nature of the propensities, reflecting as they do the priority of fundamental values within a society, emphasizes the moral relativity of the economist's criterion of profit maximization. Given the state of a society's resources it might, ideally, be possible for the economist to prescribe the optimum proportions of resources that might be devoted to fundamental science, applied science, &c., which would maximize the rate of growth of the real national income, as the economist defines that term. Such a proportioning of effort and behaviour would constitute a highly arbitrary pattern of preferences, prescribing as it would the premium to be placed on leisure as opposed to work, present consumption as opposed to material advance, security as against risk, the weight given to the full complex of motives for having children as against an economically optimum population growth, and so on. This does not mean that the economist must withdraw from making recommendations concerning means of raising the level of real income in societies. It does mean that he should be aware that his recommendations are not likely to be ethically or socially neutral or antiseptic. He is likely to be urging (consciously or not) a shift in the effective strength of the propensities and is thus confronting the deep, slow-moving social and ethical foundations of a society This, perhaps, is one way of stating the greatest lesson to be learned from American post-war experience in seeking to accelerate economic development in various regions of the world, and of defining the challenge of future policy-making in this area.

In concluding this chapter it would, perhaps, be useful to set out explicitly the place of the propensities in terms of this view and method, even at the risk of repetition. In a manner to be discussed in Chapter III, it is believed that economic growth for any particular time period is partially a function of the behaviour of a society in certain particular directions, which behaviour is not wholly a response to economic motivations. The propensities are designed to isolate and to define such selected aspects of behaviour. We are then confronted with the problem of stating the determinants of the propensities. As a first descriptive approximation they may be taken as an aspect of the scale (or scales) of values within a society (or its various segments), as effectively operating through its institutional structure; and, in turn, through this medium the propensities may be linked socially with the structure of classes and, economically, with the distribution of the working force and the techniques of production.

In a fundamental, if over-simplified, sense, then, the structure is analytically circular. A rate of growth of output in Period I, caused partially by changes in the social structure, value scales, and institutions, may yield in Period II a new strength and balance in the working force, among the social classes, in the value systems and institutions, and in the propensities. It is this partial association of the propensities with slow-changing variables in the economy which assists in permitting a limited degree of predictability concerning their future course.

But the system, thus defined, is faulty at its foundations. Value systems cannot be regarded simply, or even with a time lag, as a rationale of the composition and methods of production. Very long-run forces, operating steadily, decree a powerful accretion of attitudes and values, in societies; and they produce intransigent institutions.[1] Further, evidence for the priority of economic motivations over the pursuit of other values does not exist. Finally, it is a burden of the argument

[1] For the discussion of persistent national characteristics in terms of certain very long-run factors see, for example, George Orwell, *The English People* (London, 1947), especially pp. 7–20; and A. M. Schlesinger, *New Viewpoints in American History* (New York, 1922), chaps. i and ii, as well as *Paths to the Present* (New York, 1949), chap. i.

that the system is interacting: social and political phenomena have economic consequences.

Here, owing to the state of our knowledge of society, we face a fundamental weakness, dramatized for the economic historian, for example, by the fact that successful nineteenth-century industrialists in Britain and France settled on the land and sought objectives for their children other than the advancement of the family's wealth, while the grandsons of the great American entrepreneurs of the last quarter of the nineteenth century are often to be found in public service rather than in the family firm. The motivations and value systems of individuals and societies are complex, and models based on the elaboration of economic motives alone are unsatisfactory. We are not yet in a position to state the full determinants of the propensities; but this does not wholly strip them on the scientific attributes of conceptual measurability and predictability. The available methods of the historian and the sociologist, especially if these methods are combined, can take us a long way toward sensible, useful conclusions.

This structure, then, is not economically determinist, despite the partial long-run link it would accept between the technique of production, the composition of the working force, the social structure, and the propensities. Economic determinism is avoided by the complex nature of the forces judged capable of causing a movement in the propensities and thus setting in motion a sustained economic process, and by the recognition of the power in the value systems and institutions of a society of very long-run factors, quite apart from the current techniques of production and composition of the working force. The British industrial revolution of the late eighteenth and early nineteenth centuries certainly had important social consequences, including, in the first instance, a reinforcing effect on the propensities, as did the industrial revolutions which have taken place in other parts of the world over the past several centuries. It does not follow, however, that the early innovators of British industry or, let us say, the architects of the German or Japanese industrial revolutions were wholly or even mainly governed by economic motivations. Nor does it follow that the Industrial Revolution, having been accepted by societies of different very long-run heritage, has destroyed or even dominated that heritage and yielded societies of identical social structure, value systems, institutions, or propensities. Thus the Marxist analysis is not a valid theory of society but simply furnishes a part of the mechanism for a theory of society. Such a theory does not now exist. We know enough to assert with confidence, however, that it must exhibit, at least, the following two characteristics: it must take account of the multiple motivations of human beings; and it must be a theory, dynamically interacting over time, in which economic forces at once help determine other aspects of the society and are partially determined by them.

III

THE PROPENSITIES AND
ECONOMIC ANALYSIS

I

THE central and highly classical relationship on which this analytical structure hinges can be stated as follows: the level of output of an economy is a function of the size and quality of the working force and the size and quality of the capital stock. The qualitative elements attaching both to the working force and to the capital stock are believed to be at least conceptually capable of quantitative expression; and with this productivity element included in its determinants, output may be regarded, simply, as a function of the effective size of the working force and of the effective size of the capital stock. The rate of growth of output is taken to be a function of the rate of change in these two complex variables.

The working force is, of course, related to the size of the population with whatever time lag is appropriate. The determination of the size of the working force thus involves a consideration of prior birth-rates and prior and concurrent death-rates, depending on the extent to which changes may have occurred in infant mortality or the mortality of children as opposed to current changes in mortality among age groups within the working-force range.

The size of the working force in relation to population will depend also on the extent to which the social and political framework of the economy, interacting with the economic inducements to employ such labour, results in the entrance into the working force of women and children. The skill of the working force, which is capable of quantitative expression on a rough classification basis, must also be taken into account. The degree of skill may be regarded as a consequence of prior investment within the society in education. Finally, as noted in the preceding chapter, the propensity to seek material advance, as effective within the working classes, will help determine the response of the working force to economic incentives, and thus help to determine its effective size.

The concept of capital used in this central relationship includes the stock and productivity of natural resources available to the economy, its industrial and other forms of production and service capacity, and the accumulation of the society's stock of scientific knowledge and economic techniques, including its techniques for economic and governmental organization and management.

The use of such broad definitions for the working force and capital limits the possibilities of simple measurement of the aggregates. Nevertheless, it is precisely the complex factors included here within the aggregates which are decisive to the level of productivity in a given economy, and which must be sorted out and analysed in any comparative treatment of productivity.

II

As indicated in the preceding chapter, it is essential at this stage of the argument that the rate of growth of an economy be systematically related to the propensities; for it is on their possible role in linking economic variables with the social fabric of the society that the case for the propensities as tools of analysis rests. This involves tracing the manner in which these particular aspects of social behaviour relate to changes in the working force and changes in the stock of capital.

The major subvariables here taken as determinants of the two central variables are the following:

Related to Changes in the Size and Productivity of the Working Force

1. The (prior) birth-rate.
2. The (prior and current) death-rate.
3. The role of women and children in the working force.
4. The skill of the working force.
5. The degree of effort put forward by the working force.

Related to Changes in the Size and Productivity of the Capital Stock

1. The yield from additions to the capital stock (including natural resources, fundamental and applied science, organizational techniques, &c.).

2. The (prior) volume of resources devoted to the pursuit of fundamental science.

3. The (prior) volume of resources devoted to the pursuit of applied science.

4. The proportion of the flow (and pool) of potential innovations accepted.

5. The volume of resources allocated to current investment.

6. The appropriateness of the desired level of consumption in relation to 5, above.

We turn now to the manner in which the propensities relate to the determination of certain of these subvariables and to the character of that relationship.

The birth-rate is, as indicated earlier, determined by the interplay of certain strictly economic motives for having children and the wider motivations embraced and reflected within one of the propensities.[1] The analysis outlined earlier would distinguish two possible forms of economic motivation; namely, the long-run differences in the economic usefulness of children to be noted, for example, as between rural and urban areas; and the response of the birth-rate in a given society (or sector of a society) to short-period changes in the level of income. The propensity to have children whether it is viewed in relation to changes in income or in relation to the economic role of children in a particular economy or sector, embraces the other, social variables which might influence the birth-rate; for example, the view of the family, religion, and so on.

The death-rate is more nearly a strict economic variable. It is best regarded as determined by a form of investment, i.e. investment in the size and health of the population. Setting aside the question of fertility and birth-rates, increases in population have usually resulted, in part, from improvements in medicine and public health, which have lowered death-rates. Included in this process would be, also, changes in consumption habits, induced by, say, the coming of cheap

[1] For a consideration of this problem see, for example, Alva Myrdal, *Nation and Family* (New York, 1941), especially pp. 53 ff.; also P. H. Douglas, *The Theory of Wages* (New York, 1934), chaps. xv and xvi.

cotton textiles and soap. The decline in death-rates from such influences arose, then, from an application of science to society. In economic terms, at any given time, the society was prepared to invest a certain proportion of its talent and resources both in fundamental medical science and in discovering the applications of science to medicine and public health; it was prepared to accept to a degree the changes in outlook necessary to put these innovations into effect; and it was prepared to invest a certain proportion of its resources in medicine and public health. These allocations are, for one sector of the economy (i.e. its population), aspects of the general process which determines the scale and productivity of investment, and they are partially determined by sectoral aspects of the first three propensities. To understand, for example, the forces which helped decree a fall in the British death-rate in the mid eighteenth century, one must look back to the first development and the slow spread of the modern scientific attitude, with its implication that the physical world was governed by laws which made it capable of manipulation; one must look to the evolution of ways of looking at the world which placed a new importance on the individual and his fate; one must look to the economic and social process by which increasing numbers of men were prepared to view their environment in terms which led, on balance, to new dispositions of talent and other resources. Nothing less than the great interacting historical passages which we designate as the Renaissance, the Reformation, and the emergence of commercial capitalism is directly relevant.

Similarly, improvements in diet have contributed to declining death-rates, often, as in the classic case of Britain in the eighteenth century, resulting from the application of science to agriculture. Here, too, we can distinguish underlying social forces which leave their imprint quantitatively on economic decisions: a decision to devote a proportion of resources to the application of science to agriculture; the strength or weakness of the resistance to changes in agricultural practice; the proportionate allocation of resources to investment in agricultural improvements. These are, again, aspects of the general investment process and, thus, related to the propensities.

It is evident, however, that the broad humanitarian motives which might lead a society to allocate increased resources to medicine and public health can, to some extent, be distinguished from those which would generally lead it to place a high premium on material progress, and thus generally to produce technical possibilities, accept them, and apply them, through a high proportion of income allocated to investment. The distinction in motive, if it exists, is for the sociologist to establish. It may be, however, that a disproportionate productivity attaches to investment in medicine and public health, in the early stages of its application to a primitive society, which may help account for the dangerous spiral of over-population on the land to be observed in many parts of the world in modern times.[1]

The role of female and child labour in an economy, which would help determine the size of the working force with a given population level and age distribution, may be regarded, in first approximation, as another facet of the society's effective propensity to seek material advance. An explanation of the increased role of women in the working force of Western countries in the twentieth century would involve, for example, a consideration of the full range of forces which have changed woman's status in society and woman's own attitude toward her degree of economic independence. On balance, however, this social and historical transition has effectively enlarged the propensity to seek material advance for Western societies as a whole, and so far as the working force is concerned this is what interests the economist. Similarly, the motives and forces which lead to the increased or decreased use of child labour in an economy are likely to prove complex, but can be summarized as the effective response of a society to the yields which child labour offers in the given state of production.

In weighing the net effect of the decline in child labour on

---

[1] See, for example, *Measures for the Economic Development of Under-developed Countries*, Report by a Group of Experts appointed by the Secretary-General of the United Nations (New York, 1951), pp. 45–48.

the working force, it would be necessary to take into account, with a suitable lag, the increased effective size of the working force due to better average health, education, and skill arising from longer periods for children at home and school. And it would probably not be unfair to take into account a similar but inverse calculation with respect to the movement of women into the working force which may require increased relative outlays for domestic service, housekeeping equipment, and so on.

Like the death-rate, the degree of skill and its change within the working force can be regarded as resulting from an aspect of investment; that is, it is dependent upon the quality of the educational techniques previously generated and accepted by a society, and upon the amount of resources which a society has been prepared to allocate to education.[1] As in the case of the death-rate, the motivations for increased allocations of resources to education may not be wholly economic. In a backward area the elimination of illiteracy may be regarded as justifying outlays of resources for reasons other than increased efficiency in the working force. From the point of view of economic growth, however, this is simply another example of the general possibility that economic variables may be altered under the impact of other than economic motivations.

Finally, the degree of effort put forward by a working force of a given size may be related to the propensity to seek material advance. Working forces of similar training may exhibit differences in the effective amount of work they put forward in response to equivalent material incentives. In part, these differences may stem from the premium attached to material advance in a particular society as opposed to leisure by the working force itself. In part, it may stem from wider aspects of the society; for example, the degree of discipline which the working force accepts, habit, and so on. As

[1] For a recent clear view of education as an aspect of investment in a narrow sense, as well as in its broader social sense, see 'The Stake of Business in Public School Education', an address by Frank W. Abrams before the National Citizens Commission for the Public Schools, New York, 1951: and for a more orthodox statement of this position see Marshall's *Principles*, Book IV, chap. vi, section 7, 'Education as a National Investment'.

in the other cases, the effective strength of a propensity need not be determined by economic motivations, but may represent the balancing of economic against other motivations.[1]

Thus each of the principal determinants of the effective size of the working force—birth-rates, death-rates, the role of women and children, skill, and the degree of effort put forward—can be partially related, each in its own complex way, to the social framework of the society, through the propensities, acting alone or in combination by means of the four-stage investment process; i.e. science, applied science, acceptance of innovations, and the scale of investment input. The relationship is partial, since the analysis presented here allows for the interplay, at any particular period of time, between strictly economic incentives, generated by the working of the economy, and the social parameters. Birth-rates may decline because of depression or because a lower proportion of the population is engaged on farms, where the economic return over cost of children (although probably negative) may be relatively higher than in urban life. Factory laws may be passed not only because the society has shifted the effective premium it attaches to health, welfare, and education, as opposed to children's wages, but because of the interplay between such broad forces subsumed in the propensities and the wage-cutting competition between children and adults at a time of cyclical depression, as in Britain with respect to the Ten-Hour Bill of 1847.[2] General industrial advance in an economy, moving it away from a traditional agriculture, may raise directly the economic incentive for more intense or efficient labour, causing an increase in the working force effectively available, quite apart from any

[1] The propensities are, at this stage of the argument, examined as static phenomena, given for any period of time. In this frame of analysis they can be taken as independent of the economic incentives to which they represent a response. Over time, however, one of the determinants of the degree of effort put forward by a working force may be the economic opportunities open to it in the manner discussed in generalized terms in Chap. II, pp. 35 ff.

[2] See, for example, the author's *B.E.N.C.*, pp. 118–20. In this case it may be said that a rapid fall in the yield from using children in the factories resulting from cyclical depression confronted social parameters which were slowly shifting towards the view that unlimited hours of work were immoral; and that, if necessary, a measure of material advance should be sacrificed to a moral end.

shift in the fundamental outlook or value system of the society.

This conception of the interplay of economic incentives and yields with the basic slow-moving social parameters of a society, summarized in the propensities, raises directly the question of the economic yield to be derived from applications of resources to fundamental medical science, to public health, and to agriculture (all of which bear on the size of the population and the working force), as well as to education (which helps determine its degree of skill). It was suggested above, for example (pp. 57–58), that the initial applications to a primitive society of medicine and public health might be subject to particularly high marginal productivity, perhaps, for a time, yielding increasing marginal returns. It is evident that, with reference to the special aspects of the investment process considered here (as well as the investment process considered generally below, in relation to the growth of capital), the extent to which increasing or diminishing returns operate on increments to the capital stock (including fundamental and applied science) is directly relevant to the rate of growth of the economy. For the process of growth is here regarded as resulting from a sequence of concrete decisions, allocating resources in a particular manner, which, in turn, stem from the interaction of economic yields and the social response to the incentives they represent.

The extent to which increasing or diminishing returns operate on fundamental science, medicine, public health, agriculture, and education are, then, believed to be relevant to the long-run course of the population and the working force. Here only some very tentative observations will be made. It would obviously be foolhardy to predict that diminishing returns will, in the long run, operate in fundamental science, especially in an age where the potentialities of atomic physics are only beginning to be exploited. The course of productivity over time in applied science[1] might be

[1] Major break-throughs in fundamental and in applied science cannot be automatically or simply associated. The former may consist, in the first instance, of a new conceptual formulation of familiar data and relationships; the latter may consist of the imaginative and efficient engineering application of long-familiar concepts. Successful engineering in atomic power is, for example, to

conceived as a productivity curve made up of connected sections; each section might describe the economist's classic pattern of increasing and then diminishing returns from the application of additional increments of resources. The phase of increasing returns would represent, perhaps, a new fundamental scientific break-through, opening up fresh potentialities for application to the economy.[1] In these terms agnosticism with respect to the future of scientific potentialities would constitute ignorance of whether the long-period trend of such a segmented curve will be upward or downward.

With respect to medical science, our experience may indicate that diminishing returns operate in relation to the average age of the population. After fundamental public health measures have been instituted in a society and various forms of infectious disease brought under control, a hard core of diseases reflecting organic breakdown in the human body may remain. *Prima facie*, it would seem likely that, after a certain point, increasing applications of resources would be required to extend the average life of a population by, say, an additional year.

With respect to diminishing returns in agricultural investment, a basis for dogmatic prediction would not appear to exist despite the classic notion of long-run diminishing returns in that sector which suffuses our thought. There does not appear to be any clear-cut, *prima facie* reason why the potential applications of science and technology to agriculture should, in the long run, necessarily become less productive than their application to industry; although the acceptance of innovation in agriculture may be a particularly slow and difficult process.[2]

be distinguished from the fundamentals of atomic physics. This kind of relationship between fundamental and applied science makes the concept of the economic yield from fundamental science somewhat remote; but without some such concept the determinants of economic growth are incomplete and unrealistic.

[1] B. S. Keirstead (*The Theory of Economic Change* [Toronto, 1948], pp. 146–7) presents such segmented curves exhibiting an historical sequence of major innovations. He accepts, however, a relation between the course of innovations and the level of economic activity which, in the author's view, is not justified by modern economic history. See Chap. VI.

[2] See, especially, T. W. Schultz, *Agriculture in an Unstable Economy* (New York, 1945), and *Production and Welfare of Agriculture* (New York, 1949).

With respect to education and, in particular, education for the working force in the economy, a *prima facie* case for diminishing returns would appear to exist, although here, too, an open mind might well be kept in the absence of any serious empirical evidence. One merely feels intuitively that, after literacy and certain basic skills are universally diffused, increased outlays of resources for education may be required to raise the average level of skills of a population by some arbitrary standard unit.

It should be emphasized again that these observations are designed rather to suggest the relevance to growth of the long-run yield from these various types of investment, rather than to indicate how, in fact, those yields are likely to change. In particular they are meant to indicate the inadequacy of the common habit of generalizing the classic notion of diminishing returns to land or contrasting, without careful examination, the probable course of long-run yields in agriculture and industry.

III

As noted earlier, the capital component in the central relationship embraces the scale and productivity of natural resources in a given economy as well as the stock of capital equipment and relevant techniques of organization and management.

It is conventional and often useful to regard the stock of natural resources in an economy as fixed. And there is a sense in which, by definition, they are fixed in nature, exempting geological time periods. Analytically and historically, however, the discovery of natural resources and their effective entrance into the economy can be regarded as part of the economic process, similar to the process of the discovery and application of new techniques.[1] The discovery of natural resources has often taken place in response to an incentive arising within the economic system. A rise in price for a commodity or the prospect of the exhaustion of the existing sources of supply may, for example, lead to the outlay of investment resources for the discovery of new sources of

[1] See Chap. IV, pp. 81–86, for further discussion of this point.

supply, as has recently happened in the Western hemisphere with respect to iron ore—a process that may have to be extended over a wide range of commodities in coming years throughout the world.

Further, the operations of the economic system may result in the placing of a new valuation on a known but hitherto low-valued natural resource, as for example, in recent times, with uranium-bearing ores. Much of modern economic history centres on the changing economic importance of different fundamental natural resources and requires a flexible concept of the scope of natural resources. There is a sense in which the economic system can create new natural resources by generating incentives which lead to the application of resources in their discovery and exploitation, in much the same way that new techniques in manufacture and agriculture are invoked by the pressures and incentives of growth exerted against existing capacity and techniques.

In the long run, diminishing returns are relevant to natural resources in two separable senses. Mines can, clearly, be exhausted and forests can be cut down, if their natural growth-rates are violated. Such exhaustion may occur irrespective of the techniques and capital which are associated with their exploitation. With respect to land, however, exhaustion can be avoided by appropriate techniques and methods, and the question of long-run diminishing returns, as indicated above, remains moot.

With respect to the enlargement of the capital stock, barring the exhaustibility of certain natural resources, a general process can be defined. It may be said that the enlargement of the capital stock of a society in a given period depends on the volume of current resources devoted to new investment and on the yield of such new investment. As noted earlier, the volume of resources allocated to investment in a society is partially dependent upon the propensity to seek material advance; that is, the extent to which the relevant individuals and groups respond to possibilities of profit as against the psychic costs of (borrowers') risk, of overcoming inertia and fixed routines, of disturbing relations within the industry, &c. The yield of new investment (that is, the rate of return over cost, including interest rates relevant to different degrees of lenders' risk) is also complex. It is determined by the interplay of natural resources and the innovations which are applied to them. The effective contribution of innovations to the yield on new investment results, in turn, from the operation of the first three propensities in relation to their respective yields; that is, from the propensity to apply resources to fundamental science, to apply resources to applied science, and to accept innovations. If, as is often practical and realistic, the state of fundamental and applied science can be taken as given, from outside the particular economy or sector under analysis, only the proportion of potential innovations actually incorporated within the volume of investment input is relevant.

This approach to the analysis of investment may be related to existing models quite simply. The achievement of acts of investment requires that three separable human motives be overcome: the desire for current as opposed to future consumption; the desire for security, as against risk; and the desire for stability in method, as opposed to change. It is possible to construct models for the investment process where these three separable motives are lumped together; for example, by assuming that all investment is carried out from the savings of entrepreneurs, who exhaust effectively all opportunities for profitable investment open to them expected to yield a rate of return over cost higher than the safe rate of interest. In capitalist (and other) societies in modern times the investment process is, institutionally, sufficiently specialized to justify an analytic segregation of consumption versus saving, yield versus risk, and stability versus innovation.

In the present system the propensity to consume determines the proportion of resources available for investment input, without creating inflation, given income. The propensity to accept innovations determines what proportion of the potential innovations available will, in fact, be incorporated in the investment demand curve. Finally, the propensity to seek material advance, confronting the investment demand schedule, determines the disposition of savings as between yield and risk, and the range of interest rates (when allowance is made for the action of government).

If, as in the Keynesian model, we assume that interest rates are set in a group of money-markets, where the supply and demand for funds over different time periods and degrees of risks are in play, allowing also for the scope of fiscal policy in determining these rates, then the determination of the level of investment may be shown by a modification of the Keynesian intersection between a marginal efficiency capital curve and a rate of interest. The marginal efficiency capital curve would already exhibit the degree to which innovations would be accepted, subsuming, incidentally, borrowers' risk as it is normally conceived. In other words, one can envisage an optimum demand for capital, above the marginal efficiency of capital, which would incorporate the full possibilities for profitable investment, should all the potentialities for innovation be exploited. The optimum curve would be determined by the natural resources of the economy and the (prior) allocations to fundamental and applied science. The difference between this optimum curve and the curve showing the actual demand for capital would constitute one measure of the propensity to accept innovations. Secondly, one can envisage as deducted from the marginal efficiency of capital curve, as a cost, a risk premium; that is, the difference between the safe rate of interest and the interest appropriate to the degree of risk attached by the given society to the particular act of investment. With these two modifications, taking into account explicitly the propensity to accept innovations and the propensity to seek material advance, investment may be presented in abstract but meaningful terms, as the exhaustion of profit possibilities over and above the safe rate of interest.[1]

[1] Another device for introducing this factor has been suggested to the author by Professor Samuelson. He has suggested that the enterprise factor might be isolated by showing investment as determined by the intersection of a curve of the conventional marginal efficiency of capital and a line showing the margin between the expected rate of return and the safest available interest rate. This margin, in turn, would be determined for an economy, at any period of time, by a version of liquidity or security-preference analysis. For a given economy, at any period of time, there would be a given level of secure holdings acquired, associated with each level of the margin. Thus, given the level of secure holdings

It may be argued that some such assumptions are already contained within the conventional Keynesian analysis. If so, this manner of treating the determinants of the level of investment may be regarded merely as a way of making explicit what is often left implicit within conventional treatments of the determination of the level of investment. It is central to the argument that the response to identical profit-risk-inertia combinations may vary significantly as among national economies at the same period of time, within an economy at different periods of time, among sectors of an economy, and, looked at closely, even within sectors of an economy. With the relation of the marginal efficiency of capital curve made explicit with respect to the view of risk on the one hand and the will to accept innovations on the other, it is possible to discuss meaningfully not only short-period changes in the level of investment within a society but also the comparative performance of different societies. It is possible, for example, to treat formally the problem of generating higher and more productive levels of investment in under-developed countries, where both risk-taking and innovation capabilities are low.[1] By this method, the effective demand for capital may be explicitly contrasted with that which would exist if, in the extreme cases, there were no risk premium in society and if all possibilities of profitable innovation were exhausted; and, more important, it is possible to exhibit degrees of deviation from such an optimum. This approach should also make more natural the treatment of shifts in the effective demand for capital as caused not simply

available, one could deduce the effective margin and the intersection of the effective margin with the marginal efficiency of capital. This intersection would determine the level of investment, with income given. It should be noted, however, that Samuelson's interesting formulation would allocate the function of enterprise to those putting up the funds, whereas, in fact, the function is spread more broadly throughout the stages of the financing and production process. In particular, it might not take fully into account the forces which here determine the difference between an optimum demand for capital and the actual demand.

[1] See, for example, *Domestic Financing of Economic Development*, United Nations (New York, 1950); *Measures for the Economic Development of Under-developed Countries* United Nations (New York, 1951), especially chaps. v and vi; also Mrs. Robinson's discussion of the Supply of Finance in her 'Generalisation of *The General Theory*', *Rate of Interest and Other Essays* (London, 1951).

by changes in the yields to be derived from natural resources or from new inventions, but also by such changes in the social framework of the economy as are relevant to investment decisions.

This mode of presenting the determination of the level of investment underlines a characteristic of the first three propensities. They have been isolated as necessary for an understanding of the determination of the level of profitability at any period of time, with a given level of income. But the allocation of resources to fundamental science and to applied science and the propensity to accept, in a certain proportion, the innovations available can be regarded as aspects of the investment process itself. Under profit maximization assumptions one would assume that resources would flow to these uses in such a manner as to equate the return at the margin with that in other forms of investment. These particular forms of investment have been arbitrarily isolated because of the realistic possibility that there may be important sectoral differences as between the investment process in general and these aspects of investment. The motives and forces which determine their strength in different societies may differ from those determining in general the propensity to seek material advance. It is evident that a more generalized model might be constructed in which the propensity to seek material advance was broadened to subsume the first three propensities; and a considerable formal simplification could be achieved, for purposes where extended abstract elaboration was desirable. The author is, however, by no means clear that this approach to economic analysis will lend itself usefully to such elaboration; and even less confident that it will commend itself to the mathematical practitioner of economics.

I V

Returning now to the central relation between growth and its determinants, it may be seen that the rate of growth of capital, including its qualitative factors, can be regarded as determined by the interplay of the rate of return from natural resources and stocks of knowledge and the complex operation of the propensities reflecting the social framework of the society. The volume of resources allocated to investment, at any period of time, is a function of the relation between the supply curve of finance and the level of profitability. Both the supply curve of finance and the level of profitability are related in a particular and definable way to the propensities. Further, the volume of innovations incorporated within the input of investment resources is a function of the operation of the propensities. The character of the innovations incorporated within the volume of new investment, however, is to be understood only in terms of the process of growth, which is the subject of Chapter IV.

The argument thus far might be summarized in the form of the following six propositions:

1. The level of the output of an economy, at any period of time, is a function of the size of its working force, its stock of capital, and its stock of applied knowledge. Included within these stocks, quantitatively conceptual, are the productivity factors attaching to them.

2. The rate of growth of an economy is a function of the rate of change in these stocks.

3. These rates of change may in turn be regarded as resulting from the interplay of certain technical yields and the effective strength of the following propensities, as they operate through the existing economic, social, and political institutions in the society: the propensity to develop pure science; the propensity to apply science to the economy; the propensity to accept the possibilities of innovation; the propensity to seek material advance; the propensity to consume; the propensity to have children. The first three propensities may in a generalized manner be regarded as sectoral aspects of the propensity to seek material advance. Further, the interplay of the propensity to seek material advance and the propensity to consume determine the extent to which material resources are fully or steadily employed, and in what proportion the propensity to seek material advance is, in fact, effective in causing investment to take place.

4. The effective strengths of the propensities, in turn, are, at any moment of time, or for any limited period, a function

of the prior long-period operation of economic, social, and political forces, which determine the current social fabric, institutions, and effective political policy of the society.

5. For a given complex of institutions controlling them, the propensities, in the course of their own long-period life, may have a built-in tendency to follow an approximation of a curve of growth, stagnation, and decline. Whatever their course, it is essential to this argument that the propensities, which enter directly and technically into economic decisions, are not to be investigated or analysed in terms of wholly economic variables.

6. Quite apart from the possibility of built-in deceleration within the propensities in a given society, diminishing returns may, in the long run, operate on the size and quality of the working force, on the extractive industries, and possibly but not surely on agricultural and industrial investment as a whole.

This way of looking at economic development should permit one to talk about the growth and decline of economies in such a way as to relate the full range of underlying forces operating to their economic manifestations. This approach might be useful, for example, in permitting a more systematic description of the whole process by which, in various societies, the underlying propensities decreed a rapid take-off into industrialization; that is, an orderly account of the forces which caused an increase in the volume and productivity of investment in relation to the growth of population and the working force, such that a self-sustaining increase in *per capita* output was achieved. Similarly, it is believed possible that this approach might permit a fairly systematic account to be formulated in cases where such take-off proved abortive, where no take-off had occurred, or where increasing rates of growth have given way to decreasing rates of growth or to absolute declines.

The structure appears also to offer a framework of concepts for systematic research into the factors determining the relative productivity of investment in different societies (or in different sectors of the same economy), some aspects of which are already being effectively studied.[1] The present exposition

[1] Note, for example, pp. 23–27 and 27–28.

is designed to bring together, within a single analytic structure, the variables which are conventionally regarded as economic along with those which are non-economic, in so far as they bear on strictly economic decisions. At a time when governments have by default or necessity inherited, or have with purpose seized control over a wide range of the variables which determine the long-run course of economies, and when decision concerning them is from day to day being made on the basis of disjointed aphorisms and rules of thumb, it behoves the social scientist to order what he knows about such matters, however little it now may be.

In a narrower perspective, however, the purpose of this stage of the exposition is simply to permit the author in reasonable conscience to 'Assume a given rate of growth in real income'. Behind such an initial assumption lie assumed magnitudes for the rate of growth of the working force, investment, and the average productivity of the various relevant stocks. And behind these magnitudes lie assumptions concerning the current effective strength and prior course of the underlying social propensities, as well as the marginal yields from additions to the various stocks. The argument to this point is designed to give substance to the conception of a long-run rate of growth, independent of its possible and likely fluctuations.

V

Before turning to an examination of the process of growth as envisaged within this structure, it might be useful to compare this formulation of the determinants of growth with several others which have recently been put forward. In particular, we shall briefly examine certain observations on this problem by Spengler, Clough, and Duesenberry.

Spengler has listed, in a recent paper, nineteen 'determinants' plus a residual factor for contingencies which he believes relevant or formally related to the *per capita* net product of an economy.[1] Spengler's nineteen 'determinants' recall somewhat the state of the theory of the trade cycle before the

---

[1] J. J. Spengler, 'Theories of Socio-Economic Growth', *Problems in the Study of Economic Growth*, National Bureau of Economic Research (July 1949), pp. 52-53.

First World War. In his *A Study of Industrial Fluctuations*, D. H. Robertson began by noting that the causes of crises and depressions alleged before the various committees of Congress in the 1880's amounted to some 180 in number, and that in 1895 M. Bergmann was able to publish an exhaustive discussion in German of 230 separate opinions arranged in eight categories. Robertson concluded:

In spite of the obvious futility of many of the minor explanations that have been given, this does appear to be a case in which, in the deathless words of the Dodo, everybody has won and all must have prizes, in the sense that almost all the writers who have made any contribution to the study of the matter appear to have had a considerable measure of right on their side.[1]

The present position of our knowledge with respect to economic growth is not unlike the preliminary and formative stage of our knowledge of business cycles before the First World War. It may be predicted with some confidence that increase in knowledge will result in a narrowing of the factors which we regard as causal and an arraying of the aspects of the process of growth along lines which distinguish fundamental forces from their possible determinants on the one hand, and the consequences of their action on the other.

It may, therefore, be helpful to set out here the manner in which Spengler's nineteen 'determinants' appear to fit the present analytic system. Some of his 'determinants' would be regarded as a possible part of the background to or manifestations of the propensities; that is, they belong with the social determinants of economic decisions. Some of his 'determinants' would be regarded here as determined by the operation of the system. Briefly, they may be grouped in relation to the system as follows:

1. The following would be here regarded as among the forces which might help determine the effective strength, at a point in time, of one or more of the underlying propensities and are, themselves, capable of analysis only in terms of a combined economic, social, and political investigation:[2]

Make-up of the prevailing value system; in particular, the

[1] London, 1915, p. 1.
[2] Rearranged but directly quoted from Spengler, op. cit.

values of the socio-economic leaders and the values which significantly affect economic creativity and the disposition of man to put forth economically productive effort.

Dominant character of the politico-economic system: is it free enterprise, mixed, social-democratic, or totalitarian in character?

Effectiveness and stability of the rules, institutions, and legal arrangements designed to preserve economic, political, and civil order.

Degree of co-operation and amity obtaining between groups and classes composing the population.

Flexibility of the institutional structure and physical apparatus of the economy.

Relative amount of vertical and horizontal mobility characteristic of the population.

Distribution of the power to make and execute entrepreneurial decisions.

2. The following would be here regarded as mainly reflecting institutionally the extent to which the third propensity operated; that is, the extent to which the economic system had exploited the potentialities for higher productivity and utility open to it:

Internal geographical distribution of economic activities.

Exchange relations obtaining between the economy under study and other economies.

Degree of specialization and division of labour in effect.

Scale of economic organization and activity prevalent.

Degree to which the population's pattern of consumption is adjusted to its pattern of resource-equipment.

3. The following would be here regarded as part of the current capital stock, as determined by the past operation of the economic system:

Material equipment (i.e. resources, productive machinery, &c.) per worker.

State of the industrial arts.

State of the educational, scientific, and related cultural equipment of the population.

4. The following would be regarded as partially deter-

mined by forces operating through the system on health and on death-rates and partially by the more complex factors operating on birth-rates:

Age composition of the population.

Biological composition of the population.

Health composition of the population.

5. The present analysis would segregate the two elements in the following 'determinant', regarding the extent of disguised unemployment as reflecting the strength or weakness of the underlying propensities in exploiting available resources, while treating the extent of complete (presumably cyclical) unemployment as determined by the short-period operation of the system:

Relative amount of complete, partial, and disguised unemployment present.

In terms of the arbitrary view presented here, then, Spengler's 'determinants' would not be judged formally to constitute determinants. They would fall, in general, either among the factors determining certain of the determinants of the present system or they would be regarded as determined by the operations of the system. The author would, of course, wish to be clear that this reordering of Spengler's analysis in no way implies a criticism of it. Although the present grouping of relevant factors within concepts of greater generality, and an arraying of them as between determinants and determined variables, are judged useful, these abstract steps in no way widen our substantive knowledge of the inordinately complex process by which the propensities are determined in particular societies. Like any theoretical exercise, however, this formulation may contribute to the more fruitful ordering of data and a heightened sense of the causal forces which bind them together.

A further observation is to be made on certain of Spengler's categories, especially those grouped in (1), above. They would appear to imply that certain social characteristics of a society are necessarily linked to its economic effectiveness. Spengler, for example, might appear to hold that 'a high degree of flexibility of the institutional structure and physical apparatus of an economy' would automatically be associated with high productivity; a similar positive correlation appears to be implied with respect to the 'degree of horizontal or vertical mobility'. Our knowledge does not appear sufficiently great in these matters to justify automatically associating such social characteristics with economic effectiveness. In Japan, for example, the inflexibility of the social system may well have aided its rapid economic advance in the latter part of the nineteenth century, whereas the high degree of American social mobility almost certainly accelerated the economic advance of the United States in the same period. The great variety of social structures which have been able to move into rapid economic advance should caution against any too easy association of particular social structures and the effective strength of the propensities. Men may work hard and imaginatively for many reasons.

Clough has also formulated the determinants of economic progress in his *Prolegomenon to the Economic History of Civilization*.[1] He lists six fundamental factors in economic progress: natural resources; technology and techniques of production; labour; capital; business leadership and economic institutions; demand for goods and the technology of distribution. These may be translated into the vocabulary developed here, as including variables subsumed in the central relationship and certain propensities or manifestations of them. Clough's 'labour' would be taken account of here in the size and rate of change of the working force; 'natural resources' would be grouped with capital; 'technology and techniques of production' would also be regarded as an aspect of capital; 'business leadership and economic institutions' would be regarded as an aspect of the propensities, that is, the social frame of the society; 'the demand for goods' (as explained textually by Clough) would fall within the propensity to seek material advance as it applies to the working force; 'the technology of distribution', its efficiency or lack of efficiency, would be one aspect of the effectiveness or lack of effectiveness of the workings of the system itself; that is, methods of organization and management are treated like other more technological innovations.

[1] Shepard Clough, *Essays in Honor of Gino Luzzatto* (Milan, 1950).

Clough's theme in this article is the relation between economic growth and the general creativeness of civilizations with respect to science and culture. He is not concerned to state in any systematic way what he regards as the determinants of his six conditions of economic progress. Clough's tentative conclusion, however, bears a relation to the argument advanced here. He notes that the recognized peaks of civilization running from the third dynasty in Egypt down to the Renaissance 'were preceded or accompanied by evidence of increased productivity of goods and services per capita'. He concludes:

In the case of the rise and fall of individual civilizations, an increase in total productivity relative to that of contemporary civilizations seems to be a concomitant of rise, and a relative decline of productivity a concomitant of fall. Yet in few, if in any, instances could it be said that economic progress offered a full explanation for the achievement of great works in science or culture or for the rise and fall of an individual group.[1]

Clough is here confronted with the same complexity as that discussed in Chapter II in relation to the determinants of the propensities. It is indeed possible, in a rough way, to associate the change in one of the propensities with a rise in the power and influence of a class; and it is possible to associate the rise of a class with a change in the composition of the working force and the techniques of production. It is not possible, however, either with respect to the propensities or with respect to the high achievements of a civilization in science or culture, to make this association too simple or rigid. Changes in the propensities, like changes in the quality of a culture, are the result of a much more complex process than a simple economic determinism would suggest.

A third commentator on the social frame of economic development is James S. Duesenberry, whose article 'Some Aspects of the Theory of Economic Development'[2] includes a section on the social and psychological bases of economic

---

[1] Ibid., p. 12.
[2] *Explorations in Entrepreneurial History*, vol. iii, No. 2 (15 Dec. 1950), pp. 68–74. See also K. F. Helleiner, 'Moral Conditions of Economic Growth', *Journal of Economic History*, vol. xi, No. 2 (Spring 1951).

development. First, Duesenberry defines the process of innovation as central to economic development; he then states the conditions for innovation and, particularly, the institutional setting in which it is likely to take place. He probes, finally, at the psychological foundations for these institutions. In the terms developed here his argument would constitute a discussion of the determinants of certain of the propensities, notably the propensities to apply science, to accept the possibilities of innovations, and to seek material advance. He does not attempt to generalize his results or to lay out a general scheme for treating the social framework of a society in relation to economic development.

Like the argument presented here, Duesenberry's position would, however, emphasize the variety of institutional frameworks capable of encouraging economic development and the arbitrary character, analytically, of the economist's assumption of profit maximization. Duesenberry prefers, for example, to explain the burst of innovational activity which preceded and laid the foundations for the British industrial revolution, not in terms of the Protestant ethic, but rather in terms of a widespread belief in man's power to control his environment.

It was that belief that by reason and experiment man could bind nature to his will that led to the feverish experimentation and the innumerable projects of the seventeenth and eighteenth centuries. . . . It can be argued, then, that the necessary conditions for economic development include not only the appropriate institutional arrangements and the existence of individuals with entrepreneurial personality characteristics but a general change in attitude toward the relation of man and his environment. It is essential that there should be a widespread belief in the possibility of expanding the number of ways in which structural forces can be manipulated.[1]

Duesenberry would thus emphasize the importance of the social and psychological framework of economic development and the complexity of the forces which may determine that frame. No more than the present argument, however, has Duesenberry solved the problem of stating the funda-

[1] *Explorations in Entrepreneurial History*, vol. iii, No. 2 (15 Dec. 1952), p. 74.

mental societal and human process by which changes may come about in man's outlook on his environment and in the premium he may attach to economic advance, as against other possible goals. In the present vocabulary he has probed into some of the possible determinants of the propensities.

IV

THE PROCESS OF GROWTH

I

T HE purpose of the present chapter is, first, to define the process of economic growth under special assumptions, designed, in particular, to eliminate the possibility of short-period fluctuations in real income; and then to examine broadly the nature of the forces which might cause changing rates in such dynamic equilibrium. This highly abstract treatment of growth is introduced mainly for the purpose of clarifying the forces which have led to certain major systematic deviations from it; that is, as a basis for approaching at a later stage the analysis of the business cycle and long-period trends (Chaps. V and VI).

In the first instance, it will be assumed that full employment is continuously maintained and that investment is, somehow, perfectly and without lag directed into the appropriate channels. It will be further assumed, in the first instance, that the levels of the propensities, that is, the social framework of the society, as it is relevant to its economic decisions, are given and fixed. The growth pattern under such assumptions may be regarded as 'optimum' only with respect to full employment and the character of investment. It would take a different kind of analysis to explore another, more profound optimum; namely, an optimum balance as among material advance and other possible social goals. The assumption that the propensities are given means that we are taking from outside this system of thought, for the moment, the disposition of resources between present and future income, the priority to be given *per capita* over total real income, the proportion of real income to be taken in leisure, the priority to be accorded security in relation to progress, equity in relation to incentives, and so on.

The assumption that investment is directed into appropriate channels requires further examination. It implies that the character of investment in the various sectors of the economy is adjusted without friction or error or lag to the requirements for enlarged capacity (due to rising population and incomes, and changing tastes), and to the possibilities offered by the flow of innovations (with the strength of the propensity to accept innovations given). It implies, further, that investment may be carried out in very small units so that capacity can be enlarged in a virtually continuous manner.

The assumption of continuous full employment implies a relation between the proportions of income consumed and invested which would yield steady full employment.[1] The assumptions under which steady full employment would exist in a growing economy have been the subject of extended recent analysis; but in the first stage of the argument this issue is set aside.[2]

I I

Under these assumptions, and assuming further that the economy is growing,[3] the composition of investment would steadily change. In, let us say, wheat lands, there might be a low level of investment, sufficient to keep current capacity wheat production accommodated to the requirements of a growing population, changing food tastes, and the potentialities for profitable innovations in wheat growing.[4] If the economy were at a relatively early stage of its industrialization, one might expect to find a relatively high proportion of

[1] Formally this condition is usually achieved by assuming:
   initial full employment;
   that the proportions of income invested and saved are stable and identical proportions of income;
   that inventions, on balance, are neutral.
These highly arbitrary and unlikely assumptions evade an important and unresolved issue, namely, the dynamic relations between full employment and full capacity. For purposes of the present analysis, however, the resolution of this issue is not judged essential.
[2] See pp. 86 ff. for a discussion of this problem.
[3] Growth is defined as a relation between the rates of increase in capital and the working force, on the one hand, and in population, on the other, such that *per capita* output (not necessarily consumption) is rising.
[4] See, for example, N. Silberling's treatment of the relation between the U.S. population and food consumption, *Dynamics of Business* (New York, 1943), pp. 127–34; also building in relation to population, pp. 182–6. See also T. W. Schultz, *Agriculture in an Unstable Economy*, Part II, chap. iii, pp. 44–84.

its investment going into its textile industries; at a later stage in its development, a much lower proportion, but with higher investment allocations to steel and engineering; and so on.

Although in common-sense terms the meaning of 'appropriate character' for investment is tolerably clear, in societies with different levels of income and at different stages of development, it is difficult to deal with this concept rigorously. If technique is assumed to be constant—that is, if there is no flow of potential innovations—one can envisage the course of investment in such an optimum economy quite simply as the steady expansion of capacity in the various sectors appropriate to the growth of real income and to changing tastes, if they are formally permitted. Depending on the assumed initial level of technique—that is, on the range of finished commodities and services assumed to exist, and their production functions—the relative rates of expansion and the proportion of total capital invested in the various sectors would vary with the increase in real income, and with changes in taste. And if we rule out the discovery of new natural resources of higher than current marginal productivity, regarded here as a form of innovation, then diminishing returns might be assumed and the rate of growth of the economy would then slow down. The maintenance of full employment, under these declining circumstances, would require either an inelastic supply curve of finance (as perhaps, in a fully planned socialist state), or an increase in the proportion of income consumed.

If we assume that the propensities may change, this economy of fixed production functions might also slow down or accelerate. It might slow down if (under certain circumstances) the birth-rate were to decline; or if the propensities to seek material advance and to consume were to shift in their relations with one another in such a way as to decrease the proportion of income invested (while maintaining steady full employment); or if the society were to put forward less effort and take more of its income in leisure. It might accelerate if the propensities were so to change that the economy exploited more vigorously the possibilities offered by the environment, raising the yield from the current investment outlays, or if the volume of resources devoted to investment input were to increase (with appropriate adjustment in the propensity to consume). The simple point to emphasize in this primitive model is that changes in the rate of growth are capable of occurring not only because of changes in the yield from resources or other stocks, but also because of changes in the social or political framework, here exhibited through the propensities.

If we assume, however, that this is a society where the first three propensities operate—where resources are devoted to the development of fundamental science and to the application of science to the economy, and where there is some willingness to accept changes in production functions—then it is necessary to establish what will determine the composition of the flow of innovations available to the economy and the composition of those actually applied in various sectors. It will be recalled that, under the present assumptions, the size of the flow of innovations, as distinct from its composition, will be determined by the interplay of the various yields and the propensities which are relevant. The appropriate general proposition concerning the composition of innovations seems to be that necessity is the mother of invention.[1]

There is, of course, no guarantee that nature will always

[1] See especially A. P. Usher, *History of Mechanical Inventions* (New York, 1929); S. C. Gilfillan, *The Sociology of Invention* (Chicago, 1935); also R. S. Sayers, 'The Springs of Technical Progress in Britain, 1919–39 , *Economic Journal* (June 1950), especially pp. 282 ff.; and T. S. Ashton, *The Industrial Revolution, 1760–1830* (London, 1948), pp. 91–92. J. Schumpeter's indecisive discussion of this question should also be noted (*Business Cycles* [N.Y., 1939], vol. i, p. 85 n.). Schumpeter allows for the existence of inventions and innovations induced by necessity; but also for inventions not related to any particular requirement or not related to the requirement met by the particular innovation that incorporates them. Schumpeter states: 'It might be thought that innovation can never be anything else but an effort to cope with a given situation. In a sense this is true. For a given innovation to become possible, there must always be some 'objective needs' to be satisfied and some 'objective conditions'; but they rarely, if ever, uniquely determine what kind of innovation will satisfy them, and as a rule they can be satisfied in many different ways. Most important of all, they may remain unsatisfied for an indefinite time, which shows that they are not themselves sufficient to produce an innovation.' While admitting, of course, the possibility that nature may not always prove fruitful and that the form of the innovational response to a necessity is not determinable *ex ante*, the present argument would attach a considerable formal importance to the link between necessity, invention, and innovation. This link is judged essential to a

prove bountiful in the sense that diminishing returns will
always be conquered by science and ingenuity, in all directions toward which talent and resources are drawn by economic incentives. The notion here is that, in conception, a rate
of return exists from the application of resources to applied
science which would average relative successes and failures.
As noted earlier, the volume of resources devoted to applied
science is viewed as determined by the interaction of such
prospective yields and one of the propensities. Acceptance of
the proposition that necessity is the mother of invention
means that the composition of the flow of innovations at any
given time may be broadly related to clear (prior) economic
incentives; in practice, of course, important time lags would
be involved between the existence of an incentive and the
coming forth of an appropriate innovation.[1] Here such time
lags, along with others, are assumed away.

Although random results of economic value are likely in
creative activities of an innovational type, it does not appear
to be a violation of economic history to regard the character
of this particular form of investment (that is, the investment
of talent and other resources in the application of science to
production) as related to the expected yield. A high expected
yield from an innovation may result from the fact that, in
one sector of the economy, diminishing returns may have set
in and the price of the commodity is rising relative to that
of others. An incentive of this sort has, in the past, served to

formal explanation of the changing character of investment in the course of
growth and (see Chap. V) from cycle to cycle. While admitting the possibility
of highly productive sports and total failures in meeting necessities, this argument would regard the character of the effort expended in applying science to
the economy and the character of the potentialities accepted into the economy
as reflecting the response of the society to challenges and opportunities created
by the process of growth pressing against existing resources and techniques,
revealing themselves in profit opportunities. The processes of scientific endea-
vour and of efforts to seek applications for the economy are thus viewed as a
part of the normal investment process in the economy. It is the lack of such an
analytic link that gives to Schumpeter's major innovations their exogenous
character, and it also leads him, in the writer's judgement, to misinterpret the
analytic and historical significance of the pattern of investment outlays over
the period, roughly, 1785–1914. For further discussion see Chap. VI.

[1] See, for example, S. C. Gilfillan, 'The Lag between Invention and Application', *The Sociology of Invention* (Chicago, 1935).

stimulate the search for innovations in the form of more fertile lands, mines, sheep-grazing country, and so forth. More narrowly, we can observe in recent years the connexion, for example, between relatively high timber prices and research in timber substitutes, relatively high prices for natural textile fibres and research in synthetic textiles; and so on. Still more narrowly, we can observe a concentration of creative engineering effort, in evening up the degree of mechanization in the various stages of a given production process, as in the sequence of inventions in spinning and weaving which constituted the early revolution in cotton manufacture. Innovation in transportation may be stimulated by the general growth in size and degree of specialization of an economy, as in the case of the railways of early nineteenth-century Britain, which were designed to avoid the frustrations and high cost of road and canal transport in an expanding and industrializing economy.

Stimulus to innovation may arise not only from inelasticity of supply or diminishing returns in a sector of the economy, but also from the desire to evade the consequences for profit or rent of an elastic supply and increasing returns. In periods of agricultural depression many farmers thus survived despite of falling world prices;[1] but this case would not be relevant to the abstract circumstances presently assumed because agricultural depression of the kind historically noted is to be regarded, in terms of the whole argument developed here, as the result of prior 'inappropriate' investment.[2]

Thus, as a general proposition, it may be taken that, while the size of the flow of potential innovations is a function of certain basic propensities in conjunction with the productivity of marginal additions to the scientific stock, its composition is a function of the particular incentives offered by the pressure of growth against resources, subject to diminishing returns, or to other straightforward profit incentives arising from changes in the level of real income or in tastes. In the

[1] For a discussion of the response of various societies, in terms of innovation, to the fall of the wheat price from 1873 to 1896, see C. P. Kindleberger, 'Group Behavior and International Trade', *Journal of Political Economy* (Feb. 1951).

[2] See Chap. VI.

stylized conception of an optimum, considered at this stage, we assume that such incentives are both responded to without lag and, within the limits allowed by the underlying assumption about the acceptance of innovations, applied with promptness and accuracy of judgement.

Although, thus far, the size of the flow of innovations and the relative willingness to apply the innovations offered have been regarded as aggregates for the economy as a whole, there is no reason why they may not be distinguished as among the sectors of the economy. One might well find, for example, different values for them, at a particular period of time, in the engineering trades than in the coal industry, as may have been the case in Britain over the inter-war years; or different values for them, in a given industry, at different periods.

It should be noted that the sectoral optimum levels of capacity which emerge from this analysis, related here to the level of real income at steady, full employment, simply reflect the normal rule of equilibrium, that resources will be allocated in such a manner as to maximize yield and that the marginal yields in various directions will tend toward equality. The analysis differs from conventional analyses mainly in two respects: first, the composition of innovations is regarded as determined by the workings of the system and is not given arbitrarily from outside the system; second, the system provides, from the beginning, that account be taken of forces which, over-all or in the various sectors of the economy, may temper profit-maximization decisions with non-economic objectives as reflected in the propensities. Depending on the sectoral propensities initially assumed, the sectoral output optima would deviate in various degrees from the positions they would hold if technical potentialities were fully exploited in all sectors, or from those they would hold if it were assumed that the propensities stood in a uniform relative position in all sectors of the economy.

III

The assumption that full employment, in this system, will be steadily maintained has, thus far, eliminated from discussion the issues which have mainly engaged the attention of those economists who have combined income analysis with a consideration of over-all rates of growth. Any realistic analysis must, of course, embrace the likelihood that the determinants of investment and consumption outlays will not yield steady full employment. We must be prepared to consider, for example, that a rise in the expected level of profitability might lead to a level of investment, income, and consumption outlays which would press against the limits of the working force or capacity and raise prices and costs. The rise in costs might affect expectations of profit and, thus, the level of current investment; or, should the level of investment be sustained (the supply of investment finance being sufficiently inelastic over the relevant range), resources might be bid away from the consumer in a fashion such as to lower his real income, and with a given (or lagging) propensity to consume, lower the total level of his consumption. Similarly, a fall in expected profitability might reduce investment, income, and consumption outlays in such a manner as to yield unemployment, under suitable assumptions of wage-rate inflexibility.

The elaboration of the Keynesian system of income analysis has included a considerable effort to restate its implications under the assumption of economic growth, or under the assumption that the level of investment is systematically related to the rate of change or to the level of real income.[1] In one of its aspects this effort can be regarded as an extension of Keynes's observations on the problem of secular stagnation; that is, as a way of formalizing the possibility that the marginal efficiency of capital may move into a

[1] R. F. Harrod, *Towards a Dynamic Economics* (London 1948) and Joan Robinson, 'The Generalisation of *The General Theory*', *The Rate of In erest and Other Essays* (London, 1951). See also J. R. Hicks, *The Trade Cycle* (Oxford, 1950); N. Kaldor, 'A Model of the Trade Cycle', *Economic Journal* (Mar. 1940); E. D. Domar, 'Expansion and Employment', *American Economic Review* (Mar. 1947), and 'The Problem of Capital Accumulation', *American Economic Review* (Dec. 1948); P. A. Samuelson, 'Interaction between the Multiplier Analysis and the Principle of Acceleration', *Review of Economic Statistics* (May, 1939); R. M. Goodwin, 'A Non-Linear Theory of the Cycle', *Review of Economics and Statistics* (Nov. 1950); also Goodwin's 'Econometrics in Business-Cycle Analysis', chap. 22 in A. H. Hansen, *Business Cycles and National Income* (New York, 1951).

long-run position which, in conjunction with the consumption function, precludes the possibility of full employment in a capitalist society, without the intervention of the State. Or, more generally, these formulations constitute statements of the condition for long-run equilibrium, in terms of full employment, given the rate of growth. In another of their aspects many of these recent analyses may be regarded as an exploration of the implications of closing the Keynesian system, through the introduction of the accelerator; and they have led to business cycle analyses explicitly related to the process of growth. The connexion between such analyses and that presented here, as they relate to the treatment of the business cycle, is left for Chapter V.

Thus, for any period of time, Harrod sets out the equation:

$$GC = s.$$

G represents the increment in production; C, the increment in capital, expressed as a percentage of the increment in production; and s the fraction of income saved. Under the assumption of a constant production period (stemming from the stability of the interest rate and the average neutrality of investment) the accelerator makes GC a constant, for the condition of steady advance.

Equilibrium exists when

$$G_w C_r = s,$$

G_w being the rate of growth which leaves entrepreneurs content to persist with what they are doing and C_r being the equilibrium requirement for new capital, given G_w.

Finally comes Harrod's G_n, the maximum long-run rate of advance allowed by the increase in population and the flow of technological improvements. G_n, which also reflects the correct balance, for the given society, between work and leisure, closely approximates the conception of optimum growth defined earlier in this chapter. It includes an allowance for the social parameters of the society, and within that limitation it assumes the full exploitation of the potentialities offered by population growth and the flow of innovations coming forward. Without additional assumptions, however, it does not embrace steady full employment.

More significantly, Harrod's analysis takes population growth and the flow of innovations as given. Further, although Harrod briefly alludes to the fact that sectoral rates of growth in the economy are not likely to bear a uniform or even consistent relation to the over-all rate of growth,[1] his analysis is in over-all terms. As indicated in Chapters V and VI below, this is judged a serious weakness, in dealing with certain practical economic problems, historical or contemporary.

In terms of his assumptions, Harrod thus defines the issues that concern him: '. . . there are two distinct sets of problems both for analysis and policy, namely: (1) the divergence of G_w from G_n; and (2) the tendency of G to run away from G_w. The former is the problem of chronic unemployment, the latter the trade cycle problem.'[2]

Before approaching these issues Harrod makes arbitrary allowance, within his equation, for investment not motivated by the accelerator and for the trade balance, both expressed, like s, in terms of the level of income.

With these tools he can proceed to his central long-run question, which might be rephrased as follows: With population growth, the flow of innovations, and the social and political framework given, what can we do if s is too high to permit steady advance? The familiar devices of autonomous government investment, lowered interest rates, an export surplus, and measures to shift income to those with a high marginal propensity to consume then fall into place.

This is (or may be again) a relevant question, and the answers are germane, given both the premises and the course of modern economic history. There is no doubt that recent theoretical formulations have permitted more elegant analyses of them than we have had in the past. But, as Harrod himself was aware, they are addressed to a particular arbitrary formulation of the long-run problem. From the beginning of his

[1] Harrod, *Towards a Dynamic Economics* (London, 1948), pp. 81–82.
[2] Ibid., p. 91.

analysis Harrod sets aside the possibility of treating population and the yield from capital stocks as dependent variables:

I am interested now particularly in economies of the United States, Great Britain, Western Europe and other advanced countries. In this context we may regard the size of the population not, as in the old classical system, as a dependent but as an independent variable. To put the matter otherwise, changes in it may be regarded as exogenous changes. Secondly, I propose to discard the law of diminishing returns from land as a primary determinant in a progressive economy. Not that there was any fallacy in the classical treatment of this subject. I discard it only because in our particular context it appears that its influence may be quantitatively unimportant.[1]

Further, Harrod takes as given the flow of innovations and the quality of entrepreneurship, the latter presumably subsumed in G_w. In terms of the central equation presented here he is, simply, assuming changes in the size (and presumably quality) of the working force as given and changes in the quality of capital as given, linking the size of increments of capital to the rate of change of real income itself.[2] How, Harrod asks, may we adjust to these fixed parameters? The character of his answers stems directly from the formal assumptions he makes.

This restatement of Harrod's assumptions is not, in itself, an accusation. But it raises two questions, even aside from the self-imposed limitation with respect to advanced countries. First, is it true that the most relevant issues of our time centre on too high a level of saving, in advanced countries? Second, is it outside the scope of democratic societies to take effective action with respect to the parameters fixed in Harrod's system? It is an old story in the history of economic thought that the variables assumed as fixed or given, for purposes of formal exposition or convenience, tend to disappear from consideration among the objects of policy.

It is not the purpose of the present argument to answer these two questions definitively. It would be easily agreed, however, that with respect to under-developed countries the determinants of the size and quality of the working force and

[1] Harrod, *Towards a Dynamic Economics* (London, 1948), p. 20.
[2] Ibid., p. 21.

the quality of capital investment are highly relevant objects of policy. The aim of the non-Communist world in those regions is not to adjust smoothly to given parameters of growth but to increase in some appropriate manner (and with an appropriate composition of output) the rate of growth. It is the author's conclusion that, on balance, the great problems confronting the more advanced countries, and likely to confront them over the next decades, are more nearly like those of the under-developed countries than the formal preoccupation of economists would suggest. It is for that reason (as well as to meet the requirements of historical analysis) that the present structure is more classical than Harrod's, seeking to raise explicitly and to organize formally the old questions of the determination of population and the working force and the productivity of capital.

Harrod's analysis is directed primarily to a formal statement of the conditions for steady advance, under special assumptions; and to an analysis of certain types of deviation from steady advance and their remedy. Aside from his emphasis on the inherent instability of economic growth,[1] he does not consider systematically the relation between economic growth and full employment. The analysis made by Joan Robinson deals more explicitly with this issue; and it is to be distinguished from Harrod's analysis in several further respects.[2] Without invoking the acceleration principle Mrs. Robinson transforms the Keynesian analysis into a statement of the conditions for steady growth at full employment, underlining the unlikely assumptions required for this formal case. She then considers some of the likely lapses from these assumptions, under the heading of 'Vicissitudes of a Developing Economy': changes in thriftiness, changes in population and the labour supply, changes in the marginal productivity of land and natural resources, alterations in the supply of finance, upward or downward price trends, changes in tastes, changes in the flow of innovations, changes in the average age of the capital stock, and the instability of the business cycle. Although Mrs. Robinson does not build her

[1] Ibid., pp. 115 ff.
[2] Op. cit., 'The Generalisation of *The General Theory*'.

analysis from a systematic statement of the determinants of output, it is evident that she is prepared to consider shifts in what are here called the yields and in the propensities in a much freer way than is allowed in Harrod's system.

The distinction between analyses like those of Harrod and Mrs. Robinson and that developed here can easily be stated. Each would accept the inherent instability of a growing economic system, in which the decisions to invest and to consume are discretely taken. If the purpose of economic analysis is to demonstrate this proposition, then the analytic structures which have been developed (with or without the accelerator) are quite adequate.

If, however, one chooses to ask the question, 'What determines the rate of growth of output?' then a different formal structure is required. The determinants of the size and quality of the working force and the size and productivity of investment outlays must be introduced, including the determinants of the scale and character of innovations and their degree of diffusion through the economy.

The use of the accelerator has been a technical handicap to the development of analyses addressed to this more fundamental question; although, as Mrs. Robinson's structure indicates, the dropping of the accelerator itself does not remove the difficulty. The logical, even mathematical, attractiveness of assuming that investment is a function of the rate of increase of income has drawn attention away from a more systematic exploration of the full process of economic growth and development. Elegant explorations of the conditions for stability and steady full employment have proved possible, and extremely neat formulations of the inherent nature of the cycle. But they have been achieved by setting aside, or leaving for separate discussion, a decisive element in economic growth and fluctuations—so-called autonomous investment.[1]

[1] For an extremely interesting effort to apply the multiplier-accelerator analysis to trend problems, leaving a place for autonomous investment, see R. M. Goodwin, 'Secular and Cyclical Aspects of the Multiplier and the Accelerator', chap. v in *Income, Employment and Public Policy*, essays in honour of Alvin H. Hansen (New York, 1948), especially pp. 124–32. This analysis demonstrates that it is possible to derive values for the acceleration coefficient

The accelerator is, even in short-run economic analysis, a concept around which a considerable body of legitimate criticism has grown up.[1] For the analysis of fluctuations in relation to growth, however, it is a peculiarly unfortunate instrument, as presently formulated; for it leaves the economist with two essentially faulty constructs:

(1) That investment which simply expands capacity with existing techniques (motivated by expected increases in output) can be usefully separated from investment incorporating new techniques, and from investment motivated by profit possibilities looking beyond the current rate of increase in output;

(2) That 'autonomous investment', organized in some mysterious and irregular way by innovators (the Hegelian heroes of the economic process), comes along from time to time to set the multiplier-accelerator machine into motion.

The view presented here is that, for a time, economists might usefully sacrifice the elegance of existing formulations, and look afresh at the full economic process, which means that they must deal professionally with important aspects of the social and political process. In the end, more complex and relevant mathematical statements may be possible; but present analyses are too limited in their scope to be permitted to proceed unchallenged.

The present argument starts closer to the analytically cruder observations which have grown up around the problem of secular stagnation. These analyses emphasize that the volume of private investment may fall off, over long periods, owing to a decline in population, a rise in the proportion of income saved, the capital-saving character of investment, or

and the marginal propensity to consume, consistent with Kuznets's secular data, when population changes and the exploitation of new techniques are introduced into the equations. But it concludes: 'No analytical solution can be given if $\phi(t)$ [autonomous investment] is taken, as it must, to be an arbitrary, historically given function.' Goodwin then suggests a formal device for taking into account such an arbitrary function.

[1] See, for example, the summary analysis of its status by A. H. Hansen, *Business Cycles and National Income*, New York, 1951, pp. 183–4; also W. Fellner, 'The Capital-Output Ratio in Dynamic Economics', *Money, Trade, and Economic Growth* (New York, 1951).

the exhaustion of new areas to open up at expected high yields;[1] and that the avoidance of chronic unemployment may require measures designed to raise the proportion of income consumed and/or investment on grounds other than expected private profit. Here we are back in a more common-sense world where the rate of growth of real income is regarded as a function of the growth of the working force and the scale and character of investment. But discussions of secular stagnation and similar post-Keynesian analyses, like that of Mrs. Robinson, tend to avoid a rigorous statement of the determinants of these variables.

Thus, the first stage of the present argument takes the form of a preliminary and stylized discussion of the forces in a given society which determine the rate of growth of its working force, its capital stock, and their productivity. From this first stage emerges a view of history which is in direct conflict with what economists have derived from Schumpeter's treatment of innovations.[2] The view here is that:

(1) Innovations are best regarded as an induced phenomenon, taking the form of a continuing flow of possibilities, and represent one form of investment by a society;

(2) That the forms which investment take (including so-

---

[1] See, for example, B. Higgins, 'Concepts and Criteria of Secular Stagnation', *Income, Employment and Public Policy* (New York, 1948), chap. iv.

[2] It is ironical that Schumpeter's considerable contribution to modern economic thought, in the form of his analysis of the innovation process, should have encouraged strictly formal and exogenous treatments of this factor. Despite Schumpeter's unified, quasi-Marxist view of the social process, he did not organize his conception of economic growth rigorously in terms of this outlook. It is the arbitrariness and discontinuity of Schumpeter's presentation of innovations which is judged, in particular, to be at fault, permitting economists to proceed in good conscience with systems which isolate 'autonomous' investment. The author would not, of course, deny the importance of certain key industries in the process of growth; although he would question the role in the determination of trends that Schumpeter assigns to them. And he has tried elsewhere to emphasize, in a somewhat wider context, that history cannot usefully be regarded as inevitable *ex ante* (*B.E.N.C.*, p. 143). Nevertheless, the development of textile, iron, transport, steel, engineering, and chemical innovations is a long story of concentrated effort to apply science to production, involving the efforts of many men aware of the economic stakes in success and representing one form of society's investment. These sustained developments are not adventitious phenomena.

called autonomous investment) are related directly to
the pressure of growth against resources.

Thus, whether a given rate of growth can be sustained
depends on whether investment of a given scale and productivity is sustained. The course of investment emerges as a race
between diminishing returns, the flow of innovational possibilities, and two fundamentally sociological characteristics of
a society—namely, its response to opportunities for profit
(including profit to be derived from fundamental and applied science) and the extent to which it is prepared to
accept and apply the innovational possibilities offered.

In a wider sense an accelerator re-emerges from this way
of looking at things; for it is, of course, the interaction of the
rate of growth of income and the level (and productivity) of
investment which determines the path of growth. But analyses which would look exclusively at the interplay of these
variables aided only by the multiplier, suffer from the same
disease as the quantity theory of money; that is, they do not
isolate the mechanism by which the key relationship is maintained. And they may even mislead as to the locus of causal
factors, by making investment a derivative of changes in
income. If we must choose a point to break into the interacting operation of the economic system, history and contemporary events would argue for the determinants of the
level and productivity of investment as the appropriate point.
This is an important consideration for the historian, as it is
for others who are concerned these days to make policies
which will cause sustained rates of economic growth to take
place in many societies, old and young, throughout the world.

What the present argument would draw from modern
economic analysis of growth in relation to fluctuations is the
formal demonstration of the unlikelihood of steady full employment and uninterrupted growth. It would give, however,
a lesser place than the Keynesian analysis to the role of the
rate of interest in such fluctuations and would introduce for
consideration at least the degree of acceptance of innovations
and the position and shape of the supply curve of investment
funds; for its relative inelasticity with respect to the rate of
profit, over the relevant range, might well help to account

for the persistence of relatively high levels of investment (on average) in the face of substantial fluctuations in the rate of return; and a shift in its position or an increase in its elasticity (due to shifts in the propensity to seek material advance) might account for lower levels of investment, chronic unemployment, or a diminished rate of economic growth.

I V

Since the economic evolution of societies in modern times has occurred mainly within the framework of a cyclical pattern in employment, we know little about the rate of growth of capitalist economies under steady full employment. If we smooth the actual long-period course of real income of an economy, moving along in a cyclical pattern, adjusting in irregular spurts to the pressures and opportunities of growth, we emerge with trends of long-period growth which are not identical with the smooth full-employment optimum discussed earlier in this chapter.[1] In the first instance, on the average, resources would not be fully employed. In the second place, to some extent, the yields confronting the underlying propensities would also fluctuate with the cycles; and the effective total flow of innovations and the total size of the working force and population would probably increase somewhat less rapidly, in fact, than if full employment were steadily maintained. In the third place, the propensities themselves might shift their positions in a society where the existence of steady full employment could be assured.[2]

What we see looking backward, then, at the long-period course of British or American real income, for example, cleared for cyclical fluctuations, is a curve of growth probably somewhat below that which would have resulted if full employment had been steadily maintained. This view, that a

[1] The secular trends in production studied by S. S. Kuznets in his *Secular Movements in Production and Prices* (New York, 1930) approximate what is meant here by realistic optimum growth lines, for sectors of the economy. See below, pp. 98 ff.; also Chapter XI, for further elaboration.

[2] It is not clear, of course, that the relative security prevailing in a society where it was believed that full employment was assured would shift all the propensities in directions such that the rate of growth would be increased; *vide*, the preoccupation with the problem of incentives in Britain and elsewhere under sustained full employment.

full-employment economy would exhibit higher rates of growth than one moving in cycles, might be challenged on the grounds that the periods of false expectations of very high return during booms produced bursts of innovational activity and willingness to accept innovation, which would not occur under a steady régime of full-employment growth. This is, evidently, a debatable point, given the lack of evidence to which one might appeal, and given, in particular, our ignorance about the possible effect on the propensities of sustained full employment. On the whole, the author is inclined to the tentative view that relatively full employment, steadily maintained, is likely to produce higher growth rates than if an economy were subject to business cycles.[1]

It will be noted that the conception of optimum growth presented here contains within it the notion of an *ex ante* equilibrium. This *ex ante* optimum is highly unrealistic for two reasons. First, we cannot predict what the yield will be from applications of resources to fundamental science and to applied science. In introducing these concepts[2] the possibility was noted that scientific and technical break-throughs might occur which would result from time to time in stages of increasing return, which would, in effect, raise the historical level of the productivity curves attached to these forms of investment. We simply cannot predict the long-period course of the rate of return from science and applied science. On formal grounds this agnosticism makes an *ex ante* optimum curve of growth impossible of construction. In the second place, as indicated in Chapter II, our knowledge of the forces determining the long-period course of the propensities is not sufficiently exact to enable us to predict their course.

In practice, therefore, the concept of an *ex ante* optimum is of limited utility. Nevertheless, it is of some utility. It is exactly such an optimum which must be applied in making projections of future requirements for, let us say, raw

---

[1] See, for example, the discussion of post-war growth rates in Europe, in relation to inter-war rates, *Economic Survey of Europe in 1949*, Economic Commission for Europe, United Nations (Geneva, 1950), especially chaps. 1 and 8.

[2] See pp. 62–63.

materials. The analysis being conducted by the President's Materials Policy Commission is based on the notion that it is possible for, let us say, ten years, first, to predict the over-all rate of growth in the American economy (and perhaps even the combined economies of the non-Communist world), under appropriate assumptions concerning the average level of employment; second, to predict the rate of growth in various main sectors in relation to the over-all growth; third, to translate these growth rates into requirements for certain basic materials; and fourth, to correct these material requirements for likely changes in relative costs and in technology. The possibility of making such projections hinges, in large part, on the assumption that, within (say) ten years, only those technological changes will be effectively applied which are now known in a laboratory stage at least. Much current governmental and industrial planning of this type requires, implicitly or explicitly, an *ex ante* realistic optimum conception of this character.[1]

The second use of the *ex ante* conception is simply to raise the issue of the extent of the deviation of actual growth from its maximum potentialities; to contrast, for example, the course of growth that would occur under steady full employment with the growth rates which have, in fact, obtained in the past.

A more evident reality and usefulness attaches to the concept of an *ex post* optimum, regarded both over all and in sectors of the economy. The charts (pp. 263, 265) and Statistical Appendix I present, by way of illustration, certain trend patterns in the United States and British economies over portions of the period 1800–1949.

These actual trend patterns differ from *ex post* optimum trend patterns in several important respects. First, they are not data for closed economies. Even if the series for the sectors were cleared of net exports, we would still be dealing

[1] Analyses of this kind will also be required to employ input-output models for purposes of prediction. For a prediction over a limited time period employing this form of analysis see *European Steel Trends* (Economic Commission for Europe, United Nations, Geneva, 1949); also the forthcoming Food and Agriculture Organization–Economic Commission for Europe study of European timber requirements and supply prospects.

with data from economies whose course of development was much influenced by their place in a world market. Second, although the series are cleared for cyclical fluctuations, mainly by the use of ten- or eleven-year overlapping averages, trend periods and wars effect their course in a manner discussed in Chapter VI. Third, the social framework of the British and American economies altered significantly over the time period considered here. The conception of a realistic optimum is formulated above for a given level of the propensities; and here the changing propensities have their influence on the course of events.

Nevertheless, an examination of actual trends, thus cleared for business cycles, reveals some significant aspects of the pattern of growth.[1] In the first instance, the continuity of these curves is to be noted. Although they bear the imprint of secular trends and wars, they exhibit relatively steady or steadily changing rates of growth, when cleared of business cycles. In terms of the present analysis this fundamental aspect of the curves is attributable to a characteristic shared by both the yields and the propensities. Allowing for certain exceptions,[2] they are slow-changing phenomena. Marginal yields represent increments at the margin to a stock. They may be radically shifted upward, especially in a sector of the economy, by the discovery of a new technique or a new source of raw materials more productive than the current marginal source of supply; but, on average, one would not expect sudden major changes in the yields to be derived from the allocation of resources to investment in different directions.[3] Similarly, for reasons outlined earlier, one would

---

[1] The course of secular trends in sectors of the economy has been studied systematically by S. Kuznets (*Secular Trends in Prices and Production*, New York, 1930) and A. F. Burns (*Production Trends in the United States since 1870*, New York, 1934). In addition, W. Hoffmann has commented suggestively on trend patterns in his article 'The Growth of Industrial Production in Great Britain, a Quantitative Study', *Economic History Review* (1949). See also R. Glenday, 'Long Period Economic Trends', *Journal of the Royal Statistical Society* (1938), including the discussion of Glenday's paper.

[2] See pp. 62–63 and 44, respectively.

[3] Differences between the course of yields on average and in sectors of the economy are believed mainly to account for the greater stability of the over-all rate of growth.

expect the social framework of the society to change relatively slowly; and therefore, the response to different yields would also slowly alter. In the broadest sense it is believed that these two fundamental characteristics of an economy account for the stability or slow-changing nature of the rates of change in these trend patterns.

The principal exceptions to this kind of shapeliness in rates of change can be attributed to exogenous factors. For example, the American Civil War halted the rise in cotton consumption in both Britain and the United States, temporarily violating the continuity of its trend movement. The trend depression in Great Britain of the inter-war years, here regarded as an extra-cyclical phenomenon, leaves its imprint on both cotton consumption and steel as well as on over-all industrial production. In the United States, grain production reflects the trend history of American and world agricultural capacity, as well as the trend requirements of the American population.[1] There is, in short, some reason to believe that if business cycles alone had operated on the British and American economies over these periods the trend curves would be even more continuous in their rates of movement than they, in fact, were in a world of secular trends and wars.[2]

It will be noted that, in both cases, population follows a course different from that of the real national income. If no other factor operated, the changing course of the propensity to have children in relation to the evolution of a society would make likely a difference between the over-all rate of growth in real income and growth in that sector which constitutes the population. In addition, as noted earlier,[3] the possibly special pattern of productivity in medicine and public health, in both its increasing and decreasing return stages, may influence this outcome.

---

[1] See Chap. VI.

[2] In addition, it seems possible that some of the discontinuities in the early years of the nineteenth century are to be attributed to simple errors in the statistical data. In particular, doubt attaches to the adequacy of American data on cotton consumption and to the figures for pig-iron production in the United States in the 1830's and 1840's. See *Historical Statistics of the United States, 1789–1945* (Washington, D.C., 1949), p. 136.   [3] See pp. 59 and 63.

It is evident that certain sectors will tend to accommodate themselves over the long period to the level of population corrected for real income and tastes. The most obvious relationship included here is that between population and occupied houses in Great Britain.[1] Although the pattern of food consumption in relation to real income has changed in complex ways, as noted by Schultz and others, there is a rough conformity between American population and grain production, despite the changing position of the United States as a world supplier and other special influences operating on the demand for American grain.[2]

The most striking phenomenon presented in these charts and treated at length in the literature on secular trends is the relatively consistent rate of growth pattern in industries, over the course of their life. For present extremely limited purposes, the charts present merely a few series, relating to certain classic industries which symbolize phases of modern industrial evolution: cotton, pig-iron, steel, and automobiles. In general, although a phase of increasing rate of growth may occur in the very early stages of an industry,[3] these growth

[1] The difficulty of measuring changes in American housing in terms of uniform dwelling units has precluded the presentation of a similar series for the United States.

[2] T. W. Schultz, *Agriculture in an Unstable Economy* (New York, 1945), especially pp. 44 ff.; also N. Silberling, *The Dynamics of Business* (New York, 1943), pp. 127-34. Burns (op. cit., p. 125) also comments on the close relation between food production and population growth; but he notes, as well, the reciprocal (if partial) relation between food production and population movements. Further, Burns introduces briefly the other complex non-economic variables which are relevant: 'Our increasing material prosperity has tended to reduce the death rate, as it has promoted sanitation, medical knowledge, and medical care. The advance in material well-being has influenced also the trend of birth rates; it has improved the possibilities of increased parenthood and so released forces working in that direction, but it has also made people more mindful of their improved standard of living and so tended to promote limitation of the size of families.'

[3] W. Hoffmann (loc. cit., p. 172) notes: 'There are cases, too, when an industry has an exceptional rate of growth not because *per capita* consumption increases with rising real income but because it is a "young" industry busy creating a market for itself in the place of other products. . . . These young industries, then, owe their special rates of growth not to rising national income, falling costs, or sociological factors influencing demand but to their temporary scope for substitution.' This comment refers not only to the phases where increasing rates of growth might obtain in a sector of the economy, but, more generally, to phases where the sectoral rate of growth is high in relation, for

patterns appear to follow, roughly, the course of a logistic curve; that is, they exhibit regular retardation.

On the side of supply, the fall in costs in an industry exploiting a new scientific or technical discovery will be limited by the nature of the technical and scientific basis of the industry itself. After the initial break-through is made it is not unlikely that further refinements in its technical processes will yield diminishing marginal reductions in cost.[1] Secondly, as suggested by Merton, there may exist a systematic decline in the propensity to accept innovations, or to generate them, within a given industry.[2] In the early stages of an industry one may expect to find entrepreneurs who are 'daring, speculative, restless, imaginative', whereas in later generations their primary concern may be the safety of their investments and the assurance of stable, reasonable profits. Third, the general advance in technological progress tends to produce a multiplicity of possible methods both for satisfying a given want and for producing the same product. This possibility, emphasized in particular by Burns, would lead to a natural deceleration in a sector of the economy, given a steady over-all rate of growth for the economy—an assump-

example, to the over-all rate of growth of real income. The period between the moment when an innovation is first successfully introduced and the time when the relevant sector finds some systematic and more stable relation with the rate of growth of the economy as a whole is determined by the rate at which diffusion occurs both on the side of industrial technology and in the tastes of consumers, as they may relate to a new product. In Marshallian analysis one might exhibit an innovation as a new supply curve in an industry and (perhaps) a new demand curve, showing the adjustment to an innovation as an instantaneous process. In fact, the processes of diffusion take so long in historical time, even in societies with a high propensity to accept innovations, that the factors which Hoffmann rules out as irrelevant to the course of 'young industries' will continue to operate and leave their imprint on the actual sectoral course of output.

[1] See, for example, S. Kuznets, op. cit., p. 32: 'In a purely manufacturing industry, technical progress consists mainly in replacing manual labour by machines. When all the important operations are performed by machines which have reached a stage of comparative perfection, not much room is left for further innovations. If, in addition to that, the chemical processes are perfected to the point allowed by modern machinery, no great improvements may be expected.' Implicit in this analysis appears to be a conception of a rough but real relationship between productivity in fundamental and applied science. See also R. Glenday, op. cit., pp. 527–31, and the comment above.

[2] R. K. Merton, 'Fluctuations in the Rate of Industrial Invention', *Quarterly Journal of Economics* (1934–5), pp. 465–8.

tion which seems to be roughly appropriate to the United States over the period considered.[1]

A further factor, relevant particularly to the present illustrative trend patterns, is that the spread of technology to various regions of the world would tend to retard growth in a given industry in any one country, as it supplied a diminishing proportionate share of the world market.

On the side of demand retardation might be expected due to the inelasticity of demand with respect to both price and income. Physical limits exist to the consumption of grain, for example, or even cotton textiles, no matter how high real incomes may go or prices may fall.[2] In the case of industrial products the effective demand for raw materials or intermediate products like steel may be limited not only by the pattern of end-product demands, as real income rises, but also by the degree and character of technical progress in the consuming industries.

Briefly, then, there would appear to be some empirical justification for introducing *ex post* the concept of a realistic optimum long-run rate of growth, over all and in sectors of the economy: systematically related, over all, to the propensities and yields, on average, and related, sectorally, to the rate of growth of population, real income, and changes in taste on the one hand, and to the exploitation of the sectoral possibilities for technical advance and the yield of the relevant natural resources, on the other.

V

It may be of interest to consider briefly two issues of both historical and contemporary interest which can be examined in terms of this model: the process of take-off of a predominantly agricultural economy into industrialization, and the process of secular stagnation.

The process of take-off may be defined as an increase in the volume and productivity of investment in a society, such that

---

[1] A. F. Burns, op. cit., pp. 120–2. Burns further emphasizes that one would expect deceleration in the raw materials sectors of the economy owing to the raw materials saving character of many innovations.

[2] See, for example, Kuznets, op. cit., p. 32.

a sustained increase in *per capita* real income results. In terms of this model such an increase could arise from a substantial movement on the side, broadly, either of yields or of the propensities. The influence of both factors, in various stages of the economic history of different countries, can be discerned. Australia and New Zealand, for example, as well as many other late-developing countries in the world economy, received their impetus to growth essentially from a change in yield, or a succession of such changes over time.[1] This rise in yield took the form of an increased value placed by the markets of the world economy on raw materials or foodstuffs contained within those economies. The increases in real income resulting initially from increased output of these foodstuffs and raw materials interacted with the society in such a way as to yield a self-sustaining growth pattern which widened out to economic sectors other than the original foodstuffs and raw materials. On the other hand, economic history offers cases of societies which enjoyed, for a time, the increased real income associated with the production of

[1] For Australia see B. Fitzpatrick, *The British Empire in Australia* (2nd ed., Melbourne, 1949); Roland Wilson, *Capital Imports and the Terms of Trade* (Melbourne, 1931); and H. Burton, 'The Growth of the Australian Economy' in *Australia*, C. Hartley Gratton, ed. (Berkeley, 1947). For New Zealand see C. G. F. Simkin, *The Instability of a Dependent Economy* (Oxford, 1951). The touchstone of the underlying social resilience of these successful societies was their ability to develop intensively when the phase of high export prices for their raw products and extensive expansion (often based in part on capital imports) had passed. See, for example, the data on internal development in New Zealand during the Great Depression period, in Simkin, op. cit., especially pp. 61–65. This domestic development appeared to have been based partially on import substitutes, reflecting a will to sustain the level of consumption at a time when the foreign balance did not permit the continuance of the former relative level of imports. The case of the Argentine is of interest, in the context of this analysis, as its period of take-off would appear to have resulted primarily from a change in the effective propensities (in the form of the creation of internal security, a stronger government, and a stabilization of the currency) which permitted the profitable development of wheat and wool at a time when the world prices of these commodities were falling on trend, in the 1880's. Later, the coming of the refrigerator ship made the meat-producing resources of the region newly profitable. But, in general, while the profit possibilities of this highly productive area were central to the effort to organize it within the world economy, it was not, as in other cases, a fresh rise in the price of the commodities it might produce which was the immediate stimulant. See, for example, J. H. Williams, *Argentine Trade under Inconvertible Paper Money* (Cambridge, Mass., 1920).

scarce basic materials, but in which the interaction of this increase and the frame of the society did not yield a self-reinforcing pattern of sustained economic growth.[1]

One must distinguish the time period over which the examination of take-offs is conducted. If the time period taken is too long, one must begin to take account, in history, of the interaction of economic growth on the propensities themselves. For example, looked at narrowly, the take-off of Britain into the Industrial Revolution, if associated rigorously with developments centring on cotton textiles, can be allocated to the decade of the 1780's when the rate of increase in output rose sharply.[2] In the generalized language employed here, this take-off had its basis in a rise in yield. The basis for that rise in yield was, in turn, the application of the mule on the expiration of Arkwright's patent, coupled with the return to peaceful trade with the states of the American South. The surge of the 1780's set the stage for the invention of the cotton gin in 1793. The cheapened and enlarged supply of raw material it offered further stimulated existing inventive talent on the engineering side of the industry. The industrial development thus doubly detonated enlarged the class of manufacturers and those associated with them and produced, on balance, in British society, changed propensities, which furthered the whole process of economic development. It is not wholly unrealistic to regard the take-off, in

[1] See, for example, the story of Brazil's erratic evolution, J. F. Normano, *Brazil: A Study of Economic Types* (Chapel Hill, 1935); also H. W. Spiegel, *The Brazilian Economy* (Philadelphia, 1949).

[2] See especially E. Baines, *History of the Cotton Manufacture* (London, 1835), pp. 346–50. Baines gives the following figures for the rate of increase in the import of raw cotton into Britain, a fair trend measurement of the rate of growth of the industry (p. 348):

1741 to 1751	81%	1771 to 1781	75¾%	1801 to 1811	39½%
1751 to 1761	21½%	1781 to 1791	319½%	1811 to 1821	93%
1761 to 1771	25½%	1791 to 1801	87½%	1821 to 1831	85%

The extraordinary rate of rise between 1781 to 1791 (319½%) is partly distorted by the abnormally low figure for 1781 (5,198,778 lb., as against the average for 1776–80 of 6,766,613 lb.). Nevertheless, the rate of growth of the 1780's is unique. The subsequent rate of growth, to 1815, was, of course, damped by the pressures to invest in other directions during the years of the French Wars. Note the sharp increase in the rate of growth after 1811, which began, in fact, in 1817. For further observations on the early development of the British cotton industry, in another context, see below Chap. IX, pp. 201–7.

this narrow sense, as mainly determined by a sudden change in yield. But the long history of both technical and social preparation for the British industrial revolution cannot be ignored in a wider analysis, nor can the play-back on the economy of the social forces it later generated.

The Japanese take-off after 1868, on the other hand, can be similarly allocated, on these narrow grounds, to a shift in the propensities. The clans which had been excluded from power during the Tokugawa era (1603–1868) had shown a considerable interest in Western culture and applied science, and several of their young samurai had left the country to study Western civilization. Allen observes: 'This knowledge made them critical of the existing forms of government and apprehensive of the dangers to Japan that the growing power of the Western States might bring.'[1] The previous Shogunate had resisted the incursion of new ideas because they were believed to imperil the feudal structure. The samurai warriors, now a 'functionless and parasitic class'[2] as a result of the long period of peace, helped lead the revolt which overthrew the Shogun and mobilized a new constellation of power around the Emperor, still a rallying-point, despite his exclusion from effective power during the Tokugawa era. It was from the samurai that the administrators of the Meiji era (1868–1912) were substantially drawn. The effective propensities can be observed shifting in Japanese society after 1868, a transition summarized in the Emperor's Charter Oath, which declared *inter alia*:[3] 'Knowledge shall be sought throughout the world, so that the welfare of the Empire may be promoted.' Not only was a higher proportion of available innovations accepted, but the scale of investment input was increased. In the first instance, until a class of private capitalists was created, the State mobilized new capital in diverse ways, including the taking over of

[1] G. C. Allen, *A Short Economic History of Modern Japan* (London, 1946), pp. 18–19.   [2] Ibid., p. 11.

[3] There are various translations of the Charter Oath, of just sufficient difference to make the non-reader of Japanese faintly uneasy. The political context of the Oath made, however, a degree of ambiguity useful. The passage quoted above is Hodzuni's version, *Encyclopaedia Britannica*, 1911, quoted by G. B. Sansom, *The Western World and Japan* (New York, 1950), p. 318.

rent payments from some of the former nobility, and by means of inflationary finance.

In similar terms the familiar argument concerning secular stagnation can be restated, either from the side of the yields or from the side of the propensities. Assuming the underlying propensities as fixed, and diminishing returns from accretions in the capital stock, then investment might fall off in response to a declining level of profitability, if there is some elasticity in the supply curve of finance. This general formula would embrace the end of the Frontier hypothesis and the notion that the possibility of high yield from new industries has diminished.[1] With a fall in the level of profitability, from one or more of these causes, the maintenance of full employment may require higher levels of consumption or of investment outlays over and above those induced by the confrontation of the supply curve of (private) finance with the level of expected profitability.

The same outcome might emerge, however, if one assumes that, with a rise in income, any of the underlying propensities are weakened; that is, the propensities to develop fundamental science, to seek innovations, to apply them, to respond to profit possibilities, to consume, or to have children. This approach would cover the view that secular stagnation may result from a population decline or from a decline in the propensity to consume; and it would introduce the less familiar notion that secular stagnation may result from a fundamental failure to respond to the challenges and opportunities of growth by sufficient allocations to science or applied science, by a sufficient degree of acceptance of possibilities offered, or by a sufficient desire to achieve further material advance.

It may well be that, as our knowledge increases, we will lay greater stress than is now conventional on the possibility that secular stagnation may result from a decline in the propensities rather than from a decline in the yield from additional outlays of investment in various directions. The evidence

---

[1] To these conditions must be added the technical possibility that innovations may be sufficiently capital-saving to cause an inadequate demand for resources in investment.

for long-run diminishing returns from accretions to science and applied science is, indeed, so dubious, as is evidence for a trend toward capital-saving innovations, that in the end it is to social and political behaviour that we may look for analyses of economic stagnation and decline.

It should be noted that the cases of take-off, narrowly defined, and of secular stagnation are not symmetrical. For certain purposes the process of take-off may be arbitrarily, but not falsely, allocated to a limited time period, when the interaction between the changes in the level of income, techniques of production, and other variables in the society can properly be ignored. Secular stagnation, by definition, covers so long a period of time that the interaction between the structure of the economy and the whole social fabric cannot be ignored. The systematic analysis of declining rates of growth in an economy or of the take-off process (broadly defined) would thus constitute an exercise in the art of inter-relating economic, social, and political factors over time.

V

GROWTH AND BUSINESS CYCLES

I

THE argument thus far presented has sought to define the determinants of the rate of growth and the character of the forces likely to lead to deviations from a steady rate of growth. Both the yields from various capital stocks and the propensities which summarize a society's response to them are capable of change over time. If such changes were the only form of instability, one might expect slow alterations in the rate of growth, but regular cycles could not be deduced simply from the movements of yields, or propensities, discussed in Chapter IV. An analysis of business cycles demands the introduction of additional assumptions.

The approach to business cycles suggested here does not differ greatly from formulations which are already in the field and are widely accepted. The business cycle is presented as resulting mainly from two related aspects of the investment process: the influence of various lags on the scale and character of investment and the institutional environment of investment, when carried out by private individuals and institutions seeking profit. The special quality of the present approach to business cycles appears to consist in its emphasis on the sectoral aspects of investment as opposed to the behaviour of the total volume of investment.

It will be recalled that with given propensities, investment, under conditions of growth, is viewed as a process of selecting the most appropriate direction for investment, given the sectoral implications of the rate of growth and the potentialities offered by innovations. The allocation of resources to fundamental and to applied science is regarded here as a sectoral aspect of investment, whose prior history helps determine (along with the character of natural resources and the propensity to accept innovations) the profitability of investment, at any particular period of time. The purpose of the present chapter is to explore, in the special context of this formulation of the process of over-all and sectoral growth, the nature of the essentially cyclical pattern which growth has historically assumed in the Western world.

Formally, this must be done by relaxing certain of the assumptions which were made in the previous chapter, required to yield there a pattern of steady or slowly changing growth rates. It is believed that, in order to approximate the process of economic development, as it has taken place historically in modern times, under systems of relatively free enterprise, four types of assumptions must be dropped. First, lags must be allowed between the decision to allocate resources in certain directions and the consequences of such decisions for current capacity and its marginal yield. Second, the assumption that acts of investment may always be taken in continuous, small units must be dropped. Third, certain features of the procedures of investment under private investment must be taken into account, notably those which have caused a shortsighted view of future profitability and those which have yielded a disproportionate concentration of investment in certain directions at particular times. Fourth, allowance must be made for factors determining short-period fluctuations in the proportion of current income spent and invested.

One lag which must be noted, although its implications will not here be explored, is that between net additions to the population and the size of the working force. The various forces which decree the difference between birth- and death-rates may not have their effect on the size of the working force until an interval has passed. Their effects on the size of the total population, however, and thus on the scale and nature of the demand for certain products, comes more quickly; e.g. in the relative demand for houses and food. The course of population growth, and the nature of the factors which determine it, decree different relative burdens for the working force, in terms of the non-working force age groups; and these factors thus affect *per capita* real income.

Again, there are lags between the time when an economy sets up an incentive for innovation in a certain direction and the time when such potentialities for innovation are offered.[1] In a sense, the lag between the time when an innovation is offered and the time of its application is covered, within this system, by the third propensity, regarded dynamically—that is, by the proportion of the flow (or pool) of potential innovations accepted within the economy. Although significant for the rate and character of growth, such lags are not regarded as central to fluctuations and are not explored here.

The familiar lag believed most relevant to cyclical fluctuations and their character is that between the time of a decision to allocate resources to investment and the time when the completed investment enters into the capital stock and into production, and there exerts, through supply conditions, a direct effect on the current market position. The fact of a lag, given the nature of the investing procedure, opens the way to the misjudging of future profit prospects. The incentives to continue to undertake new acts of investment in certain directions may persist, because of this lag, beyond the point where, in fact, such investment will prove profitable in the time period envisaged by the investor. This lag, connected with the period of gestation of investment, is believed significant not only for the existence of business cycles but also for their character. It is possible to conceive of changes in the average period of gestation for investment as a whole. A shift on balance in outlays from (say) the financing of the cotton trade to canal building, or from factory extension to transcontinental railways, might well increase the average period, for investment as a whole, between the undertaking of acts of investment and their fruition. In quantity theory terms, with MV constant, T can alter (and P), due to such a shift in the average period of gestation.[2] Such relative shifts are believed to account in part for

[1] S. C. Gilfillan, 'The Lag between Invention and Application', unpublished paper.

[2] The allocation of resources to wars may be regarded as a limiting case of the lengthening of the period of gestation, in the sense that no output at all emerges from the act of investment. Similarly, taking the world economy as a whole, gold mining can be regarded as such an extreme case, except for that part of output which goes to industrial uses or personal consumption, and further assuming (not unrealistically) that the monetary system would have been adequately flexible in the absence of further gold output.

differences in the lengths of booms and the degree to which they continue into a stage of sustained rising prices. Further, as discussed in Chapter VI, the secular trends in relative prices, sectoral income distribution, and the character of current investment are judged to be linked to the history of certain types of investment, with a particularly long period of gestation.

Another fundamental characteristic of investment, related to its period of gestation, is the fact that it may not, in all cases, be possible to proceed technically, or with economy of resources, in small increments. After a time, a firm may be faced with the alternative of not expanding at all or building a whole new wing to its plant. A railway line or canal is either built, linking two places, or it is not built; building it for 20 per cent. of the route may not have any economic meaning.

In the setting of these time lags, with their possibilities for variation, and of discontinuities in the expansion of the capital stock, the method of investment by individuals and private institutions, acting under expectations of private profit, has had certain peculiar characteristics. First, there was no satisfactory method by which an investor could know what total of investment was currently planned in the sector of the economy which engaged his interest.[1] This could lead to action on the basis of some version of the primitive assumption that the present position, or the current rate of change, was likely to persist, irrespective of the action undertaken by the individual investor. Such a system of investment, based on expected profit, taken in conjunction with the technical characteristics of investment discussed above, might well yield, in itself, inappropriately high rates of investment in certain directions.[2]

[1] The increase in the self-consciousness of the investor, with respect to an 'appropriate' total level of investment in his sector of the economy, is likely to emerge as one of the most striking developments of recent times. Note, for example, recent debates in the United States and in Europe on the appropriate levels for current investment in steel capacity. The much enlarged area within which governments now determine, directly or indirectly, the character of current investment is likely to accentuate this trend. For further discussion see Chap. X.

[2] In this context appropriate investment would be the rate required to main-

Second, the tendency to overshoot might be accentuated by certain social or even human characteristics of the investors in a private economy, who did not operate atomistically, on the basis of individual judgement concerning all the possible relevant variables. Investors have tended to respond to certain current indicators of future profitability; and they tended to follow leaders within the capital markets or industry. Word would get round that certain types of investment were likely to prove profitable; or, in industry, that this was a good time to expand. In many cases the bases for the initial judgement might well be sound, in the sense that capacity had fallen behind its appropriate level given the rate of growth of the economy, its implications for the given sector, and the technical potentialities available. Since future profitability relates directly to the level of capacity in relation to an 'optimum' for the size and rate of growth of real income, the scale on which investment was undertaken in particular sectors itself helped determine future returns after the acts of investment were completed; and for some further time period, as well. Therefore, the tendency to follow the leader might accentuate the inherent tendency to overshoot the appropriate level of capacity in certain sectors of the economy; and it might well lead to an ignoring, for the time, of other potentially profitable forms of investment.

Third, one cannot ignore the tendency for the capital markets to become, as Bagehot said of Lombard Street, 'often very dull and sometimes extremely excited'. This form of statement may simply be a less exact formulation of the proposition that expectations are governed by the assumption that the present position (or rate of change) will continue over that future time period relevant to current investment. In this sense the accelerator is one formulation of an essentially psychological assumption. The historian, however, recalling the recurrent pathological manias from the tulip boom

tain capacity in the various sectors of economy at the level required by the rate of growth of real income (given the underlying propensities) and changing tastes, assuming, further, a given average level of unemployment of resources. Thus, investment fluctuations in the course of business cycles in sectors of the economy are regarded as involving the periodic overshooting and undershooting of the realistic sectoral optima, elaborated in Chap. IV.

of 1636-7 in Amsterdam to the stock-market boom of 1928-9 in New York, may doubt that such a formal abstraction of irrational social behaviour, whatever its usefulness in giving precision to a circumstance difficult to measure, is more than a crude approximation of the process whereby expectations of profitability have, in fact, been formed.

There is, of course, nothing novel about the introduction of 'errors of optimism and pessimism' into an analysis of business cycles. Professor Pigou long ago elaborated this element in the story which was not new in 1927, when his *Industrial Fluctuations* was first published.[1] The present treatment would simply introduce the concept of over-all and sectoral optima, as dependent variables, to which errors in either direction might, conceptually, be related; and it would emphasize the possibly sectoral, rather than over-all, character of the errors committed by the investment markets in the course of the cycle.

The fourth deviation from the assumptions of the previous section must embrace the possibility that the determinants of consumption and investment outlays may not yield steady full employment. We must be prepared to consider, for example, that a rise in the expected level of profitability might lead to a level of investment, income, and consumption outlays which would press against the limits of the current working force and capacity, and raise prices and costs. The rise in costs might affect expectations of profit and thus the level of current investment; or, should the level of investment be sustained (the supply curve of finance being inelastic over the relevant range), resources might be bid away from the consumer in such a fashion as to lower his real income and, with a given propensity to consume, the total level of consumption. Similarly, a fall in expected profitability might reduce investment, income, and consumption outlays in such a manner as to yield unemployment, under suitable assumptions of wage-rate inflexibility. On what might be called the inner mechanics of short-run income fluctuations, this argu-

---

[1] See A. H. Hansen, *Business Cycles and the National Income* (New York, 1951), Part III, for a tracing of the history of various strands in business-cycle analysis, including the role of psychological factors.

ment would simply absorb the currently received views, seeking to place them in a framework where the rate of growth and so-called autonomous investment are determinate, not given.

II

What sort of system emerges, then, if these factors are introduced: time lags in investment; discontinuous increments of investment; institutional tendencies for investment to concentrate and to overshoot in sectors of the economy; and the possibility of inflation and unemployment? It should be recalled as fundamental to this argument that the system is based on certain basic propensities, slow-changing in nature, which in conjunction with certain yields from stocks determine the broad shape of growth. These basic forces, for purposes of short-period cyclical analysis, can be assumed as fixed.

Starting from a position of equilibrium, as earlier defined, let us assume that the rise of real income or the flow of innovational potentialities has tended to raise expected profits in a certain sector of the economy. Perhaps this has come about because the rise in population, set against the marginal productivity of existing wheat land and technical proficiency in wheat growing, has yielded a rise in the wheat price; this has created an interest in hitherto untouched lands of believed high productivity; and capital is sought for their exploitation, at expected high yields. Or, perhaps, the rise in real income, and growth of the economy, have made previous techniques (or total capacity) of transport inadequate (reflected in rising transport costs); this has stimulated efforts to find new means of transport; and such new means appear to offer a high profit return under existing cost conditions, including interest rates. What is essential here is that persistent factors of growth or the persistent flow of innovational possibilities might yield a rise in expected profits in particular directions.[1]

[1] See pp. 117–18 for a discussion of why such a rise in expected profits might well be counted upon toward the end of the slump, in a system expanding in a cyclical pattern.

Since we are assuming a start from equilibrium (but relaxing the underlying equilibrium assumptions), full employment reigns initially. The rise in expected profitability, in a certain direction, would tend to raise total investment, if we assumed some elasticity in the finance supply curve. Resources must, however, be bid away, either from investment of lower expected yield or from consumption; prices and costs would tend to rise. But we assume that, given the capital market's reaction to the new high-yield type of investment, such rises in cost do not deter the continuance of new commitments in that direction. We are dealing, further, with a capital market which has an inherent tendency to concentrate its interests and to look rather at current indicators of future yield than to measure the impact on future yield of the investment currently under way, but not yet completed. During the period of gestation of the new form of high-yield investment, then, costs would rise, but fresh commitments might continue to be made.[1] A general inflationary situation would prevail, with a shifting of resources either away from consumption or from other forms of investment, or from both.

Two forces might bring this surge of investment in the new direction to a close: the rise in costs (including, possibly, interest rates), tending to bring down the expected level of profitability; and/or an awareness that investment in the new direction had been undertaken on such a scale (or with such faulty judgement on marginal return) that profits would be lower than originally anticipated. The latter factor would certainly come into play when the period of gestation had ended; and it might be somewhat anticipated.

---

[1] In this form of analysis, which emphasizes the role in each cycle of investment in certain key directions, it would matter where the first or most acute supply bottlenecks appeared; that is, the degree and timing of the impact on expected profitability of investment in the key directions would depend on whether and to what extent bottlenecks developed in those markets for materials and labour which entered most significantly into the particular costs relevant. This relationship defines the connexion between Hicks's sectoral capacity levels (relevant to bottlenecks) and the sectoral concept employed in the present analysis, with respect to the determination of the direction of new investment. See J. R. Hicks, *A Contribution to the Theory of the Trade Cycle* (Oxford, 1950), especially p. 132.

The loss of confidence in the new direction of investment would shift down expected profitability and lower total investment and total incomes. The psychological character-istics of the market which decreed an over-optimistic view of future returns might now decree an over-pessimistic view. With consumption relatively inelastic with respect to income, total consumption would fall somewhat, although not as sharply as investment. Unemployment would appear.

It should be noted that the process of investment con-centration in the course of the inflationary boom might well involve the physical movement of resources in certain direc-tions; e.g. the mobilization of railway gangs; a dispropor-tionate expansion of rails and railway equipment within the heavy industries; &c. It would take time, in the boom, to achieve this movement of resources and, in the slump, time would be required to shift them out.

The general nature of the forces tending to limit the extent of the slump is now fairly well agreed.[1] In terms of the present argument it is important to underline the persistent forces that would continue to operate, making for a continued rise in real income and ultimately for a new boom:

1. The relative stability of the consumption level in the face of a short-period decline in income would limit the extent of the slump.

2. The working force would continue its rise, being de-pendent on previous decisions or on forces not likely to be greatly affected by a slump (health measures); simi-larly, the total population would rise.

3. The flow of innovational potentialities coming forward would continue, even though somewhat responsive to cyclical fluctuations.[2]

4. The gap between capacity and appropriate capacity in

---

[1] See, for example, J. R. Hicks, op. cit., pp. 101–4; and A. Hansen, op. cit., p. 497.

[2] See, for example, T. S. Ashton, 'Some Statistics of the Industrial Revolu-tion in Britain', *Manchester School of Economic and Social Studies*, vol. xvi, No. 2 (May 1948), Table 1, p. 229; and E. Graue, 'Inventions and Production', *Review of Economic Statistics* (1943), pp. 221–6. The flow of innovations coming forward must, of course, be distinguished from the relative inducement of depression, in different sectors, to apply or not to apply existing potentialities.

certain sectors of the economy, relatively ignored during the previous boom, might assert itself in the form of a rise in expected profitability in directions different from those previously pursued.

5. The rise in expected profitability in certain directions (relatively slighted in the previous boom as an avenue of investment) might be reinforced by the fall in costs, during the slump.[1]

6. The low level of expected profitability might cause increased amounts of money to pile up with lending institutions, decreeing a fall in interest rates, tending in time to raise expected profitability.[3]

7. Finally, the completion of the acts of investment undertaken in the 'initial' boom might yield a rise of real income, in the form of higher productivity in a certain sector or sectors of the economy which, in itself, would help to open the way for further profitable investment.

Thus, the relatively persistent forces of growth might assert themselves, yielding a new boom, whose main directions might well differ from those of the previous expansion.

The actual process of growth, in an economy whose underlying resource-yields and propensities were sufficiently strong to sustain it, would take the form of a succession of cycles. In each, investment would tend to exploit the profit possibilities offered by the long-run pressure of growth against resources, including the (largely induced) flow of innovational potentialities. But, given the time lags inherent in the process and the nature of the investing institutions, investment in certain directions would tend to be overdone. The sectoral investment excesses would cause an over-commitment of physical resources in certain directions, requiring time for disengagement. The reaction from such excesses, when appre-

[1] The obverse of the sectoral price movements discussed above (p. 116 n.) would apply here.

[2] This is not to dispute the view of modern income analysis that the fall in the rate of interest, during the slump, is basically caused by the decline in expected profitability, with its effects on investment and income; but, rather, to assert that protracted periods of easy money in the latter stages of depression and the early stages of prosperity have, among other forces, contributed to the rise in expected profitability, helping thus to induce bursts of investment in new directions.

ciated, would yield a general downward movement in income and employment, which would be cushioned and then reversed by the action of certain strong underlying propensities, less elastic with respect to their relevant yields than the supply curve of finance. Or, it is also possible that the other relevant yields move less violently in the course of the boom and slump than the general investment profitability curve.[1]

III

The principal difference between this conception of the business cycle and more conventional formulations can best be perceived by examining somewhat more closely the character of the upper turning-point. Hansen has recently summarized as follows the modern theory of the upper turning-point:[2]

. . . the modern theory holds that there are three self-limiting factors which come into play: (1) the falling marginal efficiency of capital, partly due to a movement down the schedule as more and more investment is undertaken, and partly owing to a shift in the schedule; (2) the acceleration principle, under which induced investment necessarily fades out as the rate of increase in output tapers off when full employment of resources is approached; and (3) the slope of the consumption function, under which a widening gap of saving must be filled by investment offsets if a reversal is to be avoided.

The third of Hansen's elements in the upper turning-point can be redefined as the inability of the system to maintain a sufficient level of investment, given the consumption function, to support full employment; and attention can be concentrated on the reasons for the inadequacy of investment at the peak of the boom; that is, upon the limitation imposed by full employment on the operation of the accelerator or upon a tendency either to slide down the curve of the marginal efficiency of capital or for the curve itself to shift.

In models which use the accelerator principle, the downturn comes when a limitation on capacity prevents further rise in output, thus bringing to a halt the expansive operation

[1] See pp. 24 ff.   [2] Op. cit., pp. 495–6.

of the accelerator. This is probably to be translated into the view that a rise in the cost of new investment (including, perhaps, rises in interest rates) produces a fall in the expected yield from current investment and, thus, a decline in the volume of new investment; alternatively, it could be interpreted as reflecting an absolute decline in new orders to the investment goods industries, caused by a failure of total output to expand at its previous rate.[1]

There seems little doubt that rises in costs have played a part in producing a revision of the expected profitability of new investment in the latter stages of many booms, and they must be counted a possible factor in the downturn of new investment. Since the marginal efficiency of capital curve is a rate of return over cost, one can define the operation of the accelerator (if translated as cost increases due to bottlenecks), as a force operating on costs in such a way as to lower the marginal efficiency of capital curve.

The other agreed force operating on the level of investment is a movement down or a shift in the demand for capital induced by forces other than changes in costs. Quoting Hansen again:

. . . the available autonomous investment becomes progressively exhausted the longer the boom lasts. The new investment opportunities (opened up by advances in technique and other dynamic factors) tend to be exploited at a pace that exceeds the normal rate of growth. Innovation (progress) proceeds by spurts, by intermittent surges. . . . While this lasts the backlog of autonomous investment plus the investment induced by rapid expansion may be adequate to fill the consumption-income gap. Once the backlog is exhausted, however, and once the rate of increase in output begins to taper off, then both the autonomous and the induced investment will tend to die down. Thus the boom 'dies a natural death'. Investment has caught up with the requirements of growth and technical progress. Net investment falls off, and income recedes by a magnified amount.[2]

If one is prepared to look at the matter in terms of the total level of investment and the investment demand or

---

[1] For the discussion of this point see J. S. Duesenberry, 'Hicks on the Trade Cycle', *Quarterly Journal of Economics*, Aug. 1950, pp. 468 ff.

[2] Op. cit., p. 496.

profitability curve in general, something like this conclusion
is inescapable from the historical evidence. The author's
view would differ from Hansen's in two respects. First, as
indicated earlier, the distinction between autonomous and
induced investment is not accepted. The adjustment of capacity to changes in the level (or rate of change) of real income
and the absorption of the potentialities offered by innovation
are regarded as part of the same central process of investment
and of growth. The 'leading lines' of new investment in
booms cannot be equated with 'autonomous investment', for
they have often not involved the introduction of new techniques, but constituted simply the extension of capacity, with
existing techniques, in an effort to fill a gap between actual
and optimum capacity. Second, the author would raise the
following question: Does the boom actually exhaust the objective possibilities for profitable new investment on the
requisite scale, for the time being, or has investment simply
overshot in certain directions?[1] The answer to this latter
question can only emerge from extended empirical analysis
and measurement; but the issue is worth further preliminary
exploration.

In conception, a downturn could mark, not a general
catching up of investment with the requirements of growth
and technical progress, but simply a revision of the investor's
judgement concerning the appropriateness of capacity expansion in those particular sectors of the economy which
have led the boom. In macro-terms, it might be said that, in
the earlier stages of the boom, the investment market observes
a discrepancy between the current level of capacity in certain
sectors of the economy and the level that would be appropriate to the expansion of the economy as a whole and its
technical possibilities. Toward the latter stages of the boom
the investment market begins to observe that this discrepancy

[1] In other terms, this question raises the issue of the exact meaning of the
short-period declining shape of the marginal efficiency of capital curve used,
for example by N. Kaldor in his 'A Model of the Trade Cycle', *Economic Journal*
(1940). Does this curve reflect profit expectations, including the possibilities of
a falsely concentrated perspective in the capital market, or does it reflect in
some objective sense the relative short-period exhaustion of possibilities for
profitable investment?

has narrowed or disappeared, and the danger of relative over-capacity may come to be regarded as real. Time has passed since the new line of investment was undertaken, and the scale on which the economy as a whole has entered into this line can now be better observed. Whether or not the investing group includes in its calculations such an over-all view of the investment possibilities, certain direct market phenomena may confront it: the price of securities (or of commodities) in the new lines may cease to rise; news from the goldfields may reflect leaner yields than have been expected; and so forth. In short, a boom could turn down not only because investment prospects have been dimmed by rising costs (or by a falling off of new orders due to the failure of total output to expand at the previous rate), but also because in the leading lines of new investment the market has come to appreciate that expansion in certain sectors has proceeded beyond the optimum level, or that the decisions already taken would lead to such disproportionate expansion in terms of the optimum sectoral levels of capacity and output.

These observations, or better, this query about the trade cycle appears to open for exploration at least the view that the central phenomenon of the trade cycle is not an inappropriate total level of investment in relation to the rate of economic progress, but an inappropriate balance of investment in relation to the pattern of economic progress and its technical possibilities.[1]

The proposition that it is essentially an inappropriate composition of investment, rather than its scale, which distinguishes the boom, must confront the empirical fact that in the latter stages of many booms total investment is at an extremely high level; and the view of the future taken in

[1] Suggestive, but by no means conclusive, evidence on this proposition is information presented in another context by A. F. Burns in his study of production trends (op. cit., pp. xviii–xix): 'Each time the national economy has experienced an exceptionally rapid secular advance, the production trends of different industries have diverged so widely as to suggest a partial loss of balance, and progress has been checked by a business depression of great severity.' Implicit in this observation, as explicit here, is a notion of an appropriate balance of growth among the sectors of the economy which the boom tends first to exploit and then to violate.

many sectors is more optimistic than a reading of the long-term trends in those sectors would have justified. Could it not be possible that this generalized investment boom was simply a broad secondary response to the fact that, in certain key sectors of the economy, an inappropriately high level of investment was taking place? This limited distortion would take the form of demand curves, in the capital market and in the markets for labour and materials, which were high and inelastic. These could drive a system to inflationary full employment and hold it there for a time, depending on the period of gestation of the new form of investment or on other demand factors which might produce a revised view of its prospects which, by itself or in conjunction with rising costs, might decree a decline of new investment in the new directions.

The decline, once begun, might, through familiar reinforcing processes, have general consequences for the level of new investment in many directions. What is essential in this perspective is that in the course of expansion not all forms of investment increased to the same extent in terms of the concept of growth equilibrium earlier defined. A boom appears generally to have exhausted a line of development in one sector of the economy as a leading outlet for investment, for a period longer than a single cycle. The same direction for new enterprise seldom, if ever, dominates successive major (i.e. nine-year) cycles. This may mean that a downturn was 'unnecessary' in that not all lines of investment had exceeded their long-period equilibrium level; that the generalized downturn was an indirect product of a legitimate revulsion only from the scale on which the main lines of investment had previously been pursued. For example, a boom concentrating heavily on railway building, given the nature of the investing market, might ignore real and profitable possibilities for expansion in the housing field. The downturn might occur at a time of legitimate revulsion from the false expectations of yield in railway building, while the optimum level of housing capacity was above the current level and while, objectively regarded, real possibilities for profit existed in housing but were not being exploited.

This hypothesis requires further investigation. The history of business cycles is the history of a succession of booms in which the capital markets have seized upon certain key types of investment which have been made apparently profitable either through the prior course of growth in relation to capacity or through innovations, including the discovery of new resources. The psychological tendency of the market to concentrate its attention clearly leads to increases in capacity, in particular directions, beyond those justified by the rate of growth or the productivity of the innovations, over the time period envisaged by the investors. It is by no means clear *prima facie*, however, that the acknowledged secondary expansions of investment in all cases place the economy at the end of the boom in a position where its capacity is, over all, such, in relation to its long-run rate of growth and the potentialities of innovations, that a full employment volume of investment could not be sustained, if the composition of investment were 'appropriate'. On the other hand, further investigation might reveal that, even though important possibilities for investment were ignored towards the peak of the boom, owing to the concentration on the leading lines, the total volume of investment, profitable in terms of the long-run rate of growth, would under full employment still not be sufficient to permit maintenance of steady full employment until some time had passed in depression and the long-run forces making for further growth had been given time to operate and to yield new opportunities for investment.

The introduction of this hypothesis suggests the possibility that the problem of controlling the trade cycle is not only a problem in the appropriate level of aggregate outlays (that is, investment plus consumption), but also a problem in achieving an appropriate composition of new investment. It also reinforces the possibility, as noted earlier,[1] that the long-run rates of growth that we observe for economies growing in a cyclical sequence of this type are lower than the optimum possible, even taking the propensities as given and incapable of influence through public policy; that is, a continuing appropriate pattern of investment at the full-employment level would move real income forward at a higher rate than its trend, defined *ex post*, in terms of a succession of peak positions, or otherwise established by elimination of the cyclical movements which have taken place in the past.

Another possibility of interest—already familiar, but not fully explored—emerges from this view of the cycle; namely, that business cycles of different length are essentially of the same nature, but are to be distinguished mainly with respect to the period of gestation of the leading forms of investment which dominated their course. The inventory cycle would represent a relatively shallow deviation of production from the optimum, associated with investment in stocks of short gestation period. The conventional nine-year cycle would represent the consequence of more substantial deviations from the optimum, which took longer to appreciate. The more powerful upswings, marked by a stage of sustained inflation, to the extent that they were not the product of war outlays (for example, the expansions up to 1854 and 1873), would emerge as cases of booms where the leading forms of investment had an extraordinarily long period of gestation, and proved resistant for a longer period than the more typical boom to cost increases and a revised judgement of further prospects.

VI

GROWTH AND SECULAR TRENDS

I

THE process of cyclical fluctuations, as seen in the previous chapter, is the irregular adjustment of actual capacity, in various sectors of the economy, around realistic optimum levels, decreed by the (trend) rate of growth of real income and the potentialities for innovation, with given propensities, over-all and sectoral. This realistic optimum, in sectors of the economy, is to be distinguished from the optimum sectoral capacities of Chapter IV, under the assumptions of steady full employment and appropriate investment. Deviations between actual capacity and the realistic optimum levels appear, in a private economy, in the form of profit incentives, both to seek and to exploit innovations of a particular character and otherwise to invest in certain particular directions; or, when overshooting has occurred, deviations may appear in the form of low or negative profits to be derived in the short period from further increments of investment in particular directions. Throughout this stage of the argument we have ignored changes in the social and political context of the economy, as reflected in the propensities.

The course of modern economic history has been marked, however, not only by cyclical fluctuations, but also by protracted periods, covering several cycles in real income and employment, in which the world economy exhibited trend movements in relative intersectoral prices; intersectoral income distribution; the prevailing character of and yield from new investment; and the trend of general prices. It is believed that these trend periods are in large part to be accounted for by prolonged overshooting, in particular sectors of the economy, and by the reaction from such excessive distortions in the sectoral pattern of growth. In turn, it is believed that wars and 'lumpy' forms of (mainly agricultural and raw-material) investment, with very long periods of gestation, have been at the basis of such distortions. In this trend process, investment in the mining of the precious metals has played a part which is not wholly adventitious.[1]

It will be noted that the trends defined in this argument are not trends in the over-all rate of growth of output. Nor would they necessarily imply secular changes in the average level of unemployment; although some reflection in the average level of unemployment would not be excluded, *prima facie*, by this definition. Trends are defined primarily in terms of relative price movements, resulting from distortions in the composition of capacity, as compared to the realistic optimum compatible with the rate and technical character of long-run growth. The shifts in relative prices have their consequences on the distribution of income as among the sectors of the economy, and on the types of new investment found profitable. The exclusion from currently profitable categories of investment of types which have suffered from prior overshooting might, in conception, make the maintenance of full employment with a given supply curve of finance so difficult that the average level of employment might fall in trend periods marked by declining prices and an absence of high-yield extensive forms of investment. This might happen if the supply curve of finance were sufficiently elastic with respect to the curve of profitability, or if the decline in the profitability curve were sufficiently great. But there is nothing in the structure of the argument itself which would argue the necessity of trends in the over-all rate of growth of output or in unemployment.

Since the end of the eighteenth century what we have to explain historically are, roughly speaking, four periods when prices were rising, relatively, for agriculture. At these times the yield from investment was high and the general price level rising; and relative income movements were favourable to agriculture and to business, but less favourable to the industrial worker. These four periods may be designated, roundly: 1793–1815; 1848–73; 1896–1920; 1935 to the

---

[1] See the author's *B.E.N.C.*, pp. 21–23; and further discussion on pp. 142 and 209–10 n., below.

present. We also have three periods when the reverse trends tended to prevail: 1815-48; 1873-96; 1920-35.

These familiar time groupings do considerable violence to the complex, irregular, heterodox course of modern economic history; and they should be regarded as fairly severe abstractions, in the specific sense that the price, interest rate, and other trends which normally define them are not continuous. The course of events from 1802 to 1808 is counter to the trend movements down to 1815, for example; the boom of the 1830's, counter to those which generally characterize the period 1815-48; the character of the European boom of the 1860's runs counter to the dominant trends down to 1873, as does the boom of the late 1880's with respect to the period 1873-96.

There is nothing in the present analysis which requires a long, fifty-year cycle; and in this fundamental sense, the author's view is to be distinguished from Schumpeter's.[1] It is also to be distinguished with respect to its judgement on the causes of the periods of rising prices. Schumpeter would associate these with major industrial innovations, the present argument with periods of war and extensive expansion, of long gestation period. Wars aside, these periods are here linked to the impact of growth on existing resources and the opportunities opened up or generated by such pressures. They are not determined externally, by the appearance of innovators.

It should be noted further that there is nothing in the background of this argument which would lead automatically to the conclusion that agricultural products and raw materials in general would be consistently and simultaneously in relatively short supply or in relative over-supply. Nor, in fact, is it necessarily the case that all agricultural commodities or all raw materials would inevitably move together in terms of relative capacity and relative price. Over the past 150 years, however, the forces making for an expansion of capacity in certain basic foodstuffs often involved the open-

[1] On this view, a system at peace which incorporated the assumption that expansion in agricultural and raw-material capacity could be carried out only by the opening up of new areas, a process with a long period of gestation and not capable of execution in small increments, would exhibit periodic long cycles of the kind described here.

ing up of new areas and the exploitation of sources of supply for other foodstuffs and for raw materials which lay within the new areas. Even with this special historical fact, connected with the availability of new unexploited regions, one can note significant divergences in the output-price history, as among different foodstuff and raw-material prices.[1]

Historically, then, the overshooting process, which is believed to be central to these trend periods, arose from eras of war and/or of large-scale expansion in capacity for raw materials and foodstuffs, usually connected with the opening up of new areas. The effect of war on the sectoral structure of an economy may be fourfold: it sets up demands for products and capacity different from those which would be decreed by the peaceful process of growth; it eliminates from sectoral capacity effectively available such capacity as is located within the enemy's control or is capable of obstruction by the enemy; it drains off current investment resources, tending to lower total peaceful investment; and it may well destroy existing capital. War may also lower and distort investment in science and the application of science as well as affect, by various means, the forces determining the future size and quality of the working force and population. On the other hand, of course, war may stimulate capital development in directions appropriate to the long-period character of growth, and it may do so on a scale which is not excessive. Something of this kind almost certainly happened to the heavy industries of the North, for example, during the American Civil War and to the British light engineering industries in the Second World War. Moreover, war, in its social and political consequences, may move the propensities in directions favourable to further economic development, as has recently happened in many under-developed portions of the world.[2]

It is not difficult to see how a war can produce capacity expansion in directions inappropriate to the long-run evolution of an economy as well as produce a large backlog of gaps between actual capacity and capacity required for

[1] For a more detailed discussion of divergences of individual prices within the general foodstuff and raw-material categories, see Chap. IX.
[2] See Chap. VII for a discussion of this theme in relation to British history.

peace-time growth in various sectors. Thus, in the Napoleonic Wars, expansion was carried too far in agriculture and shipping, in the Atlantic world; and, again, in the First World War. After each of those wars a fundamental readjustment in the flows of investment was required to meet the pressures and potentialities of growth—e.g. toward housing and the cotton textile industry, after 1815.[1]

In a war where price and profit incentives still partially operate as an inducement to investment, one can relate in fairly strict sequence the sudden shift in the character of required as opposed to existing capacity; a rise in the prices and expected profits in these directions; a shifting of relative incomes in these directions; and the actual course and productivity of new investment. In the Napoleonic Wars great fortunes were made in agriculture, commerce, and shipping, while the real wages of the industrial worker diminished. Moreover, investment in housing, internal transport facilities, and industry in general was certainly lower than it would have been in the absence of war-time conditions.

The coming of peace requires an exceedingly complex readjustment in capacity and in the direction of new investments flows. The technical degree to which such adjustment can be made at all, and the rate at which it can be made, will vary. In agriculture particularly, with a tradition of fixed rents and mortgage payments, the adjustment has historically been slow and painful.[2] In any case the weight of relative over-capacity is, clearly, capable of colouring price, profit, and income distribution relations for some time after the coming of peace. New investment will tend to turn elsewhere, with a vigour decreed by the underlying propensities

---

[1] T. Tooke, in *History of Prices* (London, 1838–57), vol. i, p. 97, notes that from 1688 to 1792 war did not always result in an abnormal rise in the British wheat price, a fact no doubt connected with Britain's grain self-sufficiency and the limited scope of the manpower requirements of the wars embraced within those years. On the other hand, Mrs. D. George, *London Life in the Eighteenth Century* (London, 1925), p. 79, noted a systematic negative relation between wars and housing construction in her period. See also the author's 'Adjustments and Maladjustments after the Napoleonic Wars', *American Economic Review* Supplement, vol. xxxii, No. 1 (Mar. 1942).

[2] For a discussion of this problem in the United States see N. Silberling, *The Dynamics of Business* (New York, 1943), especially pp. 141–51.

of a society and by the yields to be derived from inventiveness and innovation in directions other than those where
overshooting has occurred.

The income distribution effects of a period of readjustment may, however, reduce effective demand for certain products. The British export industries, for example, felt in the
twenties of two centuries the weakness of demand from the
over-expanded agricultural sectors of the world economy. In
the 1820's it was the relative weakness in the American
demand that was mainly felt. The course of United States
agricultural prices and incomes after the coming of peace
and the overshooting of the post-war land boom in 1817–18
probably account for the relative depression of that decade
in the United States, reflected in real-income estimates and
in other evidence.[1] In the 1920's the income effects of low
agricultural and raw material prices were much more widely
felt throughout Britain's export markets.

The forms of current investment which appear attractive
in such a period of readjustment may be of a character
promising lower yields, involving refinement of capital stock
and its extension in new directions. Here, as noted earlier,[2]
must be introduced the possibility of changes in the average
period of gestation for current investment as a whole, and in
the degree to which investment may proceed in relatively
small increments. If one is opening up a new area for cotton,
wool, or wheat growing, time is required and it is difficult to
proceed by small increments. There are many overheads in
the form of transport and commercial facilities, which are
needed in much the same degree whether the new territory
is to be partially or totally exploited.[3] The combination of
these factors has, historically, made many agricultural expansions into new areas overshoot radically and has resulted in

[1] See R. F. Martin, *National Income in the United States* (New York, 1939);
W. B. Smith and A. H. Cole, *Fluctuations in American Business, 1790–1860* (Cambridge, Mass., 1935), section ii; and H. M. Somers, *The Performance of the American Economy before 1860*; chap. 16 in H. F. Williamson, *The Growth of the American
Economy* (New York, 1944 ed.), pp. 329–31. The continued readjustment of the
American 'war baby' industries to new and less propitious circumstances, was,
of course, another factor in the post-war decade.
[2] See pp. 109–10.
[3] In the case of the early development of the American West the inter-relations

long periods of readjustment, when the period of gestation was complete, or when peace had made available to the world similar market capacity, denied during the war interval.

In the course of expansion, whether decreed by war or by the expected profitability from new land and agricultural output, these factors had two concurrent effects. The average lengthening of the period of gestation of current investment tended to raise prices in general, by reducing the current flow of goods in relation to current total output. Second, because the period of gestation of investment was long, and an actual reckoning of yield against expectations was postponed, such expansions tended to persist in the face of rising costs; that is, the expected rate of return could be held to be abnormally high for a longer period of time than was the case in investment with a shorter gestation period, which offered the technical possibility of proceeding in smaller increments.

At a time when extensive investment of expected high yield is not available, in the sense that capacity in agricultural and raw material sectors has exceeded optimum levels, the whole curve of profitability may fall; and, after an initial breakthrough into a new territory or a new industrial technique, the curve of profitability may include, in its lower reaches, possibilities for investment not previously available. The economy may then turn to the exploitation of less exciting prospects for the refinement of its capital stock. After the transcontinental lines are laid down, railways may be double-tracked and branch lines built.[1] Rolling stock may be improved. Plants may be expanded and new, improved

between railway expansion and the opening and occupation of new lands was complex. It was the strong interest of the railway lines to see land occupied as soon and as fully as possible, and products of the land produced and moving to market. This led to policies of inducement and even subsidy to prospective farmers, both within the United States and overseas, to migrate to the new West. See, for example, J. G. Pyle, *The Life of James J. Hill* (New York, 1917), especially chaps. xiii–xv; J. B. Hedges, 'The Promotion of Immigration to the Pacific Northwest by the Railroads', *The Mississippi Valley Historical Review* (Sept. 1928); P. W. Gates, *The Illinois Central Railroad and its Colonization Work* (Cambridge, Mass., 1934); H. M. Larson, *Jay Cooke, Private Banker* (Cambridge, Mass., 1936), especially chaps. xv–xix; R. C. Overton, *Burlington West* (Cambridge, Mass., 1941), especially chaps. xiii–xiv.

[1] The railway boom of the early 1880's in the United States, as opposed to that a decade earlier, appears to have had something of this follow-up character.

machines may be installed. New industrial processes may be tried. A lag in housing, investment in which has been pushed out by apparently more attractive investment, may be made up. Service and other industries, catering to the enlarged real income of non-agricultural groups, may expand. In general, intensive investment of this character is likely to have a shorter period of gestation than the extension of basic resources; and it lends itself to expansion by smaller increments. One would expect such sectoral expansions to be marked by less overshooting than in the case of the more extensive, lumpy types of investment. Roughly speaking, this was the environment of the world economy in the periods after 1815, after 1873, and after 1920.

Historical evidence does not appear to support the view that the periods of rising trends in general prices were caused primarily by the coming of major new industries. For example, without the external events of 1793–1800, it is doubtful that the rapid growth of the British cotton industry would have caused a period of sharply rising general prices; or that, without the great extensive investments of the pre-1914 years in many parts of the world, prices would have risen owing to the growth of the automobile, electricity, and chemical industries. Even in the case of the railways, it should be noted that the great British railway boom of the 1840's was not accompanied by a sharp rise in general prices; and it is probably correct to regard railways as incidental to more profound expansionary forces in the boom of the early 1850's. In a quite literal sense several of the great American transcontinental railways were based on expected future land values; and an important part of their financing took the form of government land grants. The great expansion of the 1830's in the United States had also been accompanied by a massive expansion of transport facilities. By the 1850's, in Schumpeter's second trend upswing, the railway was in no sense a new innovation; and its extension into new regions can only be understood in terms of the trend of the wheat price and the believed profitability of investment in new Western lands.[1]

[1] The long period of gestation relevant is less that associated with the physical construction of railway lines than that which covers the interval between the

I I

It is held, then, that the course of economic history since about 1790 has yielded sustained periods of over-expansion of capacity in certain sectors of the economy decreed mainly by war and by the process of extensive expansion into new territories. The first such period took place during the Napoleonic Wars; the second in the third quarter of the nineteenth century, centred on the American Middle and Far West, as well as Australia; the third, in the decade before 1914, and during the First World War, centred on the Argentine, Canada, and various other regions within the British Empire.[1] Since the mid-1930's, impulses similar to those which yielded extensive expansions in the past have been operative in the world economy, and indeed may be observed in relative price and income movements and expansion of investment and output in many agricultural areas. Some evidence on the structural shift, as between agriculture and industry in post-war as compared with pre-war years, and on the consequent relative price and income distribution movements, follows:

World Indexes of Agricultural and Industrial Production

Agricultural Production (1934–8 = 100)	1947/8	.	. 93
Industrial Production (1938 = 100)	1947	.	. 128

Source: *Selected World Economic Indices* (U.N.), Lake Success, 1948, p. 10.

opening of an area and its effective economic exploitation. The mid-century development of the railway on the Continent is, of course, to be regarded as a technical adaptation of transport facilities to the general growth of the European economy, as in the case of Britain in the 1840's. This would in no way deny the subsequent dynamic effects on general economic development which occurred once the new lines were laid down. On the basis of the course of events in Britain in the 1840's the author would doubt, however, that the extension of European railways alone would have led to the trend developments of the third quarter of the century. It is the character of investment in the United States, Australia, and other non-European areas that is judged central to world trends over this period, rather than the extension of the railway itself.

[1] For the impact of the world-wide trend phenomena on the United States, where the major extensive expansions had already been accomplished, see T. W. Schultz, *Agriculture in an Unstable Economy*, pp. 114–16, on the 'Golden Era of American Agriculture', and P. H. Douglas, *Real Wages in the United States, 1890–1926* (Boston, 1930), on the relative stagnation of real wages outside agriculture down to the First World War.

United Kingdom and United States: Combined Unit Value Indexes of
Primary Goods and Exports of Manufactures (1938 = 100)

	1947		1948	
•	*1st half*	*2nd half*	*1st half*	*2nd half*
Imports of primary goods . .	214	223	244	251
Exports of manufactures . .	181	194	200	201
Price relation	118	115	122	125

Source: *Relative Prices of Exports and Imports of Under-developed Countries* (U.N.),
Lake Success, 1949, p. 10.

United Kingdom and United States: Farm Prices and Wage
Rates in Manufacture

	1 U.K. agricultural prices including Exchequer payments) (1936–8 = 100)	2 U.K. weekly wage rates (*Sept.* 1939 = 100)	3 U.S. prices received by farmers (1935–9 = 100)	4 U.S. average weekly earnings in manufacture (1939 = 100)
1947	242	166–7	257	209
1948	249	176–7	266	227

Source: U.K.: *Monthly Digest of Statistics*, May 1951, H.M.S.O.: col. 1, table
156, p. 124; col. 2, table 152, p. 120.
   U.S.: Calculated from *Statistical Abstract of the United States*, 1950: col. 3,
p. 582; col. 4, p. 203.
Note 1. In the course of 1949 these price and income relationships moved
somewhat counter to the general post-war trend, but reverted in the course of
1950–1.
Note 2. The comparison of agricultural and industrial output above in no
way implies that similar rates of growth in the two sectors are required to
maintain a suitable structural balance in the world economy.

A variety of events in the post-war years and the attitudes
of political leaders in agricultural areas have prevented these
forces, however, from yielding another great development
period comparable to that of the mid-century and pre-1914
periods. Now further development of this type, excepting
perhaps the Amazon region and Australia, would consist less
in the opening up of new territories than in the improvement
of productivity in existing territories, with less likelihood of

substantial overshooting.[1] Nevertheless, as we gain perspective on the period after 1945 the high levels of investment in foodstuff and raw material sectors of the world economy are likely to emerge increasingly as a major, if not a dominating, characteristic.

What detonated these expansion periods in the late 1840's and again in the mid-1890's was the catching up of the process of growth with existing capacity. In both cases rising prices in agricultural products preceded the period of great investment outlays in agricultural and raw-material development. There is some reason to feel, as well, that a British agricultural expansion would have been required, toward the end of the eighteenth century, given the rise in European population, even if war had not made grain imports from the Continent difficult after 1793.[2] The case for a similar turning point in the mid-1930's is less secure, although the combina-

[1] It should be noted that in the United States and elsewhere a consciousness of the possibility of these structural distortions (as well as an awareness of the possibilities offered by politics to turn classically competitive markets into quasi-monopolies) has led to political action designed either to avoid overshooting capacity, to evade its income-distribution effects, or both. For Latin American policy, in these circumstances, see, for example, 'Europe's Trade with Latin America', *Economic Bulletin for Europe*, United Nations (Geneva, Jan. 1951). See also Chap. X, below.

[2] The evidence here is mainly the irregular shift in the British position towards that of a consistent importer of grain and (despite the price decline of 1790–2) the rising trend in the wheat price over the pre-war decade. Note, for example, the difficulties of 1789, described by Tooke (*History of Prices* [London, 1838–57], vol. i, p. 80), which, while transitory, indicate the closeness of the European margin in a bad harvest year. This would not, of course, deny the extraordinary progress in British agricultural productivity during the eighteenth century which, in large part, permitted the rise in population to take place without a fall in standards of food consumption. D. Macpherson, *Annals of Commerce* (London, 1805), vol. iii, pp. 674–5, and vol. iv, pp. 216–17 and 532–3, gives the following data on the irregular movement toward a sustained net import position in wheat:

Period	No. of years of net export	Average annual net export (+) or import (−) in thousand quarters
1775–9	3	− 44·8
1780–4	1	−146·7
1785–9	3	+ 9·4
1790–4	1	−165·1
1795–9	0	−451·8

tion of reduced agricultural acreage in certain key areas and rising world population and real income would certainly have increased the relative profitability of agricultural and raw-material investment at some stage, even if a period of rearmament and then of war had not intervened.

The aim of this dangerously stylized rendering of modern economic history is to underline the existence in history of powerful distortions in agricultural and raw-material capacity, away from realistic optimum levels, which gave a special character in both expansion and contraction phases to relative price movements, to income distribution, and to the type of investment expected to be profitable. The great phases of large international and inter-regional capital movements were essentially a consequence of this process. The three phases of mainly intensive investment, after the overshooting had become palpable, also had much in common; that is, the decades after 1815, 1873, and 1920. In the non-agricultural sectors of the world economy, these were periods of great industrial advance, marked by sagging price and profit levels, and rising real wages. Income tended, on the whole, to shift in favour of the industrial worker. Complex problems in the readjustment of the use of resources had to be faced, which in Britain, between the wars, took place so slowly as to yield heavy chronic unemployment.

The impact of these phases of distortion in the sectoral pattern of world production can be traced in the history of international trade; or, better, in what might be called intersectoral trade, taken on a world basis. The favourable price shift, in the agricultural and raw-material producing sectors of the world economy, tended to raise relative real income there. Further, the high yields from investment in those areas at a time of relative shortage drew capital from abroad. The combination of these forces produced booms of disproportionate strength in agricultural and raw-material producing regions which helped further to shift the terms of trade in their favour. It is a process of this kind which is believed to be reflected in the calculations of Folke Hilgert in *Industrialization and Foreign Trade*.[1] These calculations exhibit a neat

[1] League of Nations, 1945, p. 18.

inverse movement between the index of relative prices of industrial and agricultural commodities and the relative quantities of those goods moving in international trade for the three trend periods incorporated within the years 1876–1938. If one were to press these calculations back into history, it is altogether likely that the behaviour of international trade during the period 1848 to 1873 would roughly conform to that shown by Hilgert for the period 1896 to 1913.[1] On the other hand, the post-Napoleonic War decades, in this as in other characteristics, might well show an affinity with the period after 1873;[2] and, despite the special and extraordinary circumstances of the world economy since 1945, in fundamental respects the years since (about) 1935 bear an affinity to the great historic periods of relative shortage in foodstuffs and raw materials; that is, to the era of the French Wars, the third quarter of the nineteenth century, and the two decades before the First World War.[3]

III

It may be useful to indicate, at this stage, the relationship between the analysis of trends set out above and certain other considerations of these familiar time periods, notably those of Kondratieff and Schumpeter.[4] In addition, it may

[1] The course of events in this period would to some degree be distorted towards conformity with Hilgert's pattern by the effects of the American Civil War on the price and flow of raw cotton in international trade.

[2] Here the special story of relative price movements in raw and manufactured cotton, commodities of key importance to the composition of world trade in this period, might shift the pattern somewhat away from that of Hilgert's three trend cases. For further discussion, see below, Chap. IX, pp. 201 ff.

[3] Note, for example, in successive editions of the annual survey of the European economy published by the United Nations Economic Commission for Europe since 1948, the gradual emergence of an analysis focusing on this factor, with its consequences for income distribution and the intersectoral terms of trade. Starting in 1948 from a conventional short-run analysis of the terms of trade and its relation to the current balance-of-payments position, the E.C.E. analysts have moved toward a general structural analysis of the relative scarcity position in sectors of the world economy. See notably, *Economic Survey for Europe in 1950*, chap. i (Geneva, 1951). See also, below, Chap. X for further observations on the post-1945 period in these terms.

[4] A part of the considerable literature of discussion and hypothesis about trend periods is summarized by A. Hansen, *Business Cycles and the National Income* (New York, 1951), chap. 4. See also the comments in Chaps. VIII and

be helpful to define the relation between the present view of trends and that presented by the author in his analysis of the British economy in the nineteenth century.[1]

Kondratieff confined himself to indicating, from a variety of data, the *prima facie* case for the existence of long cycles, offering no theoretical hypothesis of his own.[2] In particular, he examined certain price, monetary, foreign trade, and production data covering France, England, the United States, and Germany, covering portions of the period since the end of the eighteenth century. He noted, further, certain common characteristics of the periods of long-wave upswing and downswing. He pointed out, for example, the coincidence of these movements with secular prosperity and depression in agriculture; he noted that the long-wave recessions were marked by important developments in the techniques of production and communication; he noted a relation between the upswings and the discoveries of gold in the mid-century and in the 1890's; he noted a relationship between the timing of long-term trends and wars. He maintained, further, that none of these factors, including wars and gold discoveries, as well as innovations, could be regarded as exogenous; and that, therefore, the problem confronting economists and historians was to construct a view of economic development which would embrace the regular recurrence of these phenomena in their full complexity.

Kondratieff's empirical judgements also included the following:[3] 'Our investigation demonstrates that during the rise of the long waves, years of prosperity are more numerous, whereas years of depression predominate during the down-swing.'

IX on Colin Clark's views, pp. 189–92 and 208–09. Although not drawn in systematic form, the extremely suggestive observations of the late Norman Silberling, in his *Dynamics of Business*, belong with this literature, as does a portion of B. S. Keirstead's *The Theory of Economic Change*.

[1] *B.E.N.C.*, chap. i.

[2] N. B. Kondratieff, 'The Long Waves in Economic Life', *Review of Economic Statistics* (Nov. 1935), translated by W. F. Stolper from 'Die langen Wellen der Konjunktur', *Archiv für Sozialwissenschaft und Sozialpolitik*, 1926, vol. lvi, No. 3, pp. 573–609. Kondratieff himself noted that two Dutch economists anticipated his identification of these phases in economic history: Van Gelderen and De Wolff—a fact emphasized more recently by J. Tinbergen and J. J. Polak, *The Dynamics of Business Cycles* (Chicago, 1950), p. 61.

[3] Op. cit., p. 111.

Although the analysis put forth here would not preclude a systematic relationship of this kind, as the author has noted elsewhere, a firm connexion between cyclical behaviour and trend periods cannot easily be confirmed from the data available, when cyclically neutral periods are chosen for comparative measurement.[1]

In terms of the issues posed by Kondratieff, the present argument would not seek to establish any systematic time-period relationship for trends. Indeed, so important have war periods been in determining these movements that, as Kondratieff noted, one must produce an economic theory for the timing of wars in order to emerge with the theory of a recurrent long cycle. The present argument is designed rather to explain the possibility of impulses to excessive expansion in agriculture and raw-materials capacity as part of the process of growth. It would allow for wars, as one means of initiating such impulses, but would make the long period of gestation and historical lumpiness of this type of investment fundamental to an explanation of the secular upswing of the trend periods. It would offer, further, not only a mechanism, which might account for the initiation of the upswing, but also a set of relations between relative capacity positions, relative price and income movements, relative profit yields, and the direction of investment outlays, which would help explain the process, and which would inter-relate the symptoms both of the upswing and the downswing of the trend periods. In short, the scheme offered in the earlier portion of this chapter is believed to be one possible but partial answer to the question raised by Kondratieff's observations. The answer remains partial mainly because the role of wars is left exogenous.[2]

[1] *B.E.N.C.*, pp. 43–50.

[2] Kondratieff's faith in the association of wars with the upswing process of trend periods is an example of the crudity of much applied Marxist analysis. Economic factors do, indeed, enter into any serious analysis of the complex process which led to the French Revolution and the emergence of Napoleonic nationalism, the American Civil War, the Franco-Prussian War, and the First and Second World Wars. If the present analysis is correct, however, one would have to translate Kondratieff's judgement into the view that these wars were connected with the relative shortage of foodstuffs and raw materials and the consequent economic attractiveness of areas currently or potentially capable of producing such products. This is, patently, an inadequate basis for dealing

Schumpeter has, of course, erected a different mechanism to explain this recurring pattern of trends. As noted in the course of the argument, the author's analysis would differ at several points from Schumpeter's. Most notably, it would differ in the place it would assign to the development of new industries in determining trend patterns; and, more broadly, it would differ in its manner of treating innovations in relation to growth.[1] This analysis shares, however, two fundamental elements which enter Schumpeter's system. Schumpeter finds the basis for the rise in the general price level, during secular upswings, in the possibility that the innovation

seriously with the causes of any of these conflicts. The author would be inclined to assign at most a secondary role to economic motivations in determining the oncome of such major struggles for power, including the American Civil War, which superficially would best fit Kondratieff's case, focused, as indeed it was, on the political and economic destiny of the developing and currently profitable western areas of the American continent. A more superficial answer to Kondratieff's hypothesis about wars and economic trends might emphasize that they came at very different stages of the trend process: the Napoleonic and Second World War at the early stage of an upswing; the American Civil War in the middle of an upswing; the First World War and the Franco-Prussian War towards the close of an upswing.

[1] As noted (pp. 82 n.–83 n.) Schumpeter flirted with the idea of making the character of innovations a function of the workings of the system; and he clearly regarded innovation as an economic process, governed by the profit motive (e.g. *Business Cycles*, vol. i, p. 86). In the end, however, his formulation came to the proposition that historic changes were to be interpreted as a function of changes in tastes, growth, and innovation, none of which are made rigorously dependent variables. To put it another way, Schumpeter was more interested in the mechanics of the innovation process and its consequences than in its origins. And it is this view of the matter which is mainly carried over into econometric models. There is a similar ambiguity about the kinds of innovations held responsible by Schumpeter for the Kondratieff sequence. His initial definition of innovations is as broad as one could wish (ibid., p. 84), including new techniques of production, the opening up of new sources of supply or markets, greater efficiency in plant operations, improved handling of materials, and new forms of business organization. When he arrived at his historical analysis, however, he largely contented himself with an identification of the Kondratieff sequence with textiles and iron; steam, steel, and the railroads; electricity, chemistry, and motors (e.g. ibid., p. 170). Schumpeter was uneasy, however, about phases of agricultural prosperity and depression (e.g. ibid., pp. 266–70, 319–25, and 401–2). He commented on them, even roughly embraced them; but they did not truly fit a scheme which focused, in fact, on technological innovation and its consequences and which lacked both a formal conception of the determinants of growth and a mechanism for invoking expansions of capacity and innovations in response to changing relations between over-all growth and the capacity position in sectors of the economy.

period may involve credit outlays for the development of new techniques before they fully yield their cost-reducing results. It is this lengthening in the average period of gestation which is key to Schumpeter's analysis.[1]

The author would doubt that the process of innovation within the new industries, which Schumpeter regarded as central to the trend process, would in fact have so shifted the average period of gestation. But the present argument would also invoke as fundamental to trend analysis changes in the relation between current input and output. In the present argument, however, such changes are judged to have been caused (on the upswings) by the long period of development required for putting new areas effectively into production, by the wastes of war, and by the wastes of gold-mining.

The second element shared by the present analysis and that of Schumpeter is the association of the upswing of the trend periods with types of investment which promised a relatively high yield. Although, again, the author would identify somewhat differently the nature of the high-yield investment of secular upswings, he would give them a similar analytic place in his scheme.

In terms of the author's own previous writing on this subject, the present argument represents a generalization of the process described by him in terms of trends in British economy from 1790 to 1914.[2] British trends are there associated with the types of investment being pursued by Britain and by the world during the trend periods. The upswings were associated with eras of war, gold-mining, and capital exports; the downswings were associated mainly with periods of peace and intensive investment. The present argument is an extension of this approach, focused, however, on the world economy taken as a whole, rather than on a national economy. It offers an explanation for the periods of capital exports in terms of the relative shortage of foodstuffs and raw materials and the high yields which investment toward an expansion of their capacity appeared to offer; and, similarly, it would explain the intensive pattern of investment in the

---

[1] See *Business Cycles*, vol. i, chap. iv, especially pp. 130–8.
[2] *B.E.N.C.*, chap. i.

trend downswings. Although no great weight would be placed on this factor, the present argument would also regard the changing importance of gold production as endogenous to the system, in the sense that protracted periods of falling prices, in an era of stable gold standards, increased the incentive to find and to mine new gold. Wars, in the present formulation, as in the earlier one, remain exogenous, so far as economic analysis is concerned.

Professor Hansen, in summarizing various views about secular trends and business cycles, noted the existence of four broad theories designed to explain trend periods:[1] innovations and technical developments, exploitation of new resources, and the opening of new territory; government expenditures for war; gold and monetary development[1]; and developments in the field of agriculture. Leaving aside the question of wars, the present argument would link the exploitation of new resources and the opening of new territory with developments in the field of agriculture. And, further, it would systematically associate these with the relation between over-all growth and the sectoral capacity position within the world economy. So far as innovations and technological developments are concerned, it would remain sceptical that, in the past, these have had a great deal to do, as initiating forces, with the secular pattern of events. The role of gold-mining would be introduced as a secondary factor and, in large part, kept analytically within the system, in the sense that, of its nature, the trend downswing is judged to result in such cost and price declines as to raise the prospective yield from gold-mining in a world of stable gold standards.

In general, the author would emphasize his belief that the character and causes of trend periods, both when they are

[1] *Business Cycles and National Income*, chap. iv, especially pp. 59–60. The acceptance by Hansen and others of Schumpeter's association of periods of technical innovation with trend increases in price is probably a hangover of the old view that price trends are to be associated with the persistent strength of demand. *Prima facie*, the development of a new industry would keep the demand for capital high and booms 'strong'; and a rising price trend would ensue. The author would associate historical price trends primarily with changes, on balance, in the character of (current and past) investment, as it affected the relation between input and output of resources, and allot a lower place than is conventional to the relative 'strength' of booms in determining price trends.

related to the development of new resources in response to the pressures of growth against existing capacity and when they are judged to have been initiated by distortions in capacity and in requirements caused by wars, are significantly clarified by placing them against the background of a systematic conception of the process of growth in relation to sectors of the economy. When this is done, we may move directly from distortions in capacity in relation to requirements, to relative price and income shifts, and to incentives to invest in certain directions. The direction of investment becomes determined by the system. We may then treat these secular trend phenomena as special variations in the normal (cyclical) process of growth, abstractly treated in Chapters IV and V. Schumpeter's version of the Kondratieff thus returns to the mainstream of theoretical and historical analysis; and we are at once relieved from straining for a special set of causes for a doubtful fifty-year cycle and from the temptation to ignore or to slide over the flagrant exceptions to such a pattern for modern economic history.

PART II
SOME APPLICATIONS
VII
WAR AND ECONOMIC CHANGE: THE BRITISH EXPERIENCE[1]

I

LORD ACTON once enjoined the historian to study problems rather than periods. This chapter seeks to summarize the fruits of one such investigation of a problem. A virtue of compression on the scale attempted here may consist in the emergence of certain recurrent or slowly changing patterns which might be lost or concealed in a more spacious analysis, which gave proper historical weight to the uniqueness of events.

In a sense, it is manifestly absurd to consider within the compass of a single chapter the relation between war and economic change in Great Britain over a period of 750 years. To analyse the impact of war on any society, one must look at the military and physical nature of the war itself; one must examine its consequences for the disposition of material resources and manpower in agriculture, industry, and foreign trade; one must establish the principal means used for the mobilization of resources, including the techniques of finance; one must consider the effects of the process of war on the rising and falling of social classes and groups; and one must establish its consequences for the structure and efficacy of government.

A good example of what may emerge from such a study is Nef's recent volume.[2] The present chapter can be regarded as a kind of supplementary note on Professor Nef's theme. It shares his view that the direct contribution of war to

---

[1] The reader should note the special acknowledgements that attach to this chapter, stated in the Preface, p. vii.

[2] J. U. Nef, *War and Human Progress* (Cambridge, Mass., 1950).

economic change has been, on balance, negative; but, in accordance with the analysis of the propensities in Part I, it raises the question of the impact on the economic system of war-induced social and political change. This chapter is, thus, an extremely simplified exercise in the dynamic analysis of the inter-relations between the economy and its social and political framework.

I I

The major wars that Britain fought, since Richard, King of England and prince of large domains in France, led his expedition into the central and eastern Mediterranean, about 750 years ago, have a certain basic continuity. With minor exception, these wars have had two major elements; land warfare on the continent of Europe, against the predominant power; and naval operations, designed to maintain or extend British routes of trade, to maintain the links to Britain's allies and overseas forces, and to defend the British islands. Although now, finally, modern air weapons may have decisively altered the British military position, along with that of the other powers, over the years considered here, the geography of Britain in relation to the European continent, the Mediterranean, and the Atlantic, have determined a fairly stable shape for British strategy and for British warfare. There is no need to underline the parallelisms that exist between the wars of Richard and John and more recent experience: an arc of operations extending from the eastern Mediterranean to Norway; decisive operations in Normandy; a call for total mobilization (in 1205) when invasion threatened; and the subsequent British efforts to break the hold of the dominant power on the Continent by means of disruptive alliances. And the parallelisms are hardly less striking in some of the other periods.

There were, nevertheless, significant changes in British strategy, within a more or less continuous broad pattern.

First, the aims of war in relation to the Continent changed. Richard and John, Edward III, and Henry V, were, after all, mainly concerned to maintain or to reclaim their own position on the Continent. They were battling for French land and the French crown. At the end of the twelfth and the beginning of the thirteenth centuries the kingdom of Sicily was a major element in the Mediterranean manœuvres of the major powers; and the struggle with the Hansa, during the Hundred Years War, was secondary to the continental objectives. From the sixteenth century on through the eighteenth century, however, Britain engaged in a competitive struggle for trade and colonies, to which the continental operations, even when they were on a grand scale, gradually became secondary. And then there emerges over this period another theme, essentially defensive in character. If a single power dominated the Continent, mobilized its resources, and turned to the sea, the independent existence of the British Isles was endangered.

We can thus distinguish roughly three strands, related to each other, and often interwoven, but varying in their relative importance through the centuries; an early strand of offensive operations against the Continent, to maintain the British claims in Europe; a stage of competition for the stakes of trade and empire, in which the prevention of domination of the Continent by a single power is present (often focused sharply on the question of the Channel ports), but of varying relative importance; and, from Napoleon onward, the defensive wars, when Britain is primarily battling for its independent existence and the stakes of war become secondary, non-existent, or even negative.

Second, there is the changing relative importance of the navy. Down to the sixteenth century it was probably not much more than 10 per cent. of the mobilized forces in terms of manpower. In the sixteenth century the navy may have constituted about 15 per cent. of the mobilized forces, rising under Elizabeth to more than 30 per cent., as Calais was lost and Britain limited her ground force activities on the Continent. In the War of the Spanish Succession Britain's naval forces may have constituted about 40 per cent. of the mobilized effort, and an even higher proportion if we include the new Royal Marines. And the figure remained about 30 per cent., down through the Revolutionary and Napoleonic Wars. In the First World War the proportion sank again, as Britain undertook the heavy and costly responsibility of continuous continental warfare; and in the Second World War, the navy took only about 15 per cent. of total mobilized manpower, again owing to the scale of the ground forces, and the sharing of some of the classic naval functions with the R.A.F.

Third, there is the changing role of the Western Hemisphere. In the sixteenth century we find Britain obstructing the trade of Spain with its colonies and diverting as large a flow of bullion as possible to her own coffers; then, from the early eighteenth century, the colonies, conceived from the beginning in part as a supplementary source of essential raw materials for Britain, actually serve as an alternative source of naval stores to the insecure Baltic area. From the early eighteenth century onward, excepting the War of American Independence, the New World is increasingly summoned to redress the balance of the old. In the Napoleonic Wars it is the monopoly in trade with the Western Hemisphere, and then the great Latin American boom of 1808–10, that saved the British balance of payments and made possible the continental alliances. And, finally, in the First and Second World Wars, in supplies and then in troops, the New World enters fully, as it comes to appreciate that it shares with Britain an interest in avoiding control of the European continent by a single, potentially hostile power.

Fourth, there is the change in the scale of war. The wars get bigger over the centuries, both absolutely and in terms of the British population and national income, an aspect of the story that is explored somewhat further below.

III

War is a process of mobilizing and applying resources for destructive purposes. That is its essence; and it is seen most clearly if one shifts the view from the individual country to the whole area affected by war. In the short period men are diverted from agriculture, manufacturing, and trade. They continue to feed and clothe themselves at the expense of someone's economy, other people's efforts. They use, and use up, weapons which incorporate labour and raw materials. They interrupt the sowing of fields and harvesting. They disrupt trade routes or make them costly to maintain. They impoverish the production of imports and the markets for exports. Over the long period soldiers kill each other. They destroy capital equipment, houses, and ships. They drain resources away from the normal maintenance and enlargement of society's capital stock. The structure of society and of government, especially in the defeated country, may be shattered, with great long-run economic cost, as in Germany during the Thirty Years War; the American South, during the Civil War; or, less dramatically, in the case of victorious Britain's loss of manpower during the First World War.

There may be, however, some offsets to these central destructive qualities of war. In the short period, those who remain behind are, especially in modern times, more fully employed; women may come into the factories; or men may work harder or longer, with greater efficiency or enterprise. In the long period strands of activity begun under pressure of war may continue, and add to the welfare of nations at a rate which would not have existed, or existed so soon, without war. New commodities may be developed; new techniques of production, in agriculture as well as industry, may be generated and their diffusion throughout the economy accelerated.

Further, war shakes up societies, and, for better or worse, places them under pressure, accentuating the rate of social change. New and energetic classes, adjusting to the challenges and opportunities of crisis, may come forward more rapidly in war than in peace. The need for national unity may increase their bargaining power for concessions in their long-run interest. Older classes and groups, less resilient, may fade from power under the impact of war. Finally, governments, of necessity acquiring in war new functions and widened responsibilities for control and direction of the economy, may not lose them totally in peace; and they may become, thereby, more efficient instruments in the process of economic growth. There are, then, some possible economic, social, and political offsets to the essentially destructive nature of war.

These offsets may loom large if one examines not the affected area as a whole but that part of it which was victorious.

Throughout the wars examined here Britain was never invaded; and most of the British wars were won. The War of the Austrian Succession and the Seven Years War clearly show that, from the point of view of one nation, the compensation of victory can, on occasion, outweigh the costs. And this becomes particularly significant if it is appreciated that wars are not usually fought to raise absolutely the power of a single nation; they are fought to determine the relative power of two or more nations. Victory can be meaningful even if it involves lower absolute economic strength for the victorious nation. The economist's calculation of the net effects of war on the course of the real national income is by no means final.

IV

Turning to the impact of war on the various sectors of the economy, it may be useful to present some approximations concerning the proportion of the British population mobilized and the scale of direct casualties.

War	Est. population	Est. peak mobilization (British forces)	Proportion of population mobilized, %	Casualties
Richard and John	1,750,000 (Eng.)	25,000	1·4	no est.
100 Years War	2,500,000 (Eng.)	35,000	1·4	no est.
16th century	4,000,000 (Eng. & Wales)	75,000	1·9	no est.
Spanish Succession	5,475,000 (1700, Eng. & Wales)	130,000	2·4	(5,000)
Early 18th century	8,000,000 (1760, Eng. & Wales)	240,000	3·0	no est.
Revolutionary and Napoleonic .	15,700,000 (1801, U.K.)	500,000	3·2[1]	210,000
World War I .	45,222,000 (1911, U.K.)	6,000,000	13·2	750,000[2]
World War II .	47,900,000 (1941, U.K.)	5,000,000	10·5	290,000

[1] If estimated peak mobilization is measured against England, Wales, and Scotland in 1801 (10·5 million), the proportion mobilized would be as high as 4·8 per cent.

[2] This figure does not take account of the indirect loss in births, due to war

The figures in this table contain numerous ambiguities, and are not to be taken as literal quantitative measurements. Nevertheless, allowing generously for margins of error, they show some useful things.

First, from the twelfth century to the early part of the nineteenth century, the proportion of the population drawn directly into war increases slowly, from about 1·5 per cent. to somewhat over 3 per cent. The First and Second World Wars, drawing more than 10 per cent. of the population to the armed services, constituted a drain of a different order of magnitude. Second, although information on casualties before the Napoleonic Wars is almost non-existent, it seems likely that casualties, including abnormal casualties from disease, left no very severe long-term marks on British society. Most casualties in these early wars resulted from disease, rather than battle. Although there is some evidence that war spread disease, and resulted in higher than normal mortality—for example, in the ports of Plymouth and Portsmouth, which were periodically decimated—this is a factor we cannot easily measure. The heavy casualties of the eighteenth century and the Napoleonic Wars were easily borne by reason of the powerful rising trend in the British population. The casualties of the First World War, however, coming at a time when population growth was at a declining rate, were a heavy blow indeed. Thus the short-term drain of the two recent wars on manpower was greater, owing to their scale; and their long-term effects were more severe, because they came at a time when the rate of population growth was losing its momentum.

The strictly economic drain of war on manpower is not, of course, measured simply by figures for peak mobilization in relation to total population. Mobilization is a much larger proportion of the working force than of the total population: in modern times, more than twice as great. Then, too, there are diversions of civilians from peace to war production. The scale of these diversions, for which we have no simple,

and mobilization; nor does the figure for the Second World War. In the case of the First World War the figure has been estimated as high as 500,000 to 700,000. It would almost certainly be much less for the Second World War.

accurate measures, was probably rather modest, but slowly rising down through the Napoleonic Wars. And this accounts, in substantial part, for the ease with which the burdens of war were carried by the civilian population. The two great recent wars involve, on the other hand, extremely large diversions of manpower from civilian to military production, with consequently severe effects both on the standard of living and on the maintenance and increase of national capital. There are evidences of such pressures in earlier wars; but it is clear that in this respect, as in the direct drain on manpower, the two recent wars imposed strains on the British economy proportionately of a different order of magnitude than those of the past.

It is, perhaps, worth raising the question, even if it cannot be answered satisfactorily, as to whether the extent of mobilization in the pre-twentieth-century wars represented in some meaningful sense a maximum. Were the First and Second World Wars the only total wars, or were all major wars total, in their own day, given the margin of resources available to the British economy over and above a minimum standard of living?

There are at least three factors here: the will of the people to make sacrifices in their capital and consumption level for the prosecution of war; the competence and thoroughness of the government in mobilizing resources; and the absolute margin of national income and national capital, above the irreducible minimum, which is available for mobilization. The question of the degree to which wars have been total can then be rephrased: Did the willingness to make economic sacrifices and the relative administrative efficiency of government increase over time? Obviously no dogmatic generalization can be made on the evidence available. It is notable, however, that the character and duration of many of the campaigns down to the end of the eighteenth century were determined in large part by the resources available to the State. Could the British economy have mobilized greater funds and greater armies? As a matter of impressionistic judgement it seems likely that at a greater, but not intolerable sacrifice, larger forces could have been mustered and sustained. Hubert Walter, at the close of the twelfth century, does not appear to have been meeting the resistance of men brought to the point of impoverishment, but rather men who, weighing their view of the advantages of war by the king against the disadvantages of further incursions on their fortunes, decided against war and against the king. And elements of that calculation persist into the later centuries. Men of power and classes with power appear to have been prepared to acc̃ept a lesser relative decline in income and capital and still continue to prosecute war than we have come to accept in the two great wars of our time. War—and the stakes of war—were only one of the enterprises which engaged men's energies, even during hostilities. There appears to have been a subtle shading off of national policy into war, in these early centuries, a shading which was notably lacking in the First and Second World Wars, but which may be returning to the international politics of our time.

V

The vicissitudes of British argiculture in war are various. In the twelfth century one can trace the ploughing up of common land during war to furnish increased supplies of grain. And in the sixteenth century, too, land was shifted back to grain from sheep grazing. With these exceptions Britain was a surplus agricultural area down to the closing years of the eighteenth century. In these circumstances war appears to have had two contrary effects: first, as a result of heavy taxation, the sale and gift of crown lands, and for other reasons as well, the ownership of land changed during war on a large scale. And on the whole, land probably passed from the less able and energetic to more vigorous management. In net, for individual cases were bound to run both ways, the shifting of land ownership was probably a factor tending to maintain or increase agricultural productivity.

On the other hand, severe war-time taxes laid on land and the rent from land undoubtedly cut into the sums available for agricultural investment, down to 1793. Evidences of this process can be traced in the Hundred Years War and in the wars of the early decades of the eighteenth century. The effect on balance of shifting land ownership and war taxation cannot be clearly weighed. Given all the circumstances —circumstances which, in any case, have divergent implications for the productivity of agriculture—one would not expect a clear-cut relation between war and agriculture in the early instances.

In the wars of the sixteenth century, when Britain found itself somewhat short of grain self-sufficiency, a more modern consequence of war for agriculture begins to emerge. Production is increased in response to rising prices; and the beer is diluted. So it was also, on a much larger scale, during the Revolutionary and Napoleonic Wars. The inhibitions on the Baltic trade and the rise in British population required a large increase in agricultural production which was, in fact, accomplished. In the short period this rise diverted resources from war-making, from trade, and from industry. In the long run, it presented British politics and the British economy with a difficult problem of readjustment, not satisfactorily resolved until about two decades after the coming of peace in 1815.

In many ways the experience of British agriculture during the two recent great wars was similar to that of the Napoleonic Wars. But not only was total agricultural production expanded; its composition was also shifted away from meat and dairy products toward grain. This resulted mainly from the overriding need to economize on shipping space for imported foodstuff. Grain and fodder are bulky commodities. Thus, after the First World War, British agriculture faced both a reduction in scale and a reorientation from grain to the production of meat, dairy products, and other costly foodstuffs. The war-time growth of grain production in the Western Hemisphere pushed Britain farther away than ever from grain self-sufficiency in the 1920's.

The Second World War produced one trend in agriculture that is likely to persist and to constitute a real, if modest, offset to the destruction of capital in other directions. Britain has emerged with a more highly mechanized agriculture than ever before and with a substantial increase of 10 to

15 per cent. in agricultural productivity per man. Unlike the setting of the world economy after 1815 and 1920, for better or worse the world environment of British agriculture has tended to encourage further increases in investment and productivity in the post-war years.

VI

What can be said in these highly generalized terms of the impact of war on industry, foreign trade, and capital development? The issue faced here suggests a story told by Siegfried Sassoon in his volume of reminiscences.[1] A series of events led the young and troubled poet into the office of Mr. Winston Churchill, Minister of Munitions, in 1917. They discussed poetry and mutual Bloomsbury friends.

There came a point, however, [writes Sassoon] when our proceedings developed into a monologue. Pacing the room, with a big cigar in the corner of his mouth, he gave me an emphatic vindication of militarism as an instrument of policy and stimulator of glorious achievements, not only in the mechanisms of warfare, but in spheres of social progress. The present war, he asserted, had brought about inventive discoveries which would ameliorate the condition of mankind. For example, there had been immense improvement in sanitation.

It is evident that we must try to assess the significance of improvements of this type over the centuries.

Until the sixteenth century, and the large-scale use of the cannon, there does not appear to have been much stimulus from war to industrial development. Britain and her enemies were, after all, agricultural and pastoral countries. Wool was the largest of the manufacturing industries. It is possible that the wars of Richard and John may have strengthened the hold of the capitalist dyers over the trade, and guaranteed the home market, by eliminating the Flemish competitors. And the hold of British cloth manufacturers over the home market was later confirmed and strengthened by the wool export tax of the fourteenth century. This may be counted a real, if partial, offset. In the Hundred Years War, of course, the cannon makes an appearance. Tyne coal and Forest of

---

[1] *Siegfried's Journey, 1916–1920* (New York, 1946), p. 78.

Dean iron are already significant, but there is little evidence for the view that the long-run rate of development in these sectors was significantly accelerated by war at this stage.

The wars of the sixteenth century are more interesting in this respect. There we find a distinct stimulus to several lines of domestic manufacture as well as to the art or science of mathematics. There was a growth in the production of salt-petre for gunpowder; shipbuilding for the navy; home breweries for the army and to supplant the inaccessible foreign wines; and finally, development of the metallurgical industries for the building of cannon. There seems little doubt that the wars of the sixteenth century left behind some substantial long-period offsets to the wastes of war. But the impetus to metallurgy, perhaps the most important of the constructive impulses imparted by war, was largely stifled by the lack of cheap fuel in the seventeenth century; and only much later, in 1710, did Abraham Darby lay the foundations for modern metallurgy by applying coke to smelting. And Abraham Darby was a Quaker.

When we turn to the effects of sixteenth-century foreign wars on trade, a much more important sector of the economy at the time, it becomes clear that the losses far outweigh the modest long-period gains. The capital diverted to war, to war industry, and probably also, in part, to agriculture, were not without cost to its use in other directions. Perhaps the best sixteenth-century symbol of this diversion was the alloca-tion of resources from the Muscovy Company to the siege of Cadiz.

The War of the Spanish Succession witnessed, again, a significant diversion of capital from the development of trade, and perhaps even some diversion from inclosure in agricul-ture. The increase in shipbuilding is an illusory offset, in this case, simply replacing the substantial losses of war. The development of the paper and high-grade paper trades, following upon the cutting off of imports, can be rated legiti-mate compensations; but they must be judged slight. In the long run the most important new investments of the war period were, almost certainly, the bounties instituted by the Board of Trade, to stimulate the growing of hemp and flax in Ireland, and the production of naval stores in the southern colonies of North America.

In the mid-eighteenth century there is stimulus again to wool, gunpowder, iron, and shipbuilding. There are also losses in foreign trade and in the brass industry, now descended from instruments of war to luxury exports. There are losses too, in basic domestic investment—e.g. roads, bridges, and probably housing. Taking as the appropriate criterion of gain not simply increased output, as in wool or ships, but capital development which produces enlarged and cheapened production in peace, the principal offset appears to lie in the iron industry. There the absorption of the charcoal users in the production of cannon gave greater scope to the north-country coke-using furnaces and probably hastened the liberation of the industry from an inadequate timber supply. But this was, after all, a trend that ran through peace as well as war. It is only a small point that Mr. Churchill scores here.

In the case of the Napoleonic Wars, the diversion of resources to agriculture has already been noted. In part this was salutary, encouraging large-scale heavily capitalized farming. But the technical foundations for this development lay deep in the eighteenth century (or even earlier); and it might well have taken place, in any case, in response to the pressures of an enlarging population.[1] In part, however, it was an unhealthy development, bringing into production land that peace-time prices, with the given level of technology, could not support; and the disinvestment in land after 1815 was only painfully accomplished. There was also the usual expansion in shipbuilding; and a very great increase in foreign trade, especially the re-export trade, the profits from which did much to support the balance of payments during the years of heavy outlays for British and Allied armies on the Continent.

The most notable developments with long-run implications at this time came, of course, in the two stalwarts of the Industrial Revolution, cotton and iron. At first sight, viewing the curves of industrial production, one would be inclined

[1] See p. 136 n.

to associate the stimulus of the French wars with the important and even decisive two decades of the Industrial Revolution. Looked at closely, however, the case loses cogency. The great expansion in cotton textiles was based on the interplay between the new inventions spreading rapidly through the cotton-textile industry as early as the 1780's; and upon the enlarged supply and lowered price of raw cotton, due to the invention and prompt application of the cotton gin in the United States after 1793.[1] In iron and iron manufacture the impact of war was more direct. The denial of Swedish ore certainly did stimulate the British industry to solve the problem of using domestic ores. On the other hand, the trend forces pervading the years of peace were strongly in the direction of expansion in the iron industry. It is a notable fact that the rate of expansion in both cotton and iron was greater in the three decades after the Napoleonic Wars than it was in the period 1790–1815.

For this war we have, for the first time, a useful general index of domestic investment in the figures for brick production calculated by Shannon. Despite the great increase in population during the war years, there is no trend increase in brick production. Immediately after the end of the war, production begins a powerful rise, sustained over the next several decades. There is little doubt that the war itself, and the war-induced investments in agriculture, trade, and direct war industries took place again, as in the mid-eighteenth century, at the expense of housing construction and other forms of domestic investment.

In the cases down to 1815, it is indeed difficult to strike an accurate balance within the economy, as between depletion and stimulus. One is forced to compare what was with what might have been. On the whole, looking at the strictly economic aspects of British society, it seems doubtful if the long-run offsets to the destruction and diversion of war in terms of technique and manufacturing capacity were sufficient to outweigh the real costs that war imposed.

This conclusion is strengthened when one looks more closely at the course of foreign trade. In the short run, with-

[1] See below, pp. 201 ff.

out exception, major wars appear to have done injury to
foreign trade. In the first place, the normal trade routes
were obstructed and made circuitous and more dangerous,
raising the real cost of imports and of exports. By strenuous
and gallant efforts, as in the War of the Spanish Succession,
the export trade was maintained; but it was maintained only
at the cost of allocating to its protection some two-thirds of
the British fleet. Even, as in the Napoleonic Wars, when the
volume of British trade rose, the increase was accomplished
by the allocation of very large resources at the cost of the
economy as a whole. The real cost in terms of British effort
(or in the volume of British exports) of bringing to England,
say, a ton of West Indian sugar increased over the war years.
The real terms of trade tended to turn unfavourable. In the
second place, war forced Britain to sacrifice a substantial part
of her resources to loans and subsidies abroad and to the
support of armies overseas. There were various forms in
which this burden could be met. One device was, of course,
to export without receiving imports in return. From the
eighteenth century forward one can trace this process. The
Exchequer Bills and other claims on London left by British
forces in Holland, at naval bases, and in the colonies in the
mid-eighteenth century, and the loans and subsidies advanced during the Napoleonic Wars, were ultimately liqui-
dated in real British resources—either directly in British
exports or, when transferred in bullion, by the sacrifice of
the imports the bullion would have commanded in the
world's markets.

In the long run, unquestionably, the eighteenth-century
wars paid in a world of competing national economies. They
paid in terms of foreign trade, as did the Napoleonic Wars,
which confirmed and extended the earlier imperial victories.
Britain emerged with a special set of trade relations with
India and most of the Western Hemisphere that were virtually monopolistic in their effect. This cannot be said with
respect to the earlier wars; and, it should be noted, the long-
run advantage acquired was a relative advantage. It is most
unlikely that the total volume of world trade, in the long run,
was greater because of the wars between 1700 and 1815,

although the proportionate volume of British trade was undoubtedly greater than it would otherwise have been.

Against this background, what can be said of the impact on Britain of the two great recent wars? Within industry we confront again the problem of balancing cases of stimulus against cases of retardation. In foreign trade we find short-run losses accentuated by long-run loss. The First World War expanded the British heavy industries to a degree which the pattern of peace-time demands, in the 1920's and 1930's, could not sustain. It broke, perhaps irrevocably, the ties of certain British export industries, notably cotton textiles, to some of their traditional overseas markets. The British economic problem of the 1920's, often considered solely in terms of financial maladjustment, was largely a consequence of these two industrial results of the war, in the setting of world sectoral income distribution that emerged after 1920.

The Second World War has brought accelerated development to certain of the light engineering industries and to agriculture; but war was conducted at a great and damaging cost to the accumulated store of British capital, not only in the form of British investments abroad, but also the stock of capital at home. Houses were destroyed, damaged, or permitted to run down. New investment in industry and in the public services was postponed. And that precious national capital, the pool of coal miners, was permitted to decline, without adequate replacement in men or in capital equipment.

It is, of course, impossible to trace out within this chapter the full impact of the two recent wars on British industry, investment, and foreign trade. The main effects are familiar enough. And the net consequences of war on the British economy in these two instances are likely to be judged with some unanimity to have been destructive in both the short and the long run. The offsets, although inadequate, are nevertheless real; not only in Churchill's case of sanitation, but in medicine and surgery; in the accelerated development of aircraft, wireless, and radar; in automotive engineering; and now, if the world acquires in time the requisite political wisdom, in what may prove the greatest of the offsets that war has yet yielded—atomic energy.

VII

War emerges from this survey, in real terms, as a national economic enterprise, a form of communal capital investment. Like all forms of capital investment, war has been supported from some combination of five possible sources: increases in home production; increased borrowing or gifts from abroad; decreases in home consumption; decreases in forms of investment other than war; and by the depletion, in one form or another, of the accumulated national capital.

It would, indeed, be interesting if one could present at this stage a table showing the relative extent to which the various British wars were borne by each of these categories in terms of the national income. Although it would not be impossible to derive useful approximations in the case of several of the wars, this is evidently a task for further research.

It is simpler to indicate the mechanisms by which British resources were mobilized. Here the continuity in the reaction of the State to the responsibilities of war is striking. There is hardly a gambit of modern war finance which was not at least abortively attempted in the wars of Richard and John, of Edward III, and of Henry V. The government taxed; it borrowed at home; and it sought, at least, to borrow or tax abroad, the latter, for example, by means of the export tax on wool in the Hundred Years War. Down through the early years of the First World War the government, with certain exceptions noted below, was able to concentrate on the mobilization of liquid funds. It was able to count, given such funds, on somehow assembling the manpower, food, weapons, and allies that were required. The catalogue of taxes and loans, lotteries and land sales, that mark the financial history of British wars over the centuries suggest the essential brotherhood of all wartime Chancellors of the Exchequer, from Hubert Walter to Sir John Anderson.

A prevalent form of taxation in war does not appear as taxation at all. It is, of course, the diversion of resources accomplished by raising prices. The government simply bids resources from other uses. Prices rise more rapidly than incomes, and money is worth less. This form of coin clipping was, on occasion, supplemented in Britain by direct monetary measures designed to achieve or to support the inflationary process. It is a straight and consistent line from John's calling in of the coinage, through the abandonment of the bullion standard of 1797 and 1914, to the bland acceptance of direct control of resources in the Second World War. All were devices for transferring resources from private consumption and investment to the government. Direct allocation of resources and rationing, which we have known in this generation, are simply a more thorough and equitable means of accomplishing this end than inflation.

A striking aspect of the sequence of British war finance is the relation between war and the development of the capital market. In the wars of Richard and John we find the Temple extending the range of its experience and knowledgeability in international finance. At the end of the seventeenth century the Bank of England emerges, out of the financial requirements of war. Early in the eighteenth century the South Sea and East India Companies strengthen their privileges and establish precedents in the capital market that lead to the South Sea Bubble in the post-war years. In the mid-eighteenth century the techniques for mobilizing savings are extended to the individual, at home and abroad, as well as to large corporate bodies. Similarly the loans and subsidies of the Napoleonic Wars bred experience and habits in London that led immediately and directly to its great nineteenth-century role as the world's capital market.

In a sense, it is the American experience of the wars of the twentieth century that most nearly parallels the British financial experience of the earlier wars. These wars served to thrust America into a capital-exporting position, which the post-war requirements of the world economy, as well as the American interest (*pace* 1929–31) sustained. The Second World War was not, however, without its contribution to British financial practice and institutions. It was, after all, Kingsley Wood's budget of 1941 that first placed the whole British fiscal system explicitly within the framework of an analysis of the national income and its components; and it is unlikely again ever to be withdrawn from that framework.

Future historians may regard this transition as significant as the generation of the British national budget in the 1360's, a practice also induced by the requirements of war finance. Modern war finance has exercised governments in the habit of thinking of the economy as a whole, both in monetary terms and in terms of real resources; and it has forced them to assume responsibility for its course with an intimacy not known in the more recent, post-mercantilist past. The problems of the post-war period have not permitted governments to relinquish that responsibility in many of its major aspects. British planners of the future may well look back to the Second World War as the period of incubation for a new form of statecraft, a return to political arithmetic in the setting of another century.

The extent to which Britain proved able to transfer the short-term burdens of war to other countries has a history of its own. It begins with King John applying pressure on foreign merchants for loans; and it ends with the hard-earned advantages of Lend-Lease and the difficult current problem of liquidating Indian, Egyptian, and other sterling balances built up during the war years. It includes the outrageous defaulting of Edward III, which subsequently limited Henry V's ability to borrow; the loans from Antwerp in the sixteenth century; the eighteenth-century purchases abroad, accomplished with exchequer bills, and by the Dutch buying handsomely into British government issues. In most cases, however, down to the recent wars, this process of capital importing was outweighed by Britain's loans and subsidies to allies. In war Britain was normally a capital-exporting nation, transforming its liquid wealth, current or hoarded, into effective alliances or foreign troops in the field: a role to which the United States succeeded in the First and Second World Wars.

Down to the First World War, the economics of warfare was, by modern standards, disproportionately financial. Even economic warfare against the enemy was based not so much on an attempt to deny him real resources, as to deny him funds. This attitude of mind can be traced from the sixteenth-century effort by Britain to monopolize the sources of short-term credit on the Continent to the trade war with Napoleon. It was completely consistent for Napoleon to sell wheat to Britain in a bad harvest year, as indeed he did. He aimed to wreck the British balance of payments rather than to starve Britain. Nevertheless, there were always exceptions to this approach to war in financial terms. Ships, for example, were impressed for national service by John; and this appears to remain a common practice. It was John, too, who decreed general mobilization in 1205. In the eighteenth century the Militia Act and impressment add men to ships among the resources directly requisitioned; and the Office of Ordnance set up, at this time, its own gunpowder factory. In the First World War the initial approach to war economics, except for manpower, was again in financial terms. But, as the gigantic requirements became evident, step by step, case by case, the British government was forced into particular markets to take over direct control: to allocate raw materials, labour, and finished products. In this respect, where the First World War ended, the Second World War began, at least from 1940. When half the national income is being channelled into a single enterprise, that enterprise cannot behave as though it were simply another competitor for resources in free markets.

VIII

Against the background of these summary observations what can be said in general of war and economic change in British history? War has been, over these 750 years, a major avenue of British investment, determined and often imposed by the conditions under which the society of nations was conducted. It cannot be cleanly disentangled from the whole fabric of British development, economic, social, or political. To the extent that we arbitrarily abstract its economic effects for examination, however, it must be concluded that war constituted a great net waste of British resources. Looking strictly at economic variables, the rate of economic progress would appear to be slower than it would otherwise have been; and it took forms other than those which would have maximized over time the British real national income. The

direct stimulus of war to inventiveness and to creative investment by no means appears to compensate for the losses in
blood and treasure and capital. On the other hand, it is
impossible to envisage, for example, the evolution of the era
from Elizabeth to Napoleon's defeat outside the context of
war. Mercantilism is, after all, a reasonable pattern of economic policy for societies at war or living in the shadow of war.
On balance, however, a rough economist's calculation must
rate war a negative force in economic change.

If, however, one looks at the process of economic growth
more broadly, the answer becomes less clear. It seems possible
that the greatest constructive effects of war on economic
change have been social and political. In its essence war
places a society under a great strain. The king and his
government must look for help where they can find it. They
tax where they can and often weaken those groups who were
their main pillars of support in pre-war years—the older,
best-established groups in the society holding or controlling
the largest pools of cash or other resources. They bargain for
help from those who may previously have been outside the
orbit of political power or social prestige. Governments have
made in war political concessions they would not make in
peace. Many of the great shifts in social and political power
in the course of British history are intimately tied to the
pressures and the processes imposed by war. War did not
create these shifts, but it powerfully affected their timing and
the rate at which they took place. And these shifts in the
social structure and the political balance of power in Britain
may well have strengthened what are referred to earlier in
this volume as the propensities relevant to the process of
economic development.

Paralleling these shifts in the balance of political forces
within the State is, of course, the rise in importance and the
powers of the State itself. War demands leadership and a
centring of power. Despite post-war reactions, ranging from
Magna Charta to the Republican victory in the American
congressional elections of 1946, the State is rarely divested
fully of the powers it acquires in war.

Taking these two elements together—the acceleration of

social change and the increased power and competence of the State machinery—one can find in war, and consequent post-war adjustments, many of the basic transitions that make up the story of British political and constitutional development. Richard, a medieval European king—at least half French—sets off on a Mediterranean venture; a quarter of a century later John, ejected from the Continent, is making concessions to his barons, who, having felt the potential power of the national State, are determined that it should not be used without restraint against them. And England, having felt the fear of foreign invasion, is more self-consciously a nation than ever before. In a fashion the process is carried forward in the Hundred Years War, which produces its powerful great captains, on whom the king is dependent, and who are paid off in land, thus acquiring long-run stature in the society. In the fifteenth century the regents of Henry VI are effectively curbing the nation's outlays on wars. In the sixteenth century, too, war both increases the power of the State and evokes, especially in the merchants and financiers, new groups anxious to obtain an active voice in the exercise of its powers. Nor are the constitutional developments of the sixteenth and seventeenth centuries to be understood without being placed in relation to the issues arising from the economic pressures of war and their aftermath. Consider the changing composition of Parliament in the first two decades of the nineteenth century, and the extent to which the forces, placated by the Reform Bill of 1832, had gained power and leverage in British society and politics during the Napoleonic Wars. Observe the growth of the British trade unions during the First World War. Compare the status of the Labour party in the decade before 1914 with its position after 1918. And, finally, consider the effect of the Second World War in Britain on the willingness to accept the Labour programme offered in the election of 1945.

While war, in its direct economic effects, has probably slowed the rate of British economic development over the centuries, it has certainly hastened the rate of social and political change; and, in turn, these social and political changes have had consequences for the rate of growth of the British economy in, almost certainly, a positive direction.

It is, of course, impossible to strike a firm balance between the net direct negative effects of war on strictly economic variables and the probable indirect positive effects of war on the economy through social and political variables. But this appears to be the nature of the calculus which one confronts in surveying the relations of Britain's wars to its economic development.

VIII

THE TERMS OF TRADE IN THEORY

I

THE aim of this chapter is to indicate the schismatic state of economic theory and analysis with respect to the terms of trade. Chapter IX suggests and briefly illustrates a set of converging approaches to the historical analysis of the terms of trade, applying the concepts developed in Chapters IV, V, and VI. Taken together, then, Chapters VIII and IX constitute an exercise in the application of the general approach to economic analysis developed in Part I of this volume. In one of its aspects this approach is an effort to assist in the development of analytic tools which will permit a coherent and unified treatment of long-period and short-period factors. In no area of theory has the formal structure of modern doctrine, with its heavy emphasis on analyses developed within short-period assumptions, had a more limiting effect than in the analysis of prices, particularly of relative price movements in international trade.

There are some fairly persuasive reasons why this theme may also be of interest to economic historians.

In the first place, movements in the terms of trade in recent years have come to play an increased role in the exposition of modern economic history: as a shorthand index of certain complex forces operating on the balance of payments and real wages, as well as a way of isolating an important factor determining relative income changes as between one country (or sector) and the international (or national) economy. It is likely to be agreed, however, that movements in the terms of trade have not yet been satisfactorily fitted into our knowledge of the past.

In the second place, movements in the terms of trade hold a central position in the analysis of current international (and intersectoral) economic problems and in the formation of policy designed to solve them. The issues involved in the structural adjustment of world trade, which has been proceeding over recent years, are not likely to be transitory in nature, although their form and impact on different portions of the world economy will certainly change. Whether the historian wishes it or not he is likely to find historical data adduced and historical argument advanced in the process of policy formation.[1] Such considerations are, of course, not binding on the historian and his schedule of interests and priorities. But they may be judged relevant by some.

In the third place, the terms of trade, as a concept, has its roots planted in two now largely separate bodies of economic thought: the short-run theory of international trade and the theory of economic development. It is to the bringing together of these lines of theory that economists are likely to devote increasing attention during the coming years.[2] An effort in this direction is essential for the development of a coherent dynamic economic theory. To the evolution of a dynamic theory (or, more likely, a systematic body of concepts and organized historical knowledge focused directly on their inter-relations) the historian has a special contribution to make. In the evolution of the short-run theory of income fluctuations, which has dominated the attention of economists over the past several decades, no equivalent contribution was required. Economists could draw heavily on contemporary observation, on economic experience acquired, as it were, within their own lifetime. Even there, however, the nineteenth-century chroniclers and analysts of the business cycle provided important vicarious experience; and at least three of the major theorists (Mitchell, Pigou, and Robertson) conducted substantial empirical studies on their

[1] Policies now advocated, and in some countries pursued, designed to stabilize relative farm incomes, are, for example, largely based on a reading of history, especially of the inter-war years, while, similarly, the character of the development plans and aspirations of many under-developed countries stem from an interpretation of their historical relations to the world economy. Historical argument has also been much invoked in policy discussions of the dollar gap of the countries of western Europe. For the central position of an historical analysis of the terms of trade in the outlook of certain under-developed countries see *The Economic Development of Latin America*, United Nations, Economic Commission on Latin America (Lake Success, 1950).

[2] See, for example, R. F. Harrod, *Towards a Dynamic Economics* (London, 1948), especially Lecture Four, 'The Foreign Balance'.

own. But, even more, it is of the nature of the problems faced in dynamic theory—their complexity, the difficulties in measuring some of the factors, and the long periods of time envisaged—that the historical method must be invoked. A portion of the historian's contribution in these newer regions might take the form of an analysis of how and why the terms of trade have moved as they have in the past.

It is no part of the theme of these two chapters that the terms of trade are a uniquely important analytic concept, around which modern economic history should be rewritten. On the contrary, the purpose here is, in part, to indicate that a satisfactory analysis of the terms of trade can proceed, essentially as a by-product, only from a knowledge of a wide range of forces determining the course of economic development of a nation in the context of the whole international trading area.

I I

The concept of the terms of trade proceeds directly from the most fundamental classical propositions in the theory of international trade. In the first instance, the terms of trade derive from the relation between the quantity of factors of production required to produce a unit of the same commodities in different countries.[1] Only two countries and two commodities were assumed to exist. From assumptions relating to relative productivity and, later, the relative productivity of the various factors of production, a range was established within which it would be of advantage for the two countries to trade with one another. The exact 'terms of interchange', within this productivity range, on which trade would take place was determined by the relative 'strength of the demand'

---

[1] The theory of comparative advantage was, of course, first developed in terms of the labour theory of value. Despite its asymmetry with the general theory of value (see, for example, E. S. Mason, 'The Doctrine of Comparative Cost', *Quarterly Journal of Economics* [Nov. 1926], pp. 69–93), the labour theory concept proved remarkably durable as a mode of exposition. See, for example, G. Haberler, *The Theory of International Trade* (1936), pp. 125 ff. The fundamental propositions are now conventionally presented, at least alternatively, in terms of substitution or production-possibility curves, as in the general theory of production; e.g. Haberler, op. cit., pp. 175 ff., and P. Samuelson, *Economics* (New York, 1948), pp. 538 ff.

of the two countries for the two commodities in question. The possible outcomes were compared, in the fundamental propositions of theory, by assuming constant returns to scale; that is, by rigorously excluding either short- or long-period changes in real costs.

This assumption, along with the others within which classical trade doctrine was evolved,[1] permitted the transition from a fundamental productivity and real value consideration of international trade to a monetary analysis, which isolated the effects of demand shifts on international economic relations. Short-period cost changes were introduced into the structure of classical analysis, but long-period changes were mainly ruled out.[2] As Haberler wrote: 'A reduction of costs of this dynamic and "historical" nature has no place in our analysis, since it represents a change of data not to be explained by economic theory.'[3]

From an early stage—from the Bullion Report of 1810, if not earlier—what one might call the active portion of the theory of international trade was concerned with the monetary theory of international prices and their financial mechanisms: the relation between trade balances, specie movements, domestic credit policies, and the relative price levels (wage levels or exchange rates) of different countries. The propositions here were, essentially, an international extension of the quantity theory of money, with special emphasis

[1] For a recent discussion of these limiting assumptions see Joan Robinson, 'The Pure Theory of International Trade', *Review of Economic Studies* (1946–7), xiv, pp. 98–177.

[2] The treatment of the short-period elasticity of supply is a normal aspect of the exposition of the theory of international trade. See, for example, J. W. Angell, *The Theory of International Prices* (Cambridge, Mass., 1926), pp. 451–74; F. Taussig, *International Trade* (New York, 1927), pp. 76–87; C. Iversen, *International Capital Movements* (1935), pp. 489–510; Haberler, op. cit., pp. 142–4 and 198–208; J. Viner, *Studies in the Theory of International Trade* (1937), pp. 47–82. A considerable literature developed on the realism of assuming a condition of increasing returns, and especially on the problem of disentangling increasing returns from historical, long-period movements in costs. The analyses of Bertil Ohlin (*Inter-regional and International Trade*, Cambridge, Mass., 1933) and Iversen leave scope for such historical changes, although they are not brought within a strict formal analysis. All writers were, of course, aware of the importance of these changes; but the structure of classical trade theory caused them to be ignored, discussed apart, or taken as given.

[3] Op. cit., p. 202.

on the means and institutions by which monetary impulses
were transmitted from one country to another.

These two elements in the theory of international trade—
the real cost propositions and the theory of monetary (i.e.
demand) equilibrium—like the theories of value and money
of which they are a part, exhibited a powerful tendency to
remain discrete in the teaching of economics and perhaps
even in the minds of economists. One of the most modern of
elementary textbooks presents the real and monetary propositions of international trade at a distance of some 150 pages
and seven chapters; although they are to be found in orderly
sequence in Book III of Mill's *Principles*.

This schism in economic thought is reflected in different
approaches to the analysis of changes in the terms of trade.
A distinguishing of these approaches under two broad headings relates to, but is apart from, the variety of definitions
and statistical formulations of the concept.[1] It separates,

[1] Viner, op. cit., pp. 558 ff., distinguishes the following:

Commodity terms of trade. Relation between changes in export and import prices.

Single factoral terms of trade. Commodity terms of trade multiplied by reciprocal of export commodity technical coefficients index; that is, commodity terms of trade corrected for changes in productivity in producing exports.

Double factoral terms of trade. Commodity terms of trade multiplied by recipro-cal of changes in technical coefficients for imports and exports; that is, commo-dity terms of trade corrected for changes in productivity in producing imports as well as exports.

Real cost terms of trade. Single factoral terms of trade multiplied by the recipro-cal of an index of the 'disutility coefficients' of the technical coefficients for export commodities; that is, single factoral terms of trade corrected for the utility consequences of changing the methods of production and the propor-tions of resources used.

Utility terms of trade. Real cost terms of trade multiplied by an index of the relative average utility per unit of imported commodities and of native com-modities whose internal consumption is precluded by allocation of resources to production for export; that is, real cost terms of trade corrected, for example, for the displacement of domestic production by concentration on exports and increased reliance on even cheaper imports.

Index of total gain from trade. Commodity terms of trade multiplied by volume of trade, a concept designed to cover the possibility, for example, that the gain from trade may increase, despite an 'unfavourable' movement of relative prices.

The double factoral terms of trade may be regarded as the fundamental classical concept. The assumption of constant returns to scale, however, per-mitted the double factoral terms of trade to be equated with the commodity terms of trade. The main applications of the terms-of-trade concept having been made within the framework of a short-period analysis, there has been relatively little attention given to systematic measurement and analysis of rather, those analyses which have looked to changing demand relations between national economies, within a fixed short-period supply structure, from those which have focused primarily on long-period cost and supply changes, in explaining actual movements in relative prices.

Both approaches arise from the basic classic propositions. The short-period approach, however, moves over from a world of two countries and two commodities to a direct consideration of the ratio of export to import prices, in general, for a given country. And it interprets changes in the ratio mainly in terms of the changing monetary and demand position in the two regions. The long-period approach to the

movements in the single factoral or double factoral terms of trade. This has been accentuated, of course, by the greater relative difficulty of empirically establishing movements in productivity as compared with movements in market prices. It is doubtful, as Viner himself was aware, if the real cost terms of trade and the utility terms of trade could be translated into satisfactory quantitative form, although the utility factors they include were, at least once, invoked in the analysis of an important practical issue, namely, D. H. Robertson's consideration of the German reparations question ('The Transfer Problem', reprinted in *Essays in Monetary Theory* [1940], pp. 197–208).

In addition, Taussig (op. cit., pp. 113–14 and 248–51), whose 'net barter terms of trade' is equivalent to Viner's 'commodity terms of trade', distinguishes the gross barter terms of trade. This latter concept exhibits the relation between changes in the volume of exports and the volume of imports, and is designed to eliminate the effects of unilateral transactions such as tributes, immigrant remittances, &c.

Finally, G. S. Dorrance ('The Income Terms of Trade', *Review of Economic Studies* [1948–9], xvi, pp. 50–56) has defined the income terms of trade as an index of the value of exports divided by the price index for imports. This concept is designed to show the volume of imports obtainable for the actual value of exports and, in effect, to correct shifts in the commodity terms of trade for changes in the volume of trade. It would, for example, temper hasty conclusions that might be drawn from the 'deterioration' of the British commodity terms of trade early in the nineteenth century or from their 'improvement' in the years after the First World War, as compared with the pre-1914 position. It was some such concept that Keynes appeared to suggest in his 'Reply to Sir William Beveridge', *Economic Journal* (1923), pp. 481–2. T. S. Ashton has applied Dorrance's concept to the period 1798–1836 for Great Britain ('The Standard of Life of Workers in England, 1780–1830', *Tasks of Economic History, Journal of Economic History*, Supplement IX, 1949).

It seems doubtful, given the complexity of the forces operating on the prices of imports and exports and on the volume of foreign trade, that any single measure of the terms of trade will isolate all the relevant forces at work or solve, in itself, the classical problem of measuring 'the gain from trade'.

For discussion of alternative concepts see Haberler, op. cit., pp. 159–66, and Iversen, op. cit., pp. 337–42, as well as Viner.

terms of trade remains closer to the real-cost propositions of classical trade theory. It takes its shape, in part, from further propositions about the relative long-period course of productivity in different sectors of the world economy, a matter which much engaged the economists of the nineteenth century, but which has received only intermittent attention since that time.[1] It is concerned with changes in relative prices of commodity groups on an international or inter-regional basis and with the changing internal structure of economies; and it involves directly changes in relative productivity as well as in the structure of demand.

The two approaches are not, of course, incompatible, although they reflect lines of theoretical analysis which are inadequately linked. Economists have been aware of both types of forces playing on the world economy at any particular period of time. Nevertheless there is a distinction between the forces and problems which economists are merely aware of and those to which they address their energy and their formal techniques. When, for example, Taussig entered the Keynes-Beveridge-Robertson debate, on the pre-1914 course of the terms of trade for Great Britain, he ignored the concepts in which it was then being considered by the other participants.[2] And in an area of economic thought much given to exhaustive bibliographies it is almost impossible to

[1] An early discussion of the possible implications for the course and pattern of foreign trade of diminishing returns in the production of raw produce set against increasing returns in industry is R. Torrens, *An Essay on the Production of Wealth* (London, 1821), especially pp. 93–98, 115–16, and 288–9. The similarity of Torrens's analysis to some more recent gloomy views of the prospects for industrialized countries was pointed out by Viner in an address before the Manchester Statistical Society, printed in *Manchester School* (1947), 'The Prospects for Foreign Trade in the Post-War World', and reprinted in *Readings in the Theory of International Trade* (Philadelphia, 1949), pp. 514–29. The theme appears in Book IV of Mill's *Principles*, and is subtly considered in Marshall's 'Memorandum on Fiscal Policy of International Trade' (1903), *Official Papers* (1926), pp. 367 ff. An extremely interesting but little-consulted estimator and analyst of relative price movements was Michael G. Mulhall, whose *History of Prices since the Year 1850* (1885) contains estimates and discussion of the relative movement of national price levels and of agricultural as opposed to industrial prices in the nineteenth century. Some more recent discussions are referred to below.

[2] F. Taussig, 'The Change in Great Britain's Foreign Trade Terms after 1900', *Economic Journal* (1925), pp. 1–10.

find a reference to this lively debate as part of the legitimate literature of international trade.

Thus, despite a common heritage of doctrine, theories of the terms of trade can be distinguished in their techniques of analysis, in the questions for which answer is sought, in the data regarded as relevant, and in the conclusions reached. The purpose of this chapter is to characterize, in no sense fully to review, the literature from this limited perspective, separating the analyses primarily concerned with the consequences for the terms of trade of shifts in demand, as between countries (and the shape of short-period supply curves), from those taking account primarily of long-period factors, of both supply and demand. This exercise may be helpful in clearing the way for a more unified approach to the treatment of the terms of trade.

III

The modern analysis of the terms of trade may be regarded, arbitrarily, as beginning on the one hand with the work of Taussig, including the extraordinary group of pupils he inspired, and, on the other, with the Keynes-Beveridge-Robertson controversy of the early 1920s, on the terms of trade and over-population in western Europe. Both lines of thought evidently owe a good deal to Marshall's formulation of classical trade theory as well as to his speculations on the results, for international trade, of the long-period pattern of economic development.

It is important to note the question to which Taussig originally addressed himself. That question was not, Why have the terms of trade for particular countries moved as they have in the past? It was, rather, What was the mechanism of international adjustment to an increase or decrease in capital exports, and what part in that mechanism has been played by changes in the terms of trade? This latter question was a relevant variant of the classic exercise of accounting for the adjustments between two countries consequent upon the introduction of a 'disturbing' factor, such as a bad harvest or a tribute. The primary interest was the mechanism of adjustment; and the concern with the terms of trade was mainly in the extent to which their movement conformed to that assumed in classical theory.

Varying results emerged from the series of empirical studies which derived from this question, including two analyses under the special case of an inconvertible standard in the capital-importing country:[1]

1. It was established that the export of capital was, in general, accompanied sensitively by a relative increase of commodity imports into the borrowing country, a relative over-all increase of commodity exports from the lending country; and that these changes need not be bilateral, as between borrower and lender.

2. It was established that the commodity (or net barter) terms of trade of the borrowing and lending countries did not, in all cases, move against the lending and for the borrowing country; and that, therefore, they did not necessarily operate in such a way as to ease the transfer problem.[2]

3. It was established with reasonable firmness in the

---

[1] The studies of the transfer process, apart from Taussig's own work, include: John H. Williams, *Argentine International Trade under Inconvertible Paper Money* (Cambridge, Mass., 1920); Frank D. Graham, 'International Trade under Depreciated Paper. The United States, 1862–79', *Quarterly Journal of Economics* (1922); Jacob Viner, *Canada's Balance of International Indebtedness, 1900–1913* (Cambridge, Mass., 1924); Gordon Wood, *Borrowing and Business in Australia* (Oxford, 1930); Roland Wilson, *Capital Imports and the Terms of Trade* (Melbourne, 1931); Harry D. White, *The French International Accounts, 1880–1913* (Cambridge, Mass., 1933); C. Bresciani-Turroni, *Inductive Verification of the Theory of International Payments* (Egyptian University Publications of the Faculty of Law, No. 1, Cairo, n.d.—about 1933). The work of A. G. Silverman, as reflected in two articles in the *Review of Economic Statistics* ('Monthly Index Numbers of British Export and Import Prices, 1880–1913' [1930], pp. 139–48; and 'Some International Trade Factors for Great Britain, 1880–1913' [1931] pp. 114–24), is to be distinguished by the eclectic character of his approach to the terms of trade. Silverman is less concerned with the verification of classical hypotheses than with a direct accounting for changes in the terms of trade. In this sense his approach is similar to that used in the recent study of K. Martin and F. G. Thackeray, 'The Terms of Trade of Selected Countries', *Bulletin of the Oxford University Institute of Statistics*, vol. x (Nov. 1948), as well as that employed in Chap. IX below.

[2] The consideration of the transfer of German reparations led to elaborate refinement of the analysis on this point. The accepted conclusion was that, while even in terms of the classical frame of analysis there was no necessity for the terms of trade to turn against Germany, there was a presumption that this would happen. See especially D. H. Robertson, op. cit.; Viner, *Studies*, pp. 357 ff., and Iversen, op. cit., pp. 278 ff.

Canadian case, more tentatively in the Australian case, that domestic prices, during a period of capital imports, rose relative to import prices and to export prices.[1]

4. It was established that the process of transfer and the pattern of price movements were not controlled primarily by movements of specie leading to central bank interest rate policies which would move prices in the lending and the borrowing countries in opposite directions, by means of appropriate doses of deflation and inflation, respectively.

From the special perspective of this analysis, the interest of these studies is primarily their demonstration that international capital movements were not accompanied systematically by a consistent pattern of movement in the terms of trade, and that other factors and a wider frame of reference must be invoked to explain their course.[2] Positively, these studies uncovered facts and relationships which must be included in any satisfactory analysis of movements in the terms of trade, including, especially, the relative movements of domestic, import, and export prices in a capital-importing area, under conditions of rapid general development.

The literature on the terms of trade includes the work of Ohlin and Iversen. Ohlin's approach relaxed many of the assumptions which had made possible the building of a neat and compact theory of international trade. It permitted, *inter alia*, an explicit consideration of long-period factors, and had implications wider than those under examination here. His emphasis on the direct transfer of purchasing power, as opposed to the specie-flow hypothesis, helped to explain the evident promptness of the response of commodity trade to capital movements; and it was mainly in the light of this conception of the international mechanism, rather than of more fundamental aspects of Ohlin's theory, that Iversen

---

[1] Viner, *Canada's Balance*, pp. 229 ff. and Wilson, op. cit., pp. 82 ff. The American case of capital imports, under a paper standard and chronic general price deflation also appears to conform roughly to this relative pattern of price movements. See Graham, op. cit. and Iversen, op. cit., pp. 438 ff.

[2] Taussig was extremely sensitive to the complexity of the empirical setting from which he and his students were seeking to establish a verification for a narrow aspect of theory, and never tired of urging caution. See, for example, *International Trade*, pp. 239–44.

reinterpreted the empirical evidence on capital movements and their consequences. The full range of the loose structure of Ohlin's concepts was not applied systematically. And the purchasing power hypothesis, outside the context of a general income theory, either contained a variant of the assumption of full employment and constant total incomes between borrower and lender, or it yielded indeterminate results.

Thus, even including the less orthodox Scandinavians, the approach to the terms of trade, starting from the concepts of international trade theory, from the end of the First World War down to the publication of Keynes's *General Theory*, is probably best regarded as an aspect of the short-period monetary theory of prices. This does not mean that the economists concerned with this type of analysis were unaware of long-period factors. They were simply not interested in them in any primary way.[1]

The intrusion of long-period facts on short-period analysis emerges in uneasy asides which can be traced through the literature. In formulating his position on the Canadian case, for example, Viner was confronted with the hypothesis of R. H. Coats, the Dominion statistician.[2] Coats argued that the relative rise of Canadian prices in relation to world prices was part of a world-wide process of development, from 1900 to 1913. The process involved, in Canada and other rapidly developing areas, the opening up of new territories, the laying of railway lines, the building of towns, and other acts of investment with a long period of gestation. In the developing areas the supply of commodities did not increase as rapidly as the demand, and prices rose disproportionately. Viner replied, first, that only the existence of capital imports

[1] Ohlin, for example (op. cit., Appendix II, p. 563), states that his treatise resulted from an effort to explain the forces governing variations in the foreign exchanges after the First World War. It is evident that the urgent problems of reparations, war debts, and American capital movements also helped to foster a concentration of interest on short-period problems. It is another matter whether short-period concepts were wholly appropriate to those problems.

[2] Viner, *Canada's Balance*, pp. 248–53. For an excellent account of the evolution of the Canadian economy in terms which subsume capital movements as a part of the development process, see W. A. Mackintosh, *The Economic Background of Dominion Provincial Relations*, Appendix 3 to the report of the Royal Commission on Dominion-Provincial Relations (Ottawa, 1939).

permitted a general price rise to take place; and that, otherwise, a relative increase in investment would have resulted
in a rise in the prices of producers' goods and a fall in the
prices of consumers' goods.[1] Then, accepting the importance
for the period of rapid expansion in new countries, Viner
notes that this development was 'not unconnected' with capital imports; and, in passing, he refers to the possibility of
'some factor not directly connected with capital borrowings
. . . operating in any case to make the prices of foods rise
throughout the world relatively to materials . . .'[2] But the
classical theory of international trade was an inappropriate
basis from which to analyse a process of economic development. Viner was not concerned with the economic forces
which led to a flow of capital to Canada; nor, primarily,
with the underlying economic events within Canada which
yielded differential price movements.[3] His aim was to verify
a hypothesis which would link capital movements with relative price changes. That link having been, on the whole,
verified in the Canadian case, he could set aside other factors, or even alternative possible explanations of the conformity.

Similarly, Ohlin, in seeking to refute Taussig's thesis on
the relation between capital movements and the British
terms of trade after 1880, refers briefly to the long-period
effect on Britain of overseas agricultural expansion, partly
induced by previous export of British capital; and, in the
Canadian case, he accepts some of the considerations introduced by Coats, and speculates on other long-period factors

[1] R. M. Carr, in a 'Note on the Role of Price in the International Trade
Mechanism', *Quarterly Journal of Economics* (1931), criticizes Viner's static conception of the credit mechanism and notes that the rise in Canadian domestic
prices, relative to import and export prices, preceded the period of borrowing,
in the years 1900–4. He concluded, in much the same vein as Coats: 'Instead
of finding that continuous heavy borrowing was the dominating factor in this
period of Canadian history, one finds that change and industrial growth were
the outstanding features.'   [2] Viner, op. cit., p. 250.

[3] Viner's analysis of the commodity composition of Canada's exports,
designed to establish the manner in which capital imports permitted a relative
restriction of exports over the period of development, includes, however, some
extremely interesting material on the pattern of resources development in
Canada, and on the relative increase of productivity in various industries
(pp. 256 ff.).

which might have affected relative price movements, apart from capital imports.[1] Iversen's alternative explanations of the empirical data abound in references to population movements and long-period cost and supply changes; but essentially he was debating the purchasing-power versus the specie-flow transfer theory, and did not pursue or seek to measure their consequences. Williams, like Wilson, working on a case where the data were unsatisfactory and the conformity to classical theory somewhat tenuous, concluded his study with a statement of the wide range of factors operating on the Argentine economy and its foreign balance, and refused to grant the gold premium a unique causal position.[2]

In the end, two of Taussig's pupils turned dissident: John Williams and Frank Graham. Williams concluded: 'The classical theory assumes as fixed, for purposes of reasoning, the very things which, in my view, should be the chief objects of study if what we wish to know is the effects and causes of international trade, so broadly regarded that nothing of importance in the facts shall fail to find its place in the analysis.'[3] He then pointed to the role in international trade of the development, mobility, and transport of productive factors, all normally excluded from the short-period, or, in Williams's own vocabulary, 'cross-section' analysis of foreign trade.

Graham's attack on classical theory was, of course, more detailed and represented a general offensive on a wide front.[4] He protested that, for a century, the theory of international trade had 'done nothing but tread the same old Mill'; and that the exclusion of changing cost and supply considerations had led to 'fallacious doctrines'.[5] But, aside from their initial

[1] Op. cit., pp. 465–72.

[2] Op. cit., pp. 234–5. See also Wilson's flatly negative results on the correlation between capital imports and the Australian terms of trade, op. cit., pp. 101–3.

[3] 'The Theory of International Trade reconsidered', *Economic Journal* (1929), pp. 195–209.

[4] In particular, see *The Theory of International Values* (Princeton, 1948); and Graham's earlier essays, 'The Theory of International Values re-examined', *Quarterly Journal of Economics* (1923), pp. 54–86; and 'The Theory of International Values', *Quarterly Journal of Economics* (1932), pp. 581–616.

[5] *Theory of International Values*, pp. 5 and 6

empirical investigations, neither Williams nor Graham addressed himself systematically to the analysis of historical movements in the terms of trade, the latter holding, in fact, that the concept of the 'terms of trade' between one and any other single country was irrelevant to almost any conceivable purpose and probably not susceptible to any form of measurement.[1] Actual movements in the terms of trade, Graham held, were so deeply connected with changes in cost and in the composition of imports and exports, that a contemplation of relative prices for imports and exports as a whole, over periods of time, could reveal nothing that was useful.

The set of concepts developed in and from and alongside Keynes's *General Theory* has led to a reformulation of certain major propositions in the theory of international trade,[2] and it has given vitality to the analysis of short-period demand and supply situations, in relation to fluctuating world and national income.[3] Since the *General Theory*, along with the whole body of modern doctrine concerned with income fluctuation, is essentially a form of short-period analysis, these new expositions and extensions may properly be considered

[1] Ibid., pp. 284–5. For an analysis of the possible consequences for the terms of trade of different types of capital exports, developed out of Graham's emphasis on long-period cost effects, see C. R. Whittlesey, 'Foreign Investment and the Terms of Trade', *Quarterly Journal of Economics* (1932), pp. 444–64.

[2] See Joan Robinson, loc. cit.; and 'The Foreign Exchanges', from *Essays in the Theory of Employment* (Oxford, 1947). Also J. Knapp, 'The Theory of International Capital Movements and Its Verification', *Review of Economic Studies* (1942–3), vol. x, pp. 115 ff. For a simplified reflection of the manner in which the short-period theory of international trade has been subsumed in general income analysis, see *National and International Measures for Full Employment* (Lake Success, New York, 1949 [United Nations]), paras. 52–66.

[3] In this field a lively area of theoretical and empirical investigation has developed, essentially from the elimination of the assumption of full employments from the theory of international trade. A few examples are: R. Hinshaw, 'American Prosperity and the British Balance of Payments Problem', *Review of Economic Statistics* (1945), xxvii; R. Hinshaw and L. A. Metzler, 'World Prosperity and the British Balance of Payments', loc. cit.; T.-C. Chang, 'International Comparison of Demand for Imports', *Review of Economic Studies* (1945–6), XIII; 'The British Demand for Imports in the Interwar Period', *Economic Journal* (1946); 'The British Balance of Payments, 1924–1938', *Economic Journal* (1947); F. V. Meyer and W. A. Lewis, 'Effects of an Overseas Slump on the British Economy', *Manchester School* (1949). Although usually applied under short-period assumptions, this type of analysis is, conceptually, capable of application when long-period changes are assumed; see, for example, Colin Clark's attempt in 'The Value of the Pound', *Economic Journal* (1949).

here as an elaboration of the lines of thought that stretch from the classics through Marshall, Taussig, Viner, Haberler, and the others.

Mrs. Robinson, in her restatement of the classical theory of international trade, accepts, in the first instance, and even underlines, the limiting assumptions, including the assumption of full employment. Setting aside the question of the banking mechanics of adjustment, she envisages that equilibrium is maintained by movements of relative wage (or exchange) rates induced either by an inflationary excess of exports or a deflationary excess of imports. She demonstrates how, under the given classical assumptions, any deviation from the equilibrium position (say, an excess of exports) would result in a rise of wages and prices from their barely stable full-employment level, which would eliminate the export surplus. The operation of such short-period movements in the terms of trade are then examined for various supply and demand elasticity situations.

The maintenance of equilibrium is demonstrated as hinging on the sensitive adjustment of wage rates to net productivity. And, introducing briefly this long-period factor, Mrs. Robinson states: 'Since technical progress and capital accumulation proceed very unevenly over the world, while the response of wage rates to increased employment is very sluggish, the tendency to establish the equilibrium wage rates never works fast enough to catch up with changing circumstances.'

This conception of a world trade equilibrium is enunciated in general terms and applied, schematically, to a case in capital exports. The case is presented on the assumption that the rate of interest always finds the level at which world investment absorbs the rate of savings, corresponding to full employment for the world as a whole. New investment takes place where profit prospects are highest—say, in Canada. If the rate of investment, including capital imports, is greater than the rate of saving corresponding to full employment, the level of money wages (or exchange rate) for Canada must alter relative to the rest of the world so as to cause a surplus of imports equal to the difference between the rate of investment taking place and the Canadian domestic rate of savings. In the capital-exporting country, say England, where investment at home is less than the rate of savings corresponding to full employment, the level of money wages must be such as to cause a surplus of exports equal to the difference, if the assumptions are to be fulfilled.

This is a suggestive approach to the movement of capital and its consequences, in terms of a world income analysis. It avoids the *ad hoc* character of the treatment of capital movements and demand shifts, as a form of unmotivated 'disturbance'; and it relates capital movements and the transfer problem to the income level and structure in both borrowing and lending countries, which Ohlin and Iversen failed to do.

Mrs. Robinson emphasizes that any such formulation depends upon the assumption of full employment; upon the sensitive adjustment of wage (or exchange) rates to changes in relative productivity; upon perfect internal mobility of factors of production; and upon the existence of perfect competition. Although the aim of Mrs. Robinson is, in large part, to indicate the unreality of the analysis, the exposition itself is, as it is described, a restatement of the short-period classical case.

It is unlikely that historians will be able to measure the exact degree and consequences, in any given situation, of deviations from these assumptions, and thus to apply fully this reformulated classic case. It may, nevertheless, prove helpful, especially when supplemented by the tools of analysis and measurement recently developed to show the impact of income changes on economies with different short-period supply and demand elasticities. A great deal of modern economic history has occurred within the frame of a world-wide business cycle, which was almost certainly the most important short-period deviation from the classical or neo-classical formulations of the theory of foreign trade. A rough evaluation of the differing impact of the business cycle on the terms of trade of particular economies, at different phases of their development, may not be outside the scope of the data and tools of analysis available to the historian.

I V

We turn now to a literature on the terms of trade conceived in a quite different vocabulary and addressed to a different set of questions. It took its start in the last quarter of the nineteenth century, from a gathering awareness of, and technical ability to measure, the impact of price as opposed to volume changes on the British trade balance, to which, among others, Mulhall, Sauerbeck, *The Economist*, and the statisticians of the Board of Trade contributed. As a prelude to the Keynes-Beveridge-Robertson controversy one can begin, quite arbitrarily, with some calculations on Britain's import and export prices presented by Dr. Bowley in the *Economic Journal* for 1897.[1] Bowley was concerned with the technical problem of constructing meaningful index numbers for import and export prices over the period 1881–95. He notes that the movement of the import index is dominated by the prices of wheat, sugar, cotton, and wool; and that the export index is dominated by movements in the prices of iron, steel, and cotton manufactures. He concludes: 'It will be noticed that exports have fallen very generally at a slower rate than imports, a fact of the greatest importance which, however, it would be dangerous to try to interpret here.' In 1903, in the midst of Joseph Chamberlain's campaign for tariff reform, Bowley contributed two further notes on the subject: one designed to bring a touch of scientific discipline into the extravagant use of statistics during the campaign; the other a comparative measure of the British and German terms of trade over the period 1881–1900. Bowley offered no general theoretical framework for his analysis, but simply compared the trade of the two countries by commodity groups and implied that the similar movement of the two import indexes was due to the similar constitution of imports; and that a substantial part of the divergence in export price indexes was due to Germany's role as a sugar exporter and Britain's as a coal exporter, the world price of sugar having fallen over the period and that of coal having risen substantially.[2]

[1] A note on 'Import and Export Index-Numbers', pp. 274–8.
[2] *Economic Journal* (1903), 'Statistical Methods and the Fiscal Controversy',

In 1912, in a comment on the Board of Trade returns for 1911, Keynes noted that Britain was £37 million a year worse off than it would have been if all prices had moved equally between 1900 and 1911. He concluded:

The deterioration—from the point of view of this country—shown above is due, of course, to the operation of the law of diminishing returns for raw products which, after a temporary lull, has been setting in sharply in quite recent years. There is now again a steady tendency for a given unit of manufactured product to purchase year by year a diminishing quantity of raw product. The comparative advantage in trade is moving sharply against industrial countries.[1]

Here, cryptically stated, is an analytic framework, albeit incomplete, for the long-period treatment of the terms of trade. The doctrine had classic roots in the conception of the differing prospects for productivity in agriculture and the extractive industries, as opposed to manufacture; and it was fully enunciated by Torrens.[2] Keynes was to apply it, of

---

pp. 303–12; and 'The Prices of Imports and Exports of the United Kingdom and Germany', pp. 628–32.

[1] *Economic Journal* (1912), Official Papers, 'Return of Estimated Value of Foreign Trade of United Kingdom at Prices of 1900', pp. 630–1. This view was also strongly expressed by Robertson in *Industrial Fluctuations* (1915; reprinted 1948), p. 169 n. 'The general conclusion to which these figures, taken as a whole, lead (i.e. Bowley's terms of trade calculations, down to 1911) is that the normal tendency for the ratio of exchange to alter against the manufacturing and in favour of the agricultural communities was in force in the seventies, was suspended in the eighties and the nineties, and is now once more on the whole triumphing. This is perhaps the most significant economic fact in the world today. . . .' Robertson also examines (pp. 167–70) the pre-1914 cyclical behaviour of the terms of trade for Britain. It is likely that both Keynes and Robertson were influenced, in their analyses, by the views of Marshall, as incorporated in his 1903 Memorandum on Fiscal Policy, as well as by a contemplation of Bowley's terms of trade series.

[2] The bases and character of Torrens's view are indicated in the following quotations: '. . . even if the effective powers of appropriative and agricultural industry were to sustain no diminution, still, in the progress of wealth and population, the exchangeable value of wrought goods, as compared with raw produce, would gradually fall. As capital accumulates, and as labourers multiply, improvements take place in the application of machinery, and in the divisions of employment, and enable a smaller number of hands to work up the same quantity of material . . . every improvement in manufacturing industry, which enables material to be wrought up with the expenditure of a less quantity of subsistence, must, in this manner, reduce the exchangeable value of manufactured goods, as compared with fruits of the soil. . . . As the several nations of

course, as a basis for Chapter II of the *Economic Consequences of the Peace*,[1] where, thinking again of the pre-war movement of the terms of trade, he wrote: '. . . taking the world as a whole, there was no deficiency of wheat, but in order to call forth an adequate supply it was necessary to offer a higher real price'; and, later, in summing up, he referred to 'the increase in the real cost of food, and the diminishing response of Nature to any further increase in the population of the world' as one of two fundamental problems of post-1919 Europe. It was in large part on these analytic foundations that Keynes contrasted the precariousness of western Europe's position in the world with the cavalier surgery of the statesmen of 1919.

Riding into battle, Beveridge, in his Presidential Address before the British Association in 1923, loosed at Keynes a massive barrage of statistics designed to show that the rise in acreage and the yield in agriculture were keeping pace with the growth in population and the increase in industrial productivity.[2] It was only in his later article, in *Economica*, that Beveridge directly confronted the terms of trade figures;[3]

---

the world advance in wealth and population, the commercial intercourse between them must gradually become less important and beneficial . . . the species of foreign trade which has the most powerful influence in raising profits and increasing wealth, is that which is carried on between an old country in which raw produce bears a high value in relation to wrought goods, and a new country where wrought goods possess a high exchangeable power with respect to raw produce. Now, as new countries advance in population, the cultivation of inferior soils must increase the cost of raising raw produce, and the division of labour reduce the expense of working it up. Hence, in all new settlements, the increasing value of raw produce must gradually check its exportation, and the falling value of wrought goods progressively prevent their importation; until at length the commercial intercourse between nations shall be confined to those peculiar articles, in the production of which the immutable circumstances of soil and climate give one country a permanent advantage over another. . . . But [Torrens added], centuries must roll away before the full peopling of the world interposes difficulties in the way of England's exchanging her cheap manufactured goods for the cheap agricultural produce of less advanced countries.' *Essay on the Production of Wealth*, pp. 96, 98, 288–9.

[1] (1919), pp. 22 and 238.

[2] 'Population and Unemployment', *Economic Journal* (1923), pp. 447–75.

[3] 'Mr. Keynes's Evidence on Over-Population', *Economica* (1924), pp. 1–10. With only indifferent success Beveridge sought to demonstrate that there had been no significant change in the movement of Britain's terms of trade from the turn of the century. In fact, the rise of imported raw-material prices, notably

but at this stage of the argument he adduced relative British prices to show that the price of grain had fallen steadily, relative to prices as a whole, down to 1914. Beveridge was a little uneasy about the apparent stagnation of real wages between 1900 and 1914. But he ascribed it to the minor wars of the first decade of the century; to a redistribution of income in favour of property; and especially to a fairly sudden bulge in the labour supply, due to the age structure of the British population. From the present limited perspective, however, what is most significant is Beveridge's discussion, impressionistic as it essentially is, of the relative long-period movements of productivity and demand in the various sectors of the world economy. Discussing the course of the terms of trade index, he concluded: 'The course of such an index is the resultant of several independent forces, namely, efficiency of production in industry or in agriculture and demand for industrial or agricultural products. Here are four variables at least.'

Strangely enough, it was Keynes rather than Beveridge who first pointed out the dramatic reversal of the British terms of trade position in the post-war years;[1] for it might have made a most satisfying debating point for Beveridge. Keynes notes that the volume of manufactured exports given for a uniform quantity of food imports had fallen from 97 in 1913 to 77 in 1922, reflecting a 'vast improvement' in the terms of trade position, thus defined. This change, however, was accompanied by a 'disastrous falling off in the volume of British exports.' Keynes then bridged the diverse movements of the terms of trade, pre-war and post-war, with a concept that would define Britain's difficulties in both cases: 'We are no longer able to sell a growing volume of manufactured goods (or a volume increasing in proportion to population) at a better real price in terms of food.'[2]

raw cotton, was a more powerful agent in shifting the British terms of trade unfavourably in the pre-1914 years than the lesser rise in foodstuff prices. Silverman, in the second of his two articles (*Review of Economic Statistics* [1931], pp. 117–18), points out that the indexes used by Keynes and Beveridge more nearly showed the differential rise in industrial raw material import prices, in relation to food imports, than they did the volume of manufactures exchanged for a given volume of imports.

[1] 'A Reply to Sir William Beveridge', *Economic Journal* (1923), pp. 476–86.
[2] Ibid., p. 482.

With a general recognition of what had happened to the post-war terms of trade, interest among economists tended to concentrate on how the British economy should react to its sudden, and rather embarrassing, increase in real wealth. In his 'Reply' Keynes discussed the probable elasticity of demand for British exports, concluding that an attempt to restore their volume, and thus to eliminate unemployment in the export industries, might involve a sufficiently serious deterioration in the terms of trade to cause a fall in real wages, a view symmetrical with his conclusions on the German transfer problem. Robertson continued this phase of the discussion by defining three alternative methods for adjustment: 'a contrived fall in the ratio of interchange', as Keynes has proposed; a shifting of labour from export industries to production for the home market; or an increase in capital exports.[1] With respect to capital exports, it is of interest that Robertson regarded them as a rather special sort of short-run stimulant to the British export industries. He did not attempt to determine whether the causes for the favourable shift were of such a kind as to maintain the existing terms of trade relationship for Britain,[2] or whether capital exports, in their long-run effects, might not be so directed as to cushion the British economy against a more evil day.[3] And, on the whole, the terms of trade position in the interwar years tended to be regarded as if it were likely to persist. Policy discussion was addressed mainly to the most appropriate form and means of adjustment to it.[4]

[1] 'Note on the Real Ratio of International Interchange', *Economic Journal* (1924), pp. 286–91.

[2] There was, at the time, no agreed view as to the reasons for the favourable shift in relative prices, and relatively little speculation on this fundamental issue. See, for example, Keynes's further comment on Robertson's 'Note', cited above, ibid., pp. 291–2.

[3] Quite separately and for somewhat different reasons, however, Robertson sided with Keynes against Beveridge in believing that secular forces were working against 'those who make their living by tricks of manufacture as opposed to those who draw it direct from the soil' ('A Word for the Devil', *Economica* [1924], pp. 203–8). See also Robertson's evidence before the Macmillan Committee, vol. i, p. 326, para. 31.

[4] See, for example, John Inman, 'The Terms of Trade', *Manchester School* (1935), pp. 37 ff., whose method of analysis is of the same eclectic character as that of Silverman, Martin, and Thackeray, cited above, p. 176 n.

The Terms of Trade in Theory 189

The other major commentator on these matters in the 1920s was Taussig.[1] Bringing to bear the wholly different line of analysis examined above, he suggested that the movement of the terms of trade after 1900 might be related to the increase in capital exports over the period; but he did not consider in what manner, if at all, his mode of analysis, and his emphasis on the changed scale of capital exports, related to the long-period productivity concepts and the data on relative commodity prices employed by the previous contestants. The meeting of minds was asymptotic, at best.

The most substantial successor to Keynes, Beveridge, and Robertson in this range of speculation is Colin Clark, who has been followed (or paralleled) by two interpreters of Britain's position in the inter-war years, Alfred Kahn and W. Arthur Lewis.[2] In addition, for this range of speculation, there are the indispensable League of Nations' calculations of Folke Hilgert, incorporated in *Industrialization and Foreign Trade*.[3]

Clark's point of departure appears to have been, appropriately, his *ex post* measurement of the extent to which

[1] 'The Change in Great Britain's Foreign Trade Terms after 1900', *Economic Journal* (1925), pp. 1–10. It is an odd fact that none of the principal neo-classical writing examines the Keynes-Beveridge discussion, despite the tendency of writers in this field to review at length their predecessors, and to produce excellent bibliographies. Keynes is included mainly for his contribution to the reparations debate, Beveridge, for his views on the tariff. Iversen's references to the Keynes-Beveridge discussion (op. cit., pp. 364–9), are not, properly, an exception, since his theoretical framework, derived from Ohlin, lent itself to a consideration of historical changes in productivity. Iversen introduces it, however, not on its own merits, but in arguing for the 'modern' as opposed to the 'classical' mechanism of adjustment.

[2] Clark's interest in the relation between movements in the relative productivity of industry and agriculture, and the pattern and terms of world trade can be traced through *National Income and Outlay* (1938), *The Conditions of Economic Progress* (1940), and *Economics of 1960* (1942). See also 'The Value of the Pound', *Economic Journal* (1949), pp. 198–207; Alfred E. Kahn, *Great Britain in the World Economy* (1946); W. Arthur Lewis, *Economic Survey, 1919–39* (1949). See also J. Viner, 'The Prospects for Foreign Trade in the Post-War World', *Manchester School* (1947), pp. 123 ff. Although Viner's views are mainly addressed to protectionist articles by Keynes and Robertson, published in the 1930s, they apply perhaps more directly to those of Clark, Kahn, and Lewis, who are concerned with Britain's prospects after 1945.

[3] League of Nations, 1945. To the League of Nations' work in this field is to be added *Relative Prices of Exports and Imports of Under-developed Countries* (United Nations, Lake Success, 1949).

Britain, in the inter-war period, had dissipated the potential advantages accruing from highly favourable terms of trade in a high average level of unemployment.[1] After a somewhat schematic summary of partial historical evidence, he advances a Doctrine of Economic Indigestion:[2] 'During the period when potentialities of real income production are rapidly increasing, either through a genuine increase in productivity, or through an improvement in the terms of trade, it seems inevitable that a large part of this improvement should be wasted in the form of unemployment.' This notion appears later, with acknowledgements to D. H. Robertson's testimony before the Macmillan Committee, as an *ad hoc* historical hypothesis; namely, that modern economic history has been marked by successive capital-hungry and capital-sated periods. In the *Conditions* of *Economic Progress* there are further observations in this vein.[3] No hypothesis is presented to explain the successive recurrence of such periods, but Clark defined three conditions necessary for rapid economic advance: a fairly rapid increase in gold production; low interest rates; and a substantial flow of international lending, leading to a high volume of international trade.

The most advanced development of this line of Clark's thought is to be found in the *Economics of 1960*, where he presents a full-fledged set of equations of progress. In these the course of the terms of trade between industry and agriculture emerges as the key variable determining the relative distribution of income and the balance of production between the sectors of the world economy.[4]

From data of greater or lesser accuracy, on assumptions which are more or less explicit, and better or worse defended, Clark first seeks to establish the following basic factors, over the period he is considering:

1. The relation between estimated future population and the size of the working force.

---

[1] *National Income and Outlay*, chap. xiii, 'The Rate of Economic Progress'.

[2] Ibid., pp. 270-1.

[3] Chap. xiv, 'The Terms of Exchange', pp. 448-69. See also *Economics of 1960*, pp. 88-106.

[4] See especially Chap. V, 'World Equilibrium', pp. 49-69.

2. The relation between real income per head and the demand for tertiary products (transport and other services).

3. The relation between real income per head and food consumption.

4. The relation between productivity in agriculture and the density of population on the land.

5. The trend of productivity per head in secondary and tertiary industries.

6. The trend of productivity per head in agriculture.

Clark then asks the following question: Given the trend of productivity in the secondary and tertiary industries, with its consequences for real income, what level of the terms of trade will yield the food supplies appropriate to that real income? Clark holds that the numbers engaged in agriculture, and thus agricultural output, are determined by agricultural wages; and that agricultural wages are systematically related to the real income to be earned in secondary and tertiary industries. Thus, after experimenting with alternative values for the terms of trade, he establishes a value which would hold in agriculture a sufficient number of workers to yield the food supplies required at his assumed level of future real income, as determined by projected productivity trends in the secondary and tertiary sectors. He then examines the impact of these terms on the distribution of employment in the various countries and on the income level as among the various countries. Thus Clark presents the somewhat unlikely projections for 1960 on a national basis. Finally, he examines the quantity of capital investment required to fulfil the assumed trend of productivity in the secondary and tertiary industries, including the availability of capital for export, as it relates to the full-employment domestic requirements of the more developed economies, and to their respective rates of savings.

We are not concerned here with the justness of the statistical basis for Clark's analysis, with his assumptions about relative trends in productivity, his assumptions about the international flows of capital required to fulfil those trends, or with the various other necessary but arbitrary assumptions made along the way. From the present limited perspective,

Clark's work is important because it brings under explicit examination a wider range of variables than were considered by previous writers who have considered the forces determining long-period movements in the terms of trade. There is, to be sure, still a substantial (and unproved) dose of Torrens in Clark; for it is the assumed higher marginal productivity of labour (and wage rates) in industry than in agriculture which finally determines the outcome of his system of equations and the movement of the terms of trade. But Clark has at least exposed for examination relevant variables implicitly imbedded or only casually referred to in the Keynes-Beveridge-Robertson discussion.

The form in which Alfred Kahn and W. Arthur Lewis couch their conclusions on the future of British trade is significant; for they employ much the same set of terms as those evolved by Keynes, Beveridge, Robertson, and Clark.[1] Neither attempts, as did Clark, an econometric formulation of his judgements. It is to the increase in British industrial productivity, the consequences of industrialization for productivity in primary sectors of the world economy, and to the scale and character of long-term international investment that they look in their speculations. In the centre of their analysis is the future course of relative prices between industrial and agricultural products and the real effort that will be required to sustain an adequate flow of foodstuffs and raw materials to Britain.

Of its nature this type of foreign-trade analysis, in terms of long-period factors, is inter-regional or even intersectoral, rather than international, in the conventional sense. It should prove susceptible of application to national economies; and, in fact, farm policy in the United States and elsewhere has rendered extremely practical this form of domestic terms of trade analysis. A version of an intersectoral approach to the terms of trade can be found in Silberling's study of the development of the American economy.[2] He seeks to estab-

---

[1] See especially Kahn, op. cit., pp. 269–91; and Lewis, op. cit., pp. 176–201.

[2] *The Dynamics of Business* (New York, 1943), especially chaps. vii and viii, pp. 124–74. For an inter-regional study of the terms of trade, see Warren Waite, 'Indexes of Terms of Trade between Areas in the United States', *Review of Economic Statistics* (1942), vol. xxiv; also *The New England Economy*, A Report to

lish long-period trends in total production and real income from 1800 to 1940, including in his analysis the relation between farm and non-farm prices. Given the sensitivity of farm income to price movements, he then explores possible connexions between trend fluctuations in relative farm incomes and fluctuations in the national economy as a whole. Silberling's results are inconclusive. But his is a form of analysis essentially similar to that applied by others to trend movements in the volume and relative price levels of international trade—for example, Hilgert's calculations in *Industrialization and Foreign Trade*.

Thus the historian, concerned simply to account for the movement of the terms of trade for a particular country over a given period of time, is confronted with two still evolving sets of analytic tools. The application of one would direct his attention to movements in relative levels of income, as between countries, to short-period changes in costs, and to the short-period elasticities of demand for imports and exports. The application of the other would divert his interest to the character rather than the volume of investment, to shifts in the position of cost and supply curves rather than to their short-period shape, to movements in the level and the character of demand for various products as determined by population and real income trends on the one hand and the changing structure of economies on the other.

the President, prepared by Committee on the New England Economy (July 1951, Washington, D.C.), pp. 142–5.

IX

THE TERMS OF TRADE IN
PRACTICE

I

THE purpose of the present chapter is to outline and to illustrate an eclectic approach to the historical analysis of the terms of trade, bringing to bear the argument of Part I and seeking thus to unite the strands of economic doctrine traced in Chapter VIII. Illustrations will be drawn mainly from British economic history since 1790. In no sense, however, does this chapter constitute a systematic treatment of the British terms of trade.

'Terms of trade' will here be considered under its most common definition; namely, as the relation between export and import prices for a given country. Thus, an improvement or deterioration in the terms of trade will not carry with it any automatic connotation of gain or loss. The measurement of gain and loss through changes in the terms of trade, can, of course, only be conducted in real terms. This chapter does not consider, for example, the problems of formally measuring, in Viner's vocabulary, the single factoral or double factoral terms of trade.[1] The sort of historical analysis outlined for relative price movements would, however, also constitute a useful foundation for interpreting measurements of such real relationships; for, in order to judge the significance of price changes, movements in productivity must be established.

There are three forms of analysis which, if applied concurrently to the data, should furnish the historian with the materials for explaining the course of a particular terms of

---

[1] For a listing of various terms of trade definitions designed to isolate real as opposed to price relationships, see pp. 172-3 n. For indexes designed to exhibit the effects of changes in the volume as well as prices of exports and imports over the years 1798-1913, see A. H. Imlah, 'The Terms of Trade of the United Kingdom', *Journal of Economic History* (Nov. 1950), p. 177.

trade series. The three forms of analysis might be designated respectively as:

1. The comparative analysis of long-period movements in those individual prices most relevant to the terms of trade of a particular country or region.

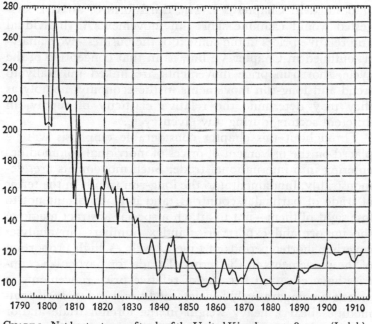

CHART 1. Net barter terms of trade of the United Kingdom, 1798–1913 (Imlah).

2. The analysis of relative price-level movements (inter-sectoral, inter-regional, or international) generated by the changing character of investment within the world economy.

3. The analysis of cyclical and short-run random movements: (a) in import and export prices, taken as indexes; and (b) in the most important individual prices which affect the course of the indexes.

It will be seen that the first form of analysis suggested requires a consideration of price movements appropriate to the conception of the process of growth, over-all and sectoral, presented in Chapter IV. It would trace the impact of changing income levels and tastes on the one hand, and the productivity of natural resources and techniques on the other, as they have their effect on the very long-run contour of individual and relative prices. The second form of analysis suggested would bring to bear the conception of trend movements in relative capacity, in different sectors of the economy, elaborated in Chapter VI. The third form of analysis suggested would examine short-run movements in individual and relative prices in the context of the business-cycle analysis outlined in Chapter V; but, as in that conception of the cycle, short-run price movements are linked integrally to trend and long-run movements in the economy, notably as they may determine the relative elasticity of supply, in different sectors, during any given cycle.

Throughout this chapter considerable emphasis will be placed on the movement of prices of individual commodities entering into international trade. Such movements are, demonstrably, fundamental to the long-run trends in the terms of trade of particular countries; and it is important not to lose sight of them—not to attach a special abstract magic to the import and export price index numbers—in analyses covering shorter periods of time as well. A high proportion of the movements in the terms of trade for particular countries have occurred because of relative price movements as among a comparatively few commodities, because such commodities bear a heavy weight in the foreign trade and/or because they were subject to relatively large amplitude in their trend or cyclical movements. Certain commodities entering into international trade do not lend themselves easily to such isolated treatment, notably engineering and chemical products and other highly processed manufactures. In such cases price indexes and sub-indexes must, of course, be used. But even in the case of advanced heterogeneous products it is often the movement in the price of a fundamental raw material (e.g. cotton or coal) which is decisive to their net movement and to their impact on the terms of trade; for changes in cost deriving from the accretion of technological development in industry have, in general, tended to be less mercurial than changes induced from the side of raw material supply.

Further, it is difficult to interpret the movement of an index of the terms of trade before one has analysed the reasons for the price movements of the main commodities determining its course. Prices rise and fall for many reasons, of differing analytic significance, responding to changes in the supply-demand relations affecting them. The reasons for price changes must be sorted out before the meaning of the movement of an import or export price index number can be determined. A series representing the terms of trade is a moving ratio which can only pose questions.

Individual commodities have, finally, a special virtue for the historian. The historian knows a good deal about cotton or iron, coal or wheat. But even such abstractions as raw materials, foodstuffs, and manufactures make it difficult for him to bring to bear his full homely knowledge and wisdom in these matters.

II

Appendix II and Charts 2 A and 2 B set out, on a common basc (1840–50), price trends for certain basic commodities of importance to the British economy over the period 1790–1945.[1] Trends are presented in the form of overlapping eleven-year averages, which effectively eliminate cyclical movements.

The most striking fact about the trend movements is that while, undoubtedly, these commodity prices were subject to a variety of common influences (notably during war periods), and while they were inter-related in subtle and complex ways, they widely diverge in their trend movements both over the period as a whole and over shorter intervals within it. Note, for example, over the whole period, the substantial net declines in the prices of cotton and sugar as compared with wheat, wool, and coal, which stand in the final decade

---

[1] Any price comparison over so long a period of time must suffer, to some extent, from changes in the quality of the products denoted. This problem is, of course, more acute in the case of manufactured articles, but would even affect the basic commodities presented here. A detailed analysis of the long-period terms of trade would have to take account systematically of this factor. It is not believed that changes in quality would alter any of the limited and illustrative conclusions here drawn from the data.

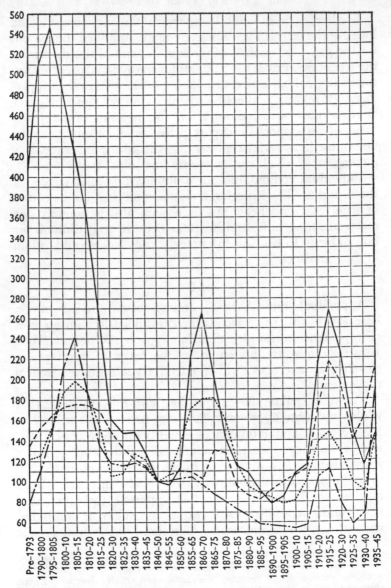

CHART 2A. Trends in selected British prices, overlapping eleven-year averages 1840–50 = 100. Key: —— cotton; – – – iron; — · — timber; . . . . wool.

not far from their initial positions, and with timber, beef, and iron, whose price levels in 1935–45 were well above the late eighteenth-century level. On firmer grounds of comparability in the quality of the commodities, note the movement from the decade 1840–50 to 1865–75, embracing the famous

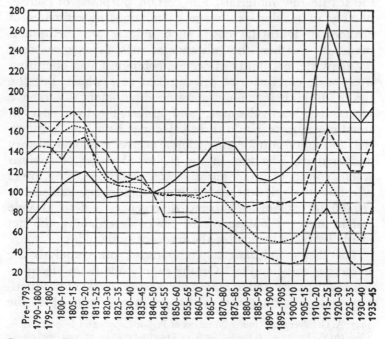

CHART 2 B. Trends in selected British prices, overlapping eleven-year averages, 1840–50 = 100. Key: —— beef: – – – coal; — · — sugar; . . . . wheat.

price-level increase of the third quarter of the century: the absolute declines in sugar, timber, and wheat; the modest increases in coal, iron, and beef; the more substantial rises in cotton and wool.[1] Excepting iron, these commodities

[1] For a recent analysis of such individual price divergences, in post-war as compared with pre-war years, with special reference to the terms of trade, see *Relative Prices of Exports and Imports of Under-developed Countries* (United Nations, Lake Success [New York, 1949]). See also Sir Walter Layton and G. Crowther, *An Introduction to the Study of Prices* (London, 1938), pp. 65, 75, 88, 108, 185, for relative movements of individual prices in trend periods over the years 1821–

might, under existing conventions, be lumped together under 'foodstuffs and raw materials'; or, broken down further, a foodstuffs sub-index might conceal strongly divergent trend movements in wheat and meat, and a raw-materials index might conceal the divergent movements of timber, coal, and the textile raw materials. For certain purposes, of course, notably in making real-wage calculations or estimates of changes in industrial costs, such indexes are useful and necessary. Further, the existence of such divergences does not deny the possibility of certain common forces operating upon wide categories of prices taken as a whole. But the prices within them cannot be assumed automatically to have moved together in the past;[1] and, in fact, the divergences in trend movements within these categories have been substantial, and significant for important aspects of economic history and analysis. The first of the suggested stages of analysis would consist in a comparative consideration of the forces affecting the relevant particular commodities, sufficiently refined to explain such trend divergences and to provide insight into the nature of the forces determining the net character of movement of the terms of trade index.

The factors relevant to comparative price analysis are numerous and complex.[2] On the supply side there are questions of capacity and acreage; of transport costs; of productivity and technique; and of changes in cost induced by the

---

1937; A. G. Silverman, 'Index Numbers of British Export and Import Prices, 1880–1913', *Review of Economic Statistics* (1930), pp. 145–7; and the classic analysis of W. C. Mitchell, *Business Cycles* (Berkeley, California, 1913), chap. iv, especially pp. 109–12.

[1] The tendency to group commodities according to 'foodstuffs and raw materials' on the one hand and 'industrial manufactures' on the other probably proceeds from three sources: the classical distinction between the productivity prospects in the two forms of economic activity; the empirical fact that there have been periods of evident relative depression and relative prosperity in agriculture, as compared with other branches of economic activity; and the empirical fact of relative inelasticity of short-period supply in 'foodstuffs and raw materials'. A recognition of the lack of uniformity of price trends within these categories should not obscure the reality of such broad uniformities in price and income behaviour as may exist among sectors of national economies or of the world economy (see pp. 208–12).

[2] See, for example, discussion of factors determining movements of individual prices in Jorgen Pedersen and O. Strange Petersen, *An Analysis of Price Behavior during the Period 1855–1913* (Copenhagen and London, 1938).

general course of wage rates in the producing areas, or by shifts in source of supply from one region to another with varying wage levels and techniques, and with natural resources of varying productivity. To these supply factors one must add the influence of tariffs and the extent to which production and sale are carried on under competitive conditions as opposed to one form or another of monopolistic arrangement.

On the demand side there are questions of the rate and character of industrial growth (for raw materials), and of population movements, changing income levels, and changing tastes (for foodstuffs and consumers' goods). In virtually all cases the cost and price history of partially competitive commodities is likely to be relevant.

One could envisage, ideally, a series of definitive econometric studies, in which these and other relevant variables were measured, related, and in the special vocabulary of econometrics, 'explained'.[1] The statistical data are not likely to be sufficiently accurate, continuous, or complete for the historian to execute such studies for the long periods of time required. Nevertheless, many of the key questions can be answered in sufficient approximation to identify and characterize the main forces determining the trend in a given price, and to compare these forces with those operating on other relevant prices. Much of conventional economic history includes, in more or less analytic form, precisely such data.[2]

Consider the relevance of this approach to the much-discussed downward trend in the British terms of trade, from 1800 to 1860.[3] Clark and Lewis have characterized this deterioration in relative prices as the passing along by Britain

---

[1] For a summary of some exploratory efforts of this type see C. F. Roos, *Dynamic Economics* (Bloomington, Indiana, 1934).

[2] See, for example, the discussion of the raw wool supply in J. H. Clapham, *The Woollen and Worsted Industries* (London, 1907), especially chap. iii, and *The Revolution in Cotton*, chap. xi; J. L. and Barbara Hammond, *The Rise of Modern Industry* (New York, 1926).

[3] C. Clark, *The Conditions of Economic Progress* (London, 1940), pp. 453–4; W. A. Lewis, *Economic Survey, 1919–1939* (London, 1949), pp. 194–5; T. S. Ashton, 'The Standard of Life of the Workers in England, 1790–1830', *The Tasks of Economic History* (1949), especially pp. 25–28; Imlah, op. cit., especially pp. 183–90.

to the rest of the world of the benefits of the Industrial Revolution at a time when British import prices were falling less sharply. More or less explicitly, they regard this movement as an example of the concurrent operation of increasing returns in industry and diminishing returns in agriculture. The Malthusian monster thus invoked for industrializing Britain is combated by Ashton, who establishes the special role of the decline in cotton goods export prices for the terms of trade movement, and emphasizes the connexion between the fall in export prices and the salutary trend rise in the volume of cotton exports.[1] Imlah, examining further the textile component of the price indexes, notes the extraordinary fall in the price of imported textile raw materials, concluding: 'The inter-relationships of import and export prices, markets, foreign investments, tariff rates, and other factors affecting the British trading position in these years need closer examination.'[2] He hazards the conclusion, however, that an exclusive emphasis on the cost-reducing effects of the new machines 'oversimplifies the matter and obscures the importance of other contributing factors'.

The decline in cotton export prices resulted, of course, mainly from the interaction of two long-period developments: the fall in the costs of growing, transporting, and cleaning raw cotton, especially in the United States; and the rising productivity of manufacture in England.[3] Not only were British manufacturers passing along the benefits of new methods of production, but the United States was also passing on to Britain the benefits of the cotton gin, transport improvements, and the new fertile cotton lands of Alabama, Mississippi, Louisiana, Arkansas, and Florida. In response to the high cotton prices of 1814–18 there was a first push into these regions; and then, in the thirties, a second great period of development of new lands.[4] It was the complex

[1] Ashton, op. cit., p. 26.   [2] Imlah, op. cit., pp. 184–5.

[3] See Ashton's discussion of the elements in the fall of real costs, op. cit., pp. 26–27.

[4] For land sales by states over the period see A. H. Cole, 'Cyclical and Sectional Variations in the Sale of Public Lands, 1816–60', *Review of Economic Statistics* (1927); or W. B. Smith and A. H. Cole, *Fluctuations in American Business before 1860* (Cambridge, U.S.A., 1935), pp. 51–58. For the course of land de-

interplay between intensive development of industry in England and extensive development of cotton growth in the United States that heavily influenced the average price of British exports and the course of the terms of trade over these years. 'Thus', wrote Baines, 'do mechanical improvements in England and agricultural improvements in America act and re-act upon each other. The spinning machinery in England gave birth to the cotton cultivation in America; and the increase in the latter is now, in turn, extending the application of the former.'[1]

TABLE 1. *English Cotton Yarn*

Description of yarn No.	Hanks per day per spindle		Price of cotton and waste, per lb.		Labour, per lb.		Cost, per lb.	
	1812	1830	1812	1830	1812	1830	1812	1830
			s. d.	s. d.	s. d.	s. d.	s. d.	s. d.
40	2·00	2·75	1 6	0 7	1 0	0 7½	2 6	1 2½
60	1·75	2·50	2 0	0 10	1 6	1 0½	3 6	1 10½
80	1·50	2·00	2 2	0 11¼	2 2	1 7½	4 4	2 6¾
100	1·40	1·80	2 4	1 1¾	2 10	2 2½	5 2	3 4¼
120	1·25	1·65	2 6	1 4	3 6	2 8	6 0	4 0
150	1·00	1·33	2 10	1 8	6 6	4 11	9 4	6 7
200	0·75	0·90	3 4	3 0	16 6	11 6	20 0	14 6
250	0·05	0·06	4 0	3 8	31 0	24 6	35 0	28 2

Table 1 indicates the rough relative influence of the two forces on the costs of yarn manufacture in Lancashire between 1812 and 1830.[2] Of the decline in cost of No. 100 yarn (totaling 21¾d.), for example, about two-thirds (14¼d.) was accounted for by the fall in raw-material costs, one-third by the decline in labour costs per pound, with wage rates estimated (by Baines) roughly constant as between 1812 and

velopment in relation to cotton prices see M. B. Hammond, *The Cotton Industry* (Ithaca, New York, 1897), especially pp. 70–72 and 247–8; L. C. Gray, *History of Agriculture in the Southern United States to 1860* (Washington, D.C., 1933), especially vol. ii, chap. 30, pp. 691 ff.; and, from the perspective of the British importer, T. Ellison, *The Cotton Trade of Great Britain* (London, 1886), pp. 89–90.

[1] Baines, *History of the Cotton Manufacture* (London, 1835), p. 317.

[2] Quoted by Baines, op. cit., p. 353; Ellison, op. cit., p. 61, gives figures consistent with these for selected years from 1779 to 1882, for No. 40 and No. 100 yarn. Ellison, however, designated 'cost per pound' as 'selling price' and 'labour per pound', as 'labour and capital'.

1830. The proportionate contribution to cost reduction of raw materials is greater in the lower grades of yarn than in the more expensive products: 71 per cent. for No. 40 yarn; only 5 per cent. for No. 250.[1]

In manufactured cotton goods the relative importance in total costs of raw materials was, of course, less than in spinning and the increase in productivity was, relatively, a larger factor in bringing down costs of production (Table 2).[2]

TABLE 2. *English Cotton Goods*

	1819–21	*1829–31*
Goods produced (lb.) . . .	80,620	143,200
Value output (£)	29,388	32,062
Average value per lb. (pence) .	86	51
Cost of cotton (£)	6,187	6,713
Cost of cotton per lb. output (pence)	18·4	11·5
Cotton as per cent. of value . .	21·1	20·9
Hands employed	250,000	275,000
Wages per lb. (pence) . . .	15·5	9·0
Total wages	10,413	11,604
Wages as per cent. of value . .	35·4	32·6
Looms at work	255,000	305,000
Output per loom (lb.) . . .	335	470

Here, the decline in cotton costs appears to account for about 20 per cent. of the decline in the unit value of output, although the base 1819–21 excludes the effects of the precipitous fall in raw cotton prices in the years 1814–20 (about 60 per cent.).

Admitting the large importance of the decline in raw-material costs for the over-all decline in the export price of British cotton manufactures, what of the net effect of the decline in the raw cotton price on the terms of trade? Raw cotton was, of course, a major direct component of the import index as well as an indirect component of export prices. Measurement is difficult, given the inadequacy of the

[1] Baines, op. cit., p. 68. These figures for the increase in productivity in spinning are only roughly consistent with those presented, in over-all terms, by Ellison which show over the decade 1820–30, a rise in output per spindle from 15·2 to 21·6 lb.; and a decline in wages paid per lb. from 64*d.* to 42*d.* Ellison thus indicates a rise in productivity for the decade roughly equal to that shown by Baines for the longer period, 1812–30.

[2] Ellison, op. cit., p. 69.

data; and the meaning of the calculation is obscure, given the fundamental interdependence of the processes of expansion and cost reduction in England and in the southern United States. Nevertheless, on balance, it would appear that between 1815 and 1830 the fall in the raw cotton price would have produced a slightly greater decline (of about 3 per cent.) in the import than the export price index for Great Britain, if no other price changes had occurred. The higher proportion cotton exports bore to total exports in 1830 than cotton imports to total imports (about 50 and 17 per cent., respectively) is outweighed mainly by the low proportion of raw cotton costs in cloth manufacture (20 per cent.).[1] The net downward effect on the terms of trade of the movement of cotton export prices down to 1830 must be accounted principally a consequence of the technological revolution. This conclusion in no way alters the basic interdependence of the productivity revolutions in manufacture and cotton growth.

It is evident that over the years down to the end of the forties nothing equivalent to the changes in cotton occurred

---

[1] Based on data in Baines (op. cit., p. 353) and Ellison (op. cit., pp. 61 and 69) the following factors were used in this arithmetic exercise:

(a) A decline of two-thirds in the raw cotton price between 1815 and 1830 was assumed; the result is not, however, significantly affected if the larger decline of about 75 per cent. from 1814 is taken.

(b) Cotton imports were taken as 15 per cent. of total imports in 1815; 17 per cent. in 1830.

(c) Cotton exports were taken as 40 per cent. of total exports in 1815; 50 per cent. in 1830.

(d) Yarn and thread were taken as 10 per cent. of total cotton exports in 1815; 20 per cent. in 1830; cloth at 90 and 80 per cent. respectively.

(e) Raw cotton was taken to represent about 50 per cent. of the sales value of yarn in 1815 and 60 per cent. in 1830; for cloth the approximate figure is 20 per cent. in both years.

With import and export indexes taken as 100 in 1815, they stand, under these abstract hypotheses, at 88 and 91, respectively, for 1830, yielding an improvement in the terms of trade due to the movement of the cotton price of about 3 per cent. If the proportion of cotton cost in cloth is taken at the figure for 1859–61, as given by Ellison (36·5 per cent.), the balance shifts, in this exercise, and the net effect of the price fall yields a greater decline in export than in import prices. This fact is worth noting, since the proportion of raw-material costs in cotton manufacture was much higher in the latter half of the century. See G. T. Jones, *Increasing Return* (Cambridge, 1933), pp. 104–6 and 192–6, for British and American data after 1845.

in the long-period development of the other major items of British imports. In wheat, after the sharp fall from 1812 to 1820, the price fell only slowly. Nevertheless, Britain and the trading world of the time were able to feed a growing population at, probably, a rising standard of consumption. The technological improvements in agriculture were real. A picture of the world sliding down a static curve of diminishing marginal productivity in agriculture would be false. The developments in food production were not, however, on a scale and of a productivity to match the special sequence in cotton. American grain and the western railways are a later story of disproportionate increase in productivity, which also leaves its imprint on the British terms of trade.

Undoubtedly it would have been better for the welfare of the British industrial working class if wheat and other basic import prices had fallen even more rapidly than, in fact, they did; and if the terms of trade had moved favourably for this reason.[1] But this is a quite different matter from regarding the decline in the British terms of trade that did take place, as, in any sense, unhealthy.[2] Relative price movements automatically measure the real gains and losses from trade only under severe, limiting short-period assumptions, unlikely to apply fully to any particular period of time, and certainly peculiarly inapplicable to the period from 1815 to 1830 in England. The real return from a unit of British labour in terms of imports was almost certainly increasing over these years; and the shape and position of the demand curve for British cotton textile exports were such as to permit, under falling costs and prices, the expansion of output

[1] One must, of course, modify such an observation with the proviso that lower import prices did not so diminish incomes among overseas customers as to counterbalance the improvement in British real wages with structural underemployment in the export industries.

[2] In the light of the literature on the advantages of 'small tariffs' one might well speculate as to whether it would have paid either the American or British cotton interests to impose export tariffs, given their relatively monopolistic positions over these years. It is likely that the strong free trade instinct of both groups (southern planters and Lancashire manufacturers) was economically justified and that it was the part of wisdom to eschew the small gains from interference with full free trade admitted, for example, by Marshall, *Official Papers* (London, 1926), 'Memorandum on the Fiscal Policy of International Trade', p. 392.

and exports on which so much of British economic development then depended.

There are other periods when the trend contours of the British terms of trade are to be understood essentially in the light of relative price movements among a few key commodities; for example, the period 1870–1914.[1] The determining relationship, at some risk of over-simplification, appears to lie mainly in the diverse course of grain and coal prices, the relation between which, while damped by other influences, helps to give the terms of trade its main lines: notably their decline from 1873 to the early eighties; their rise to 1900; their decline to 1910.[2]

Wool, meat, sugar, timber, shipping services, and many other commodities and services have their stories. And the first stage of the method of analysis suggested here would mobilize these so that their meaning for the terms of trade for particular countries and regions might be assessed. The story of an individual commodity cannot stand alone. Not only are individual commodities subject to the sort of common demand influences discussed below; they are linked as partially competing products (cotton and wool, grain and meat, &c.), and they are linked by the network of wage levels in the various economies. There are, moreover, questions of new applications of technology and changing consumers' tastes.[3] Nevertheless, a satisfactory consideration of the terms of trade for a given country or region requires that the index of relative prices be studied in the light of the comparative history of key commodities.

[1] See K. Martin and F. G. Thackeray, 'The Terms of Trade of Selected Countries, 1870–1938', *Oxford University Institute of Statistics Bulletin*, (Nov. 1948).

[2] An index of coal/wheat yields an association index of 0·75 with respect to amplitude and direction of movement when compared with year-to-year movements of Imlah's terms of trade figures; 0·8 on a simpler test of direction of movement. By themselves, of course, outside the context of knowledge of the weight and amplitude of movements of coal and wheat prices, and of the significance of their movements for other relevant prices, such correlations are not persuasive evidence.

[3] As suggested in Chap. IV, such changes in technique and even tastes may be regarded, for certain purposes, as induced by a rising relative price for a commodity, which leads to enlarged efforts to introduce cheaper substitutes and, over time, to a modification in tastes, as, for example, in the recent history of timber utilization.

I I I

The second range of factors that requires consideration was referred to above as the changing character of investment. Statistics indicating total investment and its changing constitution provide, for the period before 1914, very nearly the least satisfactory coverage that we now possess for any major economic variable. Even for more recent times there are significant ambiguities in the concepts of investment employed by economists and unsolved problems of statistical measurement. Nevertheless, such statistics as we have, combined with what we can learn from other sources, tell us a good deal about the character of new enterprise at different periods over the past century and a half. We know, for example, that British investment during the period of the French Wars was devoted heavily to fighting those wars, to expanding the capacity and productivity of agriculture, to building ships and docks, to supporting allies, to financing an expanded foreign trade, especially a re-export trade, and to expanding domestic industry. We know that after the wars, on balance, the character of investment shifted, in the direction of industry and housing and domestic transport, with a brief flier in Latin American lending in the twenties, more substantial lending to the United States in the thirties and fifties, and some interesting Far Eastern financing in the forties. We know that in the United States there were great surges of investment in new land immediately after the end of the Napoleonic Wars, in the thirties and again in the fifties. We can track the periods when an important part in the world economy was played by the development of Australia, the Argentine, South Africa, and India. We not only know the periods when British capital exports took place, and where they went, and roughly on what scale; we also know when, on balance, the world as a whole was devoting enlarged or diminished outlays to the extension of the world's resources, as opposed to their consolidation and refinement.

As discussed in Chapter VI, the character of investment in any period may be closely linked to the course of relative prices in the preceding period. It is a relationship of this type, notably with respect to foodstuffs and raw materials, that would largely explain the sequence which Colin Clark refers to as 'capital-sated' and 'capital-hungry' periods,[1] and which would give to Schumpeter's 'Kondratieff cycles' a firmer basis in history than is afforded by his emphasis on cotton textiles, railroads, and the chemicals–internal combustion engine–electricity complex. The three famous periods of extensive expansion, with rising price and interest trends (say, 1793–1815; 1848–73; 1896–1920) were part of the rough-and-ready process by which an appropriate balance of world production and a more or less appropriate distribution of population on the earth's land were maintained. Relative price movements, reflecting underlying powerful shifts in the long-run relation between the demand and supply for particular major commodities, presented apparent opportunities for profitable investment and helped to induce the periods of expansion. A reversal of these relative price trends contributed to a re-evaluation of profit possibilities and to the establishment of new patterns for current investment. Foreign investment, long associated in theory with current terms of trade movements, followed these inducements and in some cases can be demonstrated to have followed them in time.[2]

This is by no means a complete explanation of the course of price trends in relation to the pattern of investment. It would not include the influence of wars; adventitious gold discoveries;[3] and various other factors. This relation is, never-

[1] See above, pp. 189–92.

[2] It is a distinction in time of this sort which accounts for Prof. D. H. Robertson's uneasiness about the author's use of the date 1900 rather than (say) 1895, to mark a secular turn in the British economy, see 'New Light on an Old Story', *Economica* (Nov. 1948), pp. 294–5. The world-wide rise in prices of foodstuffs and raw materials certainly began in the mid-nineties; and, as R. M. Carr points out in 'Note on the Role of Price in the International Trade Mechanism', *Quarterly Journal of Economics* (1931), in Canada extensive expansion, with its attendant phenomena, began well before the international capital market turned to financing it on a large scale. In Britain, however, until the Boer War intervened, there was a bicycle boom, with a tendency for the depression phenomena to persist. On an international basis, as the author here views the matter, the classical date in the mid-nineties, upheld by Professor Robertson, would appear the more appropriate bench-mark.

[3] For a discussion of gold discoveries as an induced, rather than an adventi-

theless, an important part of the sequence of modern economic development, and it establishes a suggestive link between the first two stages of the analysis of the terms of trade presented here. The changing character of enterprise in the world economy, superimposed on, and partially related to, fundamental long-run price relationships, had important further consequences for the terms of trade for particular countries; and it had important consequences for the distribution of income among the various sectors of the world economy and for the scale and composition of international and inter-regional trade.

Consider, for example, the possible consequences for relative price levels of the bursts of extensive investment which took place in the United States during the booms of the 1830's and 1850's, and the surge of development in various parts of the British Empire in the decade before 1914.

These expansions into new areas had two important characteristics. They promised, or appeared to promise, a high yield on capital, and thus were capable of drawing investment resources both from capital-exporting countries and from other sectors of the developing economies (e.g. from the eastern seaboard of the United States). Secondly, the acts of investment had a relatively long period of gestation, meaning in turn that the passage of some time was required before the returns on investment could be compared with the expected yield, and before new supplies were coming on to the market. The consequence of these factors might well be an expansion accompanied by relatively high rates of interest, relatively resistant to rises in costs, causing (and sustaining) an upward movement in the level of wages. The profitability curve for capital might be expected to be high and relatively inelastic over the period of expansion.

The character of the process can further be understood by considering the sort of structural adjustment required both in the expanding area and in the capital-exporting area, in the course of such an expansion.

tious, phenomenon, see N. Silberling, *Dynamics of Business* (New York, 1943), pp. 74–97; A. H. Hansen, *Business Cycles and National Income* (New York, 1951), pp. 66–71; and the references above, pp. 127 and 143.

In the expanding area men were flowing in, either from other regions of the country or from abroad. They had to be grubstaked; they required food, shelter, and clothing over the period when they were transferring their residence. The mobilization of these resources had to be financed either out of their own or someone else's savings. They had to build towns, roads, and basic facilities, to say nothing of railroads, before they could begin to produce or before what they produced could find its way to market. Over this period they were not only withdrawn, in a sense, from the currently effective labour force, but, like soldiers at war, they required outlays by the community in order to continue to live and to set up the facilities for life and production in the new areas. There was, thus, a double inflationary force operating. It is little wonder that wage rates in general have been found to have risen sharply within such developing areas.

In the capital-exporting areas, in addition to the possibilities of emigration, tending to raise wage-rates, there was a sudden shift in demand in favour of the export industries. In the fifties and again in the early seventies, when railway construction was proceeding at a high rate, this pressure came to rest heavily on the capital goods industries. To the extent that domestic investment was diminished, out of competition with investment abroad, there might be idle pools of labour which might or might not be drawn promptly into production for export; although building workers do not convert easily or quickly (or, necessarily, at all) into coalminers. One might also expect in the capital-exporting areas a rise in prices and wages, but less strongly marked than in the developing area itself.

The upshot of this whole process might be a relative increase in prices and wages in the developing area, a tendency there to draw labour away from the older industries, including export industries, and a tendency to shift the terms of trade against the capital-exporting country.[1] It is in these

---

[1] In addition to the classic studies referred to in Chap. VIII (p. 176 n.), note the behaviour of the American price level in relation to the British price level and domestic *vis-à-vis* import prices in the 1830's and 1850's, as presented by W. B. Smith and A. H. Cole, *Fluctuations in American Business 1790–1860* (Cambridge, Mass., 1935), pp. 66, 68, and 100. It should be noted, however, that in

terms that one can rephrase the mechanics of Taussig's classic case, explored by Viner and others.[1]

The process need not, in itself, yield a favourable shift in the terms of trade for the developing area; for other forces of the kind considered earlier in this chapter may be in operation affecting its export prices. For reasons unconnected with the current direction and character of investment, the world-determined export prices of the developing area might be falling so rapidly that, on balance, they are not fully counteracted by the current expansion. Something of this kind appears to have happened in Australia in the eighties.[2]

It should be further noted that, in this perspective, the international movement of capital is an incident to the underlying process. One can envisage disproportionate movements of income, wages, and prices, as among various countries, without the movement of international capital;[3] and one can envisage movements of international capital, not related to such fundamental processes of development, which would not produce the described effect on the terms of trade.

The obverse of these relationships appears to have applied when periods of extensive development ceased and, on balance, world investment turned inward. The former developing areas are then producing the flow of supplies the expansion had sought to establish; and, perhaps, expansion having been carried too far, their prices are falling rapidly and the terms of trade are turning unfavourable. The former capital-exporting country, while enjoying more favourable terms of trade (after its previously inflated price position in the export industries had subsided), must shift the character of its investment and may find difficulty in sustaining employment in its export industries, both because capital exports

the capital export boom of the early seventies, so inelastic was the supply of British coal and capital goods exports that the terms of trade shifted favourably to the capital-exporting country.

[1] This description might be regarded also as a dynamic version of the process presented by Mrs. Robinson in 'The Pure Theory of International Trade', *Review of Economic Studies* (1946–7), xiv.

[2] Roland Wilson, *Capital Imports and the Terms of Trade* (Melbourne, 1931), especially pp. 101–3.

[3] One cannot, however, envisage this process without assuming inter-regional or intersectoral shifts in the direction of investment.

have decreased and because the relative price and income relations ruling in the world may relatively impoverish its export markets. After 1873 a transfer of resources of this character was, on the whole, successfully and quickly made by Great Britain; during the inter-war years, it was made only slowly and with indifferent success.

Thus, the second suggested stage in the analysis of the terms of trade for a given country is the study of the character of world investment flows and their impact on the position of that country at different times. No more than the analysis of the comparative long-period price history of selected commodities to which it relates can this approach be sufficient or conclusive; but it is an essential element in the story.

I V

The third of the suggested converging approaches to the analysis of the terms of trade would focus on short-period factors, cyclical or random in character. This is not synonymous with actual fluctuations in the terms of trade, taking place over short periods of time; for year-to-year movements are, of course, determined by the full complex of forces operating on prices in the world economy. The third approach deals with that part of the movement in the terms of trade which results from short-period fluctuations of income both within and outside the national economy and from the influence of short-period elasticities of supply and demand for import and export commodities. This portion of the analysis would also take account of harvest fluctuations, major labour disturbances, and other more or less random influences operating on prices in such a way as to leave an imprint on the terms of trade.

Throughout the period from 1790 to (say) 1931, trade fluctuations were, essentially, an international phenomenon. The various economies within the world trading area, which itself gradually expanded, accepted, on the whole, the impulses to expansion or contraction communicated from abroad and let them have their 'natural' impact on the volume and character of foreign trade as well as on internal production. Since the various national economies were of different structure and industrialized in different degree, the normal commodity constitution of their imports and their exports varied at any given moment, and they varied with the course of their development over time. One would expect that, even with a completely synchronous world trade cycle, the terms of trade, in so far as they were determined by short-period factors, would vary in short-run behaviour as among the various world economies.[1] On occasion, of course, economies did not move synchronously; and this introduced a variable factor. In addition, good and bad harvests and random factors operated. And, finally, one must take account of tariffs, wars, cartels, and other limitations on the basic notion of a freely interacting world-trading area.

Given the nature of the forces playing upon the terms of trade at any particular period in time, one would thus not expect to find a high degree of consistency in their short-run behaviour over very long time periods. And, indeed, looking back to the beginning of the nineteenth century the pattern of the British terms of trade in relation to general trade fluctuations is irregular.

Some twenty-one business cycles can be marked off for Britain between 1801 and 1914. In these the terms of trade moved in rough conformity with the business cycle in seven cases; inversely with the trade cycle in eight cases; and in six cases there is one or another kind of major irregularity with respect to general business movements. The movement of import and export prices and the net barter terms of trade (Imlah calculations) are set out by cycles in Appendix III, where indexes are calculated in terms of the average level for each cycle. Chart 3 (p. 215) presents visually the behaviour of the terms of trade cyclical indexes, with vertical lines indicating cyclical peaks, and the figure for 1914 included from Schlote. Appendix IV presents the behaviour of Silverman's monthly data on import and export prices, from 1879 to 1914, in relation to general trade fluctuations.[2]

---

[1] For a systematic analysis of the price and output responses of American commodity groups to cyclical fluctuations in different sectors or regions, relevant to terms of trade analysis over short periods, see F. C. Mills, *Price-Quantity Interactions in Business Cycles* (New York, 1946).

[2] Appendix III consists in the calculations of reference-cycle behaviour for

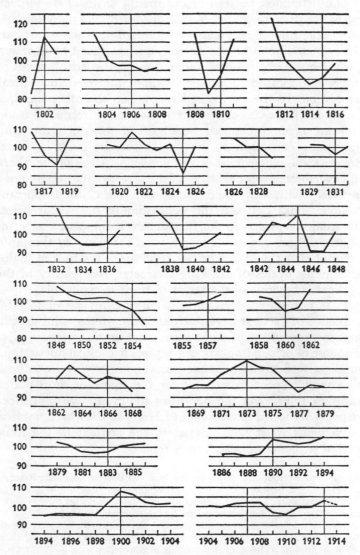

CHART. 3. The net barter terms of trade of the United Kingdom by trade cycles, 1801–1914.

The heterodox pattern of the British terms of trade over the whole period does not imply, of course, that no systematically operating forces can be detected in their short-run behaviour. The inter-war period, not examined here, saw a fairly regular inverse movement; that is, the British terms of trade deteriorated in prosperity and improved in cyclical depression. In the period 1868–1914, on the other hand, a consistent positive correlation between the terms of trade and the trade cycle can be observed to which the only important exception is the cycle with its peak in 1883. Before 1868, when most of the 'irregular' cases occur, there is, nevertheless, some tendency for the terms of trade to move inversely with the trade cycle; and there are important complex links between the behaviour of the wheat price, the quantity and value of British wheat imports, the terms of trade, and the trade cycle itself.[1] Taking further into account that the cycles before 1868 are a mixture of major and minor cycles of differing character, irregularity in the cyclical behaviour of the terms of trade is explicable.

It is not the present aim to account in detail for this sequence of cyclical irregularities and patterns. The present argument would suggest, however, that the short-period price response of British imports and exports to cyclical fluctuations in effective demand depended on the underlying trend position with respect to supply; for the shape of short-period supply curves, over the period of the cycle, was influenced strongly by trend developments. Here, as elsewhere, cyclical movements must be analysed in the context of the long-period sequence to which they relate.

the Silverman series, carried out by the National Bureau Economic Research and reproduced here by courtesy of that organization. It should be noted that the National Bureau, on the basis of monthly data, marks off a cycle with a peak in June 1903, not recognized in the tabulation of Appendix II.

[1] For a brief discussion of harvests and the British trade cycle, see the author's *B.E.N.C.*, pp. 50–52. From 1790 to 1850 the price of British wheat, taken on an annual basis, moved roughly in conformity with the trade cycle; i.e. on the average it rose during expansion and fell during general contraction. There were, however, significant deviations in this average behaviour. Nevertheless, the course of the wheat price in relation to cycles is certainly an important element in imparting an inverse bias to the British terms of trade over these years.

A satisfactory analysis of the inter-war behaviour of the British terms of trade would require an investigation of the excess capacity position in the major export industries as well as the underlying capacity and stock position for the principal items of British import, investigations that would have to reach back at least to the pattern of world investment in the pre-war decade and in the period 1914–18. In the half century before 1914 the inelasticity of the British coal supply, under boom conditions, was perhaps the most powerful single factor determining the cyclical behaviour in the terms of trade. The sharp rise of the coal price, late in prosperity, raised the price of iron, steel, and the important range of British exports which related to these prices. This inelasticity of supply was sufficient to move the terms of trade favourably during the boom; and to turn them sharply unfavourable during depression. And when the boom reaching its peak in 1873 encouraged a vast expansion in coal capacity, we observe that the following prosperity, in the early eighties, yields only a mild rise in the coal price, outweighed in its effects on the terms of trade by other factors. There is a somewhat sharper rise in the expansion reaching its peak in 1890; and something like a repetition of the experience of 1873 in 1900, both with respect to the coal price and the terms of trade.[1] Less markedly, this pattern of positive correlation persists down to 1914.

In the first half of the nineteenth century, one would not expect coal and capital goods to play so large a part in determining movements in the terms of trade. British textile exports were subject to a milder cycle in demand than the later capital goods. The price of textile exports was, moreover, sensitive to raw cotton and wool prices, which were governed by supply conditions quite different from coal in the latter decades of the century. Finally, as noted above, the harvest factor was extremely important in its effects on the

---

[1] The effects on the British terms of trade of this sequence of cyclical reactions can be roughly observed by comparing the movement of export and import prices, cycle by cycle, in Appendix IV. Excepting the boom of the early eighties, the greater amplitude of cyclical movement in export than in import prices can be noted by individual cycles, as well as in the relative average behaviour of the two series.

terms of trade. And one finds down to, roughly, the sixties a mixed bag of cyclical patterns in which fluctuations in import prices appear to be the decisive element in the ratio.

This is not to suggest that short-run movements in the British terms of trade can be satisfactorily explained, over the century before 1914, in terms of coal, cotton, and wheat alone. Their prices, it is true, were so important, and the amplitude of their movement so great, that at times they appear to dominate the net movements in the ratio. The conclusion here is more general: that the short-run movements in the terms of trade must be examined in relation to the trend position of the particular commodities most important to the given economy and to the character of investment prior to and concurrent with the short period of time under examination. There does not appear to be a simple cyclical behaviour for the terms of trade that can be neatly abstracted from the broader forces earlier discussed. Indeed, it is necessary to examine the short-run elasticities of demand and supply relevant to the foreign trade of a given country. But they are likely to be so deeply related to the longer-run forces operating on that country in the context of the world economy, that their abstraction for separate analysis may be misleading.

It is thus suggested that the course of a terms of trade series may be analysed historically in terms of relative long-run price trends as among the commodities of greatest weight and/or amplitude of movement; relative price level movements, as between regions and countries; and the impact of short-run demand fluctuations on economies of particular structure, taking account of the relation between the current position of short-run supply curves and their long-run context. Although intermingled and inter-related in any given period, each of these forces left definable imprints on the course of the terms of trade of particular countries and regions. The terms of trade for a given country or region is a ratio between price indexes; or, pressed further, between indexes of productivity. These reflect the full range of forces operating on a given economy in the context of the world trading area. A unified analysis of the terms of trade can only proceed as an outgrowth of a unified conception of the growth and fluctuations of the economic system as a whole, and of the relationship to that general process of the sectors and regions of the world economy. It is to the development of this form of analysis that the argument of Part I is meant to contribute.

X

ECONOMIC THEORY AND PUBLIC POLICY

I

THE principal conceptual achievements in economic thought over the past thirty years have been accomplished within the framework of a Marshallian short-period analysis. This is true of the monetary propositions of the 1920's, which evolved, under many hands, into what we now call Keynesian income analysis. It holds for the substantial refinement of the classical doctrine of international trade, carried out by Taussig and his pupils, and by Haberler, Harrod, and others who have lately married short-run classical trade theory to income analysis. It is also the case with respect to the fundamental analysis of monopolistic competition, developed from the propositions of E. H. Chamberlin and Mrs. Robinson. It is the present theme that these branches of economic analysis require two forms of elaboration in order to serve as an adequate scientific framework for the making of public policy in the decades which lie ahead. It appears necessary that they be placed within a systematic treatment of long-period Marshallian factors; and that they be systematically related to social and political analysis. This theme will be illustrated by observations concerning current problems in income fluctuation, foreign trade, and economic development. Although susceptible of consideration in similar terms, problems of monopoly policy are here set aside.[1]

The predominance of an interest among economists in

[1] Certain of the major issues on which the question of monopoly policy has lately come to rest conform well to the general thesis presented here. They indicate that the short-period models developed over recent decades require elaboration in such a manner as to deal formally with dynamic long-period factors as well as political and social forces. Can, for example, monopolistic units be justified in terms of their ability and willingness to generate and to apply innovations? To what extent does public (and congressional) interest temper the exploitation of the degree of monopoly open to monopolistic units, in terms of their relation to the market, narrowly conceived? To what extent (notably in Europe) can habits of co-operative action among industrialists, built up over long periods of time, be reversed by a change in the legal framework,

forms of analysis generated within a short-period framework has not, of course, prevented the execution of analyses which raised issues of the long run. Looking backward, one can always find men who foreshadow the lines of thought developed into a later orthodoxy. Keynes rediscovered Sylvio Gesell and, in a sense, Malthus. An exhaustion of the historical literature would certainly have permitted him other predecessors. Over the past thirty years, for example, Colin Clark has concerned himself persistently with issues whose treatment demands a dynamic, long-period conception of growth. Schumpeter's reflections on the relations among social, political, and economic processes, as well as his emphasis on innovations, certainly places him among the forerunners of what is likely to be a new era of orthodoxy. Kuznets's investigations of secular trends in prices and production, as well as his investigations of the long-run course and constitution of the American national income made it natural for him to raise steadily the long-run issues which did not fall within the main interests of most of his contemporaries. Arthur F. Burns's study of production trends in the United States, duly acknowledged as an interesting and proficient statistical analysis, raised fundamental issues concerning sectoral patterns of growth which were not, thus far, the concern of his contemporaries; and so with other analyses developed within the National Bureau of Economic Research, aside from those devoted to business cycles. Economic historians, in general, have gone their way concerning themselves with long-run issues quite different from those which mainly engaged the attention of their more theoretical colleagues in economics departments, as have the American institutional economists who derived their inspiration from Veblen's acute, partial observations.

and to what extent can the ultimate interests of the society in efficient production and reasonable prices be brought about only by bringing to bear on investment and market decisions interests other than those of the producer, as, for example, in the Schuman Plan? See, for example, J. K. Galbraith, 'Monopoly and the Concentration of Economic Power', chap. 3, *A Survey of Contemporary Economics*, edited by H. S. Ellis (Philadelphia–Toronto, 1948); E. S. Mason, 'Schumpeter on Monopoly and the Large Firm', *Review of Economics and Statistics* (May 1951); and E. V. Rostow, 'Market Organization and Stabilization Policy', a chapter in the forthcoming Yale University study on national policy.

Economists have, of course, been aware in particular cases of the importance of long-period factors, normally assumed fixed in the theoretical models whose elaboration was their principal concern. There is, however, a special power in the theoretical structures which are central to the thought of a generation of scientists. Keynes was quite correct when he emphasized that men would read *The General Theory* fluctuating 'between a belief that I am quite wrong and a belief that I am saying nothing new'.[1] It was Keynes's structure of analysis rather than his conclusions that were new and hard to accept. The informal, partially unorganized knowledge and awareness of scientists is something different from the knowledge which is incorporated in formal, general logical structures. It is the latter which mainly serve as guides to the selection of relevant data, in confronting a problem; and, as noted earlier,[2] the factors assumed formally to be fixed tend to disappear from among the objects of policy when issues for action are under consideration.

It appears a general characteristic of scientific progress that certain models dominate the main lines of thought in particular periods. In the meanwhile, clusters of empirical evidence and partial analyses accumulate which are not strictly explicable in terms of the current models. Then, at some stage, a new framework is created which contains the old and puts the new evidence and partial analyses into a more general frame of theory. This was the power of Keynes's analysis, notably strengthened by the measurability of the components of the national income on which it came to rest.

On this view, the strictly intellectual history of economic thought over the past three decades might justify, in terms of its own evolution, a new phase of concentration upon issues which have been set aside in order to develop fully the implications of certain short-period models. A swing back towards a consideration of long-period forces would be a natural development, quite aside from the issues of policy now being thrust upon the attention of governments and of economists. But there are powerful and urgent historical reasons for the current transition in economic thought, just

[1] p. v. For further discussion see Chapter XIV.   [2] p. 90.

as the evolution of thought in the twenties and thirties related closely to the then current issues of policy. It is often forgotten that, despite an interest in industrial fluctuations and other short-period problems among British economists before the First World War, the longer-period issue of the pattern of economic development and its relation to the British terms of trade was a matter of major concern.[1] It was this frame of thought which Keynes brought to his analysis of the Peace Conference of 1919 and its implications for Europe. It soon became apparent, however, that Britain's problem after the war would not be a problem of diminishing real returns from a given volume of exports, but rather a problem of maintaining full employment, in a society which had excess capacity in certain major export industries. Moreover, the post-war monetary developments on the continent of Europe forced economists there to rethink their monetary theory and to apply it to the most urgent short-period situations, notably to inflation and to the setting of exchange rates. Given the importance of the British economists for world thought over these years, it is not surprising that the structure of economic thought followed closely the shape of economics as developed by men concerned primarily with Britain's problems of the inter-war years. The problems of the continent were, of course, somewhat different; but they also tended to generate theoretical structures which were short-period in character. And, during the depression after 1929, a natural and proper convergence of thought among economists on the business cycle and its short-period remedy took place.

Without accepting too rigid a relation between historic problems of public policy and the scientific patterns of economic thought, it remains legitimate, broadly, to link the structures of thought which we have inherited from the past generations of economists to their interpretation of the events they confronted as citizens. Whether or not those interpretations were correct, whether or not an alternative framework

---

[1] See pp. 184–8. The view of the business cycle developed in pre-1914 thought was much closer to structural, long-run forces than it was to become when harnessed to a Keynesian analysis of fluctuations in effective demand; e.g. the early studies of W. C. Mitchell and D. H. Robertson.

of thought might have led to more fruitful recommendations for policy, is another matter.

Whatever the forces are or may have been which determined the character of the received theoretical structures in economics, it seems evident that the nature of public problems over the next decades calls for quite different structures: structures which take formally into account the process by which long-period factors are determined for any period and over time; structures which formally relate the economic process and the social and political workings of society. Some of the historical reasons for this transition can be seen by viewing the relevant branches of theory in the context of the post-war problems of unemployment and inflation, foreign trade, and economic development.

The commitment of governments and the determination of peoples to use the power of the State to maintain relatively full employment is evidently a momentous characteristic of our times. The method of income analysis generated over the past quarter century, on which full-employment policies are now largely based, was developed, however, under rather special assumptions. It led to an exploration of the forces which caused short-period fluctuations in effective demand; and it revealed some of the means open to governments to control the level of effective demand without interfering structurally in the economy. The function of governments was to supply, mainly by indirect means, an environment in which the private incentives to consume and to invest would so operate, with freedom for individuals and private institutions, that relatively full employment would be maintained. It is no accident that Keynes felt himself consciously an enemy of Marx[1] and believed that his doctrine might open

[1] In terms of modern intellectual history the following is certainly one of the most revealing quotations to be found in R. F. Harrod's *Life of John Maynard Keynes* (London, 1951), p. 462 (from a letter to George Bernard Shaw, 1 Jan. 1935):

'. . . I've had another shot at old K. M. last week, reading the Marx–Engels correspondence just published, without making much progress. I prefer Engels of the two. I can see that they invented a certain method of carrying on and a vile manner of writing, both of which their successors have maintained with fidelity. But if you tell me that they have discovered a clue to the economic riddle, still I am beaten—I can discover nothing but out-of-date controversialising.

the way to relatively steady full employment without large direct interference of the state in economic life and in the economic decisions of individuals. This remains the aspiration of a great majority of the economists and citizens of the non-Communist world.[1]

In theory one can easily envisage employment policies operating in such a way as to avoid any serious intrusion on the institutions of private enterprise and on private choice. The implementation of such policies in the context of the Western world in the post-war years has not been a good testing ground, however, for the economics of full employment, thus immaculately conceived. Quite apart from the question of whether the conception is itself wholly sound, the problems of physical reconstruction after the war, the balance of payments issues between regions in the non-Communist world, the prevalence of structural distortions in the composition of the world's capacity, the necessity for large allocations to armaments, and various other forces at work have called for a more direct interference in the workings of the economy than those envisaged in the pure Keynesian case.

Similarly, the Keynesian analysis, as joined to classical foreign trade theory, yielded a most useful framework for the treatment of short-period international trade problems. The world was so placed after the Second World War, however, that not even an International Fund with enormously greater resources could have dealt with the international trade problems which emerged. The dominant lines of thought in the

'To understand *my* state of mind, however, you have to know that I believe myself to be writing a book on economic theory which will largely revolutionise —not, I suppose, at once but in the course of the next ten years—the way the world thinks about economic problems. When my new theory has been duly assimilated and mixed with politics and feelings and passions, I can't predict what the final upshot will be in its effect on action and affairs. But there will be a great change, and, in particular, the Ricardian foundations of Marxism will be knocked away.'

[1] For a discussion of the formal basis in democratic social and political theory of this bias see, for example, M. F. Millikan, 'Objectives for Economic Policy in a Democracy', a chapter in the forthcoming Yale University study on national policy.

thirties often implicitly assumed a long-period framework which, in international trade and finance, as in domestic economies, would have left for conscious policy merely adjustments in the levels of effective demand. Further, long-period international capital movements, for which the International Bank for Reconstruction and Development was to be held partially responsible, in the post-war scheme of things, were often conceived of merely in the context of their consequences for demand and the balance of payments, rather than also in terms of appropriate rates of growth in regions of the world economy and in terms of the kinds of investment required in the interest of balance in the supply of the world's commodities. The hard fact of a dollar shortage (and of distortions in the capacity of world production in relation to requirements which are, partially, its cause) has led to a set of problems not clearly capable of treatment within the frames of conventional thought. Thus the journals have seen awkward and occasionally tense exchanges among economists, struggling either to adapt the old frame or to create a new one to deal with the facts of post-war international economic life.

Then, too, the post-war world has seen a powerful and important change in the outlook and aspirations of the hitherto under-developed countries of the world. Their desires for political independence and for rapid economic development were no new facts. The events of the war, however, much accelerated the older trends in those regions. In considerable areas of the Far East the initial military defeat of the Western colonial powers, a period of Japanese occupation under the slogan of 'Asia for the Asians', and the post-war weakness of the West, combined with the coming to maturity of another generation of men, yielded a strengthening of the long-run aspirations of the area for independence and material progress. In somewhat different ways war-time events in India, the Middle East, and Latin America operated in the same directions.

These regions emerged into a post-war world, moreover, where they were badly needed by the more industrialized powers. They were needed economically, as a source of raw materials, and as markets for industrial products, at a time when eastern Europe, Soviet Russia, and China were playing an extremely limited role in the world trading framework. They were needed because the structural balance of world production, as on occasions in the past, placed a special premium on certain kinds of output they might supply. And they were needed, for fundamental political and security reasons, as effective parts of a non-Communist coalition.

As a result, the issues of economic development from relatively primitive beginnings have increasingly occupied the minds of economists and policy makers in the West. The issues of basic economic development must clearly have for this generation a different priority than for the generations which included John Stuart Mill, Alfred Marshall, and Keynes. And all hands would agree that a fundamental analysis of economic development can neither be conducted within a short-period analytic framework nor be fruitfully carried out without a direct consideration of the interacting relations between economic decisions and social and political forces.

Against this background it may be useful to consider in greater detail the issues between theory and public policy raised by the determination of the short-run level of income, equilibrium in foreign trade, and the problem of economic development in relatively under-developed areas.

I I

The Western world entered the post-war era having absorbed and largely accepted the implications of the Keynesian analysis, and with a political determination, ranging through many sectors of Western society, that severe and protracted unemployment would never again be accepted with complacence. The events of the post-war years have raised issues, however, which would appear to underline certain inadequacies in the structure of thought originally judged sufficient for the solution of problems of short-period income control.

The Keynesian doctrine was formulated with an awareness of the importance of the problem of controlling inflation.

It is inaccurate to regard the Keynesian approach as a one-way analysis, useful only in the formulation of measures designed to increase the level of effective demand. It is, and always was, so formulated that it might be put into reverse; and its first major application, in Britain at least, was in the context of war-time inflation. The persistence in the post-war years of a high and inflationary level of demand has not made the Keynesian analysis irrelevant. Nevertheless, taken by itself, the framework of current income analysis has proved to be inadequate either in dealing with such unemployment as has marked the post-war world, or in dealing with the chronic danger of severe inflation.[1]

In Europe the most important areas of unemployment in the post-war period have been mainly structural; that is, they stem from an inappropriate balance of resources and cannot be dealt with simply by a general increase in the level of effective demand. Such has been the case with a considerable part of Italian unemployment, both in the south, where there is concealed unemployment on the land, and in the northern engineering industries. This was also the case and partially remains the case in Germany, where a large body of refugees from the east have not been satisfactorily absorbed into the German economy and German

---

[1] Modern income analysis is, patently, inappropriate to the problems of structural unemployment and unemployment in underdeveloped areas. There is, however, a further problem of linking business-cycle policy to the appropriate rate and pattern of long-run economic development. The difficulties involved emerge, for example, in the United Nations Report, *National and International Measures for Full Employment* (Lake Success, Dec. 1949), especially paras. 73–74, pp. 36–37. The United Nations experts defined the business cycle in terms of over-all levels of investment too high in the boom and too low in the slump, in relation to the long-run rate of growth. They hold that investment flows stabilized at the peak level would 'lead to a growing over-capacity of plant and equipment, and would thus require more and more compensatory public investment to maintain it (or increasing subsidies to private investment), which in turn would be likely to cause an exhaustion of useful investment opportunities'. Against this view of the relation of growth to cycles they then turn to the possible role of increasing levels of consumption in maintaining steady full employment. Whether or not the hypothesis concerning the relation of growth to business cycles, advanced in Chap. V above, is proved to be correct, the issues raised there, as well as by the analysis of the United Nations experts, indicate the need for clarifying the relation between growth and cycles, even for purposes of formulating an appropriate short-run counter-cyclical policy.

society, despite a high level of effective demand. And it may even have been true of some of the unemployment which has marked phases of the post-war period in Belgium.

Unemployment as a structural phenomenon calls for attention not only to the level of effective demand, but also to the nature of effective demand, including the character of investment which might eliminate unemployment. The kinds of spending which might eliminate Italian unemployment require consideration of the character of the skills available in the unemployed working force, and its physical location and mobility. They require thought concerning the disposal of additional products that might be produced, given the level of costs obtaining in the Italian industries. They involve a calculation of the nature and scale of the additional imports that might be required in order to produce additional output, should the pools of unemployed labour be put to work. And when one turns to the under-developed countries of the world, the relevance of short-period income analysis further diminishes. When adequate skills are lacking in the working force, when the mobility of labour is extremely low, when skill in industrial organization and high technical knowledge are lacking, measures simply to expand effective demand are of limited adequacy, if not intrinsically dangerous.[1]

Even more fundamental, the execution of the kind of 'aggressive public investment programme' widely recommended (for example, in Italy) requires qualities of public and private enterprise which cannot automatically be assumed to exist. Among the assumptions of the Keynesian analysis, usually left implicit, is that the social and institutional environment of an economy is such that once funds are made available under appropriate terms, and with an adequate level of effective demand, fruitful investment will occur. Neither in under-developed countries nor in advanced societies can this be automatically assumed; and when an appropriate environment does not exist, an analysis of the conditions and policies which might create it becomes directly relevant, in fact, central to effective public action.

[1] See, for example, *Italy Country Study*, Economic Co-operation Administration, Washington, D.C. (Feb. 1949), p. 35.

This does not mean, of course, that an environment of high effective demand may not be the most desirable environment within which structural changes in the economy might be carried out; although inflation is itself likely to produce structural changes in undesirable directions.[1] The dramatic structural evolution of the American South, over the past decade; the resilience of western Germany since the currency reform; the post-war recovery in Britain, despite its continuing acute problems; the general response of European industry to the powerful American boom of 1950–1— all would appear to attest to the usefulness of a high level of demand in the short period in accelerating long-period structural changes. It is also evident, however, that indirect manipulation of the level of effective demand is incapable, by itself, of dealing with important aspects of the problem of unemployment; and that more direct action by public policy, and a conscious consideration of the appropriate character as well as the scale of investment will be required to deal, in the real world, with the problem of unemployment as it often presents itself.

For a variety of reasons the major test of modern income analysis in the post-war years has been with respect to inflation and its control rather than with respect to unemployment. Economists have debated among themselves the abstract issue of whether a society should seek a somewhat higher level of employment, accepting as a necessary concomitant a measure of direct control, or a lesser level of employment with the maintenance of a greater degree of freedom of action.[2] Here the economist is at a disadvantage

[1] As noted above (pp. 96–97), our experience is too limited to permit us to be dogmatic about the relation between degrees of full employment (short of inflation) and the over-all rate and appropriateness of growth. In the present context one must take into account, at least, the consequences on labour and capital of diminished incentives, on the one hand, and the consequences for innovation of increased confidence in the future level of output and profits.

[2] See, notably, J. Viner, 'Full Employment at Whatever Cost', *The Quarterly Journal of Economics* (Aug. 1950) and the comment of A. Smithies (Nov. 1950). Smithies' reply to Viner's criticism of the U.N. Full Employment Report poses explicitly some of the fundamental issues of political and social policy implicit in the pursuit of degrees of full employment. These are questions normally dealt with by economists as a matter of private judgement as citizens but rarely approached with rigour as capable, potentially, of objective analysis.

because his normal working tools do not permit him to handle easily political and social data. It is evident that an analysis of the optimum balance between full employment and individual freedom of action within the economy is a matter which must reach deeply into the whole social structure of a society, into the political outlook of its people and major groupings, and, ultimately, into its scale of values. In Europe, for example, we can distinguish roughly those countries where inflation has been directly contained through a combination of rationing, allocation, and a high level of taxation, from those countries where over-all measures of credit restriction, high interest rates, and other familiar classical deflationary devices have been used. Great Britain and the Scandinavian countries have taken the former route; France, Western Germany, and Italy, the latter. The identification of the Netherlands' policy with the former group and Belgium's with the latter has been the major stumbling-block to the realization of Benelux.

The choice has not only reflected the complexion of the governments in power, with Social Democratic governments preferring the more equitable, direct controls and a higher level of employment; it has also reflected the proportion of farmers in the working force (and the electorate), the quality of the Civil Service, the sense of individual responsibility and civic self-discipline, and other more profound social facts. *Dirigisme*, as it is called by its opponents, is thus a product not of political and economic doctrines only, but also of the will and the ability of democratic societies to execute extremely complex administrative arrangements with efficiency and equity, including the collection of taxes, an art lost or never acquired in large parts of the world.

Although the ability to contain inflation by fairly direct means has, in a rough sense, measured the coherence and competence of European societies and their governments, it may be observed in passing that this fact should not obscure the fundamental weakness that the need for such policies has partially reflected.[1] A high proportion of the administrative

[1] See, notably, G. Myrdal, 'The Trend towards Economic Planning', *Manchester School* (Jan. 1951).

energy of governments has been channelled into the essentially sterile paths of guiding and controlling too high a level of effective demand and of avoiding its worst potential consequences. The tendency of democratic governments to run into inflation—to try to do too much with available resources—is one of the most disturbing phenomena of postwar Europe, and it is a problem—fundamentally a political problem—that is now even more acutely with us in the phase of rearmament into which we have entered.[1]

Confronting this issue in the Full Employment Report, the United Nations experts stated:[2] '... the situation requires such action by the government, joined with organized labor and employers' associations, that would insure that any wage increases that may be granted will not result in general price inflation.' This is, evidently, no antiseptic device of fiscal policy, but a searching political query. Moreover, it demands a revision of outlook not only by organized labour and employers' associations, but also by the farming community, whose education in means of controlling the level of their prices and income by political means has advanced, both within countries and internationally, to a point which belies the normal textbook presentation of agriculture as the last stronghold of the classic competitive market. The authors of the Full Employment Report, properly, proposed no neat formulae. They simply underlined a political condition for the successful pursuit of a sustained full-employment programme; namely, the acceptance of a common responsibility for the general price level by some groups who have normally pursued their objectives on the assumption that the general economic environment may be taken as given.

---

[1] In terms of the propensities, the tendency toward inflation is determined by the balance between the propensity to consume, on the one hand, and, on the other, the propensity to seek material advance (which helps determine the volume of investment input) and the propensities to generate and accept innovations, which determine the productivity of current investment. In the stylized argument of Part I political action, including fiscal and monetary policy, is one form in which the propensities make themselves effective (see p. 12). It should be recalled that the interacting nature of the relations among economic, social, and political forces assumed in Part I would leave full scope for important economic and social changes to be initiated by political action.

[2] Op. cit., para. 176, p. 85.

From the point of view of scientific analysis, it may be said that only the rough test of experience will be able to tell us whether, in fact, the peoples of different democratic countries will prefer relatively steady full employment at the cost of greater discipline with respect to wages and prices, to greater freedom of action with larger fluctuations in employment and profits. The possibility of a weak government neither, on the one hand, imposing (e.g. through compulsory arbitration) or negotiating adequate discipline, nor, on the other hand, instituting deflation by fiscal and monetary means cannot, of course, be ruled out, especially in the short period. But steady inflation will enforce some political as well as economic remedies.

In general, this is a problem, like many others faced by political democracies in recent times, where it is easy to demonstrate logically that the acceptance of government responsibility will strain and might threaten the fundamental liberties. The outcome is liable to depend, however, not so much on the nature of the problem as on the degree of understanding and sense of civic responsibility exhibited by the relevant groups of people, on the leadership of the government, and on the quality of its opposition. The resourcefulness of political democracy is potentially great enough to sustain a high level of employment without either protracted inflation or corruption of the social bases of democratic society. The democratic process has proved compatible in some societies with the exercise of wide governmental powers and controls; and it is feeble in many regions where there is almost unlimited scope for individual action in the economy. The strength of the democratic process is a complex phenomenon and is not correlated in any simple way with the degree and kind of economic issue settled by communal action or interplay of individual actions. Each country will, in fact, have to find its own answer and to strike its own balance between liberty and order in this field; and these balances are likely to differ from country to country, as, indeed, they differ at the present time.

All this may be said as a matter of historical generalization or of faith. But what of its implications for policy-making in

the short run? What steps must be taken within the United
States, for example, in the course of its period of rearmament,
in order to produce a political solution compatible with the
avoidance of severe inflation? The maker of policy must go
beyond the economist's controversies concerning the appropriateness of direct controls versus fiscal policy; or fiscal
policy versus a more vigorous exploitation of the potentialities of Federal Reserve action to contain the level of effective
demand. If the economist is going to take the political and
social environment of the United States in 1951 as given, his
recommendations are likely to prove of limited value to the
making of an effective policy for the period of rearmament.
In a thoroughly technical and direct sense the problem of
controlling American inflation is now a political and social
problem which deserves concentrated scientific thought to a
degree at least equal to that which is currently being given
to one or another device for diminishing or controlling the
level of effective demand.

The American people enter an era where full employment
may be chronic, with political attitudes and perhaps political
machinery ill adapted to such a setting. The American farmers now coming of age have fathers whose lives were
marked by the frustrations and relative agricultural depression of the 1920's and who had, at last, won the revolutionary
rights of parity after acute depression in the years after 1929.
They have grandfathers who lived through a part of the long
and painful fall of prices from the end of the Civil War down
to the mid-1890's. They have inherited the view that periods
of agricultural prosperity are relatively transitory and that
they should be exploited to the maximum by every means
in order to cushion the farmer's position against the evil day
of over-production that is likely again to come. In order to
play an appropriate role in the coming decades, the American farmer, like the producer of foodstuffs and raw materials
around the world, may have to trade certain apparent short-
period advantages against serious assurances of longer-run
stability in his level of real income.[1] The political lessons of

[1] A considerable range in attitudes toward the control of inflation was revealed by the major organized farm groups which testified in the *Hearings before*

parity are never likely to be unlearned in the United States: we must go forward from that point.

Turning to the industrialists, it is evident that in the United States a beginning has been made toward a responsible balancing of short-run and long-run interests. While the National Association of Manufacturers may still be able, in good conscience, to battle against effective controls and against a politically realistic programme of taxation, a significant margin of American businessmen are beginning to take into account in their current calculations the probable long-run costs for their environment of a major inflation.[1] The Committee for Economic Development has, for example, consistently supported effective anti-inflation measures for the period of rearmament.[2]

Similarly, organized labour, which historically has usually suffered, from the Napoleonic Wars forward, in times of protracted inflation, is relatively prepared to enter into a negotiation for an effective anti-inflationary policy.[3] Lacking a forum where such a negotiation might take place, however, the labour unions, like the farmers, seek a version of parity in the form of a link between cost of living and wage rates.

At every stage, then, in each of the major interested groups which is well organized there is a struggle between short-run interests, as normally pursued, and a more or less remote long-run interest in avoiding the evils and consequences of a major inflation. On occasion the machinery of American

the Committee on Banking and Currency ('Defense Production Act Amendment of 1951', U.S. Senate, 82nd Congress, First Session, G.P.O., Washington, 1951). In order of firmness in opposition to effective inflation control the three principal organizations ranked: American Farm Bureau Federation (pp. 1755 ff.); The National Grange (pp. 1200 ff.); and the National Farmers Union (pp. 2685 ff.). The degree to which these views (to the extent that they were not window-dressing) were determined by the direct economic interests of the membership, the quality of the leadership, the degree to which the membership was prepared to dilute its pressure by taking into account a general longer-run interest, &c., would be well worth intensive study.

[1] Ibid., pp. 1190 ff.
[2] Marion B. Folsom, *The CED Program to Control Inflation*, a progress report (New York, May 1951).
[3] *Hearings before the Committee on Banking and Currency*, pp. 1939 ff. (C.I.O.); 2417 ff. (A.F. of L.).

politics and of American life, in a wider sense, has proved
capable of generating relatively effective action based on a
calculus in which long-run advantages were seen to outweigh
short-run costs—for example, in the case of the Marshall
Plan.[1] Could not the lessons and methods of such passages
of public education be applied to the problem of inflation?

The attitudes of the major American groupings, however,
and the possibilities of education, persuasion, and leadership
toward more appropriate attitudes, are not the only questions
raised by the problem of inflation in the United States. There
is also the issue of whether the political process effectively
reflects the interests of all groups. Do the voices of the farm
bloc in Washington represent, on balance, the interests of all
farmers? Do the voices of industry effective in Washington
represent the interests of all business? Do the voices of organized labour in Washington effectively represent the interests
of all labour? And what of the problem of finding an effective
voice, on this issue, for the large proportion of Americans
who work on a salary basis for the government and for other
institutions? Can the interest of those who are primarily
consumers and that part of the interest of every citizen which
is his interest as a consumer be effectively mobilized?

There is a third issue of American politics which is directly
relevant to this question: namely, the adequacy of the machinery for negotiating an appropriate settlement. That machinery must lie within Congress, since Congress alone can
control the fiscal policy of the country and its farm policy.
Such negotiations as may take place within the Office of
Defence Mobilization, as between industry and labour, are
extraordinarily circumscribed in relation to the fundamental
problem of the control of inflation: Mr. Wilson held in his
hands none of the fundamental counters required to negotiate with labour a well-disciplined programme for dealing

[1] The converging motives which determined American acceptance of the
responsibilities and costs of the Marshall Plan were, of course, numerous. It is
the author's view that, on balance, the issue was determined (like the issue of
Lend-Lease, in 1941) by the American judgement that its own long-run political
and military future depended on the survival of societies in western Europe
based on a recognizably Western conception of the proper relations between the
individual and the State.

with inflation. Is there the possibility of a congressional procedure which would force the Congress at least to confront
more sharply and in their totality the fundamental issues of
income control and distribution involved in an effective anti-
inflationary policy?

Thus, the problem of the appropriate margin between the
degree of unemployment and inflation is, for a student of
society, a problem of analysing the full structure and political
procedures and capabilities of a society; and seen from the
point of view of the policy-maker, intent on controlling inflation, it is a problem of generating the attitudes and creating
the forum within which the major groups in the society
might negotiate equitable agreement to sacrifice a real or
apparent short-run interest to a common longer-run interest.
Simple appeals for a higher degree of freedom as against the
virtues of a lower level of unemployment with the acceptance
of controls, is a limited and inadequate contribution from the
economist to a debate on the fundamental question, as is
crusading for one or another special device which might
limit the level of effective demand, if it were politically
acceptable.

These issues would appear to have a considerable long-run
importance. The question of the control of inflation is likely
to be with us long after the days of rearmament have passed;
for it lies implicit in the acceptance by peoples and political
parties of the proposition that unemployment is no longer to
be regarded as an act of God.

III

The need to join modern income analysis to a consideration
of long-period forces and to the social and political environment within which these forces operate has been further
accentuated, in the post-war years after 1945, by the nature
of certain foreign-trade problems which have confronted the
Western world. These have led, in the further context of
immediate post-war reconstruction, and now of rearmament,
to a most remarkable entrance of governments into direct
control over the character of new investment, quite apart
from its scale in relation to full-employment policy.

In the classic conception of the process whereby investment takes place under private capitalism, investment is
envisaged as resulting from decisions of many individuals
and private institutions, each acting on the basis of expecta-
tion of private profit. A free, flexible price system is assumed,
indicating relative current and expected future scarcities. A
free private capital market is assumed nationally and internationally, from which the investor can draw, and within
which a range of interest rates reflects the availability of
capital and the average status of hopes and fears for various
future time periods, under various types of risk.

From the beginnings of modern European capitalism important sectors of the economy operated on a non-competi-
tive basis, notably, of course, in Germany. Between the wars
the areas of competitive practice in Europe sharply diminished. Italy and Germany went Fascist, and the character
of investment there was determined largely by government
or by private monopoly groupings. In other countries as
well, control over interest rates, discriminatory tariffs, and
exchange controls altered the setting in which investment
decisions were taken in such a way as to divert investment
from the paths it would otherwise have followed. Nationally
and internationally, the scope and power of monopolistic
arrangements in Europe grew.

In the post-war period Europe (and to a lesser extent, the
United States) may have moved irretrievably still further
from the classic competitive mechanisms of private investment. A variety of factors has contributed to this development. In the first instance, war and German occupation left
behind a heritage of shattered institutions. Almost by default,
governments had to seize the initiative in starting Europe on
the road to recovery. On the Continent, especially, neither
the private institutions nor the private investment resources
existed to reconstruct railways and other basic facilities. And
even where resources and institutions were reassembled, the
environment lacked the stability—the confidence—to induce
men responsible for other people's money to invest on a large
scale for long periods. By default rather than from ideological
persuasion, governments and their civil servants took over a

substantial part of the function of risk taking and the direction of investment. In this process the nationalization of industry has figured, but it has figured only as an incident in a much wider sequence of events.

Although in many of its functions European private enterprise has recovered remarkably since 1945, the insecurity of the international position, the continuance of a network of complex internal and external controls, the inter-governmental relations on which the balance of the world trade structure depends, the requirements of rearmament, and, perhaps, a fundamental weakening of the will of private enterprise to take risks, has left a heritage of enlarged public responsibility for the character of investment decisions. Even before large-scale rearmament, in 1949, some 40 per cent. of gross investment in Italy was undertaken by public authorities; about 30 per cent. in the United Kingdom, France, and Sweden; and only slightly less than 30 per cent. in Belgium, Norway, and Switzerland.[1]

These figures, moreover, substantially underestimate the real importance of public authorities in the investment process. Even where investment is apparently privately undertaken, the hand of government has often been upon it. A great deal of private investment has been conditioned by government grants, including E.C.A. counterpart funds and the payment of war-damage claims. In the United Kingdom, steel and timber allocations, as well as thoroughgoing control over the constitution of imports, have in fact determined in some detail the pattern of domestic investment over most of the post-war years. In France, amidst passionate protestations on behalf of private enterprise and against *dirigisme*, selective control over bank loans, in addition to more direct government interventions, has insured that investment more or less followed the lines laid down in the Monnet plan. Even medium-term foreign trade credits have tended to become the prerogative of government export guarantee boards and other governmental bodies. Finally, except for the very large flight funds that have found their way to

[1] *Economic Survey of Europe in 1949*, United Nations, Economic Commission for Europe (Geneva, 1950), pp. 48–51.

Swiss and American banks, the treasuries have had the means of insuring that British foreign investment went to the British Empire, French funds into the French Empire, Belgian funds into the Congo.

Almost irrespective of the political quality of the governments, there have been powerful forces at work converting the banker, and even in some of his functions the industrialist, into a more or less acquiescent civil servant. And the process, begun by default, has had a self-reinforcing life of its own. Once the institutions of government responsibility and action are in motion, it becomes increasingly difficult for private investment to operate in the old way. In such a setting, young men of vigour, attracted by the excitement and risks of the most responsible positions, turn increasingly to the institutions where such decisions are taken; and those institutions are now more likely to be the departments of governments than the offices of banks and industrial firms.

There has been another factor supporting this trend. From the days of U.N.R.R.A. forward through the emergency economic organizations in London and Paris, the Marshall Plan, the Economic Commission for Europe, and, now, N.A.T.O., international consultation has strongly affected the pattern of investment in Europe. The fact that financial gifts and loans were often bound up with such consultations gave them a great importance. Since 1945 a substantial proportion of western European investment has been financed by inter-governmental gifts and loans. It is mainly representatives of governments that consult internationally, though industrialists and bankers serve on the delegations, and the latter no doubt still find occasion to consult outside the presence of government officials. When governments are the agents by which capital funds are mobilized, they play, inevitably, a major part in the disposition of those funds. Even where the formal results of such international efforts have been meagre, as in the attempt of the O.E.E.C. in 1948–9 to co-ordinate western European investment plans, the effects are real. The knowledge of governments is increased by this process, and the habit of government initiative and responsibility is strengthened.

Leaving aside the influence on this process of reconstruction (defined in the limited sense of physical reconstitution of damaged plant) and the more recent effects of the accelerated rearmament of the Western world, this dramatic shift toward government control over the constitution of investment has resulted in large part from the nature of the postwar foreign-trade crisis. That crisis can be defined substantially in terms of the lack of an appropriate balance in the constitution of the world's production. Foodstuffs and raw materials, in general, have been in relatively short supply, with important consequences for the terms of trade; and too high a proportion of production available to the world market has been located in dollar areas. Looked at from the point of view of a western European government in the immediate post-war years, the problem confronted, was, in a sense, a commodity problem. Certain commodity requirements could not be met (for a politically minimum standard of living and rate of progress) unless they could be produced at home, within an accessible currency area, or somehow acquired from the United States or the dollar area. Governments were led, on this view, to encourage production in particular directions both at home and within their empires, when such were available. It was this primitive impulse which gave to the economic plans in Europe during the immediate post-war years their autarchic quality; and it was this impulse which largely led governments to invest abroad within their currency areas or empires, in commodities which could otherwise only be acquired at the expense of dollars. The commodity approach to the structural problem of international trade required concern for the character of current investment as well as its volume; and it has left the institutions of capital investment operating by means and under criteria quite different from those which are assumed to operate in a short-period analysis of income fluctuations or in classical foreign-trade theory.

It is fair to say that the taking of major investment decisions in Europe is no longer regarded by government or private institutions as wholly or even primarily a private affair. The environment and institutional arrangements for the successful existence of a classical system of private investment no longer appear to exist.

The extent and methods of government control over the pattern of investment vary widely, of course, among the European countries. This has not been an absolute Hegelian process, ending cleanly a private system and creating a government system of investment. The area of decision and of risk for private enterprise may be greater, let us say, in Belgium than in the United Kingdom. The government is more conscious of the investment pattern it wishes to achieve in France, let us say, than in Italy or in Western Germany. Further, the essence of the transition lies less in the nature of the institutional arrangements which have arisen than in this more basic characteristic of the process: investment decisions are now increasingly taken not from the essentially atomistic perspective of the individual investor but from some more or less clear, more or less articulated conception of where the national economy ought to move structurally over future years. Even where private institutions are vital and active they find themselves executing investment decisions in which they may have shared but on which have been brought to bear a conception of the national interest, or even the European regional interest, foreign to the older traditions of free enterprise and foreign also to the theoretical assumptions on which much of economic theory is based.

The problems raised by rearmament in the United States have tended to move America in somewhat the same direction. There is, first, the question of mobilizing industrial capacity in line with priorities for military end-products. This alone would heavily determine the composition of American investment during the rearmament period. Beyond this, the high levels of employment and rapid advance in output during the post-war years have revealed to the United States and the Western world generally its inadequate raw materials base, given its long-run rate of industrial development and the short-run accelerated requirements of a rearmament effort. Large industrial complexes, such as the steel firms, as well as the government itself have been forced to think in terms of their long-run requirements for certain raw materials, and the means for generating investment to yield appropriate future capacity. Although the United States retains to a greater extent than Europe the structure and procedures of a private investment system, its post-war experiences have also pushed the government to enlarged responsibilities for the composition of investment, and has altered the investment perspective in private sectors away from the classic model.

This is not to imply that the systems of investment that have emerged in European countries and in the United States are intrinsically better than those which have existed in the past, or that investment has followed a pattern designed to bring the world economy into the most rapid possible structural adjustment. There seems little doubt, for example, that the initial post-war investment plans now coming to fruition were overly nationalistic and autarchical. This reflects in part a weakness of all the 'national planning' we can observe. But more particularly, it reflects a rather primitive effort to reduce imports by substituting for them enlarged domestic production of previously imported commodities. In the immediate post-war years the perspective on future requirements and availability of various commodities was often faulty. Moreover, government action and responsibility is by no means synonymous with planning; and many forms of government action simply reflect the interests of special groups who, in other times, would have pursued their interests by private means. The increased concern of governments with hitherto private decisions has been a two-way process.

These observations on the nature of the changes in the investment process in the post-war years have a particular relevance to the maintenance of long-term foreign-trade equilibrium in the world trading area. It will be recalled that the United Nations Full Employment Report suggested that a world conference be called to link the domestic development plans of the various regions of the world to their current and prospective balance of payments positions; and it further suggested that a steady flow of dollars for development purposes be organized by the governments, acting through the International Bank. This recommendation has recently been supported by the conclusion of the United Nations experts on economic development, that some 10 billion dollars in capital imports would annually be required to sustain an appropriate $2\frac{1}{2}$ per cent. per annum rate of economic advance in backward areas.[1] Although the current phase of rearmament has somewhat altered the problem which these two groups of experts have confronted, there is little doubt that a stable world-trading system is likely to require some conscious management of its capital flows, over coming decades, and that governments will have to take a hand in the process.

Historically, adjustments in world trade have gone on steadily in response to the changing structure and requirements of national economies (including the effects of wars) which, by causing changes in relative prices, presented inducements to develop new resources. These possibilities, along with those offered by technical innovations, were exploited by national and international flows of capital, altering irregularly in their direction and character. The processes of development required to maintain a balanced flow of world production (for example, in the American West, or later in Australia, the Argentine, and Canada) themselves caused further disequilibria in world price and income-distribution relations, in the course of their operation. The history of world trade for the past century and a half is a story of unceasing structural adjustment, executed largely in response to changing price relations and technical possibilities, with lags and distortions sufficient to cause substantial trend movements in the terms of trade for particular countries and in relative income flows to different sectors of the world economy. The motive force in such movements (aside from the consequences of war) has generally been the rate and character of the structural growth of national economies, including population movements, in relation to existing capacity to produce foodstuffs and raw materials. The present trade disequilibrium is an acute version of a type of

[1] *Measures for the Economic Development of Under-developed Countries*, United Nations (New York, 1951).

problem which is the substance of much of modern economic history. Its solution must be envisaged, not in terms of a once-for-all shift, but in terms of a continuing adjustment of world trade consonant with the altering possibilities and requirements of developing national economies.

What is unique about the present situation is that the adjustment is not now taking place by means of capital flows responding sensitively to the current and expected movements of world prices and the scarcities they would reflect. The world price mechanisms and patterns of domestic and international investment are heavily controlled; and a world capital market no longer exists.

The domestic terms of trade in the United States, between agricultural and other prices, is largely determined by law; and these powerful arrangements colour world price relationships. In the Argentine, domestic investment has been shielded in recent years from the temptations of relatively high world agricultural prices. The investment programmes of the states of eastern Europe are almost wholly divorced from the considerations which would govern them under the operations of a free world economy; and in some parts of the world investment and import programmes are being pursued on the implicit assumption that dwindling hoards of foreign exchange will be somehow replaced by a stable flow. On the other hand, temporary American aid, planned in the sense that it has depended on American governmental decision, is being granted to cushion western Europe against the consequences of these 'interferences', and against a possibly lower standard of living that might emerge if aid were not granted and the economy of the United States were to adjust to the consequent volume and price level of exports.

As noted earlier, the degree and character of planning throughout the world varies widely. At the present time, however, the governments of countries with even relatively unplanned economies have one sort of grip or another on the variables which would determine the character and rate of structural development in a free world economy. It may be that a large part of the world will be able, over the years, to recreate an environment where currencies are freely convertible, effective international prices operate, capital flows speedily on expectations of private profit, direct import controls have disappeared, and structural adjustments can take place outside the consciousness of governments or even of economists. But the central fact about the world trade problem is that, consciously or not, it is being managed; and this is as true of the years dominated by reconstruction and the dollar problem as it is of the current period of rearmament.

Further, the political roots underlying some of these techniques of management (e.g. U.S. farm policy and the guided development programmes of under-developed countries) go deep, having established themselves quite independently of the post-war dollar shortage or of rearmament. We cannot assume that the elimination of the present disequilibrium in itself will restore a world economy where structural adjustment will proceed automatically; and, in fact, a good deal of contemporary management is a political response to the evils judged to have resulted from the irregularity and lags involved in unplanned structural adjustments. The secular trends in relative prices and income distribution, analysed in Chapter VI, have left a deep mark on those sectors of the world economy which suffered during its downswings. We now face the political consequences of having let the farmers and producers of raw materials suffer fully in the past, for periods running longer than a decade, the results for income and income distribution of inelastic short-run supply and demand curves, at a time when structural expansion in their sectors of the economy had gone too far, or when industrial depressions were permitted to proceed unchecked. The dilemma we confront as between stabilized incomes to primary producers and flexible structural adjustment in the world economy is quite as important in its implications for our time as that between full employment and inflation; and so is the dilemma presented by confronting the powerful and understandable desire of under-developed countries to industrialize, with the requirements for balance in the composition of world production. A solution of the former dilemma, like that between full employment and inflation, requires analytically, as well as in the formation of policy, a structure of thought which embraces within it the social and political forces operative, as well as those which are more strictly economic.

To say that the variables which determine the character and rate of structural adjustment in world trade are partially planned is not to say that they are totally planned. Here, as in other areas of economic analysis, it appears to be of importance that the debate is not conducted simply in terms of planning versus no planning. The alternatives left open to us by history appear to be not whether planning will take place, but what kind of planning; and, in particular, we must establish, within the limits of our substantive goals, what maximum areas of economic life can be left to operate on the basis of individual and private institutional decisions. More than two decades of reflection on the problem of maintaining domestic full employment by means of conscious national policy have led those concerned to seek to minimize the number and the directness of controls necessary to achieve that goal. Economists would now emphasize the potentialities of fiscal controls over the size and distribution of income as opposed to direct control over private investment or even counter-cyclical investment by governments. An equivalent approach to structural equilibrium in world trade, dynamically conceived, would appear to require the development within the non-Communist world of some practical, flexible, minimum instrument for inter-governmental examination and management of the framework of world trade. If no other force were operative, the acceptance of government and inter-governmental responsibility for determining an important margin of the flow of international investment carries with it the implication that some over-all view of appropriate capacity in sectors of the world economy, agreed upon among the various governments, is required.

I V

In the areas of income analysis and foreign trade the current theoretical formulations, in part at least, bear directly on issues of policy, although a case can be made for the necessity of widening the theoretical frame within which they are conventionally approached. In the case of the economic development of under-developed countries, the need for a new frame, wider than that incorporated in conventional analyses, would be generally admitted. As pointed out elsewhere, the systematic treatment of economic development requires a return to some of the issues of classical theory which have been set aside in recent decades.[1]

It is, perhaps, worth noting the manner in which John Stuart Mill dealt with this matter and formally disposed of the issues of economic development from a primitive base; for the terms he used are not very different from those of most economists down, let us say, to Harrod. Mill's view illustrates the extent to which economists have at once been aware of the problems of development from a primitive base, and have more or less consciously by-passed that range of problems in order to concentrate on those believed relevant to more advanced countries:[2]

From the preceding exposition it appears that the limit to the increase of production is two-fold: from deficiency of capital, or of land. Production comes to a pause either because the effective desire of accumulation is not sufficient to give rise to any further increase of capital, or because, however disposed the possessors of surplus income may be to save a portion of it, the limited land at the disposal of the community does not permit additional capital to be employed with such a return as would be an equivalent to them for their abstinence.

In countries where the principle of accumulation is as weak as it is in the various nations of Asia, the desideratum economically considered is an increase of industry, or the effective desire of accumulation. The means are, first, a better government: more complete security of property; moderate taxes, and freedom from arbitrary exaction under the name of taxes; a more permanent and more advantageous tenure of land, securing to the cultivator

[1] See pp. 4–6 and 90–92.
[2] *Principles of Political Economy*, Book I, chap. x, paras. 1–2 (Laughlin edition, New York, 1898, pp. 144–5). It would be difficult but interesting to establish the extent to which the by-passing of the social and political conditions for optimum (or maximum) growth took place because a consideration of the determination of the 'effective desire of accumulation' and the degree of 'industry' would have required forms of analysis which do not permit the use of a simple profit or relative utility maximization hypothesis.

as far as possible the undivided benefits of the industry, skill, and economy he may exert. Secondly, improvements of the public intelligence. Thirdly, the introduction of foreign arts, which raise the returns derivable from additional capital to a rate corresponding to the low strength of the desire of accumulation.

But there are other countries, and England at the head of them, in which neither the spirit of industry nor the effective desire of accumulation need any encouragement. In these countries there would never be any deficiency of capital, if its increase were never checked or brought to a stand by too great a diminution of its returns.

It was thus that classical economics largely ruled out a consideration of what are referred to in Part I as the propensities, by assuming that their relative strength and course of change did not constitute a significant problem for more advanced countries. On the other hand, Mill, and the economists who followed him, have been aware of the special case raised by societies where 'the effective desire of accumulation', the 'spirit of industry', the level of 'public intelligence', and the state of the arts was low. Mill's observations on the nations of Asia in the nineteenth century are a thoroughly relevant basic statement of policy for the practitioners of Point Four.

The issues posed by economic development may be grouped, like the issues treated in Part I of this volume, under three broad headings: the determinants of population growth; the determinants of the growth of capital; and (Chaps. IV–VI), the appropriate composition of current investment. Included here, of course, as in the formal analysis, must be the qualitative elements attaching both to population and to capital. The growing current literature addressed to the practical problems of economic development reveals an awareness of the fundamental determinants of population and capital growth, including the relevance to them of the social and political framework. Simultaneously, this literature reveals the inadequacy of the methods of analysis and the data thus far available.

The recent United Nations report *Measures for the Economic Development of Under-developed Countries* is an excellent case in point. It poses admirably the issues involved in economic development, on lines not very different from those of Mill in the passage quoted above. The substantive analysis begins (Chap. III), with a statement of the pre-conditions of economic development, emphasizing the necessity for what Mill would have called a strong 'effective desire of accumulation' and what is referred to in the course of this book as strong propensities to seek material advance and to generate and accept innovations:[1]

Economic progress will not occur unless the atmosphere is favourable to it. The people of a country must desire progress, and their social, economic, legal, and political institutions must be favourable to it. . . . Economic progress will not be desired in the community where the people do not realize that progress is possible. Progress occurs only where people believe that man can, by conscious effort, master nature.

The argument then proceeds to the forms of economic organization required to implement 'a desire for progress'; to a consideration of the role of technology, and the acceptance of innovations of a character appropriate to the stage of development; and to the problem of domestic capital formation, along lines not very different from Mrs. Robinson's treatment of the 'supply of finance'. Population growth is then examined, and the question of priorities in planning; finally, the analysis comes to rest on the relations of the under-developed countries to the world trading area, with special emphasis on the terms of trade and the import of external capital.

Although the Report abounds in *ad hoc*, wise prescriptions covering policy in various phases of the development process, its major end product is a calculation of the size of the flow of external capital required in order to permit an annual rate of growth of output of $2\frac{1}{2}$ per cent. for the under-developed areas. In terms of the central relationship used in Part I of this book, the United Nations experts largely took the propensities, the quality of the working force, and the productivity of capital investment as given and relatively fixed. Within that framework they defined the likely increase

---

[1] *Measures for the Economic Development of Under-developed Countries*, p. 13.

in the population, working force, and scale of investment financed from domestic resources in under-developed areas. Against this background they then calculated the scale of additional capital flows required to raise output at the chosen rate, which they took as a reasonable minimum standard for progress.

It would be widely agreed that the issues raised in this report are the relevant issues and the key calculation is both imaginative and interesting. However, it would also be agreed that social scientists have only begun to consider how the issues raised may be effectively handled in terms of public policy. The contrast between this United Nations report and that presented by the group of experts who reported on the problem of full employment is striking. The latter, working against the background of several decades of accumulated economic doctrine and practical experience, were able to emerge with a clear-cut, essentially quantitative programme covering the short-period issues of income control in advanced countries. Although it may be legitimately questioned whether their programme was not overly clear-cut and too quantitative in its expression, the ability of a group of economists to formulate and to agree on a programme of this kind was a tribute to the stage of advancement in an important part of the body of thought in the social sciences.

Aside from its recommendation concerning capital flows, achieved by making heroic, arbitrary assumptions, the Economic Development Report confines itself largely to posing questions rather than answering them. The question of capital growth in relation to population increase is, for example, clearly raised. The experts note: 'The rate of growth of population is now first and foremost a function of the extent to which medical knowledge is made available to the people.'[1] They note, further, that merely to maintain the standard of living of a growing population, with existing techniques, absorbs a high proportion of the internal savings of under-developed countries:

The cost of population in this sense is high. Estimates of the proportion of the national income which must be saved in order to

[1] Ibid., p. 47.

provide capital for a 1 per cent increase of population vary between 2 per cent and 5 per cent of the national income. Hence, an under-developed country, in which population is increasing at the not uncommon rate of $1\frac{1}{2}$ per cent per annum, probably needs nearly as much as it is normally likely to save, merely to cope with population growth; under these circumstances, it can do little to raise the average standard of living.[1]

Refusing to take the pessimistic view that economic development in under-developed areas must inevitably be dissipated in population growth, they note, nevertheless, that 'there are many countries where further increase of population must, all things considered, be found to be an adverse factor'. And, true to the specialist tradition of the modern social scientists, they place this momentous issue of policy—the reduction of birth-rates—before the Population Commission of the United Nations. The latter organ should, clearly, concern itself with the problem of birth-rates; but the economist cannot, in good conscience, divest himself of a partial responsibility at least, in this range of mixed social science problems.

How, in fact, can one institute a policy in a backward area designed to reduce the rate of growth of population without a reduction in allocations to public health? How does one calculate the appropriate outlays, in a given backward area, for public health as opposed to alternative forms of investment? These are the real and painful issues posed. Merely to pose them clearly is an important contribution. They are issues, however, to which the social sciences now offer no easy answer.

The report considers, in similar exploratory terms, other issues of choice in the allocation of resources: the issues of choice between consumption and investment; investment in human beings and investment in material capital; investment in public works and other productive activities; between autarchy and foreign trade; and between industry and agriculture. Leaving aside the question of choice between consumption and investment, which is a fundamental matter of social judgement as to the rate at which material progress is sought as against a minimum tolerable standard of living,

[1] *Measures for the Economic Development of Under-developed Countries*, p. 47.

the other choices all involve some conception of the appropriate balance of investment in different sectors of a developing economy. The issues posed by this presentation of choices demand a kind of sectoral analysis of the appropriate composition of investment in societies undergoing change which is not yet far advanced.

If one looks more deeply into the problem of the composition of investment, not merely in terms of broad sectors of the economy as have the United Nations experts, but in terms of particular commodities, an issue is raised which demands a form of analysis of equal importance to developed and to under-developed countries. As noted earlier, the character of post-war world-trade problems has directed the attention of governments and economists to the long-run prospects for the requirements and the supply of particular basic foodstuffs and raw materials. On the other hand, the under-developed areas are impressed with the irregular history of demand and prices in relation to supply for these basic foodstuffs and raw materials. This reading of lessons from history constitutes an important general inhibition on under-developed countries to commit their investment resources to increased output of basic commodities, just as, in another aspect, it limits American capabilities to deal with the threat of inflation. Quite aside from the question of the relative productivity of investment in these commodities, as opposed to investment in domestic industry within under-developed countries, there is the issue of whether the under-developed countries should shield themselves from the historic irregularity of income to be derived from the production of basic commodities. From the point of view of the world, it is obviously necessary that these basic commodities be produced in adequate supply and at high productivity. The problem which jointly confronts the developed and under-developed countries is how production can be undertaken without resulting in the overshooting and prolonged price and income depressions which have marked this form of activity in the past.

It seems inevitable that the world trading area will have to establish a common view of future demand requirements in certain directions, generate the capital necessary to produce supplies on an adequate scale, and make guarantees covering substantial time periods concerning the income to be derived from the furnishing of such marginal supplies. The idea of buffer stocks, to maintain a smooth flow and a stable price level for such commodities is by no means new. It must be placed, however, in the framework of a longer-run calculation of requirements and longer-run guarantees of income. Moreover, the development of basic commodity production in the backward areas must be envisaged in terms of a progressive advance in the stages of processing accomplished within the producing region, which would raise the relative income available to the backward areas, as their general economic capabilities increase.

The Economic Development Report makes some useful observations on the principles which should govern the allocations of resources:[1]

Economic analysis provides two general principles for the use of resources. One is the marginal principle. Resources should be used in such a way that a transfer of marginal units from one use to another could not increase welfare. This tautology is simple and evident; nevertheless it is frequently ignored in practice. Its most important corollary is that one should not think of any single industry or economic activity as more important than any other, and should not therefore concentrate all resources in one particular part of the economy. Progress must be made on all fronts simultaneously. In planning for a particular industry or activity, one must not put resources into it beyond the point where a transfer of marginal units to some other activity would increase total welfare.

These generalizations are to be considered in the light of the second principle which economic analysis provides. This second principle arises from the fact that large movements of resources within the economy will have effects which are disproportionately different from marginal movements. In consequence, the planner must satisfy himself not only that further marginal movements would serve no useful purpose, but also that there is nothing to be gained by large movements of resources, amounting to a considerable alteration in the structure of the economy. The first of these conditions is often satisfied where the second is not.

[1] *Measures for the Economic Development of Under-developed Countries*, p. 49.

This unexceptionable pair of general observations needs to be supplemented by a third perspective on the allocation of resources, namely, a view of optimum sectoral capacity over periods of time. As noted in Chapter IV, this approach is simply a dynamic version of 'the marginal principle'. With a full consciousness of the likely errors to be made in analyses of this type, but with a consciousness also that judgement will be made implicitly if not explicitly, we must seek to generate a conception of the implications, for particular sectors of the economy, of the rate of industrial advance being pursued over all and within particular countries. So long as a high proportion of the investment of the world is determined by the judgement of governmental and inter-governmental bodies, as opposed to that of private individuals or institutions, this issue cannot be evaded.

Two other factors argue for the urgent development of this form of sectoral analysis. One is the difficulty of generating an adequate flow of international capital; the other is the probable nature of the investment process in under-developed countries.

With respect to the first, it is noteworthy that both sets of United Nations experts, one operating from the perspective of the structural distortion of world trade, the other from the point of view of the economic development of under-developed areas, emerged with the suggestion that very large sums of capital pass regularly from the more developed to the less developed areas.

Given the peculiarly important security and political role of the under-developed countries in the balance of the world's power, it is not at all impossible that considerable sums may be allocated to them for general development purposes, on non-economic grounds. This is, however, an inadequate long-run basis for determining the scale and constitution of international capital movements.

Leaving aside political and security motives, there are at least five perspectives in which foreign lending might be judged to the national advantage of the lending country:

(1) as a means of sustaining national income without making (or at least while postponing) structural adjustments

in respect of the constitution of domestic production, or in the distribution of income flows between investment and consumption; (2) as a means of developing enlarged or cheapened production of particular commodities; (3) as a means of developing increased supply in those areas to which it is expected to be easiest to make financial payments; (4) as a means of accelerating the rise of income in foreign areas, in order to increase their ability to absorb imports; (5) as a means, in general, of enjoying the indirect consequences of a world economy in which investment was directed toward the most profitable projects.

In the foreseeable future, as well as the present, motives 2, 3, and 4 appear to be the strongest likely motives in inducing nations to enlarge their exports of capital. And with respect to 2 and 3, what interests the capital-exporting nation is not simply the general rate of increase of production induced in the under-developed area, but the character of that production.

In a world of scarcities it may be judged proper that the interests of the lending and borrowing nations be, somehow, married. This does not, of course, mean that under-developed countries should concentrate their energies on a short-run increase of output in the basic materials most urgently required, without reference to the general balance of their development programme or to the longer future. Nor does it mean that all lending from developed countries should be tied in terms of particular projects. It does mean that the developed countries and the under-developed countries must work out a clear and common perspective concerning the relative future requirements for particular commodities and must engage in negotiations which will give to the under-developed countries some guarantee that the real income obtainable from investment in foodstuffs and raw materials will be reasonably stable at a level which would constitute a fair rate of return, as opposed to the return available from investment in alternative directions.

The requirement for increased thought on the appropriate direction of investment in under-developed countries is heightened by one aspect of the post-war experience of the

International Bank. The Bank's ability to lend has not only been inhibited by the diffidence of American sources of finance and by the hesitation of some governments to borrow in dollars and thus to accept commitment for dollar interest charges and repayment. The Bank has, simply, not been presented with a sufficient number of well-designed, businesslike proposals. Its agents have occasionally presented a droll picture, combing the world for serious projects at a time when many countries are eager for and in need of capital imports. There is a tendency for economists to think in terms of a well-balanced general development programme. This is, of course, enormously important. Ultimately, however, domestic economic development must be conceived as a series of particular projects, which, in detail, as well as in broad pattern, yield a more or less rational and self-sustaining structure. There are large responsibilities here for the underdeveloped countries, and for the international authorities which might assist in the formulation of projects. Progress will require advance, in analysis as well as in policy, into the relationship between over-all rates of growth and optimum sectoral levels of capacity.

The need to develop this form of analysis is heightened by the probable institutional evolution of many of the underdeveloped areas. It has been a minor irony of the post-war experience of the United States that its agents, both in Europe and in under-developed countries, have found themselves urging an increased role for government planning in the economies of the areas where the American interest was engaged.[1] This was the consequence of no conspiracy among New Dealers or Socialists who found their way into American foreign operations. This was a realistic response to the nature of the societies where a sustained rate of economic development was sought in the American interest. It is easy to forget that, before the Industrial Revolution came to western Europe and the United States it was preceded by several

[1] See, for a not untypical example, the recommendation of the Bell Report, that a Philippine Development Corporation be established, *Report to the President of the United States by the Economic Survey Mission to the Philippines* (Washington, D.C., 1950), p. 4; also the analysis of Philippine investment over the post-war years, pp. 8–12.

centuries of commercial and early industrial development, which had formed a class of private entrepreneurs prepared morally, intellectually, and technically, to exploit the potentialities of the innovations that came forward. The middle class, in a sense, was the most important of the economic innovations of modern times; and it is not susceptible of rapid diffusion throughout the under-developed regions of the contemporary world.

Although their historical traditions differ, under-developed regions may well require a stage where the fundamental decisions of risk and innovation are taken in large part by governments rather than by private individuals and institutions.

In the longer run, of course, it is altogether possible that these regions will move away from government control toward a dispersion of authority in the making of key economic decisions. Something of this process happened rather quickly in nineteenth-century Japan, where, however, a substantial ruling class led the way to industrialization in both political life and the private sectors of the economy. A similar evolution in other under-developed areas will depend, however, on the generation of a new and responsible class adequately prepared to perform the requisite political, social, and economic functions.

If, over the foreseeable future, we must count on governmental authorities bearing not only a large part of the burden of exporting capital to under-developed countries, but also of allocating investment resources within under-developed countries, then the case for the elaboration of a systematic analysis of the optimum relationship of the sectors to over-all growth is much enhanced. If efficient private capital markets were operating, we might place a greater reliance on the profit motive, and trust that, by its power, resources would flow roughly in the appropriate directions. So long as private capital markets do not operate normally, however, a great urgency attaches to the increase of our knowledge concerning the appropriate directions of investment, dynamically conceived, under various circumstances and stages of progress.

V

It may thus be concluded that the complex and devious processes of history are forcing democratic societies to form conscious policy concerning issues which economists in recent decades have been able to set aside as irrelevant or self-resolving. What might be called the pure Keynesian hope—that the intervention of governments in democratic societies might be limited in this century mainly to the maintenance, through remote and indirect controls, of an appropriate level of effective demand—has been belied by events and by trends some of which, at least, do not appear reversible in the fore-seeable future. In different ways this appears true of the political economy of full employment, foreign trade, and economic development in the post-war setting.

If the short-period formulations generated in recent decades are an insufficient analytic framework for our times, they incorporate a spirit and an aspiration which should not be lost in the elaborations that must come. Keynes in particular was dominated by a desire to defeat the notion that the underlying individualistic moral and ethical values of the Western world must be lost if the economic problems of this century were to be conquered. He believed it within the wit of man to design conceptions and institutions which incorporated their values and which would permit a reasonable control of the economic environment while maintaining wide areas of individual choice in economic decisions and a wide area of human liberty in the broadest sense. Serious, indeed, are the issues posed for democratic societies by the need to draw a line of policy between full employment and chronic inflation and by the need to consider consciously the appropriate pattern of investment, as well as its scale. Their solution will require changes in outlook and economic analysis of a major kind, among economists and other social scientists, among politicians and civil servants, and, ultimately, among the peoples of the democratic world. These are changes no less profound than those wrought by the Keynesian revolution, which has brought the majority of men to the view that the short-run level of income is a matter that lies within the compass of conscious policy. And unless these newer issues are faced they will constitute a threat to relatively free social and political structures. They cannot be ignored with impunity any more than could the depression after 1929.

Even where the solution of these problems demands enlarged functions for the State, social scientists must struggle to establish formulations which will lead to techniques of minimum direct intervention. There is nothing in the world's history since the eighteenth century to belie that deep scepticism of human ability to wield concentrated power, economic or otherwise, which helped shape the American Constitution and which underlies, in one form or another, democratic societies everywhere. Government and intergovernmental policies which will tend to produce an appropriate balance of investment in the sectors of the world economy need not be synonymous with total government control over the direction of investment outlays. The devices of indirect influence can be fruitful, especially if action is taken before crisis situations emerge.

Further, there must be faith that intelligent democratic action is related to the degree to which problems are understood and the public is informed. In the end, it is in this underlying function of perception and education that the social scientist most importantly serves society. On this view he cannot afford to lag in his scientific formulations too far behind the events and problems of the active world.

PART III
SOME FURTHER APPLICATIONS
XI
LEADING SECTORS IN ECONOMIC GROWTH

I

CARRYING forward the argument of Chapter IV, this chapter probes the following problem: How shall we go about analysing the relation between economic growth in general and economic growth in particular sectors of an economy?

The question is of theoretical, practical, and historical interest. In theory it requires piercing the veil of present growth formulations which either segregate autonomous investment from investment via the accelerator, or which proceed by that form of 'endogenous' analysis which makes behaviour in period Two a function of circumstances given in period One. In practice, it raises the question of how, in some arbitrary, optimum sense, investment resources should be allocated. Since governments and other units in the economy increasingly make investment decisions in a macro- rather than a micro-perspective, the classic (but not necessarily optimum) solution to this problem—let the private capital markets decide—is not available for a wide range of investment outlays in our time. In history this problem suggests that our knowledge of the past would be usefully increased by studying systematically the pattern of the interacting relationship over time of total and sectoral growth.

II

The most cursory examination of the growth patterns of different economies, viewed against a background of general historical information, reveals two simple facts:

1. Growth-rates in the various sectors of the economy differ widely over any given period of time;[1]

---

[1] See, for example, A. F. Burns, *Production Trends in the United States Since 1870*, New York, 1934, especially pp. 50–62.

2. In some meaningful sense, over-all growth appears to be based, at certain periods, on the direct and indirect consequence of extremely rapid growth in certain particular key sectors.

There may be a symmetry, then, between investment patterns in relation to business cycles and investment patterns in relation to growth. In both cases there appear to be certain leading lines of investment, whose scale and productivity—including more distant secondary consequences—drive the economy as a whole forward. But, as discussed below, the leading growth sectors and the leading cyclical sectors are not necessarily identical.

In common-sense terms, the notion of leading sectors in economic growth is familiar enough. The role of the cotton industry in sustaining over-all British growth from, say, 1780 to 1840, is one of the stories on which we are all brought up. And, when cotton decelerates, the domestic and foreign rail booms of the 1840's and 1850's lift pig iron. Pig iron gives way to steel as a leading sector by the seventies and eighties; and so on down through the chemical, electrical, and light-engineering industries, the latter being perhaps the true hero of mid-century Britain, having sustained both the R.A.F. in war and the export drive since 1945.

In American economic history, somewhat more compressed in time, there is also to be observed this classic sequence of leading sectors. But, even more sharply than in the case of Britain, the western railroads of the third quarter of the century (in turn induced by the rising world wheat demand) were the instrument for launching the American industrial evolution, yielding as it did a modern centralized iron industry, and then, in the seventies and eighties, a steel industry. Like the other major industrial powers of the twentieth century, the United States then developed the chemical, electrical, and light-engineering industries, with a unique role, however, for the automobile and durable consumer goods in general, in the first half of the twentieth century.

Such stately sequences of growth, carried forward by leading sectors, are to be observed not only in the well-rounded major industrial economies—including, say, Russia, Germany, and France, as well as the United States and the United Kingdom—but also in the more specialized successful economies, for example New Zealand and Sweden.

Simkin's study of New Zealand tracks out with precision how the growth of that economy, generally dependent upon exports, was touched off in the 1860's by gold and was sustained thereafter by wool, wheat, and dairy products. In turn, the exploitation of this sequence of profitable possibilities led, given New Zealand's propensities, to considerable industrial development over a wide front. In the case of Sweden, similarly, timber in the sixties and seventies gave way, with Sweden's strong propensities,[1] to the rapid growth in pulp and paper towards the end of the century; and the vigorous exploitation of iron ore from the 1890's led on to the modern Swedish metal and engineering industries of this century. In both cases the development of export commodities, including their transport requirements, helped induce a secondary development of domestic industry, partially to meet the demands of new urban populations.

The leading sectors need not, then, repeat the classic pattern of Great Britain: cotton, pig iron, steel, engineering, and so on. They may be based on the effective exploitation of natural resources, in relation to the requirements of the world market, as well as on a succession of breakthroughs in the application of science to economic purposes.

Leaving aside the raw material and foodstuff sectors, the growth process of the modern world over the past two centuries appears to have been based on the elaboration of a finite number of major technical innovations on which leading industrial sectors are based: in textiles, metals, engineering, chemicals, and so on. In Britain, notably, but also in the

---

[1] Since, in this form of analysis, population is partially determined by the propensities, the use of the phrase 'strong propensities' must immediately be modified in two respects: (a) too strong a propensity to have children may weaken, not strengthen, the process of economic growth; (b) immigration and emigration must be allowed for. From the point of view of the world economy immigration and emigration may be largely explained and treated endogenously; but for many forms of national economic analysis it may be useful to treat population movements as a given.

United States and Western Europe, each was more or less fully exploited as it emerged over the horizon of realistic possibilities, although Germany and the United States enjoyed some of the advantages of the relative late-comer. The early stages of application of each of these technical breakthroughs, involving radical change in production functions, yielded a high productivity return from investment input, in real terms; further refinements in technique, after the initial breakthrough, appear to have yielded diminishing returns.

Discounting the other factors affecting relative growth-rates—notably, richness of natural resources and the propensities—over-all rates of growth have been partially determined by the timing of the application of these major technical possibilities. Japan and Russia, for example, have, in the twentieth century, been exploiting in much closer time sequence than did (say) Britain the accumulated backlog of technical possibilities. And this virtual simultaneity of growth in leading sectors is one explanation for the high over-all rates of growth they have enjoyed. Put another way, the yields available from the pool of applied science have been higher for the late-comers than for those who exploited the flow of possibilities more or less as they became available. The late-comers were in the position of being able to exploit simultaneously the early, high-productivity stages of past as well as current technical breakthroughs; whereas the older countries were enjoying the high-productivity stage of only the latest technical breakthroughs.[1]

III

Assuming that, at particular periods, different sectors play a strategic role in the determination of the over-all growth-rate of economies, how can we go about analysing in tolerable order the inordinately complicated process by which they have their effect?

[1] This element in the rapid rate of growth of late-comers is independent of the more familiar partial explanation; namely, that the age composition of capital is lower for late-comers and incorporates, in higher proportion, best current technical practice. This factor would operate even if diminishing returns did not apply—as it apparently does—in the technological evolution of particular sectors.

It may prove useful arbitrarily to divide the sectors of an economy into three classes:

1. *Primary Growth Sectors*, where possibilities for innovation or for the exploitation of newly profitable or hitherto unexplored resources yield a growth-rate markedly higher than the average for the economy. The cotton industry of Britain in the decades after 1780 would fall into this category, as would most of the other key sectors cited above.

2. *Supplementary Growth Sectors*, where rapid advance occurs in direct response to—or as a requirement of—advance in the primary growth sectors. These sectors may have to be tracked many stages back into the economy, as the Leontief input–output models would suggest. Arbitrarily taking, for example, the western American railways of the nineteenth century as a primary growth sector, the rapid expansion in the iron, coal, and steel industries might be properly regarded as supplementary growth phenomena.

3. *Derived Growth Sectors*, where advance occurs in some fairly steady relation to the growth of total real income, population, industrial production, or some other over-all, modestly increasing parameter. Food output in relation to population, housing in relation to family formation are classic derived relations of this order. But more complex links which might be allocated to this category exist. After a sector has gone through its rapid growth stage it may well settle down to a reasonably stable relation to over-all growth, as has steel in recent times in the more industrialized countries.

In the nineteenth century primary and supplementary growth sectors generally derived their high momentum from the introduction and diffusion of changes in the cost–supply environment (in turn, of course, partially influenced by demand changes); while the derived growth sectors are linked essentially to changes in demand (while subject also to continuing changes in production functions of a less dramatic character). In the twentieth century, with the new role in growth of durable consumer goods and services, leading sectors have been more substantially linked, in rich societies, to impulses arising from the side of demand.

Even a shallow experience of the process of growth will suggest the arbitrariness of these categories and the complexity of applying them to particular economies at particular time periods.

First, there is the problem of establishing empirically what is 'a primary growth sector'. If one makes the definition a matter of ultimate, philosophic causality, the problem is insoluble. There is a meaningful sense, for example, which we all would recognize, in which the western American railways of the nineteenth century were a primary growth sector from (say) 1850 to 1885. But they, in turn, were induced, in large part, by a rise in the world price of wheat, reflecting, in turn, an increase in population in Europe pressing against existing grain capacity. In turn, again, the rise in European population has its own complex history and causal process. While it is extremely important to recognize the complex causal chains that lie behind a given economic development, it is still possible, in a sensible arbitrary way, to isolate for different areas and time periods those sectors where the exploitation of possibilities for innovation or for developing newly profitable or hitherto unexplored resources yields ramified, creative economic results. If we are prepared to be arbitrary with respect to the chain of causation, 'primary sectors' can usefully be defined for particular areas and limited time periods.

It should be noted that while one would expect higher than average growth-rates in primary sectors, their isolation cannot be established mechanically by a simple examination of growth-rates. It is altogether possible, and even likely, that certain of the supplementary sectors will have higher growth-rates than primary sectors. It is the supplementary consequences of its expansion rather than merely its growth-rate which define a primary growth sector.

In addition to the arbitrariness of the primary growth-sector concept, there are some puzzling complexities of identification. A given sector may have, within it, for example, both primary and derived elements. The modern oil industry reflects in its growth-rate both the consequences of exploiting important new technological developments and a high marginal income elasticity of demand. This admixture of demand and supply influences is likely to operate in many cases, as, indeed, it did in the classic among primary sectors, cotton-textile manufacture of the early nineteenth century. Not only may dual forces operate on a sector's growth curve, but they may not be independent over time: a fall in price due to cost changes can produce an irreversible shift in the position and slope of its related demand curve. These difficulties would complicate and, in some cases, possibly rule out an exact statistical filling of the empty boxes. They are unlikely, how-ever, to prevent a meaningful identification of leading sectors and an approximate measurement of their impact on supple-mentary sectors over limited time periods.

There is a further weakness in conception which transcends arbitrariness and complexity; namely, the fundamentally interacting characteristic of the growth process. Wheat lands may lead to railroads, and railroads to iron and steel; but the railroads, having been built, in turn generate an endless series of further developments with a life and vitality of their own. The railroads may force the development of an engineer-ing industry, for example, from which flow many other in-dustrial innovations. A steel industry devoted heavily to the manufacture of rails, in the first instance, may help gener-ate, by its existence, other applications of steel—to bridges, ships, machinery—when the rail demand falls off. Like other forms of history, economic history is a seamless web within which we can only trace out limited chains of causation.

There is no easy formula for coping with the analysis of external economies on a macro-basis; but the successive application of these sectoral categories to particular limited time periods may give us fresh insights both into the process of growth in the past and into the problem of planning wisely future growth, if we are prepared to allow, for each time period examined, a range of external economy effects, almost certainly not derivable, *ex ante*, from the initial data, as well as for changes in the propensities, which are not wholly endo-genous economic phenomena.

Technically, this approach might permit us to unite tools

of analysis, independently developed and now proceeding in separate compartments with little communication. First, there are the historians, who have investigated how it came about that major new technological or resource possibilities were brought to application and primary growth sectors were created at particular times and places. An understanding of this phase of the whole growth process cannot evade some concern with scientific and technical history, and the human, institutional, and market environments of particular industries and societies. Second, there are those who are studying the functional relations as among the sectors of economies, with given production functions, above all Professor Leontief and his band of colleagues and students. Their measurements and insights might permit a reasonably precise analysis of the evolution of supplementary growth sectors over limited time periods. Third, this approach might open for empirical investigation a useful version of the accelerator by developing a body of systematic knowledge on the relation between overall growth parameters and capacity requirements in the slower-moving sectors of economies.

This way of looking at the economy would, then, break into the interacting process of growth at the level of key sectors. For a succession of limited time periods—the decade might be a useful unit—it would consider the primary and supplementary consequences of growth in the key sectors; it would then track out the response of sectors to the increase in real income generated in these more rapidly moving sectors, as well as the response to growth forces determined by more remote factors—notably population changes; it would, finally, allow in each period (and carry over as a given into the next period) external economy effects and changes in the propensities.

IV

We consider now the relation between this mode of analysis and three large questions: the business cycle, the capital–output ratio, and the strategy of investment allocation in underdeveloped economies.

As suggested in Chapter V the historical succession of business cycles is best regarded as the direct and secondary consequence of surges forward in certain leading lines of investment in the world economy. In each cycle the direction of the leading lines appears rational in that it was determined by profit possibilities created by the pressure of demand on capacity and/or by the potentialities of available innovations. But the scale of investment in the leading lines is somewhat irrational in the sense that, if the investors had known what the combined effect of their individual decisions would be, they would have invested less in the leading lines. In macro-terms, irrationality thus consists during a boom in a scale of expansion in capacity beyond that appropriate to the level required and made profitable by the existing level of output and its rate of growth. Thus from cycle to cycle (and, roughly, from decade to decade) the character of the leading lines changes. Over-expansion in the boom appears generally to exhaust the possibility of a sector as a leading line for a period longer than one cycle.

How do the leading lines of investment in business cycles relate to the three categories of sectors defined above for purposes of growth analysis?

It is evident that the leading growth sectors cannot be simply equated with leading cyclical sectors. While, on the average, a high rate of investment may be maintained in a leading growth sector for several cycles running, it is unlikely that this sector will in fact dominate a succession of booms. It has been more normal in cyclical history to see investment shift from a leading industrial growth sector (say, cotton-textile manufacture) to a supplementary sector (say, cotton acreage), to an induced sector (say, housing). No such pleasing symmetry of sequence is, of course, to be found in modern economic history. The point is that the leading lines in a cyclical expansion have depended on where profit is believed to lie; profitability may be created in induced sectors by prior disproportionate expansion in the more rapidly growing sectors, yielding increases in total output and real income which, for a time, may make investment in (say) housing, agriculture, or race tracks more profitable than (say) textiles or steel.

V

Thus there is no automatic equivalence between profitability as decreed in free markets by cost–price relationships, and the maximum real rate of return, in terms of the full consequences of an act of investment for the rate of growth. This lack of equivalence has long been recognized in economic theory and in the practice of even the most capitalist of societies. Where, for example, railroads and other public improvements promised important secondary advantages, not imputable to the private investor, the government stepped in, even in nineteenth-century United States.[1] More generally, it can be said that the pattern of demand set up by sovereign consumers' tastes does not necessarily result in patterns of profitability, and of private investment outlays, which maximize the rate of growth of output. This does not imply, of course, that the maximum rate of growth is, in any sense, a criterion superior to consumers' tastes, as reflected in free markets. It does suggest, however, that maximization propositions under dynamic growth conditions are likely to be quite different from those under static, or short-period, assumptions.

The shifting sectoral locus of profitability over time may help to explain why the over-all rates of growth may vary from decade to decade under conditions where the total proportion of income invested appears relatively stable.[2] Investment in different sectors may have differing productivity effects on the level of output. In his comparative analysis of Soviet and American growth-rates,[3] for example, Norman Kaplan finds that it is probably the direction rather than the scale of Soviet investment which determines its higher industrial growth-rate, notably the relative concentration of

[1] For an analysis of the types of railroad which required (and received) public financing, see the unpublished thesis of Dr. Paul Cootner, 'Transport Innovation and Economic Development: The Case of the U.S. Steam Railroads', M.I.T., 1953.

[2] See, for example, the interesting calculations of Jacob Schmookler, 'The Changing Efficiency of the American Economy, 1869–1938', *The Review of Economics and Statistics*, August 1952.

[3] 'Capital Formation and Allocation', *Soviet Economic Growth*, chapter 2, A. Bergson (ed.), Evanston, Ill., and White Plains, New York, 1953.

Soviet investment in heavy industry, with a low capital–output ratio. It is likely that, when the matter is fully investigated, we will find that the discontinuity in the rate of growth of U.S. real income *per capita*, established by Kuznets,[1] is related to changes in the character and productivity of investment from period to period.[2]

Conceived thus dynamically, the capital–output ratio becomes extremely complex. The time relationship between a given volume of investment input and its consequence for real output must be sorted out with care, taking account of at least three elements:

(*a*) *The period of gestation of the investment.* A shift, on balance, to investment with a longer period of gestation may, over any short period of time examined, impart an illusory increase in the capital–output ratio, which might disappear if a longer time period were allowed in measurement.

(*b*) *The time period over which the investment yields its service.* A shift, on balance, to investment with a longer period of life imparts an increase in the capital–output ratio, assuming that the proportion of capital services to net output is unchanged. Thus changes in the capital–output ratio must be considered both in the light of the changing life of equipment and the changing degree of capital intensity in production functions.

(*c*) *External economies.* The secondary and more remote influences of a given act of investment may be decisive to the growth process (and to the rationale for the investment) although virtually incapable of measurement by present tools.

VI

This sectoral view of growth bears as well on the problem of prescribing for economic growth. Professor C. P. Kindleberger has suggested that the proper approach to the problem of generating more rapid economic development

---

[1] S. Kuznets, *National Income: A Summary of Findings*, New York, 1946.

[2] The tables organized by Brinley Thomas suggest for exploration at least the possibility that periods of slower U.S. growth may be associated with high levels of investment in residential housing, in turn related to surges of immigration. See, especially, B. Thomas, *Migration and Economic Growth*, Cambridge, 1954.

may lie in the isolation of strategic points of attack.[1] The question arises as to whether a sectoral approach to the growth process is likely to help us in defining with any precision the strategic sectors: that is, those sectors of an economy where additional units of investment will yield the maximum increase in output, when the full range of its primary and more remote consequences is taken into account.

It is, of course, impossible to prescribe in a vacuum. But it may prove a useful exercise for planners in under-developed areas to seek to identify leading growth sectors, in the sense in which that concept is here defined. It may prove to be the case, for any given period, that a concentration of effort on one or two sectors in a given economy might drag along important supplementary sectors; and that consequent increases in real income may induce the generalized expansion of the slower-growing sectors required for balanced growth.

The identification of leading sectors is by no means simple. As noted earlier, what may be a supplementary sector for the world economy (e.g. an industrial raw material) may be a leading sector for a given region or country. Thus the strategic point of concentration may not lie in the exploitation of the classic sequence of industrial innovations but rather in the development and progressively more advanced processing of a natural resource.

Moreover, when one pierces deeper into the conditions likely to release the potentialities of a primary growth sector, one may end up with a problem of social and political policy, a problem of increasing the effective strength of the propensities. It is evident enough that the problem of accelerating economic growth in many areas lies not in a lack of natural resources or of potential innovations, but in too high a birthrate, a shortage of risk capital, a shortage of enterprising management, a shortage of technicians skilled in the application of new techniques, a shortage of competent and skilled labour, political leadership, and institutions whose objectives are inappropriate to economic growth.

At first blush it might appear that, when the growth of a

---

[1] *Review of Economics and Statistics*, November 1952, pp. 391–4. See also A. O. Hirschman, *The Strategy of Economic Development*, New Haven, Conn., 1958.

sector is obstructed by the propensities rather than the yields, concentrated action is inappropriate. The roots of the propensities lie in the institutions and value systems of societies; and their influence tends to be pervasive, although not necessarily uniform in their impact on the various sectors.

Nevertheless, there may be a meaningful sense in which a concentration of effort in key sectors may be appropriate to policy designed to shift the propensities as well as directly to exploit the yields. It may be important, for example, that the ablest technical and managerial talent be concentrated in the first instance in the key sectors, that resources devoted to labour training be not diffused too far, that applied scientists be induced to concentrate their efforts on certain key problems. In short, an acute sense of priority and a sense of the possibilities of exploiting self-reinforcing processes by powerful stimulus to strategic points might well suffuse the politics and sociology of economic growth as well as resource allocation in its more conventional sense.

XII

THE TAKE-OFF INTO
SELF-SUSTAINED GROWTH[1]

I

THIS chapter explores the following hypothesis: that the process of economic growth can usefully be regarded as centring on a relatively brief time interval of two or three decades when the economy and the society of which it is a part transform themselves in such ways that economic growth is, subsequently, more or less automatic. As indicated in Chapter IV (pp. 102–5) this decisive transformation is called the take-off.

The take-off is defined as the interval during which the rate of investment increases in such a way that real output *per capita* rises and this initial increase carries with it radical changes in production techniques and the disposition of income flows which perpetuate the new scale of investment and perpetuate thereby the rising trend in *per capita* output. Initial changes in method require that some group in the society have the will and the authority to install and diffuse new production techniques;[2] and a perpetuation of the growth process requires that such a leading group expand in authority and that the society as a whole respond to the impulses

[1] I wish to acknowledge with thanks the helpful criticisms in the development of this argument made by G. Baldwin, F. Bator, K. Berrill, A. Enthoven, E. E. Hagen, C. P. Kindleberger, L. Lefeber, W. Malenbaum, E. S. Mason, and M. F. Millikan.

[2] We shall set aside in this chapter the question of how new production techniques are generated from pure science and invention, a procedure which is legitimate, since we are examining the growth process in national (or regional) economies over relatively short periods. We shall largely set aside also the question of population pressure and size and quality of the working force, again because of the short period under examination; although, evidently, even over short periods, the rate of population increase will help determine the level of investment required to yield rising output *per capita* (see below, p. 278, note 2). By and large, this chapter is concerned with capital formation at a particular stage of economic growth; and of the array of propensities it deals only with the propensity to accept innovations and the propensity to seek material advance, the latter in relation to the supply of finance only.

set up by the initial changes, including the potentialities for external economies. Initial changes in the scale and direction of finance flows are likely to imply a command over income flows by new groups or institutions; and perpetuation of growth requires that a high proportion of the increment to real income during the take-off period be returned to productive investment. The take-off requires, therefore, a society prepared to respond actively to new possibilities for productive enterprise; and it is likely to require political, social, and institutional changes which will both perpetuate an initial increase in the scale of investment and result in the regular acceptance and absorption of innovations.

In short, this chapter is an effort to clarify the economics of industrial revolution when such a revolution is conceived of narrowly with respect to time and broadly with respect to changes in production functions.

II

The historian examining the story of a particular national economy is inevitably impressed by the long-period continuity of events. Like other forms of history, economic history is a seamless web. The cotton-textile developments in Britain of the 1780's and 1790's have a history stretching back for a half century at least; the United States of the 1840's and 1850's had been preparing itself for industrialization since the 1790's, at the latest; Russia's remarkable development during the two pre-1914 decades goes back to 1861 for its foundations, if not to the Napoleonic Wars or to Peter the Great; the remarkable economic spurt of Meiji Japan is incomprehensible outside the context of economic developments in the latter half of the Tokugawa era; and so on. It is wholly legitimate that the historian's influence should be to extend the story of the British industrial revolution back into the seventeenth century and forward far into the nineteenth century; and that Heckscher should embrace Sweden's transition in a chapter entitled 'The Great Transformation (1815–1914)'.[1] From the perspective of the economic historian

[1] E. F. Heckscher, *An Economic History of Sweden*, tr. G. Ohlin (Cambridge, Mass., 1954), chapter 6.

the isolation of a take-off period is, then, a distinctly arbitrary process. It is to be judged, like such other arbitrary exercises as the isolation of business cycles and secular trends, on whether it illuminates more of the economic process than it conceals; and it should be used, if accepted, as a way of giving a rough framework of order to the inordinately complicated biological problem of growth rather than as an exact model of reality.

There is difficulty in this set of conceptions for the statistical analyst of economic development as well as for the historian. At first sight the data mobilized, for example, by Clark, Kuznets, Buchanan, and Ellis exhibit a continuum of degrees of development both within countries over time and as among countries at a given period of time, with no prima facie case for a clearly marked watershed in the growth process.[1] In part this statistical result arises from the fact that historical data on national product and its components are only rarely available for an economy until after it has passed into a stage of more or less regular growth; that is, after the take-off. In part it arises from the fact that, by and large, these authors are more concerned with different levels of *per capita* output (or welfare)—and the structural characteristics that accompany them—than with the growth process itself. The data they mobilize do not come to grips with the inner determinants of growth. The question raised here is not how or why levels of output *per capita* have differed but rather how it has come about that particular economies have moved from stagnation—to slow, piecemeal advance—to a situation where growth was the normal economic condition. Our criterion here is not the absolute level of output *per capita* but its rate of change.

In this argument the sequence of economic development is

[1] Colin Clark, *The Conditions of Economic Progress* (London, 1951, 2nd edition); Simon Kuznets, 'International Differences in Capital Formation and Financing' (mimeographed; Conference on Capital Formation and Economic Growth, November 1953) (National Bureau of Economic Research, New York, 1953); Norman Buchanan and Howard Ellis, *Approaches to Economic Development* (Twentieth Century Fund, New York, 1955). See also the United Nations data presented as a frontispiece to H. F. Williamson and John A. Buttrick, *Economic Development* (New York, 1954).

taken to consist of three periods: a long period (up to a century or, conceivably, more) when the preconditions for take-off are established; the take-off itself, defined within two or three decades; and a long period when growth becomes normal and relatively automatic. These three divisions would, of course, not exclude the possibility of growth giving way to secular stagnation or decline in the long term. It would exclude from the concept of a growing economy, however, one which experiences a brief spurt of expansion which is not subsequently sustained; for example, the United States' industrial boom of the War of 1812 or the ill-fated spurts of certain Latin American economies in the early stages of their modern history.

Take-offs have occurred in two quite different types of societies; and, therefore, the process of establishing preconditions for take-off has varied. In the first and most general case the achievement of preconditions for take-off required major change in political and social structure and, even, in effective cultural values. In the vocabulary of this book, important changes in the propensities preceded the take-off. In the second case take-off was delayed not by political, social, and cultural obstacles but by the high (and even expanding) levels of welfare that could be achieved by exploiting land and natural resources. In this second case take-off was initiated by a more narrowly economic process, as, for example, in the northern United States, Australia, and, perhaps, Sweden. The take-off was initiated primarily by a change in the yields; although subsequent growth brought with it changes in the propensities as well. As one would expect in the essentially biological field of economic growth, history offers mixed as well as pure cases.

In the first case the process of establishing preconditions for take-off might be generalized in impressionistic terms as follows:

We start with a reasonably stable and traditional society containing an economy mainly agricultural, using more or less unchanging production methods, saving and investing productively little more than is required to meet depreciation. Usually from outside the society, but sometimes out of its own dynamics, comes the idea that economic progress is possible; and this idea spreads within the established *élite* or, more usually, in some disadvantaged group whose lack of status does not prevent the exercise of some economic initiative. More often than not the economic motives for seeking economic progress converge with some non-economic motive, such as the desire for increased social power and prestige, national pride, political ambition, and so on. Education, for some at least, broadens and changes to suit the needs of modern economic activity. New enterprising men come forward willing to mobilize savings and to take risks in pursuit of profit, notably in commerce. The commercial markets for agricultural products, domestic handicrafts, and consumption-goods imports widen. Institutions for mobilizing capital appear; or they expand from primitive levels in the scale, surety, and time horizon for loans. Basic capital is expanded, notably in transport and communications, often to bring to market raw materials in which other nations have an economic interest, often financed by foreign capital. And, here and there, modern manufacturing enterprise appears, usually in substitution for imports.

Since public-health measures are enormously productive in their early stages of application and, as innovations go, meet relatively low resistance in most cultures, the death-rate may fall and the population begin to rise, putting pressure on the food supply and the institutional structure of agriculture, creating thereby an economic depressant or stimulus (or both in turn), depending on the society's response.[1]

The rate of productive investment may rise up to 5 per cent. of national income;[2] but this is unlikely to do much more

[1] Historically, disruptive population pressure has been generated in pre-take-off societies not only by the easy spread of highly productive measures of public health but also the easy acceptance of high-yield new crops, permitting a fragmentation of land-holdings, earlier marriage, and a rise in the birth-rate; e.g. Ireland and China.

[2] The relation of the investment rate to growth depends, of course, on the rate of population rise. With stagnant population or slow rise a 5 per cent. investment rate could yield substantial growth in real output *per capita*, as indeed it did in pre-1914 France. On the other hand, as noted below (p. 290), investment rates much higher than 5 per cent. can persist in primitive economies which lack the preconditions for growth, based on capital imports, without initiating sustained

than keep ahead of the population increase. And, in general, all this activity proceeds on a limited basis, within an economy and a society still mainly characterized by traditional low-productivity techniques and by old values and institutions which developed in conjunction with them. The rural proportion of the population is likely to stand at 75 per cent. or over.

In the second case, of naturally wealthy nations, with a highly favourable balance between population and natural resources and with a population deriving by emigration from reasonably acquisitive cultures, the story of establishing the preconditions differs mainly in that there is no major problem of overcoming traditional values inappropriate to economic growth and the inert or resistant institutions which incorporate them; there is less difficulty in developing an *élite* effective in the investment process; and there is no population problem.[1] Technically, much the same slow-moving process of change occurs at high (and, perhaps, even expanding) levels of *per capita* output, and with an extensive growth of population and output still based on rich land and other natural resources. Take-off fails to occur mainly because the comparative advantage of exploiting productive land and other natural resources delays the time when self-reinforcing industrial growth can profitably get under way.[2]

growth. For some useful arithmetic on the scale and composition of capital requirements in a growing economy with a 1 per cent. population increase see A. K. Cairncross, *Home and Foreign Investment* (Cambridge, 1953), chapter 1.

[1] Even in these cases there have often been significant political and social restraints which had to be reduced or eliminated before take-off could occur; for example, in Canada, the Argentine, and the American South.

[2] Theoretically, such fortunate societies could continue to grow in *per capita* output until diminishing returns damped down their progress. Theoretically, they might go on as growing non-industrial societies, absorbing agricultural innovations which successfully countered diminishing returns. Something like this might describe, for example, the rich agricultural regions of the United States. But, in general, it seems to be the case that the conditions required to sustain a progressive increase in agricultural productivity will also lead on to self-reinforcing industrial growth. This result emerges not merely from the fact that many agricultural improvements are labour-saving, and that industrial employment can be stimulated by the availability of surplus labour and is required to draw it off; it also derives from the fact that the production and use of materials and devices which raise agricultural productivity in themselves stimulate the growth of a self-sustaining industrial sector.

The beginning of take-off can usually be traced to a particular sharp stimulus. The stimulus may take the form of a political revolution which affects directly the balance of social power and effective values, the character of economic institutions, the distribution of income, the pattern of investment outlays, and the proportion of potential innovations actually applied; that is, it operates through the propensities. It may come about through a technological (including transport) innovation, which sets in motion a chain of secondary expansion in modern sectors and has powerful potential external economy effects which the society exploits. It may take the form of a newly favourable international environment, such as the opening of British and French markets to Swedish timber in the 1860's or a sharp relative rise in export prices and/or large new capital imports, as in the case of the United States from the late 1840's, Canada and Russia from the mid-1890's; but it may also come as a challenge posed by an unfavourable shift in the international environment, such as a sharp fall in terms of trade (or a wartime blockage of foreign trade) requiring the rapid development of manufactured import substitutes, as in the case of the Argentine and Australia in the 1930's and during the Second World War.[1] All these latter cases raise sharply the profitability of certain lines of enterprise and can be regarded as changes in the yields.

What is essential here, however, is not the form of stimulus but the fact that the prior development of the society and its economy result in a positive sustained, and self-reinforcing, response to it: the result is not a once-over change in production functions or in the volume of investment, but a higher proportion of potential innovations accepted in a more or less regular flow, and a higher rate of investment.

In short, the forces which have yielded marginal bursts of activity now expand and became quantitatively significant as rapid-moving trends. New industries expand at high rates,

[1] Historically, the imposition of tariffs has played some role in take-offs, e.g. the American Tariffs of 1828 (cotton textiles) and 1841–2 (rail iron); the Russian tariffs of the 1890's, &c. Although these actions undoubtedly served to assist take-off in leading sectors, they usually reflected an energy and purpose among key entrepreneurial groups which would, in any case, probably have done the trick.

yielding profits which are substantially reinvested in new capacity; and their expansion induces a more general expansion of the modern sectors of the economy where a high rate of plough-back prevails. The institutions for mobilizing savings (including the fiscal and sometimes the capital-levy activities of government) increase in scope and efficiency. New techniques spread in agriculture as well as in industry, as increasing numbers of persons are prepared to accept them and the deep changes they bring to ways of life. A new class of business-men (usually private, sometimes public servants) emerges and acquires control over the key decisions determining the use of savings. New possibilities for export develop and are exploited; new import requirements emerge. The economy exploits hitherto unused backlogs in technique and natural resources. Although there are a few notable exceptions, all this momentum historically attracted substantial foreign capital.

The use of aggregative national-income terms evidently reveals little of the process which is occurring. It is nevertheless useful to regard as a necessary but not sufficient condition for the take-off the fact that the proportion of net investment to national income (or net national product) rises from (say) 5 per cent. to over 10 per cent., definitely outstripping the likely population pressure (since under the assumed take-off circumstances the capital–output ratio is low),[1] and yielding

---

[1] The author is aware of the substantial ambiguities which overhang the concept of the capital–output ratio and, especially, of the dangers of applying an over-all aggregate measure. But since the arithmetic of economic growth requires some such concept, implicitly or explicitly, we had better refine the tool rather than abandon it. In the early stages of economic development two contrary forces operate on the capital–output ratio. On the one hand there is a vast requirement of basic overhead capital in transport, power, education, &c. Here, due mainly to the long period over which such investment yields its return, the apparent (short-run) capital–output ratio is high. On the other hand, there are generally large unexploited backlogs of known techniques and available natural resources to be put to work; and these backlogs make for a low capital–output ratio. We can assume formally a low capital–output ratio for the take-off period because we are assuming that the preconditions have been created, including a good deal of social overhead capital. In fact, the aggregate marginal capital–output ratio is likely to be kept up during the take-off by the requirement of continuing large outlays for overhead items which yield their return only over long periods. Nevertheless, a ratio of 3–1 or 3·5–1 on average seems realistic as a rough bench-mark until we have learned more about capital–output ratios on a sectoral basis.

a distinct rise in real output *per capita*. Whether real consumption *per capita* rises depends on the pattern of income distribution and population pressure, as well as on the magnitude, character, and productivity of investment itself.

As indicated in the accompanying table, I believe it possible to identify at least tentatively such take-off periods for

Some Tentative, Approximate Take-off Dates

Country	Take-off	Country	Take-off
Great Britain . .	1783–1802	Russia . . .	1890–1914
France . . .	1830–60	Canada . .	1896–1914
Belgium . . .	1833–60	Argentine‡ . .	1935–
United States* .	1843–60	Turkey§ . .	1937–
Germany . .	1850–73	India‖ . .	1952–
Sweden . .	1868–90	China‖ . . .	1952–
Japan† . . .	1878–1900		

* The American take-off is here viewed as the upshot of two different periods of expansion: the first, that of the 1840's, marked by railway and manufacturing development, mainly confined to the East—this occurred while the West and South digested the extensive agricultural expansion of the previous decade; the second the great railway push into the Middle West during the 1850's marked by a heavy inflow of foreign capital. By the opening of the Civil War the American economy of North and West, with real momentum in its heavy-industry sector, is judged to have taken off.

† Lacking adequate data, there is some question about the timing of the Japanese take-off. Some part of the post-1868 period was certainly, by the present set of definitions, devoted to firming up the preconditions for take-off. By 1914 the Japanese economy had certainly taken off. The question is whether the period from about 1878 to the Sino-Japanese War in the mid-1890's is to be regarded as the completion of the preconditions or as take-off. On present evidence, I incline to the latter view.

‡ In one sense the Argentine economy began its take-off during the First World War. But by and large, down to the pit of the post-1929 depression, the growth of its modern sector, stimulated during the war, tended to slacken; and, like a good part of the Western world, the Argentine sought during the 1920's to return to a pre-1914 normalcy. It was not until the mid-1930's that a sustained take-off was inaugurated, which by and large can now be judged to have been successful despite the structural vicissitudes of that economy.

§ Against the background of industrialization measures inaugurated in the mid-1930's the Turkish economy has exhibited remarkable momentum in the past five years founded in the increase in agricultural income and productivity. It still remains to be seen whether these two surges, conducted under quite different national policies, will constitute a transition to self-sustaining growth, and whether Turkey can overcome its current structural problems.

‖ As noted in the text is it still too soon (for quite different reasons) to judge either the Indian or Chinese Communist take-off efforts as successful.

a number of countries which have passed into the stage of growth.

The third stage is, of course, the long, fluctuating story of sustained economic progress. Over-all capital per head increases as the economy matures. The structure of the economy changes increasingly. The initial key industries, which sparked the take-off, decelerate as diminishing returns operate on the original set of industrial tricks and the original band of pioneering entrepreneurs give way to less single-minded industrial leaders in those sectors; but the average rate of growth is maintained by a succession of new, rapidly growing sectors, with a new set of pioneering leaders. The proportion of the population in rural pursuits declines. The economy finds its (changing) place in the international economy. The society makes such terms as it will with the requirements for maximizing modern and efficient production, balancing off, as it will, the new values against those retarding values which persist with deeper roots, or adapting the latter in such ways as to support rather than retard the growth process. This sociological calculus interweaves with basic resource endowments to determine the pace of deceleration.

It is with the problems and vicissitudes of such growing economies of the third stage (and especially with cyclical fluctuations and the threat of chronic unemployment) that the bulk of modern theoretical economics is concerned, including much recent work on the formal properties of growth models. The student of history and of contemporary underdeveloped areas[1] is more likely to be concerned with the

---

[1] A number of so-called underdeveloped areas may have, in fact, either passed through the take-off process or are in the midst of it, e.g. Mexico, Brazil, Turkey, the Argentine, and India. I would commend for consideration—certainly no more until the concept of take-off is disproved or verified—the dropping of the concept of 'underdeveloped areas' and the substitution for it of a quadripartite distinction among economies: traditional; pre-take-off; take-off; and growing. Against the background of this set of distinctions we might then consider systematically two separable questions now often confused. First, the stage of growth, as among growing economies. It is legitimate to regard Mexico and the United States, Great Britain and Australia, France and Japan, as growing economies, although they stand at very different points along their national growth curves. Second, the foreseeable long-run potential of growing economies. Over the long pull, even after they are 'fully developed', the *per capita* output levels that different economies are likely to achieve will undoubtedly

economics of the first two stages; that is, the economics of the preconditions and the take-off. If we are to have a serious theory of economic growth or (more likely) some useful theories about economic growth, they must obviously seek to embrace these two early stages—and notably the economics of the take-off. The balance of this chapter is designed to mobilize tentatively and in a preliminary way what an economic historian can contribute to the economics of take-off.

III

There are several problems of choice involved in defining the take-off with precision. We might begin with one arbitrary definition and consider briefly the two major alternatives.

For the present purposes the take-off is defined as requiring all three of the following related conditions:

(*a*) a rise in the rate of productive investment from (say) 5 per cent. or less to over 10 per cent. of national income (or net national product);

(*b*) the development of one or more substantial manufacturing[1] sectors, with a high rate of growth;

(*c*) the existence or quick emergence of a political, social, and institutional framework which exploits the impulses to expansion in the modern sector and the potential external economy effects of the take-off and gives to growth an on-going character.

The third condition implies a considerable capability to mobilize capital from domestic sources. Some take-offs have

vary greatly, depending notably on resource endowments in relation to population. The arraying of levels of output *per capita* for different economies, now conventional, fails to distinguish these three elements; that is, the current rate of growth; the stage of growth; and the foreseeable horizon for growth. For further discussion of stages beyond take-off see Chapter XIII.

[1] In this context 'manufacturing' is taken to include the processing of agricultural products or raw materials by modern methods; e.g. timber in Sweden; meat in Australia; dairy products in Denmark. The dual requirement of a 'manufacturing' sector is that its processes set in motion a chain of further modern sector requirements and that its expansion provides the potentiality of external economy effects.

occurred with virtually no capital imports; e.g. Britain and Japan. Some take-offs have had a substantial component of foreign capital; e.g. the United States, Russia, and Canada. But some countries have imported large quantities of foreign capital for long periods, which undoubtedly contributed to creating the preconditions for take-off, without actually initiating take-off; e.g. the Argentine before 1914, Venezuela down to recent years, the Belgian Congo currently. In short, whatever the role of capital imports, the preconditions for take-off include an initial ability to mobilize domestic savings productively, as well as a structure which subsequently permits a high marginal rate of savings.

This definition is designed to isolate the early stage when industrialization takes hold rather than the later stage when industrialization becomes a more massive and statistically more impressive phenomenon. In Britain, for example, there is no doubt that it was between 1815 and 1850 that industrialization fully took hold. If the criterion chosen for take-off was the period of most rapid over-all industrial growth, or the period when large-scale industry matured, all our take-off dates would have to be set forward: Britain, for example, to 1819–48; the United States to 1868–93; Sweden to 1890–1920; Japan to 1900–20; Russia to 1928–40. The earlier dating is chosen here because it is believed, on present (often inadequate) evidence, that the decisive transformations (including a decisive shift in the investment rate) occur in the first industrial phases; and later industrial maturity can be directly traced back to foundations laid in these first phases.

This definition is also designed to rule out from the take-off the quite substantial economic progress which can occur in an economy before a truly self-reinforcing growth process gets under way. British economic expansion between (say) 1750 and 1783, Russian economic expansion between (say) 1861 and 1890, Canadian economic expansion between 1867 and the mid-1890's—such periods—for which there is an equivalent in the economic history of almost every growing economy—were marked by extremely important, even decisive, developments. The transport network expanded, and with it both internal and external commerce; new institutions for mobilizing savings were developed; a class of commercial and even industrial entrepreneurs began to emerge; industrial enterprise on a limited scale (or in limited sectors) grew. And yet, however essential these pre-take-off periods were for later development, their scale and momentum were insufficient to transform the economy radically or, in some cases, to outstrip population growth and to yield an increase in *per capita* output.

With a sense of the considerable violence done to economic history, I am here seeking to isolate a period when the scale of productive economic activity reaches a critical level and produces changes which lead to a massive and progressive structural transformation in economies and the societies of which they are a part, better viewed as changes in kind than merely in degree.

IV

The case for the concept of take-off hinges, in part, on quantitative evidence on the scale and productivity of investment in relation to population growth. Here, as noted earlier, we face a difficult problem; investment data are not now available historically for early stages in economic history. Following is such case as there is for regarding the shift from a productive investment rate of about 5 per cent. of NNP to 10 per cent. or more as central to the process.[1]

---

[1] In his important article, 'Economic Development with Unlimited Supplies of Labour', *Manchester School*, May 1954, W. Arthur Lewis indicates a similar spread as defining the transition to economic growth:

'The central problem in the theory of economic development is to understand the process by which a community which was previously saving and investing 4 or 5 per cent. of its national income or less, converts itself into an economy where voluntary saving is running at about 12–15 per cent. of national income or more. This is the central problem because the central fact of economic development is rapid capital accumulation (including knowledge and skills with capital). We cannot explain any "industrial" revolution (as the economic historians pretend to do) until we can explain why saving increased relatively to national income.'

Presumably Mr. Lewis based this range on empirical observation of contemporary 'under-developed' areas on which some data are presented below. As in note 2, p. 278, above, it should be emphasized that the choice of investment proportions to symbolize the transition to growth hinges on the assumptions made about the rate of population increase.

1. *A Prima Facie Case*

If we take the aggregate marginal capital–output ratio for an economy in its early stage of economic development at 3·5–1 and if we assume, as is not abnormal, a population rise of 1–1·5% per annum it is clear that something between 3·5 and 5·25% of NNP must be regularly invested if NNP *per capita* is to be sustained. An increase of 2% per annum in NNP *per capita* requires, under these assumptions, that something between 10·5 and 12·5% of NNP be regularly invested. By definition and assumption, then, a transition from relatively stagnant to substantial regular rise in NNP *per capita*, under typical population conditions, requires that the proportion of national product productively invested move from somewhere in the vicinity of 5% to something in the vicinity of 10%.

2. *The Swedish Case*

In the appendix to his paper on international differences in capital formation, cited above, Kuznets gives gross and net capital-formation figures in relation to gross and net national product for a substantial group of countries where reasonably good statistical data exist. Excepting Sweden, these data do not go back clearly to pre-take-off stages.[1] The Swedish data begin in the decade 1861–70; and the Swedish take-off is to be dated from the latter years of the decade.

Kuznets's table of calculations for Sweden follows:

Decade	Domestic GCF GNP (%)	Domestic NCF NNP (%)	Depreciation to DGCF (%)
1. 1861–70 . . .	5·8	3·5	(42)
2. 1871–80 . . .	8·8	5·3	(42)
3. 1881–90 . . .	10·8	6·6	(42)
4. 1891–1900 . . .	13·7	8·1	43·9
5. 1901–10 . . .	18·0	11·6	40·0
6. 1911–20 . . .	20·2	13·5	38·3
7. 1921–30 . . .	19·0	11·4	45·2

Note (Kuznets): Based on estimates in Eric Lindahl, Einan Dahlgren, and Karin Kock, *National Income of Sweden, 1861–1930* (London: P. J. Kingston, 1937), Parts One and Two, particularly the details in Part Two.

These underlying totals of capital formation exclude changes in inventories.

While gross totals are directly from the volumes referred to above, depreciation for the first three decades was not given. We assumed that it formed 42 per cent. of gross domestic capital formation.

[1] The Danish data are on the margin. They begin with the decade 1870–79,

3. *The Canadian Case*

The data developed by O. J. Firestone[1] for Canada indicates a similar transition for net capital formation in its take-
off (say, 1896–1914); but the gross investment proportion in
the period from Confederation to the mid-nineties was higher

probably the first decade of take-off itself. They show net and gross domestic
capital formation rates well over 10 per cent. In view of the sketch of the Danish
economy presented in Kjeld Bjerke's 'Preliminary Estimates of the Danish
National Product from 1870–1950' (Preliminary paper mimeographed for the
1953 Conference of the International Association for Research on Income and
Wealth), pp. 32–34, it seems likely that further research would identify the years
1830–70 as a period when the preconditions were actively established, 1870–
1900 as a period of take-off. This view is supported by scattered and highly
approximate estimates of Danish National Wealth which exhibit a remarkable
surge in capital formation between 1864 and 1884.

Estimates of National Wealth in Denmark

	1,000 millions of kroner	Source
1864	3·5	Falbe-Hansen, *Danmarks statistik*, 1885.
1884	6·5	Falbe-Hansen, *Danmarks statistik*, 1885.
1899	7·2	Tax commission of 1903.
1909	10·0	Jens Warming, *Danmarks statistik*, 1913.
1927	24·0	Jens Warming, *Danmarks erhvervs- or samfundsliv*, 1930.
1939	28·8	Economic expert committee of 1943, *Økonomiske efterkrigsproblemer*, 1945.
1950	54·5	N. Banke, N. P. Jacobsen og Vedel-Petersen, *Danske erhvervsliv*, 1951.

(Furnished in correspondence by Einar Cohn and Kjeld Bjerke.) It should
again be emphasized, however, that we are dealing with a hypothesis whose
empirical foundations are still fragmentary. For a recent discussion of Swedish
and Danish take-off periods see A. J. Youngson, *Possibilities of Economic Progress*,
Cambridge, 1959, chapters ix and x.

[1] O. J. Firestone, *Canada's Economic Development, 1867–1952, with Special Reference to Changes in the Country's National Wealth*, paper prepared for the International Association for Research in Income and Wealth, 1953, to which Mr.
Firestone has kindly furnished me certain revisions, shortly to be published.
By 1900 Canada already had about 18,000 miles of railway line; but the territory served had been developed to a limited degree only. By 1900 Canada
already had a net balance of foreign indebtedness over $1 billion. Although this
figure was almost quadrupled in the next two decades, capital imports represented an important increment to domestic capital sources from the period
of Confederation down to the pre-1914 Canadian boom, which begins in the
mid-1890's.

than appears to have marked other periods when the pre-conditions were established, possibly due to investment in the railway net, abnormally large for a nation of Canada's population, and to relatively heavy foreign investment, even before the great capital import boom of the pre-1914 decade:

Canada: Gross and Net Investment in
Durable Physical Assets as Percentage of Gross and Net National
Expenditure (for Selected Years)

	$\frac{GCF}{GNP}$	$\frac{NCF}{NNP}$	Capital consumption as percentage of gross investment
1870	15·0	7·1	56·2
1900	13·1	4·0	72·5
1920	16·6	10·6	41·3
1929	23·0	12·1	53·3
1952	16·8	9·3	49·7

4. *The Pattern of Contemporary Evidence in General*[1]

In the years after 1945 the number of countries for which reasonably respectable national income (or product) data exist has grown; and with such data there have developed some tolerable savings and investment estimates for countries at different stages of the growth process. Within the category of nations usually grouped as 'underdeveloped' one can distinguish four types.[2]

(*a*) *Pre-take-off economies*, where the apparent savings and investment rates, including limited net capital imports, probably come to under 5% of net national product. In general, data for such countries are not satisfactory, and one's judgement that capital formation is low must rest on frag-mentary data and partially subjective judgement. Examples

[1] I am indebted to Prof. Everett Hagen for mobilizing the statistical data in this section, except where otherwise indicated.

[2] The percentages given are of net capital formation to net domestic product. The latter is the product net of depreciation of the geographic area. It includes the value of output produced in the area, regardless of whether the income flows abroad. Since indirect business taxes are not deducted, it tends to be larger than national income; hence the percentages are lower than if national income was used as the denominator in computing them.

are Ethiopia, Kenya, Thailand, Cambodia, Afghanistan, and perhaps Indonesia.[1]

(*b*) *Economies attempting take-off*, where the apparent savings and investment rates, including limited net capital imports, have risen over 5% of net national product.[2] For example, Mexico (1950) NCF/NDP 7·2%; Chile (1950) NCF/NDP 9·5%; Panama (1950) NCF/NDP 7·5%; Philippines (1952) NCF/NDP 6·4%; Puerto Rico (1952) NCF (Private)/NDP 7·6%; India (1953) NCF/NDP, perhaps about 7%. Whether the take-off period will, in fact, be successful remains in most of these cases still to be seen.

(*c*) *Growing economies*, where the apparent savings and investment rates, including limited net capital imports, have reached 10% or over; for example, Colombia (1950) NCF/NDP, 16·3%.

(*d*) *Enclave economies*. (1) Cases where the apparent savings and investment rates, including substantial net capital imports, have reached 10% or over, but the domestic preconditions for sustained growth have not been achieved. These economies, associated with major export industries, lack the third condition for take-off suggested above (p. 284). They include the Belgian Congo (1951) NCF/NDP 21·7%; Southern Rhodesia (1950) GCF/GDP 45·5%, (1952) GCF/GDP 45·4%. (2) Cases where net capital exports are large.

---

[1] The Office of Intelligence Research of the Department of State, Washington, D.C., gives the following estimated ratios of investment (presumably gross) to GNP in its Report No. 6672 of 25 August 1954, p. 3, based on the latest data available to that point, for countries which would probably fall into the pre-take-off category:

	%		%
Afghanistan	5	Pakistan	6
Ceylon	5	Indonesia	5

[2] The Department of State estimates (ibid.) for economies which are either attempting take-off or which have, perhaps, passed into a stage of regular growth include:

	%		%
The Argentine	13	Colombia	14
Brazil	14	Philippines	8
Chile	11	Venezuela	23

Venezuela has been for some time an 'enclave economy', with a high investment rate concentrated in a modern export sector whose growth did not generate general economic momentum in the Venezuelan economy; but in the past few years Venezuela may have moved over into the category of economies experiencing an authentic take-off.

For example, Burma (1938) NCF/NDP, 7·1%; net capital exports/NDP, 11·5%; Nigeria (1950–1) NCF/NDP 5·1%; net capital exports/NDP 5·6%.

5. *The Cases of India and Communist China*

The two outstanding contemporary cases of economies attempting purposefully to take off are India and Communist China, both operating under national plans. The Indian First Five Year Plan projects the growth process envisaged under assumptions similar to those in paragraph 1, p. 287, above. The Indian Planning Commission estimated investment as 5% of NNP in the initial year of the plan, 1950–1.[1] Using a 3/1 marginal capital–output ratio, they envisaged a marginal savings rate of 20% for the First Five Year Plan, a 50% rate thereafter, down to 1968–9, when the average proportion of income invested would level off at 20% of NNP. As one would expect, the sectoral composition of this process is not fully worked out in the initial plan; but the Indian effort may well be remembered in economic history as the first take-off defined *ex ante* in national product terms.

So far as the aggregates are concerned, what we can say is that the Indian planned figures fall well within the range of *prima facie* hypothesis and historical experience, if India in fact fulfils the full requirements for take-off, notably the achievement of industrial momentum. The Chinese Communist figures are somewhat more ambitious in both agriculture and industry. As of 1959, the momentum achieved over the previous six years in China appeared somewhat greater than that in India, but it will be some time before the accounts of progress can be assessed with confidence— notably with respect to agricultural development, which must play so large a role in each.

We have, evidently, much still to learn about the quantitative aspects of this problem; and, especially, much further quantitative research and imaginative manipulation of historical evidence will be required before the hypothesis

[1] Government of India, Planning Commission, *The First Five Year Plan*, 1952, vol. i, chapter 1.

tentatively advanced here can be regarded as proved or disproved. What we can say is that *prima facie* thought and a
scattering of historical and contemporary evidence suggest
that it is not unreasonable to consider the take-off as including as a necessary but not sufficient condition a quantitative
transition in the proportion of income productively invested
of the kind indicated here.

V

Whatever the importance and virtue of viewing the take-
off in aggregative terms—embracing national output, the
proportion of output invested, and an aggregate marginal
capital–output ratio—that approach tells us relatively little
of what actually happens and of the causal processes at work
in a take-off; nor is the investment-rate criterion conclusive.

Following the definition of take-off (p. 284 above), we
must consider not merely how a rise in the investment rate is
brought about, from both supply and demand perspectives,
but how rapidly growing manufacturing sectors emerged and
imparted their primary and secondary growth impulses to
the economy.

Perhaps the most important thing to be said about the behaviour of these variables in historical cases of take-off is that
they have assumed many different forms. There is no single
pattern. The rate and productivity of investment can rise,
and the consequences of this rise can be diffused into a self-
reinforcing general growth process by many different technical and economic routes, under the aegis of many different
political, social, and cultural settings, driven along by a wide
variety of human motivations.

The purpose of the following paragraphs is to suggest
briefly, and by way of illustration only, certain elements of
both uniformity and variety in the variables whose movement has determined the inner structure of the take-off.

1. *The Supply of Loanable Funds*

By and large, the loanable funds required to finance the
take-off have come from two types of sources: from shifts in
the control over income flows, including income-distribution

changes and capital imports;[1] and from the plough-back of profits in rapidly expanding particular sectors.

The notion of economic development occurring as the result of income shifts from those who will spend (hoard[2] or lend) less productively to those who will spend (or lend) more productively is one of the oldest and most fundamental notions in economics. It is basic to the *Wealth of Nations*,[3] and it is applied by W. Arthur Lewis in his recent elaboration of the classical model.[4] Lewis builds his model in part on an expansion of the capitalist sector, with the bulk of additional savings arising from an enlarging pool of capitalist profits.

Historically, income shifts conducive to economic development have assumed many forms. In Meiji Japan and also in Czarist Russia the substitution of government bonds for the great landholders' claim on the flow of rent payments led to a highly Smithian redistribution of income into the hands of those with higher propensities to seek material advance and to accept innovations. In both cases the real value of the government bonds exchanged for land depreciated; and, in general, the feudal landlords emerged with a less attractive arrangement than had first appeared to be offered. Apart from the confiscation effect, two positive impulses arose from land reform: the State itself used the flow of payments from peasants, now diverted from landlords' hands, for activity which encouraged economic development; and a certain number of the more enterprising former landlords directly invested in commerce and industry. In contemporary India and China

[1] Prof. Everett Hagen has pointed out that the increase in savings may well arise from a shift in the propensity to save, as new and exciting horizons open up, rather than merely from a shift of income to groups with a higher (but static) propensity to save. He may well be right. This is, evidently, a matter for further investigation.

[2] Hoarding can, of course, be helpful to the growth process by depressing consumption and freeing resources for investment if, in fact, non-hoarding persons or institutions acquire the resources and possess the will to expand productive investment. A direct transfer of income is, evidently, not required.

[3] See, especially, Smith's observations on the 'perversion' of wealth by 'prodigality'—that is, unproductive consumption expenditures—and on the virtues of 'parsimony' which transfers income to those who will increase 'the fund which is destined for the maintenance of productive hands'. Routledge edition, London, 1890, pp. 259–60.

[4] Op. cit., especially pp. 156–9.

we can observe quite different degrees of income transfer by this route. India is relying to only a very limited extent on the elimination of large incomes unproductively spent by large landlords; although this element figures in a small way in its programme. Communist China has systematically transferred all non-governmental pools of capital into the hands of the State, in a series of undisguised or barely disguised capital levies; and it is drawing heavily for capital resources on the mass of middle and poor peasants who remain.

In addition to confiscatory and taxation devices, which can operate effectively when the State is spending more productively than the taxed individuals, inflation has been important to several take-offs. In Britain of the late 1790's, the United States of the 1850's, Japan of the 1870's there is no doubt that capital formation was aided by price inflation, which shifted resources away from consumption to profits.

The shift of income flows into more productive hands has, of course, been aided historically not only by government fiscal measures but also by banks and capital markets. Virtually without exception, the take-off periods have been marked by the extension of banking institutions which expanded the supply of working capital; and in most cases also by an expansion in the range of long-range financing done by a central, formally organized, capital market.

Although these familiar capital-supply functions of the State and private institutions have been important to the take-off, it is likely to prove the case, on close examination, that a necessary condition for take-off was the existence of one or more rapidly growing sectors whose entrepreneurs (private or public) ploughed back into new capacity a very high proportion of profits. Put another way, the demand side of the investment process, rather than the supply of loanable funds, may be the decisive element in the take-off, as opposed to the period of creating the preconditions, or of sustaining growth once it is under way. The distinction is, historically, sometimes difficult to make, notably when the State simultaneously acts both to mobilize supplies of finance and to undertake major entrepreneurial acts. There are, nevertheless, periods in economic history when quite substantial improvements in the machinery of capital supply do not, in themselves, initiate a take-off, but fall within the period when the preconditions are created: e.g. British banking developments in the century before 1783; Russian banking developments before 1890, &c.

One extremely important version of the plough-back process has taken place through foreign trade. Developing economies have created from their natural resources major export industries; and the rapid expansion in exports has been used to finance the import of capital equipment and to service the foreign debt during the take-off. United States, Russian, and Canadian grain fulfilled this function, Swedish timber and pulp, Japanese silk, &c. Currently Chinese exports to the Communist Bloc, wrung at great administrative and human cost from the agricultural sector, play this decisive role. It should be noted that the development of such export sectors has not in itself guaranteed accelerated capital formation. Enlarged foreign-exchange proceeds have been used in many familiar cases to finance hoards (as in the famous case of Indian bullion imports) or unproductive consumption outlays.

It should be noted that one possible mechanism for inducing a high rate of plough-back into productive investment is a rapid expansion in the effective demand for domestically manufactured consumer goods, which would direct into the hands of vigorous entrepreneurs an increasing proportion of income flows under circumstances which would lead them to expand their own capacity and to increase their requirements for industrial raw materials, semi-manufactured products, and manufactured components.

A final element in the supply of loanable funds is, of course, capital imports. Foreign capital has played a major role in the take-off stage of many economies: e.g. the United States, Russia, Sweden, Canada. The cases of Britain and Japan indicate, however, that it cannot be regarded as an essential condition. Foreign capital was notably useful when the construction of railways or other large overhead capital items with a long period of gestation played an important role in

the take-off. After all, whatever its strategic role, the proportion of investment required for growth which goes into
industry is relatively small compared to that required for
utilities, transport, and the housing of enlarged urban populations. And foreign capital can be mightily useful in helping
carry the burden of these overhead items either directly or
indirectly.

What can we say, in general then, about the supply of
finance during the take-off period? First, as a precondition,
it appears necessary that the community's surplus above the
mass-consumption level does not flow into the hands of those
who will sterilize it by hoarding, luxury consumption, or low-
productivity investment outlays. Second, as a precondition,
it appears necessary that institutions be developed which provide cheap and adequate working capital. Third, as a necessary condition, it appears that one or more sectors of the
economy must grow rapidly, inducing a more general industrialization process; and that the entrepreneurs in such
sectors plough back a substantial proportion of their profits
in further productive investment, one possible and recurrent
version of the plough-back process being the investment of
proceeds from a rapidly growing export sector.

The devices, confiscatory and fiscal, for ensuring the first
and second preconditions have been historically various.
And, as indicated below, the types of leading manufacturing
sectors which have served to initiate the take-off have varied
greatly. Finally, foreign capital flows have, in significant
cases, proved extremely important to the take-off, notably
when lumpy overhead capital construction of long gestation
period was required; but take-offs have also occurred based
almost wholly on domestic sources of finance.

2. *The Sources of Entrepreneurship*

It is evident that the take-off required the existence and
the successful activity of some group in the society which
accepts borrowers' risk, when such risk is so defined as to
include the propensity to accept innovations. As noted above,
the problem of entrepreneurship in the take-off has not been

profound in a limited group of wealthy agricultural nations whose populations derived by emigration mainly from north-western Europe. There the problem of take-off was primarily economic; and when economic incentives for industrialization emerged commercial and banking groups moved over easily into industrial entrepreneurship. In many other countries, however, the development of adequate entrepreneurship was a more searching social process.

Under some human motivation or other, a group must come to perceive it to be both possible and good to undertake acts of capital investment; and, for their efforts to be tolerably successful, they must act with approximate rationality in selecting the directions towards which their enterprise is directed. They must not only produce growth but tolerably balanced growth. We cannot quite say that it is necessary for them to act as if they were trying to maximize profit; for the criteria for private profit maximization do not necessarily converge with the criteria for an optimum rate and pattern of growth in various sectors.[1] But in a growing economy, over periods longer than the business cycle, economic history is reasonably tolerant of deviations from rationality, in the sense that excess capacity is finally put to productive use. Leaving aside the question of ultimate human motivation, and assuming that the major overhead items are generated, if necessary, by some form of state initiative (including subsidy), we can say as a first approximation that some group must successfully emerge which behaves as if it were moved by the profit motive, in a dynamic economy with changing production functions; although, risk being the slippery variable, it is under such assumptions that Keynes's dictum should be borne in mind: 'If human nature felt no temptation to take a chance, no satisfaction (profit apart) in constructing a factory, a railway, a mine or a farm, there might not be much investment merely as a result of cold calculation.'[2]

In this connexion it is increasingly conventional for economists to pay their respects to the Protestant ethic.[3] The

[1] See above, Chapter XI. [2] *General Theory*, p. 150.
[3] See, for example, N. Kaldor, 'Economic Growth and Cyclical Fluctuations', *Economic Journal*, March 1954, p. 67.

historian should not be ungrateful for this light on the grey horizon of formal growth models. But the known cases of economic growth which theory must seek to explain take us beyond the orbit of Protestantism. In a world where Samurai, Parsees, Jews, North Italians, Turkish, Russian, and Chinese civil servants (as well as Huguenots, Scotsmen, and British North-countrymen) have played the role of a leading *élite* in economic growth John Calvin should not be made to bear quite this weight. More fundamentally, allusion to a positive scale of religious or other values conducive to profit-maximizing activities is an insufficient sociological basis for this important phenomenon. What appears to be required for the emergence of such *élites* is not merely an appropriate value system but two further conditions: first, the new *élite* must feel itself denied the conventional routes to prestige and power by the traditional, less acquisitive society of which it is a part; second, the traditional society must be sufficiently flexible (or weak) to permit its members to seek material advance (or political power) as a route upwards alternative to conformity.

Although an *élite* entrepreneurial class appears to be required for take-off, with significant power over aggregate income flows and industrial investment decisions, most take-offs have been preceded or accompanied by radical change in agricultural techniques and market organization. By and large the agricultural entrepreneur has been the individual land-owning farmer. A requirement for take-off is, therefore, a class of farmers willing and able to respond to the possibilities opened up for them by new techniques, land-holding arrangements, transport facilities, and forms of market and credit organization. A small purposeful *élite* can go a long way in initiating economic growth; but, especially in agriculture (and to some extent in the industrial working force), a wider-based revolution in outlook must come about.[1]

[1] Like the population question, agriculture is mainly excluded from this analysis, which considers the take-off rather than the whole development process. Nevertheless, it should be noted that, as a matter of history, agricultural revolutions have generally preceded or accompanied the take-off. In theory we can envisage a take-off which did not require a radical improvement in agricultural productivity: if, for example, the growth and productivity of the indus-

Whatever further empirical research may reveal about the motives which have led men to undertake the constructive entrepreneurial acts of the take-off period, this much appears sure: these motives have varied greatly, from one society to another; and they have rarely, if ever, been motives of an unmixed material character.

3. *Leading Sectors in the Take-off*

Chapter XI presents, it will be recalled, the notion that the over-all rate of growth of an economy must be regarded in the first instance as the consequence of differing growth rates in particular sectors of the economy, such sectoral growth-rates being in part derived from certain over-all demand parameters (e.g. population, consumers' income, tastes, &c.), in part from the primary and secondary effects of changing supply factors, when these are effectively exploited.

On this view, it will be recalled, the sectors of an economy may be grouped in three categories:

(a) *Primary growth sectors*, where possibilities for innovation or for the exploitation of newly profitable or hitherto unexplored resources yield a high growth-rate and set in motion expansionary forces elsewhere in the economy.

(b) *Supplementary growth sectors*, where rapid advance occurs in direct response to—or as a requirement of—advance in the primary growth sectors; e.g., coal, iron, and engineering in relation to railroads. These sectors may have to be tracked many stages back into the economy, as the Leontief input–output models would suggest.

(c) *Derived growth sectors*, where advance occurs in some fairly steady relation to the growth of total real income,

trial sector permitted a withering away of traditional agriculture and a substitution for it of imports. In fact, agricultural revolutions have been required to permit rapidly growing (and urbanizing) populations to be fed without exhausting foreign-exchange resources in food imports or creating excessive hunger in the rural sector; and, as noted at several points in this argument, agricultural revolutions have in fact played an essential and positive role, not merely by both releasing workers to the cities and feeding them, but also by earning foreign exchange for general capital-formation purposes.

population, industrial production, or some other over-all, modestly increasing parameter. Food output in relation to population, housing in relation to family formation are classic derived relations of this order.

Very roughly speaking, primary and supplementary growth sectors derive their high momentum essentially from the introduction and diffusion of changes in the cost–supply environment (in turn, of course, partially influenced by demand changes); while the derived-growth sectors are linked essentially to changes in demand (while subject also to continuing changes in production functions of a less dramatic character).

At any period of time it appears to be true even in a mature and growing economy that forward momentum is maintained as the result of rapid expansion in a limited number of primary sectors, whose expansion has significant external economy and other secondary effects. From this perspective the behaviour of sectors during the take-off is merely a special version of the growth process in general; or, put another way, growth proceeds by repeating endlessly, in different patterns with different leading sectors, the experience of the take-off. Like the take-off, long-term growth requires that the society not only generate vast quantities of capital for depreciation and maintenance, for housing and for a balanced complement of utilities and other overheads, but also a sequence of highly productive primary sectors, growing rapidly, based on new production functions. Only thus has the aggregate marginal capital–output ratio been kept low.

Once again history is full of variety: a considerable array of sectors appears to have played this key role in the take-off process.

The development of a cotton-textile industry sufficient to meet domestic requirements has not generally imparted a sufficient impulse in itself to launch a self-sustaining growth process. The development of modern cotton-textile industries in substitution for imports has, more typically, marked the pre-take-off period, as for example in India, China, and Mexico.

There is, however, the famous exception of Britain's industrial revolution. Baines's table on raw-cotton imports and his comment on it are worth quoting, covering as they do the original leading sector in the first take-off.[1]

Rates of Increase in the Import of Cotton-wool,
in Periods of Ten Years from 1741 to 1831

	%		%
1741–51	81	1791–1801	67½
1751–61	21½	1801–11	39½
1761–71	25½	1811–21	93
1771–81	75¾	1821–31	85
1781–91	319½		

From 1697 to 1741 the increase was trifling: between 1741 and 1751 the manufacture, though still insignificant in extent, made a considerable spring: during the next twenty years the increase was moderate: from 1771 to 1781, owing to the invention of the jenny and the water-frame, a rapid increase took place: in the ten years from 1781 to 1791, being those which immediately following the invention of the mule and the expiration of Arkwright's patent, the rate of advancement was prodigiously accelerated, being nearly 320 per cent.: and from that time to the present, and especially since the close of the war, the increase, though considerably moderated, has been rapid and steady, far beyond all precedent in any other manufacture.

Why did the development of a modern factory system in cotton textiles lead on in Britain to a self-sustaining growth process, whereas it failed to do so in other cases? Part of the answer lies in the fact that, by the late eighteenth century, the preconditions for take-off in Britain were fully developed. Progress in textiles, coal, iron, and even steam power had been considerable through the eighteenth century; and the social and institutional environment was propitious. But two further technical elements helped determine the upshot. First, the British cotton-textile industry was large in relation to the total size of the economy. From its modern beginnings, but notably from the 1780's forward, a very high proportion of total cotton-textile output was directed abroad, reaching 60 per cent. by the 1820's.[2] The evolution of this industry was

---

[1] E. Baines, *History of the Cotton Manufacture* (London, 1835), p. 348.

[2] The volume (official value) of British cotton-goods exports rose from £355,060 in 1780 to £7,624,505 in 1802 (Baines, op. cit., p. 350). See also the calculation of R. C. O. Matthews, *A Study in Trade Cycle History* (Cambridge, 1954), pp. 127–9.

a more massive fact, with wider secondary repercussions, than if it were simply supplying the domestic market. Industrial enterprise on this scale had secondary reactions on the development of urban areas, the demand for coal, iron, and machinery, the demand for working capital and ultimately the demand for cheap transport, which powerfully stimulated industrial development in other directions.[1]

Second, a source of effective demand for rapid expansion in British cotton textiles was supplied, in the first instance, by the sharp reduction in real costs and prices which accompanied the technological developments in manufacture and the cheapening real cost of raw cotton induced by the cotton gin. In this Britain had an advantage not enjoyed by those who came later; for they merely substituted domestic for foreign-manufactured cotton textiles. The substitution undoubtedly had important secondary effects by introducing a modern industrial sector and releasing in net a pool of foreign exchange for other purposes; but there was no sharp fall in the real cost of acquiring cotton textiles and no equivalent lift in real income.

The introduction of the railroad has been historically the most powerful single initiator of take-offs.[2] It was decisive in the United States, Germany, and Russia; it has played an extremely important part in the Swedish, Japanese, and other cases. The railroad has had three major kinds of impact on economic growth during the take-off period. First, it has lowered internal transport costs, brought new areas and products into commercial markets, and, in general, performed the Smithian function of widening the market. Second, it has been a prerequisite in many cases to the development of a major new and rapidly enlarging export sector which, in

[1] If we are prepared to treat New England of the first half of the nineteenth century as a separable economy, its take-off into sustained growth can be allocated to the period, roughly 1820–50, and, again, a disproportionately large cotton-textile industry based substantially on exports (that is, from New England to the rest of the United States) is the regional foundation for sustained growth.

[2] For a detailed analysis of the routes of impact of the railroad on economic development see Paul H. Cootner, *Transport Innovation and Economic Development: The Case of the U.S. Steam Railroads*, 1953, unpublished doctoral thesis, M.I.T.

turn, has served to generate capital for internal development; as, for example, the American railroads of the 1850's, the Russian and Canadian railways before 1914. Third, and perhaps most important for the take-off itself, the development of railways has led on to the development of modern coal, iron, and engineering industries. In many countries the growth of modern basic industrial sectors can be traced in the most direct way to the requirements for building and, especially, for maintaining substantial railway systems. When a society has developed deeper institutional, social, and political prerequisites for take-off, the rapid growth of a railway system with these powerful triple effects has often served to lift it into self-sustaining growth. Where the prerequisites have not existed, however, very substantial railway building has failed to initiate a take-off, as, for example, in India, China, pre-1895 Canada, pre-1914 Argentine, &c.

It is clear that an enlargement and modernization of armed forces could play the role of a leading sector in take-off. It was a factor in the Russian, Japanese, and German take-offs; and it figures heavily in current Chinese Communist plans. But historically the role of modern armaments has been ancillary rather than central to the take-off.

Quite apart from their role in supplying foreign exchange for general capital-formation purposes, raw materials and foodstuffs can play the role of leading sectors in the take-off if they involve the application of modern processing techniques. The timber industry, built on the steam saw, fulfilled this function in the first phase of Sweden's take-off, to be followed shortly by the pulp industry. Similarly, the shift of Denmark to meat and dairy products, after 1873, appears to have reinforced the development of a manufacturing sector in the economy, as well as providing a major source of foreign exchange. And as Lockwood notes, even the export of Japanese silk thread had important secondary effects which developed modern production techniques.[1]

'To satisfy the demands of American weaving and hosiery mills for uniform, high-grade yarn, however, it was necessary to im-

[1] W. W. Lockwood, *The Economic Development of Japan* (Princeton, 1954), pp. 338–9.

prove the quality of the product, from the silkworm egg on through to the bale of silk. In sericulture this meant the introduction of scientific methods of breeding and disease control; in reeling it stimulated the shift to large filatures equipped with machinery; in marketing it led to large-scale organization in the collection and sale of cocoons and raw silk . . . it exerted steady pressure in favor of the application of science, machinery, and modern business enterprise.

The role of leading sector has been assumed, finally, by the accelerated development of domestic manufacture of consumption goods over a wide range in substitution for imports, as, for example, in Australia, the Argentine, and perhaps in contemporary Turkey.

What can we say, then, in general about these leading sectors? Historically they have ranged from cotton textiles, through heavy-industry complexes based on railroads and military end products, to timber, pulp, dairy products, and finally a wide variety of consumer goods. There is, clearly, no one sectoral sequence for take-off, no single sector which constitutes the magic key. There is no need for a growing society to recapitulate the structural sequence and pattern of Britain, the United States, or Russia. Four basic factors must be present:

1. There must be enlarged effective demand for the product or products of sectors which yield a foundation for a rapid rate of growth in output. Historically this has been brought about initially by the transfer of income from consumption or hoarding to productive investment; by capital imports; by a sharp increase in the productivity of current investment inputs, yielding an increase in consumers' real income expended on domestic manufactures; or by a combination of these routes.

2. There must be an introduction into these sectors of new production functions as well as an expansion of capacity.

3. The society must be capable of generating capital initially required to induce momentum in these key sectors; and especially, there must be a high rate of plough-back by the (private or state) entrepreneurs controlling capacity and

technique in these sectors and in the supplementary growth sectors they stimulated to expand.

4. Finally, the leading sector or sectors must be such that their expansion and technical transformation induce a chain of Leontief input–output requirements for increased capacity and the potentiality for new production functions in other sectors, to which the society, in fact, progressively responds.

VI

This hypothesis is, then, a return to a rather old-fashioned way of looking at economic development. The take-off is described as an industrial revolution, tied directly to radical changes in methods of production, having their decisive consequence over a relatively short period of time.

This view would not deny the role of longer, slower changes in the whole process of economic growth. On the contrary, take-off requires a massive set of preconditions going to the heart of a society's economic organization and its effective scale of values. Moreover, for the take-off to be successful, it must lead on progressively to sustained growth; and this implies further deep and often slow-moving changes in the economy and the society as a whole, of the kind considered in Chapter XIII, in the treatment of the drive to maturity.

What this argument does assert is that the rapid growth of one or more new manufacturing sectors is a powerful and essential engine of economic transformation. Its power derives from the multiplicity of its forms of impact, when a society is prepared to respond positively to this impact. Growth in such sectors, with new production functions of high productivity, in itself tends to raise output per head; it places incomes in the hands of men who will not merely save a high proportion of an expanding income but who will plough it into highly productive investment; it sets up a chain of effective demand for other manufactured products; it sets up a requirement for enlarged urban areas, whose capital costs may be high, but whose population and market organization help to make industrialization an on-going process; and, finally, it opens up a range of external economy effects which, in the end, help to produce new leading sectors when the initial impulse of the take-off's leading sectors begins to wane.

We can observe in history and in the contemporary world important changes in production functions in non-manufacturing sectors which have powerful effects on whole societies. If natural resources are rich enough or the new agricultural tricks are productive enough such changes can even outstrip population growth and yield a rise in real output per head. Moreover, they may be a necessary prior condition for take-off or a necessary concomitant for take-off. Nothing in this analysis should be read as deprecating the importance of productivity changes in agriculture to the whole process of economic growth. But in the end take-off requires that a society find a way to apply effectively to its own peculiar resources what D. H. Robertson once called the 'tricks of manufacture'; and continued growth requires that it so organize itself as to continue to apply them in an unending flow, of changing composition. Only thus, as we have all been correctly taught, can that old demon, diminishing returns, be held at bay.

XIII

THE STAGES OF ECONOMIC GROWTH

BUILDING on the whole argument thus far developed in this book, this chapter summarizes a way of generalizing the sweep of modern economic history. The form of this generalization is a set of stages of growth, which can be designated as follows: the traditional society; the preconditions for take-off; the take-off; the drive to maturity; the age of high mass consumption. Beyond the age of high mass consumption lie the problems which are beginning to arise in a few societies, and which may arise generally when diminishing relative marginal utility sets in for real income itself.

These descriptive categories are rooted in the dynamic propositions about supply, demand, and the pattern of production, elaborated in Part I; and before indicating the historical content of the categories I shall briefly restate the underlying dynamic propositions.

A Dynamic Theory of Production

The classical theory of production is formulated under essentially static assumptions which freeze—or permit only once-over change—in the variables most relevant to the process of economic growth. As modern economists have sought to merge classical production theory with Keynesian income analysis they have introduced the dynamic variables: population, technology, entrepreneurship, &c. But they have tended to do so in forms so rigid and general that their models cannot grip the essential phenomena of growth, as they appear to an economic historian. We require a dynamic theory of production which isolates not only the distribution of income between consumption, saving, and investment (and the balance of production between consumer and capital goods) but which focuses directly and in some detail on the composition of investment and on developments within particular sectors of the economy. The argument that follows is based on such a flexible, disaggregated theory of production.

When the conventional limits on the theory of production are widened, it is possible to define theoretical equilibrium positions not only for output, investment, and consumption as a whole, but for each sector of the economy.

Within the framework set by forces determining the total level of output, sectoral optimum positions are determined on the side of demand, by the levels of income and of population, and by the character of tastes; on the side of supply, by the state of technology and the quality of entrepreneurship, as the latter determines the proportion of technically available and potentially profitable innovations actually incorporated in the capital stock.[1]

In addition, one must introduce an extremely significant empirical hypothesis: namely, that deceleration is the normal optimum path of a sector, due to a variety of factors operating on it, from the side of both supply and demand.

The equilibria which emerge from the application of these criteria are a set of sectoral paths, from which flows, as first derivatives, a sequence of optimum patterns of investment.

Historical patterns of investment did not, of course, exactly follow these optimum patterns. They were distorted by imperfections in the private investment process; by the policies of governments; and by the impact of wars. Wars temporarily altered the profitable directions of investment by setting up arbitrary demands and by changing the conditions of supply; they destroyed capital; and, occasionally, they accelerated the development of new technology relevant to the peacetime economy and shifted the political and social framework in ways conducive to peace-time growth. The historical sequence of business cycles and trend periods results from these deviations of actual from optimal patterns; and such fluctuations, along with the impact of wars, yield historical paths of growth which differ from those which the optima, calculated before the event, would have yielded.

---

[1] In a closed model, a dynamic theory of production must account for changing stocks of basic and applied science, as sectoral aspects of investment, as is done in Chapter IV.

Nevertheless, the economic history of growing societies takes a part of its rude shape—as a first approximation—from the effort of societies to approximate the optimum sectoral paths.

At any period of time, the rate of growth in the sectors will vary greatly; and it is possible to isolate empirically certain leading sectors, at early stages of their evolution, whose rapid rate of expansion plays an essential direct and indirect role in maintaining the over-all momentum of the economy. For some purposes it is useful to characterize an economy in terms of its leading sectors; and a part of the technical basis for the stages of growth lies in the changing sequence of leading sectors. In essence it is the fact that sectors tend to have a rapid growth phase, early in their life, that makes it possible and useful to regard economic history as a sequence of stages rather than merely as a continuum, within which nature never makes a jump.

The stages of growth also require, however, that clasticities of demand be taken into account, and that this familiar concept be widened; for these rapid growth phases in the sectors derive not merely from the discontinuity of production functions but also from high price or income elasticities of demand. Leading sectors are determined not merely by the changing flow of technology and the changing willingness of entrepreneurs to accept available innovations: they are also partially determined by those types of demand which have exhibited high elasticity with respect to price, income, or both.

The demand for resources has resulted, however, not merely from demands set up by private taste and choice, but also from social decisions and from the policies of governments—whether democratically responsive or not. It is necessary, therefore, to look at the choices made by societies in the disposition of their resources in terms which transcend conventional market processes. It is necessary to look at their welfare functions, in the widest sense, including the non-economic processes which determined them.

The course of birth-rates, for example, represents one form of welfare choice made by societies, as income has changed;

and population curves reflect (in addition to changing death-rates) how the calculus about family size was made in the various stages: from the usual (but not universal) decline in birth-rates, during or soon after the take-off, as urbanization took hold and progress became a palpable possibility, to the recent rise, as Americans (and others in societies marked by high mass consumption) have appeared to seek, in larger families, values beyond those afforded by economic security and by an ample supply of durable consumer goods and services.

And there are other decisions as well that societies have made as the choices open to them have been altered by the unfolding process of economic growth; and these broad collective decisions, determined by many factors—deep in history, culture, and the active political process—outside the market-place, have interplayed with the dynamics of market demand, risk-taking, technology, and entrepreneurship, to determine the specific content of the stages of growth for each society.

How, for example, should the traditional society react to the intrusion of a more advanced power—with cohesion, promptness, and vigour, like the Japanese; by virtue of fecklessness, like the oppressed Irish of the eighteenth century; by slowly and reluctantly altering the traditional society, like the Chinese?

When independent modern nationhood was achieved, how should the national energies be disposed—in external aggression, to right old wrongs or to exploit newly created or perceived possibilities for enlarged national power; in completing and refining the political victory of the new national government over old regional interests; or in modernizing the economy?

Once growth is under way, with the take-off, to what extent should the requirements of diffusing modern technology and maximizing the rate of growth be moderated by the desire to increase consumption *per capita* and to increase welfare?

When technological maturity is reached, and the nation has at its command a modernized and differentiated industrial machine, to what ends should it be put, and in what proportions—to increase social security, through the welfare state; to expand mass consumption into the range of durable consumer goods and services; to increase the nation's stature and power on the world scene; or to increase leisure?

And then the question beyond, where history offers us only fragments: what to do when the increase in real income itself loses its charm? Babies; boredom; three-day week-ends; the moon, or the creation of new inner, human frontiers in substitution for the imperatives of scarcity?

In surveying now the broad contours of each stage of growth, we are examining, then, not merely the sectoral structure of economies, as they transformed themselves for growth, and grew; we are also examining a succession of strategic choices made by various societies concerning the disposition of their resources, which include but transcend the income and price elasticities of demand.

The Traditional Society

The central economic fact about traditional societies is that they evolved within limited production functions. Both in the more distant past and in recent times the story of traditional societies is a story of endless change, reflected in the scale and patterns of trade, the level of agricultural output and productivity, the scale of manufactures, fluctuations in population and real income. But limitations of technology decreed a ceiling beyond which they could not penetrate. They did not lack inventiveness and innovations, some of high productivity. But they did lack a systematic understanding of their physical environment capable of making invention a more or less regular current flow, rather than a stock of *ad hoc* achievements inherited from the past. They lacked, in short, the tools and the outlook towards the physical world of the post-Newtonian era.

It followed from this productivity ceiling that food production absorbed 75 per cent. or more of the working force and that a high proportion of income above minimum consumption levels was spent in non-productive or low-productivity outlays: religious and other monuments, wars, high living for those who controlled land rents; and for poorer folk there was a beggar-thy-neighbour struggle for land or the dissipation of the occasional surplus in an expensive wedding or funeral.

Social values were geared to the limited horizons which men could perceive to be open to them; and social structures tended to hierarchy, although the traditional societies never wholly lacked paths for vertical mobility.

The centre of gravity of political power tended to reside in the regions, with the landowners, despite a fluctuating tension with those who—along with their soldiers and civil servants—exercised a degree of central authority.

The Preconditions for Take-off

The initial preconditions for take-off were created in Western Europe out of two characteristics of the post-medieval world which interacted and reinforced each other: the gradual evolution of modern science and the modern scientific attitude; and the lateral innovation that came with the discovery of new lands and the rediscovery of old, converging with the impulse to create new technology at certain strategic points. The widening of the market—both within Europe and overseas—brought not only trade but increased specialization of production, increased inter-regional and international dependence, enlarged institutions of finance, and increased market incentives to create new production functions. The whole process was heightened by the extension to trade and colonies of the old dynastic competition for control over European territories, inherited from the world of traditional societies.[1]

Britain was the first of the European nations to move from the stage of preconditions into take-off, a fact capable of

[1] This analysis shares with Schumpeter's the view that the ultimate causes of war were inherited from traditional societies, and were not a consequence of the more or less rational pursuit of direct economic interests. But, whereas Schumpeter tends to emphasize the persistence of irrational and romantic nationalist attitudes, this analysis would underline the structural fact that, once national sovereignty was accepted as a rule of the world arena, nations found themselves gripped in an almost inescapable oligopolistic struggle for power, which did have elements of non-economic rationality. See also Raymond Aron, *War and Industrial Society*, London, Oxford University Press, 1958.

various explanations but certainly influenced by these circumstances: its achicvement of a political and religious settlement by 1688; the area of social latitude and the limited but powerful incentives offered to nonconformists, who played a remarkable role in the process of industrial innovation; its naval and, thus, trading advantages, partly determined by a greater freedom from commitments to land warfare than the French, an endowment in industrial raw materials superior to the Dutch.

The existence of the British take-off from, say, 1783 set in motion a series of positive and negative demonstration effects which progressively unhinged other traditional societies or accelerated the creation of the preconditions for take-off, where the preconditions process was already under way.[1] Before examining the manner in which these demonstration effects were communicated, however, the structural characteristics of the preconditions period should be defined.

Technically, the preconditions for sustained industrialization have generally required radical change in three nonindustrial sectors. First, a build-up of social overhead capital, notably in transport. This build-up was necessary not merely to permit an economical national market to be created and to allow natural resources to be productively exploited, but also to permit the national government effectively to rule. Second, a technological revolution in agriculture. The processes at work during the preconditions generally yielded both a general rise in population and a disproportionate rise in urban populations. Increased productivity in agriculture has been generally a necessary condition for preventing the process of modernization from being throttled. Third, an expansion in imports financed by the more efficient production and marketing of some natural resources plus, where possible, capital imports. Such increased access to foreign exchange was required to permit the less advanced region or nation

[1] This chapter will not examine the preconditions process in the nations which, in Louis Hartz's phrase, were 'born free' of traditional societies, mainly deriving from a British society already well advanced in the preconditions process or in regular growth. I refer to the United States, Canada, New Zealand, Australia, &c. The nature of the preconditions for take-off in such societies is, however, briefly considered in Chapter XII, p. 277.

to increase the supply of the equipment and industrial raw materials it could not then itself supply as well as to preserve the level of real income while social overhead capital of long gestation period was being created.

Framed by these three forms of sectoral development, yielding both new markets and new inputs for industry, the initially small enclaves of modern industrial activity could begin to expand, and then sustain expansion, mainly by the plough-back of profits.

These technical developments required, in turn, prior or concurrent changes in the non-economic dimensions of the traditional society : a willingness of the agricultural community to accept new techniques and to respond to the possibilities of the widened commercial markets; the existence and freedom to operate of a new group of industrial entrepreneurs; and, above all, a national government capable not only of providing a setting of peaceful order which encouraged the new modernizing activities but also capable and willing to take a degree of direct responsibility for the build-up of social overhead capital (including its finance), for an appropriate trade policy, and often, as well, for the diffusion of new agricultural and industrial techniques.

The political dimension of the preconditions deserves a further word, due to the peculiar mixture of positive and negative ways in which the demonstration effects of industrialization were transmitted from more advanced societies.

In part the transmission consisted in making men in less advanced societies perceive that new positive choices were open to them: longer life for themselves and their children; new ranges of consumption; new devices of productivity; higher levels of welfare. At least equally powerful, however, was the negative demonstration that more advanced societies could impose their will on the less advanced, through the exercise of military force. A reactive nationalist sentiment— rooted in a perception of the link between industrialization and effective power in the world arena—came to be an extremely important factor in leading men to take the steps necessary to unhinge and transform the traditional society in such ways as to permit growth to become its normal condition.

Without the affront to human and national dignity caused by the intrusion of more advanced powers, the rate of modernization of traditional societies over the past century and a half would have been much slower than, in fact, it has been.

Thus, it was not merely the German merchants but the German nationalists that led the way after 1848; not merely the Japanese merchants but the samurai after 1868; not merely the Russian middle class, but a political, military, and civil service *élite*, smarting from the harsh lesson of the Crimean War and from a widening perception of the national costs of Russian backwardness; not merely the Chinese merchants, but the intellectuals and the younger soldiers, who sought effective modernization by various routes in the whole long, turbulent sweep from the Opium War and the Taiping Rebellion forward.[1] Ataturk's role in Turkey—and his motivation—constitutes a more typical case of the preconditions process than, let us say, the role and motivation of the innovating British nonconformists of the eighteenth century.

The evolution of colonial areas is also a version of the general case. There the positive and negative demonstration effects intermingled, under colonial rule; but they yielded, in the end, a local *élite* which accorded to political independence an overriding and urgent priority.

[1] An element of reactive nationalism is not wholly lacking from earlier cases, as well, apparently more purely economic in their motivation. The more rapid evolution in Britain than on the Continent of the preconditions for take-off can be viewed, in part, as the product of a series of nationalist reactions to intrusion from more powerful or advanced neighbours: the Spanish in the sixteenth century; the Dutch in the seventeenth; the French in the eighteenth. These threats and national struggles may have yielded a sentiment which softened the rigidities of the traditional society, accelerated a new national settlement, and permitted Britain to get on with the tasks of economic growth more effectively than others in the eighteenth century. And in the United States, too, the acceptance of the Constitution—reluctant at best—may have been made possible by a convergence of the desire of men of property to avoid the anarchy of a fragmented market and a certain casualness towards property rights, with the widespread perception in the mid-1780's that the United States might not be able to cope with more powerful nation states, intruding on the Confederation in one way or another, unless an effective central government existed. Hamilton's nationalism, and his conviction that American industrialization was necessary, transcended motives of private economic advantage.

While a reactive nationalism has been a powerful engine of modernization it also posed problems for economic development; for it did not immediately and directly prepare men to face and handle the homely economic tasks of the preconditions and the take-off. On the contrary, when a new national government was achieved—in the face of the colonial power, the traditional society, or both in combination—its leaders were tempted to go on with the familiar game of politics and power rather than to turn promptly to the domestic tasks of modernization. There were real or believed external wrongs and humiliations to be righted; there were still rear-guard actions from elements in the traditional society to be dealt with; and much energy and resource could be allocated to the political—and sometimes military—problem of consolidating the power of the centre over the old regional forces.

In short, some time often had to pass before men emerged in authority willing to accept the fact that the larger objectives of resurgent nationalism could not be achieved without turning wholeheartedly to the technical tasks of economic growth.[1] Both in the more distant past and in the contemporary world it is possible and useful to view societies in the stage of preconditions in terms of the changing balances struck among these three possible expressions of reactive nationalism. Until a definitive political transformation occurs—which harnesses national energies, talents, and resources around the concrete tasks of economic growth—the take-off is likely to be postponed: negatively, because the thin layer of modern technical and administrative talent in the society (as well as the society's margin of savings) is likely to be dissipated in activities of low or negative productivity; positively, because the government is unlikely to play its role effectively in the

[1] In his forthcoming study of the preconditions process in Japan, Turkey, and India, Mr. Lawrence Barss, of M.I.T., advances the hypothesis that it may be useful to distinguish two political stages, which he designates the Transition and the Transformation. In the Transition, political life is dominated by men who want for their nations the benefits of modern independent status, but they are inhibited by many factors, including attitudes and ties of interest to the traditional society, from doing what must be done for economic growth. In the Transformation, a political leadership takes hold that, at last, means business.

three sectoral developments—in social overhead capital, agriculture, and trade—necessary to create the matrix for sustained industrial growth.

The Take-off

As suggested in Chapter XII, the take-off consists, in essence, of the achievement of rapid growth in a limited group of sectors, where modern industrial techniques are applied. Historically, the leading sectors in take-off have ranged from cotton textiles (Britain and New England); to railroads (the United States, France, Germany, Canada, Russia); to modern timber-cutting and railroads (Sweden). In addition, agricultural processing, oil, import-substitution industries, ship-building, and rapid expansions in military output have helped to provide the initial industrial surge.

The take-off is distinguished from earlier industrial surges by the fact that prior and concurrent developments make the application of modern industrial techniques a self-sustained rather than an abortive process. Not only must the momentum in the three key sectors of the preconditions be maintained but the corps of entrepreneurs and technicians must be enlarged, and the sources of capital must be institutionalized in such a way as to permit the economy to suffer structural shocks; to redispose its investment resources; and to resume growth. It is the requirement that the economy exhibit this resilience that justifies defining the take-off as embracing an interval of about two decades.

A result—and one key manifestation—of take-off is the ability of the society to sustain an annual rate of net investment of the order of, at least, 10 per cent. This familiar (but essentially tautological) way of defining the take-off should not conceal the full range of transformations required before growth becomes a built-in feature of a society's habits and institutions.

In non-economic terms, the take-off usually witnesses a definitive social, political, and cultural victory of those who would modernize the economy over those who would either cling to the traditional society or seek other goals; but—

because nationalism can be a social solvent as well as a diversionary force—the victory can assume forms of mutual accommodation, rather than the destruction of the traditional groups by the more modern; see, for example, the role of the Junkers in nascent industrial Germany and the persistence of much of traditional Japan beyond 1880. By and large, the maintenance of momentum for a generation persuades the society to persist, and to concentrate its efforts on extending the tricks of modern technology out beyond the sectors modernized during take-off.

The Drive to Maturity

After take-off there follows, then, what might be called the drive to maturity. There is a variety of ways in which a stage of economic maturity might be defined; but for these purposes it is defined as the period when a society has effectively applied the range of (then) modern technology to the bulk of its resources.

During the drive to maturity the industrial process is differentiated, with new leading sectors gathering momentum to supplant the older leading sectors of the take-off, where deceleration has increasingly slowed the pace of expansion. After the railway take-offs of the third quarter of the nineteenth century—with coal, iron, and heavy engineering at the centre of the growth process—it is steel, the new ships, chemicals, electricity, and the products of the modern machine tool that come to dominate the economy and sustain the over-all rate of growth. This is also, essentially, the case with the later Russian drive to maturity, after 1929. But in Sweden after 1890 it was the evolution from timber to woodpulp and paper; from ore to high-grade steel and finely machined metal products. The leading sectors in the drive to maturity will be determined, then, not merely by the pool of technology but by the nature of resource endowments; and it may be shaped to a degree, as well, by the policies of governments.

Although much further detailed analysis would be required

to apply this definition rigorously, I would offer the following sample as rough symbolic dates for technological maturity.[1]

Great Britain	1850
United States	1900
Germany	1910
France	1910
Sweden	1930
Japan	1940
Russia	1950
Canada	1950

The meaning of this technological definition of maturity—and its limits—may be better perceived by considering briefly a few specific problems posed by these particular dates.

Is France, for example, on the eve of the First World War, to be regarded as technologically mature, despite its large, comfortable, but technologically backward peasantry and its tendency to export large amounts of capital, despite certain technologically lagging industrial sectors? The case can, of course, be argued either way; but it does dramatize the need to allow, within the present definition, for regions of a nation or sectors of the economy to resist—for whatever reason—the full application of the range of modern technology. And this turns out to be generally true of nations which, by and large, one would judge mature. The United States of 1900 contained, after all, the South, whose take-off can only be dated from the 1930's; and contemporary mature Canada contains the still lagging province of Quebec. The technological definition of maturity must, then, be an approximation, when applied to a whole national society.

Japan as of 1940 poses a somewhat different problem. Can one rate as mature an economy with so labour-intensive an agricultural sector? The answer is affirmative only if one is prepared to take as a given—outside the definition of

[1] An oddity is to be noted. These dates, independently derived, come more or less sixty years after the dates established, on quite different criteria, for the beginning of take-off. There is no body of argument or evidence I can now offer to make rational such a uniformity. But it may be that when we explore the implications of some six decades of compound interest applied to the capital stock, in combination with three generations of men living under an environment of growth, elements of rationality will emerge.

maturity—a society's decision about its population size. Within the Japanese population–resource balance, its agriculture, with extraordinary refinement in the use of both water and chemical fertilizers, does indeed reflect a high form of modern technological achievement, even if modern farm machinery, designed to save labour, is capable of only limited use.

What about contemporary Russia, with more than 40 per cent. of the working force still in agriculture and much modern technology still unapplied in consumer-goods industries? Here again, the present definition of maturity would not predetermine how a society chooses to allocate its technological capabilities. By and large contemporary Russia is to be judged a mature economy despite the fact that its leaders have chosen for political reasons to bear the costs of a low-productivity agriculture and have chosen to concentrate capital and technology in sectors other than manufactured consumption goods. Put another way, the obstacles to full modernization of the Russian economic structure do not lie in the supply of capital, entrepreneurial administrators, or technicians.

Finally, there is the case of Britain, mature on this definition as early, say, as the Crystal Palace Exhibition. How is one to deal with the long interval between the stages of its maturity, in terms of the effective application of mid-nineteenth-century technology, and the next stage of growth: the age of high mass consumption, when the radical improvements in housing and durable consumer goods and services become the economy's leading sectors?

The reasons for the gap in the British sequence lie in the nature of this next stage. The age of high mass consumption represents a direction of development a society may choose when it has achieved both technological maturity and a certain level of real income per head. Although income per head—and usually consumption per head—will rise in the drive to maturity, it is evident that there is no fixed connexion between technological maturity and any particular level of real consumption per head. The course of these variables after take-off will depend primarily on the society's population–resource balance and on its income-distribution policy. The process of growth, by definition, raises income per head, but it does not necessarily lead to uniformity of *per capita* income among nations or, even, among regions within nations. There are—and there are likely to be—technologically mature societies that are, so to speak, both rich and poor. When historical data on national income are developed to permit systematic comparison, we are likely to find that incomes per head, at maturity, vary over a considerable range. Mid-century Britain would, presumably, stand low in that range. The improvements in real income and consumption per head that occurred in the second half of the nineteenth century took the form of improvements in diet, housing, and urban overhead capital which, while substantial, did not create within Britain new leading industrial sectors—at least down to the bicycle boom of the 1890's.[1]

[1] In a different perspective, it is possible to dismiss the gap between mid-nineteenth-century British technological maturity and twentieth-century high mass consumption as a simple product of technological history; that is, the technology of modern transportation, suburban housing, and household gadgetry did not exist in, say, the third quarter of the nineteenth century. And for many purposes that is a quite satisfactory way to look at the matter.

On the other hand, three considerations argue that it is worth regarding the British sequence in the second half of the nineteenth century as involving a gap. First, technology itself is, in its widest sense, not an independent variable (see above, pp. 83–86). If the level of British incomes and consumption had been high enough, incentives might have existed which would have yielded a quite different evolution of technology. Second, the phenomenon of a gap in time between the attainment of technological maturity and the age of high mass consumption—the existence of relatively poor as well as rich mature societies—is more general than the British case. And a view of Britain in the second half of the nineteenth century as in the process of closing the gap may, for certain purposes, be linked suggestively to similar transitions in other societies. Third, much in British social, political, and even entrepreneurial history in the second half of the nineteenth century is typical of transformations in attitude and policy which have occurred in other societies after technological maturity has been attained: the beginnings of serious welfare legislation, with the Ten Hours Bill; the pressures and reflections which led the society to accept the Second and Third Reform Bills; the emergence of political coalitions which damped the power of industrial interests; the mounting intellectual attention and public sentiment focused on problems of social reform, laying the bases for the pre-1914 Liberal measures and the emergence of the Labour Party. In short, even narrowly examined, much in British history in the period 1850–1900 is illuminated by the notion that this was a society which took its technological virtuosity as a given and, at a decorous rate, proceeded to seek, at the margin, welfare objectives beyond.

And so Britain, after Crystal Palace, moved onward in growth at a modest pace, using its capital and entrepreneurship substantially to help acquire resources with which it was not sufficiently endowed and to help build the preconditions and assist the take-offs of other societies, suffering along the way some of the costs of having led in the process of industrialization, to enter the new century with most of its initial lead gone.[1] Put another way, the achievement of maturity by Western Europe and the United States early in the twentieth century, at the then existing level of technology, found Britain in a roughly equivalent position: while the newer nations had moved from take-off to maturity in the sixty years before the First World War, Britain had moved, in terms of income levels, from being a relatively poor mature society to being a relatively rich mature society.

As societies move to technological maturity, the structure and quality of the working force change. The proportion of the population in agriculture and rural life decreases; and within the urban population the proportion of semi-skilled and white-collar workers increases.[2] This emergent working force is likely not only to organize itself with increasing effectiveness in the labour markets, but also to perceive that the industrial civilization of which it is a part can offer levels and types of consumption not previously regarded as a realistic possibility on a mass basis. And the rise in real income per head is likely to make these new tastes effective.

Further, the new working force, increasingly born to the city rather than transferred from the lower margins of rural life, is likely to perceive that it can bring its weight to bear on the political process in such ways as to make the government increasingly provide measures of social and economic security.

---

[1] The forces which relatively damped the rate of increase in British income and permitted its technological lead to be dissipated are, evidently, more complex than this sentence can suggest; but it would be inappropriate to this exposition to examine them at greater length here.

[2] Although Colin Clark's categories—of primary, secondary, and tertiary activity—do not precisely fit this analysis, his pioneer compilations suggest that considerable uniformities in the structure of the working force of mature economies do exist.

Moreover, the character of leadership in industry begins to change as well. The take-off is usually managed by relatively modest, creative men with an insight as to how output in their sector can be radically expanded: the Boultons and Lowells. In the drive to maturity men take over with more grandiose visions, with a more acute sense of scale and of power: although there are vast differences between post-Civil War United States and Stalin's Russia, there is, nevertheless, a distant family resemblance between some of the great entrepreneurs of the American drive to maturity and the men who administered the Five Year Plans between, say, 1929 and 1953. At maturity, however, the professional managers become more important—the nameless comfortable, cautious committee-men who inherit and manage large sectors of the economy, while the society begins to seek objectives which include but transcend the application of modern technology to resources.

These sea-changes in the outlook and objectives of the working force and industrial management are likely to be accompanied by wider shifts in the society's mood, which the intellectuals and politicians articulate. They react against the harshness and social costs of the drive to maturity. The extension of industrialization ceases to be acceptable as an overriding goal: in an extension of the law of diminishing relative marginal utility, men appear to place a lowered valuation on further increments to what they have in abundance, and, at the margin, to seek new satisfactions. In the pre-1914 drive to maturity of Western Europe and the United States one can find, in each nation, reflections of this mood gradually gathering strength, centred about the question: How shall the mature industrial machine, with compound interest built firmly into its structure, be used? In the 1930's it was faced by Japan; and in the 1950's it confronts Russia.

The Age of High Mass Consumption

There have been, essentially, three directions in which the mature economy could be turned once the society ceased to accept the extension of modern technology as a primary, if not an overriding objective: to offer, by public measures, increased security, welfare, and, perhaps, leisure to the working force; to provide enlarged private consumption—including single family homes and durable consumer goods and services —on a mass basis; to seek enlarged power for the mature nation on the world scene. A good deal of the history of the first half of the twentieth century can be told in terms of the pattern and succession of choices made by various mature societies as among these three alternatives.

After a brief and superficial flirtation with the attractions of world power at the turn of the century and after imposing a set of mild measures of social reform, during the Progressive period, the United States opted whole-heartedly in the 1920's for the second choice.[1] The boom of that decade was built squarely on the migration to suburbia, the mass extension of the automobile, and the household gadgetry which modern industry could provide. And these decisions to relocate the population and provide it with mobility brought in their train not only new leading sectors—housing, automobiles, petroleum, rubber, electric-powered household devices, &c. —but also vast commitments to build new social overhead capital and commercial centres.

Down to 1914 Britain and Western Europe opted more substantially for public measures of social security, influenced perhaps by the higher proportions of urban population and by the greater power of socialist thought and political influence than existed in the United States. In addition, Germany was more seriously tempted than the United States to translate industrial maturity into enlarged world power; and in the inherently oligopolistic circumstances of the European arena of power, this decision led to a greater relative enlargement of military expenditures in Europe as a whole than in pre-1914 United States.

[1] The time-lag in the United States between the achievement of technological maturity in, say, 1900, and the high mass-consumption boom of the 1920's is to be accounted for in part by the relative stagnation of industrial real wages in the pre-1914 trend period, due to rising living-costs (see above, Chapter VI). The more protracted lag of Western Europe is partly a consequence of pre-1914 real-wage trends; partly also a consequence of the economic impact of the First World War and of the public policies and dominant social attitudes of the inter-war years.

During the 1920's Britain, in effect, took its favourable terms of trade in the form of chronic unemployment in the export industries. Only in the 1930's did a persuasive recovery occur. This phase did begin to exhibit a shift into the age of high mass consumption: suburban housing, automobiles, and durable consumer goods began to assert themselves more strongly as leading sectors. But rearmament and war postponed the immediate fruition of this trend.

Although the post-1920 terms of trade problem struck the Continent with less force than Britain, there too the return to relative prosperity, of 1925–9, did not move the economies far beyond pre-1914 patterns. France, on the whole, continued to stagnate down to the Second World War; and German recovery, while reflecting certain symptoms of the new phase, was dominated by rearmament.

Svennilson presents calculations of motor-vehicle production (private and commercial) which suggest the relative movements of the United States and Western Europe between the wars. In 1929 the four major European nations (Great Britain, Germany, France, and Italy) produced 702,000 vehicles; the United States 5·4 million. After a decade of protracted depression in the United States (marked by a compensatory turn to the welfare state) and a considerably greater degree of European recovery, the European figure was 1·1 million in 1938; the American 2·5 million.[1]

In the decade 1946–56 the United States resumed a pattern of recovery and growth markedly similar to that of the 1920's:

[1] Ingvar Svennilson, *Growth and Stagnation in the European Economy*, United Nations, Geneva, 1954, pp. 144–52. I am inclined to believe that the length of the American depression and its intractability in the 1930's stems from the character of leading sectors in the age of high mass consumption. The diffusion of single-family housing, the automobile, &c., requires expanding levels of private income and, in effect, full employment. Moreover, until the diffusion process is actively under way certain major forms of investment are likely to be slack, because of idle capacity. Full employment is needed, in a sense, to maintain full employment when the leading sectors are consumption sectors. This was not true in pre-1914 when, even with unemployment high and incomes low, it might well have paid to press on with railroadization, steel ships, &c., where the high expected rate of return over costs derived primarily from lowered costs. Put another way, in the age of high mass consumption a higher proportion of investment becomes endogenous, rather than exogenous, when the latter term is used to embrace investment stimulated by new technological possibilities.

the migration to suburbia; and the extension of the automobile and the standard mix of durable consumer household gadgets to 75 per cent. or more of American families. And, after an interval of post-war reconstruction, Western Europe resumed with force the similar but more laggard development of the 1930's. By the late 1950's Western European growth was based on the fact that this region had at last fully entered the age of durable consumer goods and services, experiencing a version of the American 1920's. The patterns of consumption, as among the various European countries, emerge as largely explicable in terms of income and price elasticities of demand.[1] And in Russia, as well, the inexorable attraction of the sewing-machine, washing-machine, refrigerator, and television was beginning to assert itself; and the first satellite town was under construction.[2] It was evident, however, from the pattern of future plans that the Soviet government was not yet prepared to give the vast hostages to fortune that follow a society's commitment to the mass automobile.

Beyond Consumption

While Western Europe (and to a degree, also, Japan) was entering the era of high mass consumption, and the Soviet Union was dallying on its fringes, an important new element entered the world economic system in the form of a quite unexpected tendency of birth-rates to rise in rich societies.[3] Although the tendency can be observed in a number of countries, it is most marked in the United States. During the years of the Second World War the American birth-rate rose from 18 to about 22 per 1,000. This was judged at the time, and to a large degree it certainly was, a phenomenon of resumed full employment and early war-time marriages. In the post-war years, however, it moved up and has stayed at about 25 per 1,000. An official forecast in 1946 estimated that the

[1] See, notably, Milton Gilbert and Associates, *Comparative National Products and Price Levels*, O.E.E.C., Paris, 1958.

[2] *Economic Survey of Europe in 1957*, United Nations, Geneva, 1958, pp. 14 and 22 n.

[3] There have also been remarkable declines in birth-rates in Japan and Italy in the 1950's, as new horizons of economic progress have opened up for large segments of the population.

American population would reach 165 million in 1990; an official forecast of 1958 estimated that the figure might be of the order of 240 million by 1980.

The human motivations and social processes which have yielded this extraordinary result are not yet well understood; but Americans have behaved as if diminishing relative marginal utility set in to the expansion of real income along the old paths. They have opted at the margin for larger families; and this trend may be related to the high rate of expansion in family trips to national parks, motor-boats, do-it-yourself implements, and even to a widely noted tendency to turn away from the pursuit of income and authority within the large-scale bureaucratic establishments where a high proportion of the population do their work.[1]

Whatever the motivation, however, an expansion of population on this scale will set up requirements for the lateral extension of the society's resources, including its requirements of social overhead capital. These requirements in any case had been enlarged by the consequences of the previous phase of extension in automobile ownership and suburban housing:[2] there is a vast American backlog of investment to be carried out in roads and in the reconstruction of old depopulated urban centres. Finally, a quite significant change in the dependency ratio is under way. After falling for about a century, the number of persons under 20 and over 65 in the American population supported by each 100 members of the working force had reached 74 in 1935; by 1955 the figure was 81; and if present population patterns persist it is estimated that the figure will rise to 98 by 1975.[3]

The pattern of American economic growth over the next several decades is likely to differ, then, from that of either the 1920's or the 1946–56 decade; and it is likely to be based on somewhat different leading sectors. In any case, it is clear that

[1] See, notably, Clyde Kluckhohn, 'Have There Been Discernible Shifts in American Values in the Past Generation?', in *The American Style* (E. E. Morison, ed.), New York, 1958.

[2] See, notably, the calculations on social overhead requirements in *The Challenge to America: Its Economic and Social Aspects*, Special Studies Project Report IV, Rockefeller Brothers Fund, New York, 1958.

[3] C. and I. B. Taeuber, *The Changing Population of the United States*, New York and London, 1958, p. 325.

American society, by its quiet collective decision about birth-rates, has postponed the problems of a time of true affluence, when the full utilization of resources would not much matter.

The somewhat strenuous choice made by Americans as they pushed high mass consumption to a kind of logical con-clusion, in the first decade after the Second World War, need not prove to be universal: the income elasticity of demand for children may vary. It is evident, however, that the march of compound interest is bringing some societies close to the point where the pursuit of food, shelter, clothing, as well as durable consumer goods and public and private services, may no longer dominate their lives. A new and revolutionary set of choices is being confronted, or is a mere generation or so over the horizon.

This is not to say that the richer societies are without challenge. There is the problem of escaping from a treacher-ous nuclear-arms race. And there is the equal problem of organizing the planet, as the whole southern half of the globe and China move through the preconditions into take-off and regular growth. But the era when the human agenda were imposed by the fact of scarcity is coming towards an end: the day when, in Marx's phrase, labour 'has of itself become the prime necessity of life' is not all that far off, if nuclear destruction and the grosser forms of international disorder can be avoided.

A Comparison with Marxism

The analysis of stages of growth summarized here invites comparison with Marxism; for Marxism is also a theory of how societies came to build compound interest into their structures and of what then transpired; Marxism also begins with the impact on feudal (traditional) societies of the new discoveries and the expansion of trade; and it ends with com-munism—the stage beyond high mass consumption—when men need no longer work very hard for the material things they may want.

There are differences between the two systems at every point; but the most consequential difference centres on the assumptions made about human motivation. Marx derived several of his essential analytic tools from classical economics, as he interpreted it: a labour theory of value; an essentially Malthusian law of population and labour supply; and a version of diminishing returns, applied to the capital stock. But his most important derivation was the notion of treating human behaviour as an exercise in profit maximization.

The exact form of the function relating economic interest to non-economic behaviour varies in Marx's writings and in the subsequent Marxist literature. Much in the original texts —and virtually all the operational conclusions derived from them—depends on a view of the function as simple and direct as the dictum in the *Communist Manifesto* that capitalism 'left no other nexus between man and man than naked self-interest, than callous "cash payment"'. Elsewhere the function is developed in a more sophisticated form. Non-economic behaviour is seen as related not immediately and directly to economic self-interest but to the ideology and loyalties of class. Since, however, class interests and ideologies are presented as essentially a function of the techniques of production, and the social relationships arising from them, this indirect formulation yields much the same results as the more primitive statement of connexion. In the main stream of Marxist literature, from beginning to end, it is only in seeking, protecting, and enlarging property and income that men are really serious. Finally, there are a few passages in Marx—and more in Engels—which reveal a perception that human behaviour is affected by motives and objectives which need not be related to or converge with economic self-interest. This perception, if systematically elaborated, would have altered radically the whole flow of the Marxist argument and its conclusions.

It is with this perception that my analysis begins; for in the stages of growth human behaviour is seen not as an act of maximization, but as an act of balancing alternative and often conflicting independent human objectives in the face of the changing range of alternatives men perceive to be open to them. Men seek not merely economic advantage, but personal and national power as well; not merely adventure but security and continuity of social and cultural experience;

not merely personal expression, but the joys of family, and a bit of fun down at the local.

Applied to societies, this innately paradoxical view of the human condition—a view which regards man as a complex household rather than a maximizing unit—does not yield rigid, inevitable stages of history. It leads to a succession of patterns of choice—varying in their balance—made within the framework permitted by the changing setting of society: a setting itself the product of both objective material conditions and of the prior choices made by men.

It follows directly from this view of how individuals act that the performance of societies is not uniquely determined by the locus of property-ownership or by the nature of production techniques. The sectors of society interact: cultural, social, and political forces, reflecting different facets of human aspiration, have their own authentic impact on the evolution of societies, including their economic evolution. They are not a superstructure derived from the economy.

This view alters the specific stages of growth away from the Marxist pattern in quite particular ways.

First, the preconditions period is seen as a searching process of restructuring all dimensions of the traditional society, in which a reactive nationalism plays an important role; and decisions about the direction of national objectives which transcend material interests must be made before the take-off can get under way.

Second, neither in nor out of the market-place is the power of the new property-owners such as necessarily to deny the working force a share in expanding output once regular growth begins with the take-off; and the fact of progress, combined with urbanization, has generally set in motion a non-Malthusian decline in birth-rates, tending to reinforce the rise in real wages.

Third, with the fact of regular progress in income, the income elasticity of demand comes into play as an independent force, altering the range of perceived alternatives, the pattern of effective demand, and the sectoral structure of the economy; whereas in Marxism the income elasticity of demand appears only in the perverse form of rising income from surplus value in the hands of a narrowing band of the *bour-geoisie*, capable of use which will only further distort the sectoral structure of the economy and hasten its ultimate crisis.

Fourth, in wider terms as well, the choices made by the society are determined by the existence of independently powerful political and social processes where effective influence is not weighted by property-ownership; and, notably when maturity is reached, these areas of influence help determine how, and in what sequence, the resources of the mature economy will be used, including the possibility of a welfare state based on progressive taxation.

Fifth, the choices open to men when affluence is achieved appear to include but to transcend Marx's somewhat romantic vision of 'labour as a prime necessity of life'. There are, as suggested earlier, the possibilities of a population surge; outer space; boredom; an elevation of the quality of life; or the devil making work for idle hands.

The basic error in Marxism is, then, not a technical error in his economics; although such errors can be identified. In building on the western intellectual and moral tradition he failed to perceive that the body of thought about society, of which classical economics was a part, was a spacious, complex, and essentially paradoxical creed. As Myrdal and Robbins have pointed out in this generation,[1] the individualist–utilitarian creed did, indeed, make the case for free competitive markets and for private property; but it also contained within its presuppositions the case for free elections, on a one-man-one-vote basis; for destroying or controlling monopolies; for social legislation which would set considerations of human welfare off against profit incentives; and, above all, for the progressive income tax.

In wrestling loyally with the dilemmas posed by the individualist–utilitarian creed, in finding balances that respected its conflicting imperatives, the societies of the West have thus made their way to the brink of communism without succumbing to Marx's prognosis.

[1] G. Myrdal, *The Political Element in the Development of Economic Theory* (tr. from the German edition of 1932 by Paul Streeten), London, 1953; L. Robbins, *The Theory of Economic Policy in English Classical Political Economy*, London, 1952.

XIV

THE INTERRELATION OF THEORY
AND ECONOMIC HISTORY

I

I DO not much hold with ardent debate about method. An historian's method is as individual—as private—a matter as a novelist's style. There is good reason for reserve—even reticence—on this subject, except in so far as we seek to share each other's unique professional adventures and to listen occasionally, in a mood of interest tempered with scepticism, to such general reflections as we each would draw from those adventures.

Moreover, as a practical matter, no good cause is likely to be served by further exhortation to the historian to use more theory or to the theorist to read more history. Progress in this old contentious terrain is made only by meeting a payroll; that is, by demonstrating that something interesting and worth while can be generated by working with historical data within a conscious and orderly theoretical framework, or by adding to the structure of theory through historical generalization. This chapter is thus justified only to the extent that it sets down some tentative and interim personal reflections drawn from practical work; for I take it to be agreed that man has open to him no alternative but to use theoretical concepts in trying to make sense of empirical data, past or present; I take it to be agreed that, as Keynes said in the preface to the blue Cambridge economics handbooks, 'The Theory of Economics . . . is a method rather than a doctrine, an apparatus of mind, a technique of thinking' rather than 'a body of settled conclusions'; in terms of this definition I take it to be agreed that we all wish to bring to bear in our work the most relevant 'technique of thinking' available and would be pleased to use the corpus of received economic theory for all it is worth. The real questions are how, if at all, the theoretical structures developed in modern social science can be used by the working historian and how, if at all, the historian should link his insights to the bodies of theory developing in the social sciences which surround him.

My own answers to these questions are directly coloured by a pleasant but somewhat bizarre education. As a relatively innocent sophomore student of modern history at Yale in the autumn of 1934, I was first introduced to an important philosophical notion. This event can hardly be ranked as revolutionary, since the notion has been part of the received Western tradition for some twenty-five centuries; namely, that human perception works through arbitrary abstract concepts and therefore the reality of what we call facts is not without a certain ambiguity. If historical narration of the most responsible and professional kind was thus shot through with implicit, arbitrary theory, why not make it explicit? And, since I was then beginning to study economics, why not see what happened if the machinery of economic theory was brought to bear on modern economic history?

This line of reflection soon opened up two quite distinct areas for experiment: the application of modern economic theory to economic history; and the application of the modern social sciences to the interaction among the economic, political, social, and cultural sectors of whole societies. I was drawn to this latter area in part because I was repelled by Marx's economic determinism without, however, finding a satisfactory alternative answer to the question he posed.

In one way or another I have been experimenting ever since with these two issues; that is, with the reciprocal relations of economic theory and dynamic economic data and with the effort to analyse whole societies in motion. They have given a private unity to study ranging from the analysis of the Great Depression after 1873 to the selection of bombing targets in World War II; from the likely consequences of Stalin's death to the pattern of the British take-off in the 1780's and 1790's; from the historical application of the National Bureau method of cyclical analysis to the formulation of some general hypotheses about economic growth.

What I have to say about the reciprocal relations of theory and history flows directly from these and similar exercises.

The argument will take the form of a few concrete, arbitrary, possibly useful assertions which aim partially to answer these questions from one arbitrary and personal perspective. The assertions are essentially three: first, the problem is the most useful link between theory and empirical data; second, of the nature of an economic historian's problems he is fated to be mainly a theorist of the Marshallian long period; and third, of the nature of the Marshallian long period, the economic historian can avoid only with great difficulty being something of a general dynamic theorist of whole societies. From these assertions I derive a final proposition; namely, that in our generation the most natural meeting-place of theory and history is the study of comparative patterns of dynamic change in different societies, focused around the problems of economic growth.

II

The problem approach to history can have two meanings. It can mean that history is viewed (and rewritten) in the light of contemporary problems of public policy—as, for example, Pigou reviewed the adjustment of the British economy after November 1918 during World War II, and as, in the shadow of impending legislation, O. M. W. Sprague examined crises under the National Banking Act. Or the problem approach can mean that history is re-examined to throw light on an unresolved intellectual problem of contemporary interest—as, for example, Schumpeter's hypothesis about entrepreneurship in a capitalist society is now being historically tested. The two meanings are generally related because most of the intellectual issues within the social sciences, no matter how antiseptic their scientific form and articulation, are at no great remove from debate over public policy.

Economic history, as a field of academic study, is peculiarly associated with the problem approach in both senses. Thumbing through the files of our journals or the listing of doctoral dissertations one can still detect the series of fighting issues, arrayed in geological layers, out of which we have evolved. There is first the argument over the universal wisdom of free trade in which the German scholars, then Cun-

ningham and Thorold Rogers, evoked historical evidence
against the repeal of the tariffs.[1] The debate quickly broadened to embrace the legitimacy of state intervention into the
workings of the economy, the legitimacy of social-welfare legislation, the legitimacy of labour unions. Then economic history was pushed into narrower and more technical areas by
the debate over monetary and trade policy (and theory) in
the 1920's and by the concern of the 1930's with the cause and
cure for the business cycle. At the same time longer-term reflections about the historical evolution and viability of
capitalism stirred by the cloudy interwar years—notably
those of Schumpeter—opened up the thriving field of entrepreneurial study, bringing *inter alia* a phalanx of economic
historians to debate against their naughty muckraking
parents (or occasionally against their libertine youth). And
it is not too much to say that a good part of the contemporary
effort in economic history is directly shaped by the concern
with public policy designed to accelerate growth in the under-
developed regions of the world, which emerged in the decade
after World War II.

Although it is no great trick to identify the historical
foundations of our respective interests as economic historians,
the conventions of academic life tend to conceal our origins
in the rude forum of social and political conflict and policy-
formation. Contemporary graduate schools—their methods
and their manners—have a peculiar power to denature
problem-oriented thought (in either sense) and to tame it to
departmentally organized disciplines; for a real problem, involving whole people, rarely if ever breaks down along the
lines into which the study of human affairs is professionally
fragmented.

In history what begins as an analytic insight of some power
and subtlety often ends in the second and third generations as
a flow of monographs, high in empirical content, but increasingly divorced from the living problem that opened up
the new terrain. Turner's essay on the frontier, for example,

---

[1] We can, of course, track our ancestry to Adam Smith, in which case we
have done briefs for both sides on the issue of free trade, as indeed we (and other
historians) have done on most major issues of public policy.

has served as the intellectual basis for two further generations' study. The frontier process has now been explored by regions, by states, and occasionally by counties. Few of these empirical exegeses have, however, added anything of analytic importance to Turner's formulation. Despite a massive empirical effort, the great historical watershed of the 1890's—a part (but only a part) of whose meaning Turner sensed—remains still to be dealt with analytically. And it is often true that the academic approach to history divests propositions of their analytic content and converts them into respectable, institutionalized specialties within which graduate students can be safely encouraged to write doctoral dissertations, researchable within a year after their general examinations have been completed.

There is, of course, another side to the medal. However much the historian may be (consciously or unconsciously) guided by abstract conceptions, his profession requires that, for a considerable portion of his working life, he pore over data, sort out reliable from unreliable sources, and (whatever the philosophical ambiguities) assemble facts. No man can be an historian unless he has at least a touch of the antiquarian about him, unless he derives some simple-minded satisfaction from knowing how things really were in a part of the past. Whatever his loyalty to the creation of generalized knowledge, he must derive some sly pleasure at the exception to the broad historical rule. Moreover, even if one acknowledges that the economic historian's activity should in the end be related to the solution of general problems, and even if one accepts it to be the duty of economic history to contribute to the formation of a wiser public policy, these higher-order activities need not concern the economic historian all the time, nor need they concern every economic historian. There is room for students of every bent and taste within our field over the spectrum from pure theory to statistical compilation.

When all this is said, I would still assert that economic history is a less interesting field than it could be, because we do not remain sufficiently and steadily loyal to the problem approach, which in fact underlies and directs our efforts. Take a favourable case: the studies in the transfer problem and in the balance of payments under inflationary conditions, inspired by Taussig. Here clear issues were posed, capable of orderly empirical examination; the results could be brought directly into the main stream of one of the oldest and most mature branches of economic thought, foreign trade theory; and in the post-1919 world of reparations and inflation the results bore directly on major issues of public policy. It is no accident that Taussig's inspiration yielded four of the best works in economic history ever written by Americans, namely, the balance-of-payments studies of Williams, Viner, Graham, and White. And if it is objected that we have not all been regularly favoured with doctoral students of this quality, the answer in part is that economic history has not regularly posed to its students issues as clearly relevant to major problems of theory and public policy.

Take a case closer to us, the modern study of entrepreneurial and business history. All the returns are by no means in. We cannot firmly judge the net contribution to knowledge of the enormous post-war effort in this area. Several things can, however, be said with confidence. First, there has been a considerable amount of low-order effort, where the authors have lost touch with their problem, where the analytic terms of reference derive mainly from a firm's books, and where the results can be meaningfully linked to no generally useful bodies of knowledge. Second, the most interesting efforts have been those which sought actively to overcome the built-in tendency to antiquarianism and to relate conclusions about entrepreneurship to problems within two quite distinct general bodies of knowledge: either to the process of capital formation as a whole; or to the social structure and values of the society and period whose entrepreneurs were examined. Third, the final evaluation of the worth of this effort is likely to be made not in terms of the number of firms studied—or the empirical gaps 'closed'—but in terms of the extent and the character of the problems it solves and the general insights it provides or fails to provide into the workings of economic and social processes that transcend but embrace the field of business history.

What I am asserting, then, is that a heightened and more

conscious loyalty to the problem could strengthen in several dimensions the relations between theory and history. The problem helps prevent the historian from becoming the prisoner of a received theoretical hypothesis; for by definition he is dealing with a question unresolved in theory, policy, or both. At the same time, by giving the historian a point of departure independent of his data, the problem helps prevent him from accepting in a fit of absent-mindedness the categories and analytic concepts built into his data. And, finally, the problem—if it is well and carefully defined—provides an area of common discourse, of useful, professional communication between the historian and the theorist, where results can be compared, where the historian can learn how the theorist poses the question and the historian can teach the theorist how things really worked. And should the latter statement be regarded as a mere verbal courtesy to our profession, it should be recalled that the classical concept of the movement of the terms of trade in consequence of capital flows never recovered from even moderately systematic historical inquiry, and that Clapham's pointed questions about empty boxes led directly (on one side of the Atlantic) to the upsetting of perfect competition as the theorist's norm. Seriously undertaken—that is, focused around clearly defined problems of common interest—the relationship between theorists and historians can be a two-way street.

III

Having held up the bright vision of theorist and historian solving problems in cheerful, productive collaboration I come to the lion in the path to its attainment: the theorist has generally been uneasy if not awkward if forced to work outside Marshallian short-period assumptions; the historian—like the human beings he writes about—cannot avoid working in a world of changing tastes and institutions, changing population, technology, and capacity.

The difficulty goes deep. The weakness of economic theory derives from its main strength; namely, that it is the most substantial body of useful thought about human behaviour that is Newtonian in character. It represents the logical elaboration of a minimum number of basic assumptions that of their nature permit of maximization propositions and thus permit static equilibrium situations to be rigorously defined. Value and distribution theory are essentially an extensive development of one proposition about man, another about his environment; that is, they derive from the laws of diminishing relative marginal utility and from diminishing returns. And these propositions remain essential, even, in modern income analysis, in the elegant world of interacting multiplier and accelerator.[1]

In both major branches—value theory and income analysis —long-period factors must be handled on an extremely restricted basis if the structure of theory is to retain its shape. For a theorist it is fair enough to say, as Marshall did, that a case of increasing return is 'deprived of practical interest by the inapplicability of the Statical Method'; but this is a curiously chill definition of 'practical interest' for an historian. Similarly, in modern income analysis, when efforts are made to introduce changes in population, technology, entrepreneurship, and other long-period factors, they are made on so formal and abstract a basis as to constitute very little change from the older conventional assumption that they were fixed and constant. To Keynes's famous dictum—'in the long run we are all dead'—the historian is committed by profession flatly to reply, 'Nonsense! the long run is with us, a powerful active force every day of our lives.'

Indeed the long series of debates between classical theorists and their more empirical opponents reduces substantially to a difference between those committed to the primacy of short-period factors and those who held that long-period factors might be dominant over particular short periods of time: so it was between the authors of the Bullion Report

[1] The upper turning-point in modern business-cycle theories, for example, is usually traced back to a short-period rise in saving (reflecting the diminished relative marginal utility of consumption with a rise in income); to supply bottlenecks and cost increases (reflecting short-period diminishing returns); to a short- or long-period exhaustion of avenues for profitable investment adequate to sustain full employment (again reflecting diminishing returns); or to some combination of these factors.

and its opponents in explaining the war-time rise in prices; between free traders and the would-be protectors of infant industries; between the opponents and advocates of legal limitation on hours of work; between those who advocated large-scale government intervention to deal with unemployment and those who feared its revolutionary long-run consequences.[1] In one sense this issue is at the core of the ideological race between Indian and Chinese Communist methods for take-off: will victory go to the system which uses force to constrain consumption and to maximize the short-period volume of investment or to that which creates a long-run setting of human incentives and institutions more conducive to spontaneous self-sustaining growth, designed to yield (through normal plough-backs and a democratically controlled national policy) levels of investment and productivity adequate substantially to outstrip population growth? (I might say parenthetically that, whatever the outcome of this competitive historical exercise, the structure of modern income analysis, as applied to economic growth, biases the case unrealistically in favour of the Chinese Communist method.)

Are we to conclude, then, that by the nature of their professions the economic theorist and the economic historian are doomed to work different sides of a street so wide that it is hardly worth shouting across? Should the theorist, equipped with powerful mechanisms for analysing economies under short-period assumptions, be left to deal with problems where such assumptions are useful and relevant, leaving the historian and other less disciplined but less inhibited investigators to handle the murky world of long-period change? After all, that is roughly the way our textbooks are written and our courses set up; and there is often wisdom in apparently irrational arrangements that persist.

On the whole, I would take the view that such complacent (or pessimistic) conservatism is both inappropriate and unnecessary.

It is inappropriate because whether we look to the under-

[1] This case could, of course, be reversed; that is, it could be regarded as a debate between those who held to classic assumptions and those who faced the long-period reality of inflexible money wage rates. Politically, the Keynesians were the men of the short period; in theory, the Pigovians.

developed areas, caught up in the early stages of the process of growth, or to the industrial societies that have learned to vote themselves chronic full employment, the economic problems of the foreseeable future, both of policy and of intellectual interest, require the systematic understanding and manipulation of long-period factors. This is self-evident in the under-developed areas, where new economic institutions must be created, skills and attitudes appropriate to growth imparted, capacity expanded in appropriate balance, the possibilities of external economies examined and exploited. Even the most classically short-period of economic activities—fiscal policy—must, in the under-developed areas, be touched with an acute awareness of changing capital–output ratios, with the need to transfer income flows from traditional to modern sectors, and with other long-period considerations which assume a peculiar urgency in the transition to self-sustaining growth. The industrialized societies are only a little less obviously enmeshed in long-period problems: radical shifts in birth-rates, with important consequences for the structure of the population and the working force; radical changes in technology and in the sectoral composition of output; the deepening commitment to make an overt political distribution of resources among security outlays, social overhead capital, and the private sector; and so on.

In short, if the work of the economist is to be relevant, he must work to an important degree outside the theoretical structures that have mainly interested him since, say, J. S. Mill.

There is, however, no need for pessimism if one looks not merely to the formal structure of theory but also to the total capabilities of economists; and if one looks to the whole long tradition of economic thought, not merely to the theorems of greatest interest in the past several generations. Economists, it is true, receive their contemporary training and develop their professional virtuosity mainly by manipulating a relatively narrow range of propositions; but it has long been in the best tradition of economists to go forth into the world as it is, full of long-period forces; to analyse whole problems; and to prescribe for them. Sometimes those analyses and

prescriptions have exhibited the bias of a training disproportionately devoted to the manipulation of short-period forces
in static equilibrium situations. On the whole, however, the
ablest economists transcended the limits of their most refined
tools: from Marshall's testimony on the Great Depression to
the Paley Commission Report; from D. H. Robertson's study
of industrial fluctuations to the contemporary pilgrimage of
Western economists to New Delhi.

Once out in the real world, what relation does economic
theory bear to the virtues of economists when they perform
virtuously? Are they merely smart fellows, handy to have
around when considering a tough practical problem; or does
the structure of their formal thought have a useful as well as
an inhibiting effect? Put another way, what are the uses of
economic theory in analysing problems where long-period
factors are important, particularly problems in history?

Theory can be useful in three distinguishable ways. First,
in defining the problem. Although the best-developed areas
of theory take the form of short-period propositions, economics offers an orderly way of looking at and defining the
totality of factors at work in an economic system. Formal
economics can help map a problem, even if it has little to suggest by way of a solution. It can help pose the questions and
set up empty boxes in fields as remote from the main streams
of theoretical effort as population change, the generation of
new technology, and the quality of entrepreneurship.
Although economists may have done little in modern times
to analyse long-period factors, they are well trained in listing
exhaustively the factors they are assuming fixed; and this is
most helpful.

Second, although the nature of long-period change may
make impossible the development of a long-period economic
theory—for example, a theory of economic growth—it by no
means bars the development of important theoretical propositions about long-period change. For example, income
analysis has been successfully adapted as a rough and ready
but indispensable aggregative framework for the planning of
economic growth;[1] the classical analysis of factor proportions

[1] See, for example, *The First Indian Five-Year Plan* (New Delhi, 1951), ch. ii.

in the theory of production has been adapted to throw important light on certain growth problems;[1] and, in general, the familiar technique of isolating one variable or relationship in movement, within a system otherwise held constant, while inappropriate for the general treatment of a whole interacting historical process, can be an extremely fruitful partial technique of analysis.[2] In short, there are many more uses for theory in dealing with long-period problems than have yet been developed. Neo-Marshallian pessimism on this score— a conviction that rigour has to be abandoned when the economist departs from the short period, that there is no middle ground between geometry and description—can easily be overdone.

There is a third role for economic theory and theorists in history: that is, to contribute actively to the systematic organization of knowledge about the past in terms of analytic categories that permit cross-comparison and generalization. This role requires that economists, in addition to maintaining and developing the Newtonian sectors of their science, begin to take seriously the biological strands in their heritage embedded in the *Wealth of Nations*, evoked in our time by Mitchell's leadership in the study of the trade cycle and by Schumpeter's fruitful suggestions. It is only in terms of some such grand conception focused around some clear concrete problems shared between economists and historians that the full possibilities of interrelationship can be developed. And it is to some of its implications—which most obviously bear on the study of economic growth—that I now turn.

IV

In one sense it is distinctly anticlimactic to suggest that the major common task and meeting-place of economists and historians are to be found in the analysis of economic growth; and that the systematic isolation of similarities and differences among national patterns of growth is likely to be the most

[1] See R. S. Eckaus, 'The Factor Proportion Problems in Underdeveloped Areas', *American Economic Review*, xlv (Sept. 1955), 539–65.

[2] See, for example, T. Haavelmo, *A Study in the Theory of Economic Evolution* (Amsterdam, 1954).

productive method jointly to pursue. What, after all, have we been doing in recent years? A high proportion of recent articles in the economic history journals has been designed to translate aspects of national economic history into the more universal language of economic growth; and articles on economic growth—in fact or in name—have hit the economic journals like a biblical plague. Papers prepared for special meetings—such as the 1954 conference on capital formation—indicate not merely a convergence of interest among historians, statisticians, theorists, and functional specialists but the beginnings, at least, of an ability to communicate when a problem as relatively clearcut as capital formation is explored.[1] Moreover, comparative analysis of national growth experiences is increasingly a feature of the landscape: from, as it were, our little family difficulty with nineteenth-century France and Germany to the study of Brazil, Japan, and India.[2]

We have found, it might appear, an optimum focus for our efforts as economic historians: economic growth permits us to use in a shapely way much of the cumulative work of our predecessors; it provides a problem area in both policy and problem senses; in the analysis of growth the Marshallian long period, in whose treatment we historians enjoy a comparative advantage, cannot be ignored; and since by definition growth takes place over long periods of time, the economist must either study history or call us in on a basis of equal partnership at least.

But I would make two final observations before agreeing that the golden age of economic history and of collaboration between theory and history has already arrived.

First, I do not believe that the efforts now going forward, from many technical perspectives, focused around economic growth are going to yield a usable body of biological theory unless a conscious effort is made to develop that theory. I do not believe that the organization, side by side on a country

---

[1] See *Capital Formation and Economic Growth* (Princeton: Princeton University Press, 1955).

[2] S. Kuznets, W. E. Moore, and J. J. Spengler, *Economic Growth: Brazil, India, Japan* (Durham: Duke University Press, 1955).

basis, of statistical data, industry analyses, entrepreneurial studies, and monographs on technology, with experts in Harrod-Domar models benevolently looking on, is going to yield automatically, by osmosis, the corpus of organized concepts we shall require if the golden age is to come to pass. In the three-quarters of a century or so since the Americans created their graduate schools, and the professional study of history and the social sciences, based on German models mixed with American empiricism, we have managed to create many barren acres of factually accurate volumes, bearing on interesting issues, in which the authors left the problem of intellectual synthesis to someone else. Ironically this persistent philosophical disease—apparently a disease of modesty and intellectual scruple—has left American academic life, by default, particularly vulnerable to the brilliant, casual, and not wholly responsible insights of a Veblen, a Beard, or a Schumpeter who did not fear to generalize.

I would warn, then, on the basis of our common experience and our ingrained national style, against assuming that theoretical synthesis comes about without special, conscious effort.

But to what kind of synthesis should we look? What kind of framework is capable of posing researching questions for historians that, if answered, permit empirical results to be compared and generalized and also permit easy and useful intercommunication with the theorist?

Each answer to this question will inevitably be shaped by unique interests and experiences; mine is affected in particular by the job of trying to teach coherently the story of the evolution of the world economy over the past two centuries. I have leaned to a concept of historical stages held together by a bone structure of more conventional dynamic theory. I have suggested that it may be useful to regard the period, after a relatively static traditional society begins to break up, as divisible into stages of preconditions, take-off, and sustained growth. And as Chapter XIII indicates I have developed subdivisions of the sustained growth stage, with stages of technological maturity and of dominance by durable consumer goods and services, both of which are, I believe, capable of reasonably precise definition and approximately historical dating for those societies which have experienced them. (It may be that after the age of durable consumer goods—when diminishing relative marginal utility has set in sharply for the extra car or portable TV—babies will take over as a leading sector; but it is a bit too soon to lay this down as immutable natural law.) I doubt that stages by themselves in the old German style will serve our purpose; but if we can link them to a modified corpus of conventional economic theory—and especially provide some definitions that are at least conceptually quantitative and permit reasonably accurate dating —we may generate something of intellectual power and utility.

I would certainly not be dogmatic about the forms of synthesis likely to prove most useful; but I would urge with some confidence that, as we gain an increasing knowledge of each other's work, and as the data pile up, we must allocate more time to building and applying a synthesis than we have in the past.

I come now to a final observation. It is quite simply that the explicit analysis of growth is likely to force economic history in somewhat new ways into the analysis of politics, social structure, and culture. A glance at our textbooks indicates that economic historians are not strangers to these fields. Clapham's affectionate and precise evocation of the round of British life at various historical epochs is as good as anything social history affords; and the role of the state in economic life has embedded us all in the study of politics at one time or another. It is, indeed, possible to criticize much of conventional economic history as too political and social and not sufficiently economic. My point is that the systematic treatment of growth will pose some new problems of relationship between economic and other factors and some old problems in new forms.

The comparative study of periods of preconditioning for take-off must, for example, focus sharply in most cases around two related questions: the formation of an effective, modern, central government capable of exercising fiscal power over old regionally based interests; and the emergence of a group

(or usually a coalition) with vested interests in the development of an effective national government and the technical
talents and motivation to operate the modern sectors of the
economy. From post-medieval western Europe to contemporary Egypt and India, from Canada to the Argentine, from
Japan to Turkey, the political and social patterns that have
accompanied the stage of preconditions have, of course,
varied, and yet they have been shot through with recognizable common features. The orderly sorting out of both common features and variations, in their relations to more familiar
patterns of economic change, will prove, I believe, an essential aspect of the development of a general biological theory
of economic growth. (If we move in this direction we should,
incidentally, be able to get much assistance from the current
generation of political scientists who are increasingly committed to the study of comparative politics in non-Western
societies.[1]) Nor will these extra-economic concerns end when
we have seen our respective countries into sustained growth;
for social structure, politics, and culture are not the monopoly
of economically under-developed areas. As time goes on we
shall, I suspect, be studying differences in the sociological
bases and political consequences of growth stages dominated
by heavy as opposed to light engineering industries, not excluding the significance of the differences within Communist
societies; we shall be exploring the social and cultural, as well
as the economic, anatomy of the durable consumer-goods and
service stages, which we entered in the 1920's and the entrance
into which of western Europe and Japan constitutes one of the
most surprising and revolutionary features of the post-war
decade; and we may even learn a little about the dynamic
determinants of the birth-rate.

In short, in accepting economic growth as a central problem we shall, from one perspective, be forced to become
general theorists of whole societies; for the motives of men
and the human institutions and activities which bear directly

[1] See, notably, D. Rustow, 'New Horizons for Comparative Politics', *World Politics*, ix (July 1957), 530–49. See also George McT. Kahin, Guy J. Pauker, and Lucian Pye, 'Comparative Politics of non-Western Countries', *American Political Science Review*, xlix (Dec. 1955), 1022–41.

and technically on the rate of increase of output *per capita* are not narrowly limited. And our loyalty should be to the problem of economic growth, wherever it may take us, not to the bureaucratic confines of economic history or of economics as they are at present consecrated in our graduate schools.

APPENDIXES

APPENDIX I

Illustrative Statistics of the Pattern of Growth:
the United States and the United Kingdom

UNITED STATES

1. Population of the Continental United States, 1790–1940
(in millions)

1790	. 3·93	1830 .	12·87	1870 .	39·82	1910	91·97
1800	. 5·31	1840 .	17·07	1880 .	50·16	1920	105·71
1810	. 7·24	1850 .	23·19	1890 .	62·95	1930	122·78
1820	. 9·64	1860 .	31·44	1900 .	75·99	1940	131·67

Source: U.S. Bureau of the Census, *Historical Statistics of the United States, 1789–1945*. Washington, D.C., 1949, Series B2, p. 25.

2. National Income of the United States, 1799–1938
($ billions at 1913 prices)

1799–1809	. 0·87	1869–79	. 7·47	1909–18	. 33·04
1809–19	. 1·00	1879–88	. 12·43	1914–23	. 37·63
1819–29	. 1·19	1884–93	. 14·22	1919–28	. 42·20
1829–39	. 1·68	1889–98	. 15·77	1924–33	. 43·57
1839–49	. 2·76	1894–1903	. 18·64	1929–38	. 40·58
1849–59	. 4·75	1899–1908	. 22·95		..
1859–69	. 5·97	1904–13	. 27·95		..

Sources: R. B. Martin, *National Income in the United States, 1789–1938*, New York, 1939.
S. Kuznets, *National Product since 1869*, New York, 1946.

Martin's figures (op. cit., Table I, p. 6) are used for the estimates for 1799–1809 to 1869–79. (Kuznets's figures are available from 1869, but he admits (op. cit., p. 86) that his estimates for the first decade he covers may be too low.) To avoid the distortions which would arise from the fact that individual years may be at different stages of the business cycle, and from the Civil War, we have taken the geometric mean of adjacent pairs of estimates of money national income from Martin's table, and divided by the arithmetic mean of the pairs of figures for the relevant years in the Snyder-Tucker general price index. (*U.S. Historical Statistics*, series li, pp. 231–2.)

From· 1879 onward we have used Kuznets's series (op. cit., Table II, 16, col. 5, p. 119) and divided by the arithmetic mean of the Snyder-Tucker figures for the relevant ten-year period.

As Kuznets points out (op. cit., pp. 86–87) the differences in coverage between his figures and Martin's are likely to be quantitatively insignificant in earlier years, and it is believed that the present series gives a rough indication of the movement of real income over the period.

3. *Manufacturing Production in the United States (1799–1928)*
(*$ millions at prices of 1910–14*)

1799–1809	. 15	1849–59	. 283	1899–1908	. 3,622
1809–19.	. 22	1859–69	. 417	1909–18	. 6,064
1819–29.	. 35	1869–79	. 606	1919–28	. 9,134
1829–39.	. 64	1879–89	. 1,206	..	
1839–49.	. 137	1889–99	. 2,066	..	

Source: Martin, op. cit.

Martin's figures for Realized Private Production Income derived from manufacturing (op. cit., p. 58) were taken as a base, and divided by a very rough price index for manufactured goods, constructed by taking the arithmetic mean of the indexes for Textile Products and Metals and Metal Products in Warren and Pearson's index of wholesale prices.[1] For the estimates from 1799–1809 to 1889–99, the geometric mean of adjacent pairs of the resulting figures was taken. For the last three decades we took the arithmetic mean of Martin's figures, and divided by the arithmetic mean of our price-indexes, for the relevant ten-year period.

4. *Consumption of Raw Cotton in the United States (1789–1944)*
(*millions of pounds: eleven-year overlapping averages*)

1789–99	. 4·3	1839–49	. 162·2	1889–99	. 1,385·2
1794–1804	. 13·0	1844–54	. 239·0	1894–1904.	1,688·0
1799–1809	. 26·9	1849–59	. 307·7	1899–1909.	2,109·2
1804–14	. 32·5	1854–64	. 298·5	1904–14	. 2,393·6
1809–19	. 37·0	1859–69	. 313·6	1909–19	. 2,920·0
1814–24	. 45·8	1864–74	. 416·0	1914–24	. 3,198·3
1819–29	. 56·8	1869–79	. 590·4	1919–29	. 3,330·5
1824–34	. 64·8	1874–84	. 791·0	1924–34	. 3,336·2
1829–39	. 72·2	1879–89	. 985·3	1929–39	. 3,371·2
1834–44	. 101·9	1884–94	. 1,146·1	1934–44	. 4,422·0

[1] *Historical Statistics of the U.S.*, Series L7 and L9, p. 232. These two items are weighted equally in Warren and Pearson's index for all commodities. See *Journal of the American Statistical Society, Proceedings, 1931*, p. 246.

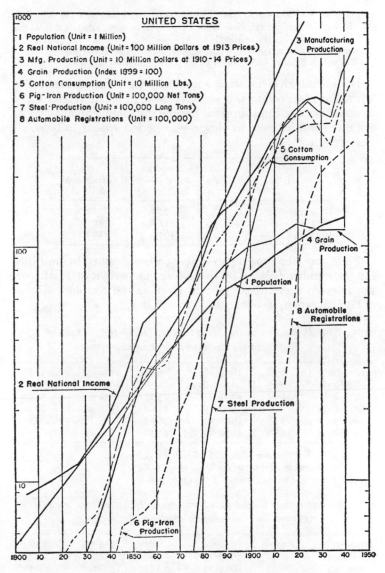

Illustrative trend patterns in the United States and British economies
(1800–1949). United States.

Sources: M. B. Hammond, *The Cotton Industry*, Publications of the American Economic Association, New Series, No. 1, New York, 1897. Table at end of book gives figures to 1897.
Statistical Abstract of the United States, 1921, p. 602, for 1898–1904.
Historical Statistics of U.S., Series J 179, p. 187, for 1905–44.

Hammond gives no data specifically for consumption before 1827. For years before this we have taken production less exports as an estimate of consumption. Despite the complication of stocks, the discrepancies over an eleven-year period appear to be small. For example:

	Production minus exports (million lb.)	Consumption (million lb.)
1829–39 . . .	75·6	72·2
1834–44 . . .	111·3	101·9
1839–49 . . .	164·9	162·2

The figures for 1904–14 to 1934–44 were obtained by multiplying the number of bales by the average net weight of a bale over the relevant eleven-year period, given in the *Statistical Abstract of the U.S.*, 1949, p. 696.

5. *Steel Production in the United States (1869–1949) (millions of long tons: eleven-year overlapping averages)*

1865–74[1]	. 0·08	1894–1904	. 9·96	1924–34	. 37·65
1869–79 .	. 0·35	1899–1909	. 16·58	1929–39	. 35·82
1874–84 .	. 1·02	1904–14	. 23·13	1934–44	. 54·90
1879–89 .	. 2·06	1909–19	. 32·63	1939–49	. 70·20
1884–94 .	. 3·36	1914–24	. 36·64	..	
1889–99 .	. 5·73	1919–29	. 41·97 ·	..	

Source: *Historical Statistics of the U.S.*, Series J 165, pp. 186–7.
1946–8: *Statistical Abstract of the U.S.*, 1950, p. 809.
1949: *Survey of Current Business*, Feb. 1950, p. S 32.

6. *Automobile Registrations in the United States (1900–44) (in millions: eleven-year overlapping averages)*

1900–9[1]	. 0·10	1914–24	. 6·82	1929–39	. 23·14
1904–14 .	. 0·52	1919–29	. 14·97	1934–44	. 25·54
1909–19 .	. 2·53	1924–34	. 20·44	1939–48	. 28·01[1]

Source: *Historical Statistics of the U.S.*, Series K 230, p. 223.
Statistical Abstract of the U.S., 1950, p. 487.

[1] Average of ten years.

7. *Index of Grain Production in the United States (1839–1939)*
(*1899 = 100*)

1839 .	. (14·8)	1879 .	. 63·8	1919 .	. 124·8
1849 .	. (21·4)	1889 .	. 83·5	1929 .	. 117·7
1859 .	. (30·7)	1899 .	. 100·0	1939 .	. 117·7
1869 .	. 38·4	1909 .	. 106·6		..

We have figures for the wheat, corn, and oats crops for the census years 1839, 1849, and 1859, and for every year from 1866 onward.[1] For the figures from 1869 onward we took the average crop for the five-year period centred on the year named. These figures were weighted in accordance with the relative prices per bushel of the three products from 1865 to 1944[2] (the weights thus arrived at were: wheat 5, corn 3, oats 2), and the resulting series was reduced to an index with 1899 = 100.

8. *Pig-Iron Production in the United States (1810–1949)*
(*millions of net tons*)

1810–20 .	·04	1874–84 .	3·53	1914–24 .	36·04
1825–35 .	·19	1879–89 .	5·53	1919–29 .	38·39
1840–50 .	·65	1884–94 .	7·61	1924–34 .	31·79
1849–59 .	·74	1889–99 .	10·30	1929–39 .	27·18
1854–64 .	·84	1894–1904 .	14·43	1934–44 .	41·18
1859–69 .	1·15	1899–1909 .	21·51	1939–49 .	53·34
1864–74 .	1·87	1904–14 .	27·21		..
1869–79 .	2·40	1909–19 .	34·50		..

Sources: *Historical Statistics of the U.S.*, Series G 96, p. 149.
   1946–8: *Statistical Abstract of the U.S.*, 1950, p. 808. Adjusted for comparability with *Historical Statistics of the U.S.*
   1949: *Survey of Current Business*, Feb. 1950, p. S 32. Adjusted for comparability with *Historical Statistics of the U.S.*

Figures are not continuous until 1854. Thus the figure given above for 1810–20 is an average of only two years; that for 1825–1835, of five years; for 1840–50, of seven years; for 1849–59, of nine years. The remaining figures are overlapping eleven-year averages.

[1] *Historical Statistics of the U.S.*, Series E 182, 187, and 197, pp. 106–7.
[2] *Statistical Abstract of the U.S.*, 1950, p. 610.

Appendix I

1. *Population* (*in millions*)

	England and Wales	Great Britain[1]	United Kingdom[2]
1811	10·16	11·97	17·91
1821	12·00	14·09	20·89
1831	13·90	16·26	24·03
1841	15·91	18·53	26·73
1851	17·93	20·82	27·39
1861	20·07	23·13	28·93
1871	22·71	26·07	31·48
1881	25·97	29·71	34·88
1891	29·00	33·03	37·73
1901	32·53	37·00	41·46
1911	36·07	40·83	45·22
1921	37·89	42·77	44·03
1931	39·95	44·79	46·03[3]
1941	41·74[4]	46·88[4]	48·17[3]

Sources: Census returns, except where otherwise indicated.

1811–1911: Recorded in W. Page, *Commerce and Industry*, Statistical Tables, London, 1919, p. 1.

1921–41: *Annual Abstract of Statistics, 1935–6*, H.M.S.O., London, 1948, p. 7.

2. *National Income of the United Kingdom at 1900 prices* (£ *billions*)

1801–10	0·30	1880–9	1·12
..		1890–9	1·53
1830–9	0·43	1900–9	1·81
1840–9	0·50	1910–19	(2·01)[5]
1850–9	0·56	1920–9	2·08[6]
1860–9	0·73	1930–8	2·51
1870–9	0·86	..	

This series is probably the most unreliable of all those presented. For years before 1870 we have used Colin Clark's estimates. For 1801–10 we took the geometric mean of his estimates of National Income in millions of international units in Great Britain in 1801 and 1812,[7] added them to his figure for Ireland

[1] England, Wales, Scotland.

[2] Until 1911 Great Britain and the whole of Ireland. From 1921 onwards, Great Britain and Northern Ireland only.

[3] Figure for Northern Ireland estimated.   [4] Estimated.

[5] From 1915 to 1919 the figures are very approximate. See Prest., op. cit., p. 59, n. 4.

[6] From 1920 onwards Southern Ireland is excluded. See Prest, loc. cit., n. 1.

[7] Colin Clark, *Conditions of Economic Progress*, 2nd ed., London, 1951, p. 71.

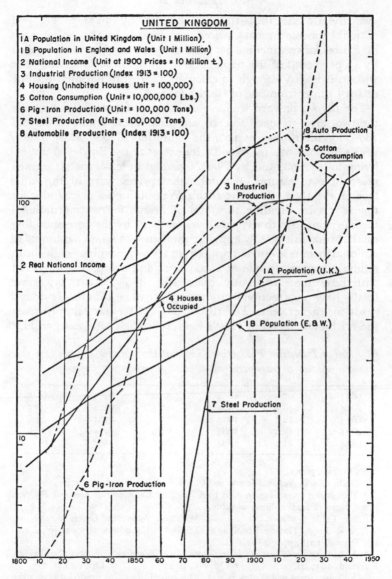

UNITED KINGDOM

1A Population in United Kingdom (Unit 1 Million)
1B Population in England and Wales (Unit 1 Million)
2 National Income (Unit at 1900 Prices = 10 Million £)
3 Industrial Production (Index 1913 = 100)
4 Housing (Inhabited Houses Unit = 100,000)
5 Cotton Consumption (Unit = 10,000,000 Lbs.)
6 Pig-Iron Production (Unit = 100,000 Tons)
7 Steel Production (Unit = 100,000 Tons)
8 Automobile Production (Index 1913 = 100)

8 Auto Production

5 Cotton Consumption

3 Industrial Production

100

2 Real National Income

1A Population (U.K.)

4 Houses Occupied

1B Population (E. & W.)

7 Steel Production

10

6 Pig-Iron Production

1800 10 20 30 40 1850 60 70 80 90 1900 10 20 30 40 1950

Illustrative trend patterns in the United States and British economies (1800–1949). United Kingdom.

over the decade 1801–10,[1] and divided by 9·25[2] to get real national income in 1913 prices. For 1830–9 to 1850–9 we took his figures for real income per head in 1913 prices,[3] and multiplied by 45 per cent.[4] of the population of the United Kingdom.[5] For 1860–9 it is easy enough to calculate aggregate national income at 1913 prices from one of Clark's tables.[6]

For 1870–9 onward we have used Prest's figures.[7] To combine the two series we need to compare price-levels in the 1860's and 1870's. With 1860–9 as 100, the figure for 1870–9 is, by Sauerbeck's index,[8] 97, by Wood's index[9] 102, by Bowley's cost-of-living index[10] 98, and by Clark's general index[11] 102. It seemed reasonable to assume, therefore, that prices were at the same level in the 1860's as in the 1870's. We obtained a price index for the 1870's by dividing the total of Prest's figures for national income from 1870 to 1879 at current prices[12] by the corresponding total at 1900 prices.[13] By applying this figure to Clark's estimate of national income in current prices from 1860–9,[14] which results in an estimate for this decade at 1900 prices, and comparing the result with the estimate previously obtained for 1860–9 at 1913 prices, we finally have a correction factor to apply to the estimates previously made for earlier years. For 1870–9 onward we have simply taken the arithmetic mean of Prest's figures for each ten-year period.[15]

3. *Index of Industrial Production[16] in Great Britain, 1804–1934 (ten-year moving averages centred on years given) (1913 = 100)*

1804 .	. 7·3	1854 .	. 32·0	1904 .	. 96·5
1814 .	. 8·8	1864 .	. 43·4	1914 .	. 99·3
1824 .	. 12·1	1874 .	. 57·5	1924 .	. 99·6
1834 .	. 16·7	1884 .	. 67·5	1934 .	. 126·6
1844 .	. 22·9	1894 .	. 80·6		..

[1] Op. cit., p. 70. [2] Ibid.
[3] Colin Clark, *National Income and Outlay*, London, 1937, p. 247.
[4] This is the rough figure used by Clark. See *Conditions of Economic Progress*, p. 72, head of final column of table.
[5] See Table 1, above. [6] *National Income and Outlay*, p. 232.
[7] A. R. Prest, 'National Income of the United Kingdom, 1870–1946', *Economic Journal*, 1948, pp. 31–62.
[8] A. L. Bowley, *Wages and Income in the United Kingdom since 1860*, Cambridge, England, 1937, p. 99. [9] Op. cit., p. 124. [10] Op. cit., p. 123.
[11] *National Income and Outlay*, p. 231. This calculation was made by giving the 1870–6 figure a weight of 7 and the 1877–85 figure a weight of 3.
[12] Op. cit., p. 58, col. 2. [13] Loc. cit., col. 7.
[14] *National Income and Outlay*, p. 232. [15] Prest, op. cit., pp. 58–59, col. 7.
[16] Including building.

Source: Walther Hoffmann, *Wachstum und Wachstumsformen der englischen Indus-triewirtschaft von 1700 bis zur Gegenwart, Jena, 1940.*

4. *Housing in England and Wales, 1811–1911 (millions of inhabited houses)*

1811 .	. 1·80	1851 .	. 3·28	1891 .	. 5·45
1821 .	. 2·09	1861 .	. 3·74	1901 .	. 6·26
1831 .	. 2·48	1871 .	. 4·26	1911 .	. 7·14
1841 .	. 2·94	1881 .	. 4·83		..

Source: H. Barnes, *Housing: The Facts and the Future*, London, 1923, Tables 1–6, pp. 337–41.

5. *Cotton Consumption[1] in Great Britain (1811–1934) (in millions of pounds; ten-year overlapping averages)*

1811–19	. 89[2]	1850–9	. 797	1890–9	. 1,635
1815–24	. 121	1855–64	. 778	1895–1904.	1,641
1820–9	. 165	1860–9	. 786	1909–18	. 1,865
1825–34	. 233	1865–74	. 1,031	1914–24	. 1,562[4]
1830–9	. 322	1870–9	. 1,197	1920–9	. 1,394
1835–44	. 422	1875–84	. 1,319	1925–34	. 1,282
1840–9	. 525	1880–9	. 1,456[3]	1930–9	. 1,221
1845–54	. 640	1885–94	. 1,529	1935–44	. 1,148

			Great Britain	United Kingdom
1855–64 .	.	.	778	806
1860–9 .	.	.	786	812
1865–74 .	.	.	1,031	1,047
1870–9 .	.	.	1,197	1,210
1875–84 .	.	.	1,319	1,333

Sources: To 1875–84: Thomas Ellison, *The Cotton Trade of Great Britain*, London, 1886, Table No. 1 at end of book.

1880–9 to 1925–34, W. R. Layton and G. Crowther, *An Introduction to the Study of Prices*, 3rd ed., London, 1938, p. 268.

Figures for 1935 to 1944: *Annual Abstract of Statistics*, 1935–46, H.M.S.O., London, 1948, p. 146.

[1] No deduction is made for raw cotton included in textile products exported from Great Britain.

[2] Average of nine years.

[3] From 1880–9 onward the figures are for the United Kingdom. The differences between the two series, however, are not very great.

[4] Average of ten years, 1919 excluded.

6. *Steel Production in the United Kingdom, 1865–1949 (millions of tons, ten-year overlapping averages)*

1865–74	.	0·35	1895–1904	.	4·55	1925–34	.	7·2
1870–9	.	0·7	1900–9	.	5·45	1930–9	.	9·2
1875–84	.	1·35	1905–14	.	6·5	1935–44	.	12·15
1880–9	.	2·4	1910–19	.	7·95	1940–9	.	13·1
1885–94	.	3·1	1915–24	.	8·1		..
1890–9	.	3·7	1920–9	.	7·5		..

Source: Layton and Crowther, op. cit., p. 269.

Figures from 1935–46 from *Annual Abstracts of Statistics, 1935–1946*, p. 140, and *1937–1947*, p. 125.

Figures for 1947–1949 from *Monthly Digest of Statistics*, July 1951, p. 35.

7. *Pig-Iron Production in the United Kingdom, 1806–1949 (millions of tons: ten-year overlapping averages unless otherwise stated)*

1806[1]	.	0·24	1880–9	.	7·91
1815–24[2]	.	0·38	1885–94	.	7·47
1820–9[4]	.	0·57	1890–9	.	7·96
1825–34[4]	.	0·67	1895–1904	.	8·64
1830–9[3]	.	0·91	1900–9	.	9·17
1835–44[6]	.	1·32	1905–14	.	9·60
1840–9[5]	.	1·54	1910–19	.	9·10
1845–54[4]	..	2·31	1915–24	.	7·38
1850–9[7]	.	3·21	1920–9	.	6·05
1855–64	.	3·84	1925–34	.	5·39
1860–9	.	4·53	1930–9	.	6·10
1865–74	.	5·64	1935–44	.	7·46
1870–9	.	6·28	1940–9	.	7·85
1875–84	.	7·18		..

Sources: To 1914: S. Kuznets, *Secular Movements in Production and Prices*, Boston and New York, 1930, pp. 417–19.

1915–46 various *Statistical Abstracts of the U.K.*

1947–9 from *Monthly Digest of Statistics*, July 1951, p. 35.

8. *Automobile Production in Great Britain, 1907–34 (index, 1913 = 100: ten-year overlapping averages)*

1907–16	.	.	.	.	61
1910–19	.	.	.	.	88
1915–24	.	.	.	.	149
1920–9	.	.	.	.	319
1925–34	.	.	.	.	526

Source: Hoffmann, op. cit.

[1] One year.	[2] Three years.	[3] Four years.	[4] Five years.
[5] Six years.	[5] Seven years.	[7] Eight years.	

APPENDIX II

Trends in Selected British Prices

(*Overlapping eleven-year averages, 1840–50 = 100*)

	Wheat	Cotton	Wool	Coal	Beef	Timber	Iron	Sugar
Pre-1793 .	83·3	406·8	121·3	174·1	68·7	79·1	134·2	137·8
1790–1800	111·9	510·8	125·2	170·5	81·1	110·8	151·2	146·0
1795–1805	139·4	546·6	153·9	159·8	95·9	149·3	165·0	144·3
1800–10 .	159·1	489·4	187·2	172·5	108·5	212·9	173·2	132·7
1805–15 .	167·0	430·5	198·6	180·8	116·4	240·8	175·4	150·5
1810–20 .	163·8	367·5	188·3	168·4	121·7	187·1	174·8	154·5
1815–25 .	126·2	266·8	155·1	149·1	109·1	136·0	169·4	134·8
1820–30 .	110·5	161·5	106·5	139·8	95·4	117·4	149·4	115·7
1825–35 .	106·8	147·8	108·1	120·0	97·0	115·7	132·8	109·4
1830–40 .	105·7	148·3	128·0	114·1	101·3	118·9	121·4	111·5
1835–45 .	103·3	128·7	120·9	111·5	100·0	113·4	114·9	117·6
1840–50 .	100·0	100·0	100·0	100·0	100·0	100·0	100·0	100·0
1845–55 .	98·4	97·3	106·7	97·2	105·5	100·7	107·0	76·1
1850–60 .	97·8	113·9	136·2	97·5	113·8	103·3	110·1	75·2
1855–65 .	96·5	224·5	172·0	97·9	124·3	104·1	109·9	76·1
1860–70 .	94·1	265·8	180·7	97·7	129·6	96·6	102·4	70·1
1865–75 .	98·2	201·5	182·1	111·1	145·5	87·5	130·2	70·7
1870–80 .	93·1	141·6	160·5	109·2	150·0	80·0	128·1	69·1
1875–85 .	80·6	115·6	117·1	93·1	145·5	72·7	95·5	60·3
1880–90 .	67·1	108·4	95·2	85·7	129·9	66·3	86·1	48·8
1885–95 .	55·0	90·9	89·1	87·8	114·6	58·5	82·1	40·2
1890–1900	52·5	78·9	84·7	91·0	111·9	56·8	92·6	36·0
1895–1905	51·0	85·6	79·0	88·3	117·6	55·9	99·7	30·5
1900–10 .	54·4	108·4	81·3	92·0	127·5	54·1	106·9	30·1
1905–15 .	62·8	116·8	100·5	100·5	140·5	57·4	112·1	33·4
1910–20 .	96·6	217·9	138·7	136·8	221·4	103·5	173·3	72·2
1915–25 .	113·2	268·9	147·4	163·0	267·7	111·8	217·7	85·0
1920–30 .	94·8	226·2	128·2	143·7	233·6	78·9	198·3	63·6
1925–35 .	65·1	149·8	99·4	121·8	181·4	57·7	139·7	33·3
1930–40 .	52·1	115·2	90·9	121·3	169·6	69·1	161·1	23·8
1935–45 .	85·6	146·7	143·5	151·2	184·9	189·1	209·3	27·0

Note. The data for these indexes were derived as follows:

(*a*) Pre-1790 prices are from Jevons (wheat, cotton, wool, timber, iron) and Mulhall (coal, beef, and sugar).

(*b*) 1790–1850 prices are from data organized in the course of the forth-coming study of the 'Growth and fluctuations of the British economy, 1790–1850' directed by A. D. Gayer.

(*c*) 1850–1945 prices are from the data given annually in the *Journal of the Royal Statistical Society*.

(*d*) The 'pre-1793' figures represent the average level in the period 1783–93, when Jevons data are available; 1782–90, in the case of the Mulhall data.

APPENDIX III

Cyclical Movements of Import Prices, Export Prices, and Net Barter Terms of Trade, 1801–1913, United Kingdom (Imlah)

	Import prices	Export prices	Terms of trade	Average standing for cycle (1880 = 100) Import prices	Export prices	Terms of trade
1801	112·2	93·5	82·3	183·1	444·1	245·5
1802	89·8	102·8	113·1	—	—	—
1803	97·9	103·6	104·6	—	—	—
1803	96·8	110·5	114·0	185·2	416·7	225·1
1804	102·6	103·0	100·4	—	—	—
1805	102·5	99·7	97·2	—	—	—
1806	98·8	96·8	97·9	—	—	—
1807	103·1	97·4	94·5	—	—	—
1808	96·4	92·7	96·1	—	—	—
1808	89·8	104·5	114·6	198·9	369·7	188·8
1809	116·7	97·4	82·2	—	—	—
1810	105·0	98·1	92·0	—	—	—
1811	88·5	100·0	111·3	—	—	—
1811	88·8	110·1	122·8	198·1	335·9	171·1
1812	105·9	107·3	100·5	—	—	—
1814	114·9	100·9	87·1	—	—	—
1815	101·7	93·1	90·8	—	—	—
1816	88·6	88·5	98·9	—	—	—
1816	98·4	107·3	108·6	178·5	277·1	155·9
1817	99·6	95·8	95·8	—	—	—
1818	110·3	100·3	90·6	—	—	—
1819	91·5	96·6	105·0	—	—	—
1819	118·9	121·3	101·8	137·6	220·7	160·7
1820	109·4	109·7	100·0	—	—	—
1821	95·4	103·8	108·5	—	—	—
1822	94·5	96·6	102·0	—	—	—
1823	94·4	93·5	98·8	—	—	—
1824	89·2	91·0	101·8	—	—	—
1825	110·3	95·2	86·1	—	—	—
1826	88·0	88·9	100·9	—	—	—
1826	104·3	109·3	105·0	116·2	179·6	154·4
1827	101·2	101·1	100·0	—	—	—
1828	98·8	99·0	100·3	—	—	—
1829	95·7	90·6	94·7	—	—	—
1829	101·1	103·1	101·9	110·0	157·9	143·6
1830	99·7	101·1	101·4	—	—	—
1831	102·7	98·9	96·3	—	—	—

Cyclical Movements (cont.)

		Import prices	Export prices	Terms of trade	Average standing for cycle (1880 = 100)		
					Import prices	Export prices	Terms of trade
1832	.	96·5	96·9	100·4	—	—	—
1832	.	88·6	101·7	114·2	119·8	150·5	126·2
1833	.	96·5	96·1	99·1	—	—	—
1834	.	100·5	95·6	94·7	—	—	—
1835	.	107·6	102·3	94·7	—	—	—
1836	.	111·1	106·1	95·0	—	—	—
1837	.	95·7	98·3	102·3	—	—	—
1837	.	97·4	110·3	112·9	117·6	134·1	114·3
1838	.	99·3	105·0	105·4	—	—	—
1839	.	113·0	104·0	91·9	—	—	—
1840	.	102·5	95·3	92·8	—	—	—
1841	.	99·0	95·3	96·0	—	—	—
1842	.	88·8	90·0	100·9	—	—	—
1842	.	108·1	105·5	97·1	—	—	—
1843	.	92·6	98·4	106·3	96·7	114·3	118·8
1844	.	94·8	99·3	104·3	—	—	—
1845	.	95·4	105·8	110·3	—	—	—
1846	.	106·9	97·9	90·7	—	—	—
1847	.	115·0	104·2	90·2	—	—	—
1848	.	87·3	88·8	101·2	—	—	—
1848	.	87·9	95·9	108·5	—	—	—
1849	.	89·5	93·3	103·7	96·0	105·3	110·9
1850	.	94·8	96·6	101·3	—	—	—
1851	.	91·6	93·9	101·9	—	—	—
1852	.	93·0	95·9	102·6	—	—	—
1853	.	112·6	111·3	98·3	—	—	—
1854	.	115·5	111·3	95·8	—	—	—
1855	.	115·1	101·7	87·9	—	—	—
1855	.	97·0	95·0	97·8	—	—	—
1856	.	102·5	100·8	98·1	113·9	113·3	99·6
1857	.	107·6	107·6	100·2	—	—	—
1858	.	92·9	96·6	103·8	—	—	—
1858	.	93·7	95·6	102·2	—	—	—
1859	.	97·0	97·8	101·0	112·9	114·4	101·2
1860	.	101·2	95·9	94·5	—	—	—
1861	.	100·2	96·2	96·1	—	—	—
1862	.	107·9	114·6	106·2	—	—	—
1862	.	96·5	95·8	99·3	—	—	—
1863	.	98·8	105·8	107·1	126·3	136·9	108·3
1864	.	109·6	111·9	102·2	—	—	—
1865	.	101·2	98·8	97·7	—	—	—
1866	.	101·2	102·2	101·1	—	—	—
1867	.	96·6	95·9	99·4	—	—	—
1868	.	96·2	89·6	93·2	—	—	—

Appendix III

Cyclical Movements (cont.)

		Import prices	Export prices	Terms of trade	Average standing for cycle (1880 = 100)		
					Import prices	Export prices	Terms of trade
1868	.	110·3	104·4	94·6	110·1	117·5	106·6
1869	.	107·1	103·7	96·9	—	—	—
1870	.	104·9	101·0	96·4	—	—	—
1871	.	98·5	100·7	102·3	—	—	—
1872	.	105·2	111·2	105·8	—	—	—
1873	.	105·1	114·9	109·4	—	—	—
1874	.	102·6	108·7	106·0	—	—	—
1875	.	97·3	102·1	105·0	—	—	—
1876	.	95·1	93·9	98·7	—	—	—
1877	.	97·3	90·3	92·9	—	—	—
1878	.	90·3	87·1	96·5	—	—	—
1879	.	86·2	82·1	95·4	—	—	—
1879	.	102·8	105·7	102·8	92·3	91·3	98·9
1880	.	108·3	109·6	101·1	—	—	—
1881	.	107·4	105·1	97·8	—	—	—
1882	.	106·8	103·8	97·0	—	—	—
1883	.	102·8	100·5	97·6	—	—	—
1884	.	96·0	96·4	100·4	—	—	—
1885	.	90·8	92·0	101·3	—	—	—
1886	.	85·2	87·0	102·0	—	—	—
1886	.	101·8	97·8	96·0	77·3	81·2	105·1
1887	.	100·6	97·2	96·4	—	—	—
1888	.	103·2	98·1	95·0	—	—	—
1889	.	104·3	100·5	96·2	—	—	—
1890	.	102·3	106·6	104·1	—	—	—
1891	.	102·6	105·8	103·0	—	—	—
1892	.	99·0	100·6	101·6	—	—	—
1893	.	96·6	99·0	102·3	—	—	—
1894	.	89·6	94·4	105·3	—	—	—
1894	.	110·8	95·5	94·9	68·8	80·3	116·6
1895	.	96·7	92·6	95·8	—	—	—
1896	.	97·7	93·7	95·9	—	—	—
1897	.	96·9	92·6	95·7	—	—	—
1898	.	97·0	92·3	95·2	—	—	—
1899	.	97·9	99·8	102·0	—	—	—
1900	.	105·4	113·9	108·1	—	—	—
1901	.	102·0	108·5	106·6	—	—	—
1902	.	100·8	103·4	102·7	—	—	—
1903	.	102·1	103·3	101·2	—	—	—
1904	.	102·7	104·5	101·8	—	—	—
1904	.	93·3	98·6	100·2	75·7	89·7	118·5
1905	.	93·6	93·5	99·9	—	—	—
1906	.	97·5	98·9	101·4	—	—	—
1907	.	102·0	103·8	101·8	—	—	—

Cyclical Movements (cont.)

	Import prices	Export prices	Terms of trade	Average standing for cycle (1880 = 100)		
				Import prices	Export prices	Terms of trade
1908 .	98·2	99·9	101·8	—	—	—
1909 .	99·3	96·1	96·9	—	—	—
1910 .	104·9	100·3	95·5	—	—	—
1911 .	102·3	102·1	99·7	—	—	—
1912 .	104·2	103·8	99·7	—	—	—
1913 .	104·7	108·0	103·1	—	—	—

APPENDIX IV[1]

Cyclical Behaviour of British Export and Import Prices, 1879–1914 (Silverman Monthly Data)

(Average rates of change per month from stage to stage of reference cycles—Great Britain—Index of Export Prices, Total, A. G. Silverman.)

Dates of business cycles Revival peak trough (1)	Rate of change per month in reference cycle relatives from stage to stage of the cycles							
	Expansion				Contraction			
	I–II Revival to first third (2)	II–III First to middle third (3)	III–IV Middle to last third (4)	IV–V Last third to recession (5)	V–VI Recession to first third (6)	VI–VII First to middle third (7)	VII–VIII Middle to last third (8)	VIII–IX Last third to revival (9)
(1) July 1879, Dec. 1882, June 1886	−a	−0.7	..	−0.5	−0.4	−0.3	−0.4	−0.4
(2) July 1886, Sept. 1890, Feb. 1895	+0.2	+0.3	+0.6	..	−0.9	−0.5	−0.3	−0.8
(3) Mar. 1895, June 1900, Sept. 1901	+0.5	..	+0.9	+1.7	−0.4	−3.1	−1.0	−0.3
(4) Oct. 1901, June 1903, Nov. 1904	−0.6	+0.2	+0.3	+0.8	−0.3	+0.6	−0.9	..
(5) Dec. 1904, June 1907, Nov. 1908	+0.2	+0.9	+0.7	+1.1	−1.0	−2.0	−0.9	−0.9
(6) Dec. 1908, Dec. 1912, Sept. 1914	+0.7	+0.6	+0.2	+0.6	..	−0.3	−a	−a
Averages 6 cycles, 1879–1914	+0.2b	+0.2	+0.4	+0.6	−0.5	−0.9	−0.7b	−0.5b
Average deviations	0.3b	0.4	0.3	0.6	0.3	1.1	0.3b	0.3b
Average interval in months	7.3	13.9	14.2	7.6	4.7	8.6	9.1	5.2

(Average rates of change per month from stage to stage of reference cycles—Great Britain—Index of Import Prices, Total, A. G. Silverman.)

Dates of business cycles Revival peak trough (1)	(2)	(3)	(4)	(5)	(6)	(7)	(8)	(9)
(1) July 1879, Dec. 1882, June 1886	−c	−0.2	+0.1	−0.7	−0.4	−0.6	−0.6	−0.3
(2) July 1886, Sept. 1890, Feb. 1895	+0.2	+0.3	..	−0.3	..	−0.3	−0.6	−0.6
(3) Mar. 1895, June 1900, Sept. 1901	+0.5	+0.1	+0.4	+0.8	..	−0.9	−0.8	..
(4) Oct. 1901, June 1903, Nov. 1904	+0.3	+0.5	+0.1	+0.5	−0.3	+0.4	−0.2	+0.3
(5) Dec. 1904, June 1907, Nov. 1908	..	+0.5	+0.4	+0.5	−0.3	−0.6	−0.2	..d
(6) Dec. 1908, Dec. 1912, Sept. 1914	+0.9	+0.1	+0.2	+0.2	−0.6	+0.2	−d	−d
Averages 6 cycles, 1879–1914	+0.4e	+0.2	+0.2	+0.2	−0.3	−0.3	−0.5e	−0.1e
Average deviations	0.3e	0.2	0.1	0.4	0.2b	0.4	0.2e	0.3e
Average interval in months	7.3	13.9	14.2	7.6	4.7	8.6	9.1	5.2

a Data begin January 1880, end December 1913. No data November 1893 and March 1912. b Five items only. c Data begin January 1880. d Data end December 1913. e Five cycles.

1 The measures of cyclical behaviour presented here were calculated by the method described in the *National Bureau of Economic Research Bulletin* 57, 'The National Bureau's Measures of Cyclical Behaviour', Wesley, C. Mitchell and Arthur F. Burns, New York, July 1935. The current modified method is described by the same authors in their more recent *Measuring Business Cycles*. The changes, which correct a ...

INDEX

(The designation (t) or (c) following a page number indicates that the reference is to a table (t) or chart (c).)